Renaissance Society
and
Culture

Photo by Russell Maynor

Eugene F. Rice, Jr.

RENAISSANCE SOCIETY

AND

CULTURE

ESSAYS IN HONOR OF
EUGENE F. RICE, JR.

❧

EDITED BY
JOHN MONFASANI
AND
RONALD G. MUSTO

ITALICA PRESS
NEW YORK
1991

ITALICA PRESS, INC.
595 Main Street
New York, New York 10044

Library of Congress Cataloging-in-Publication Data

Renaissance society and culture : essays in honor of Eugene F. Rice,
    Jr. / edited by John Monfasani and Ronald G. Musto.
        p.   cm.
    Includes bibliographical references and index.
    ISBN 0-934977-24-0 : $50.00 (pre-publication)
    1. Renaissance. I. Rice, Eugene F.   II. Monfasani, John.
III. Musto, Ronald G.
CB361.R472   1991
940.2' 1--dc20
                                                        90-55872
                                                             CIP

Printed in the United States of America
5 4 3 2 1

CONTENTS

CONTENTS

PREFACE

After a distinguished academic career encompassing more than forty years at Harvard, Cornell, and Columbia universities, nearly twenty years as executive director of the Renaissance Society of America, and approximately a decade in the governance of the American Historical Association, Eugene F. Rice, Jr. has drawn to himself a wide circle of scholarly friends, students and colleagues who could justly claim a place in a volume of essays written in his honor. The twenty-one scholars whose contributions make up this collection therefore represent only a selection from the nearly impossibly large body of possible participants.

We have chosen to present a volume in celebration of Gene's long tenure as a teacher of Renaissance history at Columbia University. Hence the title and the participants of this Festschrift. Two illustrious friends, now retired from Columbia (Kristeller and Mundy), have contributed their appreciations; his daughter Louise, trained in art history at Columbia, has compiled his bibliography; five colleagues presently in the departments of history (Bean and Harris), art history (Beck and Rosand) and religion (Somerville) have written essays in tribute; ten of his former doctoral students (Edelstein, Gosselin, Hankins, Jorgensen, Kraye, Mathers, Monfasani, Musto, Rainey, and Rappaport) have requited in kind the scholarship that he so enthusiastically inculcated in them; one senior scholar (Rostenberg) received a doctorate from Columbia with Gene's support; while two younger scholars (Bullard and Knox), whose careers Gene has encouraged, herein honor their latter-day mentor.

Because of the appreciations of Professors Kristeller and Mundy further on in this volume, there is no need for us here to dilate on our admiration for Eugene Rice. Let us only say that the preparation of this Festschrift has been a deeply satisfying experience, one that we hope expresses in fitting form and measure the gratitude we feel toward this extraordinary teacher, scholar, and friend.

John Monfasani
Ronald G. Musto
February 1991

TABULA GRATULATORIA

Michael J. B. Allen
Christy Anderson
Pamela Askew
Guy Bedouelle, O.P.
Harry Berger
David A. Berry
Phyllis Pray Bober
K.Weil-Garris Brandt
Frieda S. Brown
Howard M. Brown
Virginia Brown
George Bull
Caroline W. Bynum
Ron Caldwell
Fritz Caspari
Centre for Reformation &
   Renaissance Studies
Mary Jane Chase
Cecil H. Clough
Louise George Clubb
James A. Colaiaco
F. Edward Cranz
Lawrence J. Crockett
Julie E. Cumming
Alan Phipps Darr
Istvan Deak
Jerome H. Delamater
Mario & Lee Di Cesare
John Patrick Donnelly, S.J.
Elizabeth Story Donno
John Dooley
Robert S. Du Plessis
Wayne Dynes
Barbara J. Fields
Mike Foster
Alison Frazier
Roland M. Frye
Edward J. Furcha
Nina G. Garsoïan
Hilary Gatti
Joseph D. Gauthier

Donna Gavak
Luce Giard
Creighton Gilbert
Felix Gilbert
Neal W. Gilbert
Paolo A. Giordano
Rona Goffen
Richard A. Goldthwaite
Phyllis W. G. Gordon
George & Naomi Gorse
Rita Guerlac
Phyllis A. Hall
Barbara McClung Hallman
Richard Harrier
A. Kent Hieatt
History Department,
   Columbia University
R. Po-chia Hsia
Dominick A. Iorio
Donald R. Kelley
Margaret King
Benjamin G. Kohl
Carolyn Kolb
Patricia & George Labalme
F. J. Levy
Lewis Lockwood
Bridget Gellert Lyons
Edward P. Mahoney
Michael Mallett
Germain Marc'hadour
Christine Meek
Charles E. Mercier
James V. Mirollo
Michael L. Monheit
Henry Muniz
Bernard O'Kelly
Heiko A. Oberman
Robert Oresko
Myra D. Orth
W. Brown Patterson
William Percy

Leeman L. Perkins
Maria Grazia Pernis
Emil Polak
Ann Lake Prescott
Sesto Prete
Wayne Proudfoot
Albert Rabil, Jr.
Renaissance Society of America
Marjorie A. Riley
J. B. Rives
Nicolai Rubenstein
Walter Rüegg
H. D. Saffrey
Jane Schuyler
Karl-Ludwig Selig
Paul Seton
Barbara A. Shailor

Charles Shively
Ann Shukman
Anne Simonson
Nancy G. Siraisi
Louis Charles Stagg
James M. Stayer
Anders Stephanson
Christopher Stocker
Jeffrey Stockwell
Michael Suozzi
John A. Tedeschi
Amadeu Rodrigues Torres
J. B. Trapp
Charles Trinkhaus
Pauline Watts Trinkhaus
Bernerd C. Weber

A Tribute to
Eugene F. Rice, Jr.

PAUL OSKAR KRISTELLER

This month, as I write, Eugene Rice is celebrating his sixty-fifth birthday. I am pleased that his friends, colleagues, and former students are honoring him on this occasion with a volume of studies and that I have been given the opportunity to pay my tribute to him as a scholar and as a cherished colleague and friend of long standing.

As most leading American Renaissance historians of his generation, Gene owes his training to the excellent instruction and guidance received at Harvard from the late Myron Gilmore. Gene's special interest in the French Renaissance may be due to his stay in France during the Second World War, and especially to the two years he spent as a graduate fellow, prior to his doctorate, at the École Normale Supérieure. His career as a scholar began when he was still a graduate student at Harvard and wrote a research paper on Erasmus and the religious tradition that was immediately published in the *Journal of the History of Ideas* and republished many years later in a volume of Renaissance essays from that journal edited by Philip Wiener and myself.

Gene's first major publication was an excellent book, based on his dissertation and entitled *The Renaissance Idea of Wisdom*, in which he gave a comprehensive and well documented history of a major philosophical concept, tracing it from Petrarch to Montaigne and Charron. In a series of substantial articles, Gene has dealt with Colet, Cusanus, Lefèvre d'Étaples, and Grolier, with the influence of the Greek medical writer Paul of Aegina, and with such significant topics as the Renaissance idea of Christian antiquity and the impact of patristic literature on Renaissance thought, a subject to which he also dedicated his contribution to the voluminous recent work on Renaissance humanism edited by Albert Rabil. In its size as well as in its masterful command of historical and philological methods and techniques, Gene's most impressive contribution is his annotated edition of the prefatory epistles of Jacques Lefèvre d'Étaples. It puts into proper perspective the work of a leading French scholar and thinker of the late fifteenth and early sixteenth centuries who was in close touch with many distinguished contemporaries and had a very great impact, not always appreciated, on the history of Aristotelianism, Platonism, Hermeticism, and magic during the sixteenth century.

xiii

Equally important, especially for the wealth of its detail and the variety of its perspectives, is Gene's latest book, based on lectures given at the Johns Hopkins University and entitled *Saint Jerome in the Renaissance*. It conveys a rich picture of St. Jerome's influence, especially from the fourteenth to the sixteenth century, not only by describing this influence in theology and biblical scholarship, but also by paying great attention to the interpretation of Jerome and his work as reflected in the religious orders and congregations named after him and in the way he is represented in the visual arts of the period. This heavily documented and mature work will long be read by scholars and laymen alike and provides an excellent model for further investigations of related or similar topics.

As a loyal colleague and friend, Gene edited the medieval and Renaissance studies of the late Theodore E. Mommsen, and contributed valuable papers to the volumes dedicated to Wallace K. Ferguson, Hans Baron, and myself.

In addition to his learned studies read and appreciated by his professional colleagues, Gene has written a very successful volume, *The Foundations of Early Modern Europe, 1460-1559*, intended for the general public and the college student. He also contributed to several popular books intended for the same general audience, such as the *Columbia History of the World, Studies in World Civilization,* and *The Western Experience.*

No less important than his scholarly contribution has been his activity as a teacher, administrator, and editor. He began his teaching career at Harvard (1953-1959) and spent a number of fruitful years at Cornell (1959-1964), where I first met him and enjoyed the exquisite hospitality of his late wife Lotte. In 1964 he came to Columbia, where he has taught ever since, recently as the William R. Shepherd Professor of History. His long presence at Columbia has been a great blessing, not only for the numerous students whom he trained and supervised, and some of whom have since become distinguished scholars in their own right, but also for his colleagues and for the University itself. He has exercised great influence in his department (which he served as chairman for three years), in the Graduate School, and in the Society of Fellows in the Humanities, in the University Seminars, and in the University as a whole. He has always used his authority and influence to maintain high standards of scholarship and to promote or invite faculty members who would maintain or enhance through their work the reputation and standing of the University in the various areas of the humanities. He has greatly influenced the policy of the University as a member of the Arts and Sciences Committee (1976-77) and of the Presidential Committee on the Future of the University (1984-87) and as co-author of the widely discussed report entitled "Strategies of Renewal" (1987). He also has played an active role in the Renaissance Society of America, serving as its executive director for many years, as board member, as delegate to the American

Council of Learned Societies, and as chairman of the committee in charge of publications.

Gene's presence at Columbia and in New York, his company and friendship (which included his wife, Lotte, becoming the friend of my wife, Edith, and me) has been one of the greatest privileges I have enjoyed during the last twenty-five years. We shared the supervision of several excellent dissertations. We often discussed scholarly problems, and I have always profited from his knowledge and judgment. We also discussed scholarly and academic policy in matters concerning the University or the affairs of the Renaissance Society, in which we were heavily involved, and I am glad to say that we have always seen eye to eye on the major issues of scholarly standards and policy. In a more personal way, we shared a strong interest not only in cultural history, but also in art and music, as well as in traveling. We often exchanged our experiences and impressions in these areas. Apart from this, Gene has been a cherished friend, whom I have often consulted on a number of great and small personal decisions and whose wise counsel has always been available and helpful to me.

It is thus with great enthusiasm that I join the chorus of well wishers on this happy occasion, send him my warmest congratulations on his birthday and on his past achievement, and add my best wishes for many more years of productive scholarship and personal fulfillment.

New York City
August 1989

Eugene F. Rice, Jr.
An Appreciation

JOHN HINE MUNDY

Eugene Rice was born in Lexington, Kentucky on August 20, 1924. His father, Eugene Franklin Rice, Sr., a descendent of two signers of the Declaration of Independence, one of whom contributed the name Franklin, was also from Lexington, a town that remained home in the eyes of his wife Lula Hammond Piper. Employed by a Boston-based sugar company, the Rice couple moved to Puerto Rico in 1920, living in plantations in and around Central Aguirre, a center of the sugar industry on the island's southern shore. Gene was soon joined by a sister named Lucy, born in Puerto Rico. Essential persons in and around Aguirre were a Doctor Bonelli, an Italian, living in the nearby town of Guayama, who delivered Lucy and saw the young Gene through diphtheria; Miss Elizabeth Watkins from Lexington, who taught first through fourth grades in a school for the children of the company's managers; and Miss Sally Ann Claiborne from Lynchburg, Virginia, for grades five through eight in another school the children attended. Eugene Rice Senior remained in the service of the sugar company until his retirement in 1965, when he and his wife returned to live in the United States until their deaths in 1977.

In a foreign world with few friends, Eugene Junior early became interested in books. Lucy was more gregarious, soon speaking very colloquial Spanish. After eighth grade in Puerto Rico, Gene was sent to the Eaglebrook School, Deerfield, Massachusetts, entering in 1937, graduating in 1939. While there, he became seriously interested in music and headed the Glee Club. At the conclusion of his Sixth Form, he was voted "best student" and "most likely to succeed," and was among the "most popular." He was also secretary of the Town Council and managing editor of the school newspaper, and once played Nanki-Poo in the school production of *The Mikado*. He then went to Phillips Exeter Academy in New Hampshire, from which he graduated in 1942 with honors, after serving in the choir, glee club and senate, and also as manager for the soccer team. Of the eight students whose pictures appeared on the page of the yearbook where this information was recorded, three opted for Harvard, two for Princeton, one each for Dartmouth and Amherst, and one for Michigan.

Gene entered Harvard in June 1942 but was soon drafted for service in the Second World War. In the European theater of Operations, he served as sergeant (T3) in the Intelligence Section of a Signal Corps cryptanalysis company. His sister recalls an older person sharing their table in a railway diner who, after looking at Gene for a time, finally said "Son, I know you must be older than you look, but you're the youngest dam sergeant I've ever seen!" Gene and I shipped out together to spend a month or so in and about London in the latter part of the war, when the V-ls and V-2s were falling. Our friends in the unit handled that grey, dangerous and unhappy wartime city in different ways. One bought second-hand scholarly books, another busied himself meeting the aristocracy and still another searched out and found elegant restaurants. Gene enjoyed what he does today: music, ballet and opera, delighted by the sounds and scenes of the London theater.

When he returned to Harvard, he was again active in the Glee Club and Music Club, graduating in 1947 *magna cum laude* and Phi Beta Kappa. At Harvard in 1948 he completed his masters and won the doctorate in 1953 under the direction of Myron Gilmore. During his graduate years there, Gene shared quarters with Bernard Bailyn, now Adams University Professor. Bailyn remembers that Gilmore, "on his way to ice-skate, called on him in our graduate dormitory room, skates in hand, to tell [Gene] personally that he had just read his first term seminar paper, that it was excellent, and that it should be published." It was: "Erasmus and the Religious Tradition" in the 1950 *Journal of the History of Ideas*.

Before gaining the doctorate, Gene went to France, registered, in fact, at the École Normale Supérieure from 1951 to 1953. In Paris he met and married Charlotte Bloch in 1952. Born in Prague in 1918, Lotte was the daughter of a successful lawyer, Arthur Bloch. Sometime in 1941, both he and his wife, Louise Stein, died in the infamous Nazi ghetto at Lodz. The Blochs had three children, all of whom escaped. One son reached Sweden and the other the United States. Lotte left Prague in 1938 for Britain, where she studied at University College, London, and received the baccalaureate. She enlisted in British service during the war and was teaching English and attending the Sorbonne in Paris when the two met. Typical of their travels in later life, they met on a train going to Geneva. The Rices had three children, Eugene, John and Louise. All three eventually received doctorates, respectively, in physics, music and art history.

Lotte and Gene delighted in travel: their children especially remember a trip on a freighter to Norway with a heavy schedule of tourism there and in Sweden. This was followed by a sleeper rail trip to South Germany and then on to Venice, where the family stayed in a *pensione* on the Giudecca with a spectacular view. Typical of Gene's attitudes about his environment is a remark in the preface to his *Saint Jerome* (p. xi). He thanks the officers of the American Academy at Rome for assigning "my wife and me a home on the summit of the Gianicolo, an enchanted spot protected by the Aurelian wall and hedged with laurel." I myself remember Lotte's passion for South German rococo buildings and churches. With deep conviction, their interests were centered on Europe and European civilization, but they once went as far afield as Istanbul, really, I suppose, for Justinian's Hagia Sophia.

From their earliest days in Paris, both were art collectors, initially of contemporary French tapestries (Lurçat), later of Italian seventeenth-century drawings. Had she not been cut off prematurely by the cancer that killed her in 1982, Lotte planned to write her dissertation on the seventeenth-century Italian painter and print-maker Salvator Rosa. Both loved opera. Since I rarely go to concerts, ballet or opera, I cannot add much when Gene talks about them, and it worried me that a one-sided conversation might soon peter out. Such is Gene's extraordinary enthusiasm, however, that one merely starts him talking about a performance, a conductor or singer, and he's off, full of joy, criticism and description. About music and the theater, Lotte and Gene had only one divergence: she did not share his love of ballet, a devotion especially directed to Balanchine's New York City Ballet. But everything balances. Gene's passable as a cook, but Lotte was extraordinary. Mary and Israel Shenker were good friends of the Rices, Mary having met Lotte in the Maison Franco-Britannique in the Cité Universitaire in Paris in 1947. The Shenkers record: "Lotte was a superb cook, one of those wonders of nature who was fantastically quick and knowing. Gene loved good food and did very nicely on the regime. The one thing he took charge of in the kitchen was making the pancakes for breakfast on Sunday – Lotte's concession to her American husband. At Christmas they would serve goose – the traditional Czech dish for the holiday." Having taken refuge there during the war, Lotte loved England, and Gene did also. With a flat in Oxford, they spent summers there.

Gene has had a full share of academic honors. After teaching for two years at Harvard, he went to Cornell in 1955, where he was promoted professor. In 1963, he came to Columbia and, after his chairmanship of the History Department from 1970 to 1973, was given the title of "William R. Shepherd Professor of History." A fellow of the American Academy of Arts and Sciences, he has had fellowships and memberships in the American Academy at Rome, American Council of Learned Societies, Fulbright, Guggenheim, the Institute for Advanced Study in Princeton, and the National Endowment of the Humanities. He was Executive Director of the Renaissance Society of America from 1966 to 1982 and again from 1985 to 1987, and is on its board as ACLS representative. From 1979 to 1981, he was also Vice-President for Research of the American Historical Association. He is currently a member of the editorial boards of the *Journal of the History of Ideas* and the *Renaissance Quarterly*.

The present volume is a testimonial to Gene's ability as a trainer of scholars in Renaissance history. What strikes me about his work is its balance between monographs, general history and text editing, the last surely the noblest part of a scholar's enterprise. His *Saint Jerome* won plaudits from a larger audience, as is shown by its winning prizes from the American Catholic Historical Association, the American Society of Church History and the American Academy of Religion. Recently, he has shifted his interests to the intellectual and social history of homosexuality. In 1989 he instituted Columbia University's first university "Seminar on Homosexualities," and currently offers an introductory course on the history of the same subject in western Europe and North America from antiquity to the present.

Gene is a first-class public lecturer. His timing is terrific, and the flow of words Niagara-like, the whole delivered with a distinctively Harvard accent. One amazed student reported in the *Course Guide* that this "Ole' Man River" flowed irresistibly but stopped the very second the bell rang. The Society of Columbia Graduates awarded him its Great Teacher Award in 1984.

Bibliography of the Works of Eugene F. Rice, Jr., 1950-1989

LOUISE RICE

DISSERTATION

"Varieties of Renaissance Wisdom. A Study of the Secularization of an Idea." Harvard University, 1953.

BOOKS AND ARTICLES

1950. "Erasmus and the Religious Tradition, 1495-1499," *Journal of the History of Ideas* 11:387-411.

1952. "John Colet and the Annihilation of the Natural," *Harvard Theological Review* 45:141-63.

1957. "Nicolas of Cusa's Idea of Wisdom," *Traditio* 13:345-68.

1958. *The Renaissance Idea of Wisdom.* Cambridge, MA: Harvard University Press.

1959. Editor, *Medieval and Renaissance Studies,* by T. E. Mommsen. Ithaca, NY: Cornell University Press.

1959. Review of R. Trame, *Rodrigo Sánchez de Arévalo, 1404-1470. Spanish Diplomat and Champion of the Papacy.* Washington, DC: Catholic University of America Press, 1958, in *Renaissance News* 12:105-7.

1960. Review of E. L. Surtz, *The Praise of Wisdom. A Commentary on the Religious and Moral Problems and Backgrounds of St. Thomas More's* Utopia. Chicago: Loyola University Press, 1957, in *Archiv für Reformationsgeschichte* 57:112-13.

1961. "Report on Non-western Material in the Undergraduate Curriculum," *ACLS Newsletter* 12, 7:7.

1961. "Reply to the Editor, *ACLS Newsletter* 12, 10:17-18.

1962. "The Humanist Idea of Christian Antiquity: Jacques Lefèvre d'Étaples and his Circle," *Studies in the Renaissance* 9:126-60.

1962. Review of N. W. Gilbert, *Renaissance Concepts of Method.* New York: Columbia University Press, 1960, in *The Philosophical Review* 71:263-64.

1963. "Foreword," to W. H. Woodward, *Vittorio da Feltre and Other Humanist Educators.* New York: Teachers College, Columbia University, pp. vii-xix.

1963. Review of R. W. Gibson, *St. Thomas More: A Preliminary Bibliography of his Works*. New Haven: Yale University Press, 1961, in *Archiv für Reformationsgeschichte* 54:276-77.

1964. Review of R. Ridolfi, *The Life of Niccolò Machiavelli*, trans. C. Grayson. Chicago: University of Chicago Press, 1963, in *Political Science Quarterly* 79:442-44.

1964. Review of B. L. Ullman, *The Humanism of Coluccio Salutati*. Padua: Editrice Antenore, 1963, in *Speculum* 39:569-70.

1964. Review of *A Translation of St. Thomas More's 'Responsio ad Lutherum,'* ed. G. J. Donnelly. Washington, DC: Catholic University of America, 1962, in *Archiv für Reformationsgeschichte* 55:274-75.

1964. Review of *Erasmus and Cambridge: the Cambridge Letters of Erasmus*, ed. H. C. Porter. Toronto: University of Toronto Press, 1963, in *American Historical Review* 69:1122.

1964. Review of S. R. Jayne, *John Colet and Marsilio Ficino*. Oxford: Oxford University Press, 1963, in *Renaissance News* 17:107-10.

1965. "Recent Studies on the Population of Europe, 1348-1620," *Renaissance News* 18:180-87.

1965. Review of J. Lefèvre d'Étaples, *Epistres & Évangiles pour les cinquante & deux septmaines de l'an. Fac-similé de la première édition de Simon du Bois*, ed. M. A. Screech. Geneva: Droz, 1964, in *American Historical Review* 70:531-32.

1966. Editor. Reissue of *Medieval and Renaissance Studies*, by T. E. Mommsen (1959). Ithaca, NY: Cornell University Press.

1966. Review of F. Gilbert, *Machiavelli and Guicciardini: Politics and History in Sixteenth-Century Florence*. Princeton: Princeton University Press, 1965, in *Political Science Quarterly* 81:114-16.

1968. Reprint of "Erasmus and the Religious Tradition, 1495-1499" (1950), in *Renaissance Essays from the Journal of the History of Ideas*, eds. P. O. Kristeller and P. Wiener. New York: Harper & Row, pp. 162-86.

1968. Review of M. L. Bush, *Renaissance, Reformation and the Outer World*, New York: Humanities Press, 1967, in *American Historical Review* 74:577-78.

1969. Reprint of "The Humanist Idea of Christian Antiquity: Jacques Lefèvre d'Étaples and his Circle" (1962), in *French Humanism, 1470-1600*, ed. W. Gundersheimer. London: Macmillan, pp. 163-80.

1969-1972. Consulting Editor, *Studies in World Civilization*. 6 vols. New York: Alfred A. Knopf.

1970. *The Foundations of Early Modern Europe, 1460-1559*. New York: W. W. Norton.

1970. "Humanist Aristotelianism in France: Jacques Lefèvre d'Étaples and his Circle," in *Humanism in France at the End of the Middle Ages and in the Early Renaissance*, ed. A. H. T. Levi. New York: Barnes & Noble, pp. 132-49.

1971. "Jacques Lefèvre d'Étaples and the Medieval Christian Mystics," in *Florilegium Historiale: Essays presented to Wallace K.*

Ferguson, eds. J. G. Rowe and W. B. Stockdale. Toronto: University of Toronto Press, pp. 89-124.

1971. "The Patrons of French Humanism, 1490-1520," in *Renaissance Studies in Honor of Hans Baron*, eds. A. Molho and J. Tedeschi. Florence: G. C. Sansoni, pp. 687-702.

1972. *The Prefatory Epistles of Jacques Lefèvre d'Étaples and Related Texts*. New York and London: Columbia University Press.

1972. Contributor, *The Columbia History of the World*, eds. J. Garraty and P. Gay. New York: Harper & Row, chapters 39-43.

1973. Reissue of *The Renaissance Idea of Wisdom* (1958). Westport, CT: Greenwood Press.

1974. Advisory editor, *The Western Experience*, by M. Chambers, R. Grew, D. Herlihy, T. Rabb, and I. Woloch. 2 vols. New York: Alfred A. Knopf. (4th ed. 1987.)

1974. "The Idea of the Evangelical," in *The Pursuit of Holiness in Late Medieval and Renaissance Religion*, eds. C. Trinkaus and H. Oberman. Leiden: Brill, pp. 472-76.

1974. Review of E. Jodelle, Le Receuil des inscriptions, 1558. *A Literary and Iconographical Exegesis*, eds. V. E. Graham and W. M. Johnson. Toronto: University of Toronto Press, 1972, in *Renaissance Quarterly* 27:344-46.

1974. Review of *The Collected Works of Erasmus*, I. *The Correspondence of Erasmus*. I. trans. R. A. B. Mynors and D. F. S. Thomson, ed. W. K. Ferguson. Toronto: University of Toronto Press, 1974, in *The Times Literary Supplement*, November 1, p. 1223.

1976. "The 'De magia naturali' of Jacques Lefèvre d'Étaples," in *Philosophy and Humanism: Renaissance Essays in Honor of Paul Oskar Kristeller*, ed. E. Mahoney. New York: Columbia University Press, pp. 19-29.

1976. "The Humanist Idea of Christian Antiquity and the Impact of Greek Patristic Work on Sixteenth-Century Thought," in *Classical Influences on European Culture, A.D. 1500-1700*, ed. R. R. Bolgar. Cambridge: Cambridge University Press, pp. 199-203.

1979. "The Social World of Jean Grolier," *Gazette of the Grolier Club*, N.S. 30/31:51-66.

1980. "Paulus Aegineta," in *Catalogus Translationum et Commentariorum*, vol. 4, ed. P. O. Kristeller and F. E. Cranz. Washington, DC: Catholic University of America Press, pp. 145-91.

1983. "St Jerome's 'Vision of the Trinity': an iconographical note," *The Burlington Magazine* 66:151-55.

1985. *Saint Jerome in the Renaissance*. Baltimore and London: The Johns Hopkins University Press.

1985. "Philosophy," in *A Critical Bibliography of French Literature: The Sixteenth Century*, ed. R. La Charité. Syracuse, NY: Syracuse University Press, pp. 93-107.

1985. "John Hine Mundy: An Appreciation," in *Women of the Medieval World. Essays in Honor of John H. Mundy*, eds. J.

Kirshner and S. Wemple. Oxford and New York: B. Blackwell, pp. 1-5.

1985. Review of B. Ridderbos, *Saint and Symbol. Images of Saint Jerome in Early Italian Art*. Groningen: Bouma's Boekhuis, 1984, in *Burlington Magazine* 127:233-34.

1986. Review of S. L. Reames, *The Legenda Aurea: A Reexamination of its Paradoxical History*. Madison, WI: University of Wisconsin Press, 1985, in *Renaissance Quarterly* 39:279-80.

1986. Review of R. M. Bell, *Holy Anorexia*. Chicago: University of Chicago Press, 1985, in *Renaissance Quarterly* 39:733-35.

1988. Reissue and first paperback ed. *Saint Jerome in the Renaissance* (1985). Baltimore and London: The Johns Hopkins University Press.

1988. "The Renaissance Idea of Christian Antiquity: Humanist Patristic Scholarship;" and "Humanism in France," in *Renaissance Humanism: Foundations, Forms, and Legacy*, ed. A. Rabil. 3 vols. Philadelphia: University of Pennsylvania Press, 1:17-28, 2:109-22.

1988. Review of R. Carrasco, *Inquisición y represión sexual en Valencia. Historia de los sodomitas (1565-1785)*. Barcelona: Laetes S.A. de Ediciones, 1985, in *Commitee on Lesbian and Gay History Newsletter*, n.s. 2, 3:23-25.

I

The Pelham Family
and the Lancastrian Usurpation,
July-September 1399

J. M. W. BEAN

An episode in the campaign of July-September 1399 that deprived Richard II of his throne had always been regarded as belonging primarily to the history of a family that played a leading role in the affairs of Sussex during the succeeding centuries, especially in connection with the Hastings area. The castle of Hastings was held and defended successfully in the Lancastrian interest by Joan, the wife of John Pelham.[1] The husband had served as a squire in the retinue of Henry of Bolingbroke, earl of Derby, a decade earlier.[2] On 7 December 1394 he was granted the office of constable of Hastings castle for life by his lord's father, John of Gaunt, duke of Lancaster.[3] Some years later the duke also granted him all the

1. For accounts of the incident see A. Collins, *The Peerage of England*, ed. Sir Egerton Brydges, 9 vols. (London: F. C. & J. Rivington, etc. 1812; reprinted New York: AMS, 1970), 5:491; T. W. Horsfield, *The History, Antiquities and Topography of the County of Sussex*, 2 vols., (Lewes: Sussex Press, 1835), 1:315; M. A. Lower, *Historical and Genealogical Notices of the Pelham Family* (privately printed, 1873), p. 11; J. H. Wylie, *History of England under Henry the Fourth*, 4 vols. (London: Longman's, 1884-98), 2:112; *Dictionary of National Biography*, 15:693; C. Dawson, *History of Hastings Castle*, 2 vols. (London: Constable, 1909), 1:229; E. G. Pelham and D. McLean, *Some Early Pelhams* (Hove: Combridges, 1931), pp. 62-64; J. S. Roskell, *The Commons in the Parliament of 1422* (Manchester: Manchester University Press, 1954), p. 209; N. Saul, *Scenes from Provincial Life: Knightly Families in Sussex, 1280-1400* (Oxford: Clarendon Press, 1986), p. 71. Throughout the discussion that follows the name "Hastings" is used for the castle, rather than the "Pevensey" of contemporary documents.
2. See R. L. Storey, "Liveries and Commissions of the Peace, 1388-90," in *The Reign of Richard II: Essays in Honour of May McKisack*, ed. F. R. H. Du Boulay and C. M. Barron (London: Athlone Press, 1971), pp. 134-35.
3. Collins, *Peerage*, 5:491. It seems certain, however, that the year given by Collins (17 Richard II) is an error. In July 1396 in a Chancery exemplification Roger Newent was described as constable. See *Calendar of Patent Rolls 1396-99* (henceforth *Cal.Pat.R.*), p. 14. Pelham, however, was mentioned as constable in the account of the bailiff of the court of Pevensey covering the year following Michaelmas 1394 (18-19 Richard II). See Public Record Office (henceforth *PRO*), DL29/441/7096. It is likely that the year of Pelham's

lands in the marshes of Pevensey.[4] Pelham's services in the
events that brought his lord to the throne as Henry IV were
rewarded with a knighthood. And on 24 October 1399 he was
given the honor of the right to carry the king's sword in his
presence.[5] He became a leading councillor of Henry IV; and
further rewards laid the foundations of his family's position in
the upper ranks of the Sussex gentry.[6]

Our knowledge of Joan Pelham's defence of Hastings castle is
entirely based on a single letter. This was first printed by Arthur
Collins in the edition of his *Peerage* published in 1735 and was
reprinted in subsequent editions. The letter was not among the
family muniments in which it had been found by Collins when
these – "the Newcastle MSS" – were deposited in the British
Museum by the earl of Chichester in 1887.

No further trace has survived of the original of this letter or of
other letters and documents from the family muniments that
Collins transcribed or cited in his account of the Pelham family
during the fourteenth and fifteenth centuries. Aside from the
attention given the letter in histories of Hastings, Sussex and the
Pelham family, the letter has also been accorded a place in the
history of the English language. In 1837 Henry Hallam described it
as "one of the earliest instances of female penmanship," adding
"till any other shall prefer a claim, it may pass for the oldest
private letter in the English language." On the basis of "the
badness of the grammar" he assumed the letter was in Joan
Pelham's own hand.[7]

Although copies already exist in print,[8] it is worthwhile providing another for the purpose of the present discussion. Several
phrases are printed in italics because of the need to refer to them.

My dere Lord,

I recommande me to yowr hie Lordeschipp wyth hert and body
and all my pore myght, and wyth all this I think zow, as my dere
Lorde, *derest and best yloved off all erthlyche Lordes:* I say for me, and
thanke yhow my dere Lord, with all thys that I say before, off
your comfortable lettre, that ze send me from Pownefraite, that
com to me on Mary Magdaleyn day: ffor by my trowth I was
never so gladd as when I herd by your lettre, that ye warr stronge
ynogh wyth the grace off God, for to kepe yow fro the malyce of

---

appointment was 18 Richard II. The Chancery document must have contained
an error.
4.   Collins, *Peerage*, 5:491. See also note 14 below.
5.   *Cal. Pat.R.,1399-1401*, p. 45.
6.   See, e.g., Roskell, *Commons in the Parliament of 1422*, pp. 209-11.
7.   H. Hallam, *Introduction to the Literature of Europe in the Fifteenth,
Sixteenth and Seventeenth Centuries*, 4 vols. (London: John Murray, 1837-39), 1:55
and n. 7.
8.   Copies of Collins' text can be found in Horsfield, *History of the County of
Sussex*, 1:315; Lower, *Historical Notices*, p. 11; Dawson, *History of Hastings Castle*,
1:229; Pelham and McLean, *Some Early Pelhams*, p. 65. Modernized versions can
be found in Hallam, *Introduction to Literature*, 1:55 n. 7; L. Lyell, *A Mediaeval
Postbag* (London: Jonathan Cape, 1934), pp. 267-68.

your ennemys. And dere Lord yff it lyk to your hyee Lordeschipp that als son als ye myght, that I myght her off your gracious spede, whych God Allmyghty contynue and encrease. And my dere Lorde if it lyk zow for to know off my ffare, I am here by layd in manner off a sege, wyth the counte of Sussex, Sudray, and a great parcyll off Kentte: so that I ne may noght out, nor none vitayles gette me, bot with myche hard. Wharfore, *my dere* if it lyk zow, by the awyse off zowr wyse counsell, for to sette remedye off the salvation off *yhower castell*, and withstand the malyce off ther schires foresayde. And also that ye be fullyche enformed off these grett malyce wykers in these schyres, whyche yat haffes so dispytffuly wroght to zow, and *to zowr castell, to zhow men, and to zour tenaunts* ffore this cuntree, have yai wastede for a gret whyle.

Fare wel my dere Lorde, the Holy Trinyte zow kepe fro zour ennemys, and son send me gud tythyngs off yhow.

Ywryten at Pevensay in the castell, on Saynt Jacobe day last past.

By yhour awnn pore J. PELHAM.
To my trew Lorde.

In 1928 L. F. Salzman disturbed the consensus that had existed about this letter ever since it had been printed by Collins. He drew attention[9] to a serious difficulty in ascribing its authorship to a wife of John Pelham whose name was Joan. The only known wife with the initial "J." was the widow of Sir Hugh Zouche. But he died on 11 July 1399, and the letter was written on 25 July. The Joan in question had certainly married Pelham by 24 May 1400, when Henry IV granted a pardon to Pelham for marrying the widow of a tenant-in-chief without royal licence.[10]

Salzman understandably dismissed the possibility that Joan married Pelham within two weeks of the death of her first husband. To his judgment that this was *a priori* unlikely we may add another consideration. The lady Joan was an heiress in her own right. It is difficult to believe that such a widow, who also was to receive a dower interest in her late husband's lands, would have risked her future as a desirable match by marrying herself to the squire of a magnate, the success of whose return from exile was by no means a foregone conclusion at the time of her supposed marriage. It is not, of course, absolutely impossible, as Salzman admitted, that Pelham was married at the time to another Joan who must have died within a few months or so of the letter being written. But, if so, no trace of her has survived, let alone her survival at the time the letter was written. In the light of the fact that the signatory of the letter was the only Joan who was definitely known to have married John Pelham, Salzman was

9.   L. F. Salzman, "The Early Heraldry of Pelham," *Sussex Archaeological Collections*, 69 (1928): 55-56. R. Somerville, *History of the Duchy of Lancaster*, (London: Her Majesty's Stationery Office, 1953), 1:137 n. 1, regards the letter as "apocryphal." Cf. the fanciful and romantic treatment in Pelham and McLean, *Some Early Pelhams*, pp. 63-64.
10.   *Cal. Pat.R., 1399-1401*, p. 287.

driven to entertain the possibility that the letter is a forgery. It is, however, necessary to reject this suggestion. Doubts about the letter's style and orthography to which Salzman drew attention do not provide a convincing argument. It is more than likely that the copy provided by Collins contains errors of transcription. The transcript of a valor of Pelham's estates that he printed in a later edition (that of 1756) is wrongly dated[11] and contains inaccurate extensions of manuscript abbreviations.[12]

More important, it is impossible to understand why such a letter would have been forged. It would hardly have been necessary at the time to manufacture a piece of evidence in order to convince the new king of the worth of Pelham's services during the events that led to his accession. Nor does it seem possible that the letter was forged generations later as part of the Pelham family's efforts to add distinction to their origins. It apparently formed part of a group of documents[13] in the duke of Newcastle's muniments relating to the career of John Pelham before he was knighted in 1399; and surviving accounts of the duchy of Lancaster corroborate the authenticity of two cited by Collins – John of Gaunt's grant of the constableship of Hastings castle and that of lands within the lordship.[14] Moreover, the date on which the letter was written – 25 July – fits with what we know of Bolingbroke's movements at the time. He landed in Yorkshire, probably at Ravenspur. He must have reached Pontefract by 11 or 12 July.[15] It is unlikely that he spent more than a day or two there.[16] But a letter sent from there at some point in the period 11-14 July is quite likely[17] to have reached its recipient in Hastings on 22 July, the date mentioned in the Pelham letter.

11. For this see Collins, *Peerage*, 5:494-95. The valor includes the rape of Hastings together with the manors of Crowhurst, Burwash, and Bevilham. On 21 November 1412 Henry IV granted these to Pelham in reversion after the death of Ralph Neville, earl of Westmorland (*Cal.Pat.R.,1408-13*, p. 457; Brit. Lib., Addit. Ch., 29,972 and 30,045). The earl did not die until 21 October 1425. Pelham then entered into these estates (*PRO*, C139/39/9/m. 2). If we can assume that Collins transcribed the number "5" correctly, the valor must be assigned to 5 Henry VI (1426-27). This would have been the regnal year that included the beginning (Michaelmas 1426) of the first full financial year of Pelham's occupation. It is not surprising that a valor was drawn up about this time and that this survived in the family's archives.
12. E.g., *Receptoria* instead of *Recepte* and *particularit* instead of *particulariter*. There is a lack of consistency in the handling of MS abbreviations (Collins, *Peerage*, 5:494-95). It is likely that this was due to Collins' lack of experience of this sort of document, especially in the case of the transcription *Feodar*.
13. Ibid., 5:491.
14. A portreeve's account of 1396-97 indicates that Pelham held a farm of the demesne lands from Michaelmas 1397 for a term of ten years (*PRO*, DL29/441/ 7097). See also note 3 above.
15. J. L. Kirby, *Henry IV of England* (London: Constable, 1970), p. 55.
16. Cf. ibid., p. 55.
17. See the times listed in C. A. J. Armstrong, "Some Examples of the Distribution and Speed of News at the Time of the Wars of the Roses," *Studies in Medieval History Presented to Frederick Maurice Powicke*, ed. R. W. Hunt, W. A. Pantin and R. W. Southern (Oxford: Clarendon Press, 1948), pp. 429-54,

In view of the doubts raised by Salzman, it is odd that neither he nor any other scholar has sought to question the accepted attribution of the letter to the wife of John Pelham and to consider the possibility that the author was Pelham himself. In fact, the only support for the wife's authorship, apart from the initial "J." appears to be a family tradition that Collins accepted. It has also been assumed that Pelham was with Bolingbroke at the time the letter was written; but this rests entirely on family tradition.[18]

In fact, both the style and the content of the letter give strong support to Pelham's authorship. With one exception, the language, especially the repetition of the phrase "my dere lorde," is no different from what we would expect from a loyal squire writing to a great lord he was anxious to impress. The exception is the single phrase "my dere." But the omission of the noun "lorde" can be readily explained in terms of careless transcription, either on the part of the original scribe or that of Collins. Furthermore, it is odd that, if the "J." in the signature stood for Joan, there was no other language indicating that the writer was the intended recipient's wife. In contrast, the letters from wives in the Paston family collection give Christian names in full and contain other indications of a conjugal relationship between the writer and the recipient.[19]

The most solid evidence, however, that helps to destroy the assumption that the writer was Pelham's wife lies in the words "yhower castell" and "to zowr castell, to zhow men and to zour tenaunts." By no stretch of the imagination could the wife of a constable of a castle who was holding it in his stead employ such language about the castle itself or the tenants of the surrounding lordship. To be sure, Pelham himself held a life-estate within the lordship[20] and may have had subtenants; but the lands involved were not substantial, and the letter's language clearly implies that the writer was thinking in terms of the lordship as a whole. The words "castell" and "tenaunts" only make sense if we understand that the intended recipient was Bolingbroke himself and that the writer was the actual constable of the castle.

---

reprinted in Armstrong, *England, France and Burgundy in the Fifteenth Century* (London: The Hambledon Press, 1983), pp. 97-122. The best comparison is the time taken by the news of Edward IV's victory at Towton sent by him from York on 30 March 1461, which reached his mother in the early morning of 4 April (ibid., pp. 114-15). We must also allow additional time for the further distance to Hastings.

18. According to this tradition, Pelham went into exile with Bolingbroke. This can be dismissed, since he was apparently in Sussex on 25 October 1398 (*Cal.Pat.R., 1396-99*, p. 524). He also appears to have been there on the following 29 December when he witnessed a charter as constable of Hastings castle (Brit. Lib., Addit. Ch., 30,717), though it seems unlikely that he exercised the duties of that office so long after Richard II's seizure of the Lancastrian inheritance. He may, of course, have crossed the Channel to join his lord after this date.

19. *The Paston Letters and Papers of the Fifteenth Century*, ed. N. Davis, 2 parts (Oxford: Clarendon Press, 1971-76), passim.

20. See above notes 4 and 14.

These arguments are supported by the explanation that Henry IV as duke of Lancaster gave for a special reward conferred on John Pelham, now a knight, on 12 February 1400. His constableship was now granted to him and his heirs in tail male, it being stated that as constable "at our late arrival in England took by force and held to our use our said castle of Pevensey and did other noble and pleasing services for which we are bound to reward him."[21] It is clear that Pelham was in personal command of the castle's defence.

There is only one possible objection to this conclusion. Why, if the recipient was Bolingbroke, was the letter found among the muniments of the Pelham family, and not those of the Crown or the duchy of Lancaster? It is, of course, possible that the document transcribed by Collins was either a draft of the letter that was sent or a copy made at the time. But it is more likely that shortly after it was written it was overtaken by events and either not sent or not delivered. Edmund, duke of York, whom Richard II had left in charge of the kingdom when he left for Ireland, met Bolingbroke at Berkeley castle on 27 July and joined forces with him;[22] and news of his intentions may well have been known before this.

If these arguments are accepted, the Pelham letter loses its claim to be regarded as the earliest letter written in the English language by a woman. The attribution to John Pelham has, however, implications that transcend the history of the Pelham family and that of Hastings castle. We now obtain a new insight into the strategy that lay behind Bolingbroke's landing in early July 1399. He chose to arrive in person in a region where the territorial power of the house of Lancaster was strongest. But the fact that he wrote to Pelham from Pontefract and the clear indications in Pelham's reply that he had expected to hear from his lord together suggest that there was a deliberate intervention in the south as well as the north.[23]

The holdings of the house of Lancaster south of the Thames consisted mainly of manors, Hastings being the only castle. It made sense for Bolingbroke to create a presence in his name in the south, even though his main effort was elsewhere. The result would be some diversion of efforts directed against the force he led in person. Indeed, the language of Pelham's letter indicates that the government laid siege to Hastings castle with forces drawn from Kent and Surrey, as well as Sussex.

21.   For the copy entered in the Chancery register of the Duchy of Lancaster see *PRO*, DL 42/15/fol. 21v. Brit. Lib, Addit. Ch. 31,577 is a copy kept in the family's muniments. See also *Sir Christopher Hatton's Book of Seals*, ed. L. C. Loyd and D. M. Stenton. Publications of the Northamptonshire Record Society 15 (Oxford: Northamptonshire Record Society, 1950), p. 340.
22.   Kirby, *Henry IV*, p. 57.
23.   It has been suggested that Pelham was put ashore when Bolingbroke touched on the Sussex coast. See E. F. Jacob, *The Fifteenth Century* (Oxford: Clarendon Press, 1961), pp. 1-2. Although this is possible, there is no evidence. See note 18 above.

It is also possible that Bolingbroke had in mind the risks of intervention from France and wished to discourage this. To be sure, he had made an agreement with the duke of Orleans, who controlled the government of France[24] at the time of his departure. But this did not totally remove the risk of some sort of intervention from France, since Richard II was married to a daughter of the French king. If a Lancastrian presence was to be established south of the Thames, Hastings castle was the obvious choice for a base. And it may not be entirely fanciful to suggest that this had a propaganda value, because it encouraged memories of a successful invasion three centuries earlier. This reconstruction of the events of Bolingbroke's invasion has the merit of explaining why a few months later, after his lord's accession to the throne, a mere squire was not only knighted for his services but also given the signal honor of bearing the the king's sword in his presence.

It is also worthwhile examining Pelham's choice of language at one point in his letter. He described Bolingbroke as the "derest and best yloved off all erthlyche Lordes." At the time these words were written Richard II still lawfully occupied the throne. And such language in law could only be used of the king by any loyal subject. Caution must obviously be employed in discussing the meaning and implications of Pelham's language. These were the words of a retainer who was making a special effort to impress his lord. At the same time, Pelham must have been aware of the implications of his language and must have felt that his lord would at least find it acceptable. In any event, this portion of Pelham's letter deserves serious attention in any discussion of Bolingbroke's intentions when he landed in Yorkshire in July 1399.

Scholars have engaged in a great deal of discussion of the one piece of evidence that bears directly on this issue – Bolingbroke's claim that he returned to England merely to secure his rights of inheritance. Whether or not an oath was taken by him to this effect and perjury was then committed by him and leading supporters, the correct attribution of Pelham's letter provides reason to believe that a follower who occupied a position in the inner circle of Bolingbroke's supporters and must have been privy to his intentions addressed his lord in terms that were appropriate for a lawful ruler.

24. Kirby, *Henry IV*, p. 54. See also M. Nordberg, *Les ducs et la Royauté. Études sur la rivalité des ducs d'Orleans et de Bourgogne, 1392-1407.* Studia historica upsaliensia 12 (Upsala: Studia historica upsaliensia, 1964), p. 111; J. J. N. Palmer, *England, France and Christendom 1377-99* (London: Routledge and Kegan Paul, 1972), p. 225.

II

Michelangelo's *Sacrifice* on the Sistine Ceiling*

JAMES BECK

Amazingly enough, the proper identification of the third scene on the main field of the Sistine Ceiling, reading from the entrance or the seventh reading from the altar, has not been determined in the vast body of modern scholarly literature devoted to Michelangelo. For example, recent studies of the ceiling, including the authoritative accounts of J. O'Malley and A. Chastel, have referred to the fresco as the *Sacrifice of Noah*[1] (fig. 1). Also of like opinion are Frederick Hartt and Esther G. Dotson, as are, really, all modern scholars.[2] They are fully aware that the identification goes contrary to the 1553 biography by Ascanio Condivi, who is properly regarded as registering Michelangelo's own "corrections" to Vasari's first life of the master of 1550.[3] Condivi unequivocally reports: "Nel settimo è il sacrificio di Abel e di Cain: quello grato e accetto a Dio, questo odioso e reprobato."[4]

*   I trust that Gene Rice will not be displeased if I offered on this occasion results of ongoing research. The conclusions reached thus far are based largely upon textual interpretation, a procedure that he has always held to be worthy.

1.   J. O'Malley, S.J. "The Theology Behind Michelangelo's Ceiling," in *The Sistine Chapel. The Art, the History, and the Restoration*, ed. C. Pietrangeli (New York: Harmony Books, 1986), p. 130; and A. Chastel, "First reactions to the Ceiling," in op. cit., pp. 154-57.
2.   F. Hartt, "'Lignum vitae in medio paradisi': The Stanza di Eliodoro and the Sistine Ceiling," *Art Bulletin* 32 (1951): 131, 186. E. G. Dotson, "An Augustinian Interpretation of Michelangelo's Sistine Ceiling, Part 1," *Art Bulletin* 61 (1979): 242 ff. J. D. Oremland follows the same tradition by calling the scene the *Sacrifice of Noah*, although he describes the action as "a complicated representation of the paternal side of the generational struggle," in *Michelangelo's Sistine Ceiling. A Psychoanalytic Study of Creativity* (New York: International Universities Press, 1989), p. 81. A summary of earlier scholarly opinion may be found in G. Vasari, *La Vita di Michelangelo nelle redazioni del 1550 e del 1568*, ed. with notes by P. Barocchi (Milan: Ricciardi, 1962), 2:541-43, who concludes that the identification as Noah's Sacrifice is the more probable.
3.   See T. S. R. Boase, *Giorgio Vasari: The Man and the Book* (Princeton, NJ: Princeton University Press 1979), pp. 249-50.
4.   A. Condivi, *Vita di Michelangelo* (Florence: Rinascimento del libro, 1938), p. 81.

Vasari had referred previously to the depiction as the *Sacrifice of Noah:* "Nè è di minor bellezza la storia del sacrifizio di Noè dove sono chi porta le legne e chi soffia chinato nel fuoco et altri che scannano la vittima...," so that Condivi's designation was in effect an emendation of Vasari.

Condivi's explanation was followed by Vasari in his second edition published in 1568, which reads "Nè di minor bellezza è la storia del sacrificio di Caino ed Abel; dove sono, chi porta le legne, e chi soffia chinato nel fuoco, ed altri che scannono la vittima...."[5] That is, Vasari retains the language of his first edition, except that the title of the scene is changed to conform to Condivi (and Michelangelo).

Despite their loyalty to the identification of the scene as the *Sacrifice of Noah,* modern scholars have been keenly aware that, so identified, it is out of chronological order. The biblical account calls for the scene to come *after* the *Flood,* not before it. O'Malley argues, as support for the correctness of the identification and its idiosyncratic placement, that according to legend the Erythraean Sibyl married one of Noah's sons, which would explain why she sits near this scene. This historian goes on to assert: "The presence of the *Sacrifice of Noah* was appropriate, surely, in a chapel intended for the celebration of the sacrifice of the mass of which it was a 'type'."[6] Chastel dismisses the Cain and Abel identification, judging it as "certainly impossible" because, he claims, Cain and Abel are nowhere to be found. Chastel continues by maintaining that the subject represented is quite clearly *Noah sacrificing* as described in Genesis 8:20-21, when Noah is said to have taken every clean beast and fowl and offered burnt offerings on the altar, and the Lord smelled a sweet odor.[7] Dotson agrees: "The Sacrifice *cannot* [emphasis mine] be that of Cain and Abel: there are too many participants, and only the acceptable animal sacrifice is shown. In both respects, the representation conforms perfectly to the biblical account of the *Sacrifice of Noah.*" The scene would present no problem of identification if its position did not disrupt biblical order, she observed.[8] Dotson, however, does not associate the representation with the postdiluvian passage in Genesis as does Chastel, Gen. 8:20, but with an earlier reference, Gen. 4:2-5, a reference that must represent a *lapsis mentis,* because the biblical citation is to the Sacrifices of Cain and Abel, the identification she has rejected.[9]

5. G. Vasari, *La vita de Michelangelo,* ed Barocchi, 1:45.
6. O'Malley, "The Theology Behind Michelangelo's Ceiling," p. 130.
7. Chastel, "First Reactions to the Ceiling," p. 155.
8. Dotson, "An Augustinian Interpretation," p. 232; F. Hartt, "'Lignum vitae'," pp. 131, 186.
9. Dotson, "An Augustinian Interpretation," p. 234 n. 62. An effort to connect the scene to a time before the Flood was made by G. Parroni in "Una rivelazione della Sistina: L'Offerta degli empi," in *Illustrazione vaticana* 4 (1933): 639, cited in C. de Tolnay, *Michelangelo* (Princeton, NJ: Princeton University Press, 1945), 2:133, who finds it unlikely. Tolnay, in fact, raises the following objections to the scene in question being the *Sacrifice of Cain and*

The biblical texts might be compared at this point for the sake of clarification.

[Gen. 4:2-5. Cain and Abel Sacrificing]

(2) And she [Eve] again bare his brother Abel. And Abel was a keeper of sheep but Cain was a tiller of the ground. (3) And in process of time it came to pass, that Cain brought of the fruit of the ground an offering unto the Lord. (4) And Abel, he also brought of the firstlings of his flock and of the fat thereof. And the Lord had respect unto Abel and to his offerings: (5) But unto Cain and to his offering he had not respect. And Cain was very wroth, and his countenance fell.

[Vulgate, Gen. 4:2-5]

(2) Rursumque peperit fratrem eius Abel. Fuit autem Abel pastor ovium, et Cain agricola. (3) Factum est autem post multos dies ut offerret Cain de fructibus terrae munera Domino. (4) Abel quoque obtulit de primogenitis gregis sui, et de adipibus eorum: et respexit Dominus ad Abel, et ad munera eius. (5) Ad Cain vero, et ad munera illius non respexit: iratusque est Cain vehementer, et concidit vultus eius.

[Gen. 8:20-21. Noah Sacrificing]

(20) And Noah builded an altar unto the Lord; and took of every clean beast. and of every clean fowl, and offered burnt offerings on the altar. (21) And the Lord smelled a sweet savour....

[Vulgate, Gen. 8:20-21]

(20) Ædificavit autem Noe altare Domino: et tollens de cunctis pecoribus et volucribus mundis, obtulit holocausta super altare. (21) Odoratusque est Dominus odorem suavitatis....

A detailed description of the fresco seems desirable at this point if one recognizes, as did Tolnay but not the other experts mentioned herein, that the fresco had undergone extensive repainting by the Modenese master Domenico Carnevale (or Carnevali), between 1566 and 1572. As far was we know, the *Sacrifice* was the only one of the nine histories to have been so subjected, apparently because it was required by severe cracking of the *intonaco*. The women in the front plane near the central axis and the nude youth to the left by her side holding the ram have been totally repainted, except for the extremities, along with the head of the ram.[10] Obviously the newly painted replacement

---

Abel: (l) the type of "Noah" found at the altar corresponds to that in the other representations of Noah on the Ceiling; (2) because of the animals that come out of the ark and can be related only with the *Sacrifice of Noah;* (3) the number of figures, eight, corresponds to the family of Noah.

10.   E. Steinmann, *Die Sixtinische Kapelle*, 3 vols. (Munich: Bruckmann, 1901-1905), 2:314 n. 3; and especially G. Bottari, ed., *G. Vasari, Vita di Michelangelo* (Rome: N. & N. Pagliarini, 1760), pp. 176-77. Alessandro Conti, who does not question the *Noah Sacrificing* identification of the scene in his recent monograph on the Sistine Ceiling, effectively raises the problem of the

portions cannot be wholly dependent upon when considering the iconography. Furthermore even portions that had not been damaged may have received some retouchings, simply because, in the course of filling in the lost sections, the others have required adjustments in order to conform to the newly painted elements. That is, we must imagine that Carnevale had to integrate what he had produced with what had remained essentially undamaged. I am assuming, notwithstanding the repainting, however, that the composition and the general details as they are now presented closely reflect Michelangelo's original intention.

The *Sacrifice*, a rectangular panel with a proportion of 1 [h.] to 1.5, is surrounded by a marble frame obscured from view at the corners by four *ignudi*. Although the space appears rather crowded, there are but eight figures, an acceptable number for an Albertian *istoria*, plus two rams and, in the upper left corner, the heads of an ox and an ass, the head and neck of a horse, and the partially visible trunk and head of an elephant.[11]

The composition is divided vertically by the edge of the foreshortened altar, which is located obliquely in the rather shallow pictorial space that consists of two planes. On the first plane, reading from left to right, a nude youth holds a ram with his right knee, and with his arm he grabs one of its twisted horns. His left foot virtually rests upon the lower edge of the picture, while the toes appear to break or at least touch the picture plane. This figure looks towards the right, at a red-colored object held by the woman next to him. She presents it (a fowl or "clean" bird for Chastel; more likely, a piece of bloody meat or "fat" is my suggestion) to another youth at the right who is sitting on the other ram.[12] She also looks across to the right to the lad: both of their heads are in profile. Beneath the woman is another nude boy whose head is turned sharply into the pictorial space; he appears to be crawling on the ground, his head framed by the fire in the altar, which he seems to be tending, at least as Vasari would have it. The nude youth who straddles the ram at the center right is strongly contrappostal in pose; his left arm is slung across the body, while the legs move in the opposite direction. The fifth figure on the near plane who holds a oversized bundle of stripped

sixteenth-century restoration. See *Michelangelo e la pittura a fresco. Tecnica e conservazione della Volta Sistina* (Florence: La Casa Usher, 1986), pp. 77-80.

11.   Dotson, "An Augustinian Interpretation," pp. 253-54, makes a good deal out of the juxtaposition of the ox and the ass, which are time-honored symbols of the Jews and Gentiles, the Old and New Law. She adds to the equation the horse, which continues the structure of threes that are commonly associated with the entire ceiling, in which the third animal stands for the church. This argumentation fails to take into account the massive head and trunk of an elephant behind the other animals.

12.   From the detail reproduced Pietrangeli, *Sistine Chapel*, p. 156, I find it difficult to read a bird or fowl there, as does Chastel, who finds it necessary to have such an element to correspond to the biblical text for Noah's thanksgiving. In Jacopo della Quercia's *Noah Giving Thanks (Sacrifice of Noah)* fowls are prominently in evidence (fig. 3).

branches also looks down at the unidentified object. The uneasily posed and awkwardly rendered ram on the left appears to be struggling: he too looks off to his right. His sad-eyed counterpart on the other side with his head foreshortened rests on the ground, revealing a deadly wound in the throat.

In the second plane, which can be readily determined in the upper portion of the pictorial field, are three frontally posed figures at the back of the altar that seems to be placed obliquely in space; off to the left are the four animals. The central figure, a bearded and bald old men who presides over the event, is clothed in a red garment. Standing in front of a marble building, he holds his right hand raised with the index finger turned upward, seeming to be in the act of speaking. His left hand rests on the altar table beside the burning offerings. The flames lick upward in the middle directly in front of the old man but bend off sideways near the women on the left, who seems to be stirring the flames with an object in her left hand.[13] Her right hand is raised, perhaps in a gesture of awe, amazement or revulsion, as she looks down upon the red object being presented below. The other women who wears a white shawl over her head is very aged, a contemporary of the man with whom she seems to be communicating.

Is this scene *Noah Sacrificing,* as modern criticism would have it, or the *Sacrifice of Cain and Abel,* as reported by Condivi and Vasari? Herein lies a question that affects not merely the appropriate evaluation of the scene itself, but its relation to the other eight histories and, ultimately, the entire fresco. A look at some earlier and contemporary representations might supply clues.

Ghiberti's second doors for the Baptistry, familiar to Michelangelo and often cited as having offered insight to the master for aspects of the ceiling's imagery, contain both representations: the *Sacrifice of Cain and Abel* and the *Sacrifice of Noah* (fig. 2). Actually Michelangelo's scene does not appear to be connected specifically with either, although in Ghiberti's *Cain and Abel,* which occurs in the second panel of the Paradise doors, the flames of Abel's offering rise upward from the altar table, while Cain's is smothered on a separate altar, as appears to be the case with the fire on Michelangelo's single altar. The bearded God the Father blesses Abel.[14] The third panel of Ghiberti's doors are devoted to events related to Noah, including his *Sacrifice,* which is located on the lower right. Here a number of elements are, in fact, shared with the *Sacrifice* on the Sistine ceiling: the altar, the fire, a bundle of sticks for burning, a ram and the number of figures, which totals eight, including Noah (fig. 2). While not strictly

13.   It was the manner in which the flames operated on the altar that first alerted me to inherent problem with the Noah Sacrificing identification.
14.   In an oversight R. Krautheimer and T. Krautheimer-Hess, *Lorenzo Ghiberti* (Princeton: Princeton University Press, 1956), p. 160, does not single out this sub-scene in his schema of the Gates of Paradise for the second panel.

speaking in the same area, there are animals within the larger framework of the scene, including many birds and a conspicuous eagle.

Another cycle from the early *quattrocento* contains both scenes: Jacopo della Quercia's Portal of San Petronio in Bologna, long recognized as a mine for Michelangelo, especially because he was in Bologna shortly (February) before beginning the painting of the ceiling on 10 May 1508. Quercia's cycle must have have been fresh in his mind (figs. 3 and 4). In his treatment of the *Sacrifice of Cain and Abel*, unlike Ghiberti's, Jacopo della Quercia has a single altar with both offerings burning on it, analogous to the altar in the scene from the Sistine ceiling. Here too the flame of Abel's offering burns high, while the flame of Cain's offering is smothered, as a sign of rejection.[15] Abel, located in the space beneath his offering, is rendered in profile, seemingly a preferential attitude.

Jacopo's *Sacrifice of Noah* on the same pilaster does not show Noah literally supervising or officiating over the sacrifice. Rather he is giving thanks, his hands clasped in prayer. Noah is accompanied by family members whose total number is eight, together with an array of animals and fowls of the air; the latter element is totally missing in the Sistine treatment. In both Ghiberti's and Jacopo della Quercia's interpretations, Noah is shown in prayer and located off to one side, as it were, not specifically at the altar. The same arrangement is found in the fresco in the Vatican from "Raphael's Bible" illustrating *Noah's Sacrifice*, produced by the Urbanite's shop, which by then had easy access to Michelangelo's Ceiling, as is verified by other examples from the same cycle as well as by the stucco decorations of the *logge*. In this late contemporary example, although several elements are shared, in particular the two rams and the presence of an ox and an ass, the figures in the Raphaelesque composition are six in number, not eight; the number is influential, it may be recalled, for the association of Michelangelo's scene with Noah by some specialists.[16] Noah in profile is shown in grateful prayer,

15. In the rendering of the so-called "Florentine Picture Chronicle" in the British Museum the sheet with *The Fall of Adam and Eve* (above) is united with that of the *The Sacrifice of Cain and Abel* (below), which is, in turn, conflated with the Murder of Abel. Here too the flames of Abel's sacrifice wind upward to God, while those of Cain whirl chaotically. See S. Colvin, *A Florentine Picture-Chronicle by Maso Finiguerra* (reprint, New York: B. Blom, 1970), plate 1. The *Murder of Abel* follows the scene of the *Fall* and the *Expulsion of Adam and Eve* in the mid-fourteenth century relief cycle on the Silver Altar of St. Jacopo in Pistoia, for which see L. Gai, *L'altare argenteo di San Jacopo nel Duomo di Pistoia* (Turin: Allemandi, 1984), p. 102.

16. Paolo Uccello's *Sacrifice of Noah* among the frescoes in the Chiostro Verde in Florence seems to have had seven figures for the event. Its poor state of preservation provides difficulties for an accurate reconstruction. On the other hand, from the evidence available it appears that Noah is behind the altar, and that there is a woman by his side. The actual slaughter of the ram is not shown, however; apparently there was once the head of the burnt animal on the altar. There also seem to have been birds in Uccello's treatment.

not in the role of an officiating priest, as is the case with Michelangelo's *Sacrifice*.[17] Furthermore, Noah is alone, in distinction to the Sistine Chapel treatment, where he is accompanied by two other figures, presumably his wife and a daughter(?), if we accept the conventional modern designation.

Although precise identifications of all the figures in Michelangelo's *Sacrifice* are not readily apparent when read as either alternative, when understood as the *Sacrifice of Cain and Abel*, the nude youth on the lower right shown with his head in profile has good claims to being Abel; his repainted counterpart on the opposite side of the scene is plausibly interpreted as Cain. Perhaps a better possibility for Cain, however, is the draped figure holding the bundle of heavy sticks on the extreme right who moves out of the sacred environment as he glances back angrily toward the center of the scene.[18] Abel is in close proximity to the flaming sacrifice associated with him.[19]

THE MEDALLIONS

Not only is there difficulty in specifying all the figures in the *Sacrifice*, but the appropriate definitions of the subjects of the medallions in general, and in particular those located on either side of the *Sacrifice*, have not achieved a consensus. Condivi stated, as one might indeed expect, that these bronze or gold colored medallions are related to the histories beside them ("son fatte varie storie, tutte a proposito però della principale [storia]").[20] Hence, in seeking the proper interpretation for the main scenes, the monochromatic reliefs might prove useful.

Tolnay has identified the subjects of the two medallions on either side of the *Sacrifice* as (left) *The Destruction of Baal* (2 Kings

---

17.   See B. F. Davidson, *Raphael's Bible. A Study of the Vatican Logge* (University Park, PA and London: Pennsylvania State University Press, 1985), p. 67 and passim.   A Raphaelesque scene from the ceiling of the Stanza d'Eliodoro in the Vatican is commonly identified as *God Appearing to Noah After the Flood*.   Noah is shown in profile, hands clasped in prayer before the bearded figure of God the Father.   There are strong reflections from Michelangelo's ceiling that are even more evident in Marcantonio's engraving of the subject, datable to 1513-15; for which see I. H. Shoemaker, ed., *The Engravings of Marcantonio Raimondi* (Lawrence, KS: Spencer Museum of Art, 1981), pp. 104-5.
18.   This suggestion was made to me by Dr. Maria Grazia Pernis, whom I take this opportunity to thank cordially.
19.   The most difficult identifications are the figures behind the altar.   The central figure could be God the Father or, perhaps, Adam and with him, on the right, Eve.   They are both aged and, oddly enough, have a certain correspondence to Piero della Francesca's figures of the same personages in the *Death of Adam* in his Arezzo frescoes.   Parenthetically, I cannot say that I am particularly pleased with this solution.
20.   Tolnay, *Michelangelo*, 2:171 and Condivi, *Vita*, p. 85. Vasari in the second edition (p. 97) said that they were scenes taken from the Book of Kings.   Of course, these two ideas are not in conflict. Tolnay, loc. cit., gives a summary of previous interpretations.

10:25-29) and (right) *The Death of Uriah* (2 Samuel 11:16-17).[21] The biblical text for the former begins with an account of a burnt offering and the slaying of the soldiers of Jehu and says that "they brake down the image of Baal." The so-called Baal Medallion, which may well be unfinished, shows a nude idol standing in profile on a high altar with his left arm extended; it is in a proportion of about 1 to 2 to the living figures on the ground. A helmeted soldier who occupies the main position in the composition holds a stick with his left hand, with which he seems to be about to hit the idol. Tolnay suggested that an assistant who executed the medallion used a drawing by Michelangelo, which he reversed: hence the left-handedness of the idol and of the main figure. Speaking against this theory, the figure to the left of the central one holds his staff in his right hand. It should be recalled that Michelangelo himself was left-handed. The soldiers on the left side of the altar are juxtaposed with two figures on the right behind the altar who seem to be civilians: they are unfinished, as Tolnay has observed. In terms of the biblical text, which deals with Jehu in 2 Kings 10:25, we find the following, which is quite relevant to the Sacrifice nearby: "And it came to pass, as soon as he had made an end of offering the burnt offering, that Jehu said to the guard and to the captains, Go in, and slay them..." and a few lines later in verse 27: "And they brake down the images of Baal...." I see no reason to discard Tolnay's identification of the medallion; although, as shall be mentioned shortly, alternatives for this subject have been proposed.

The *Death of Uriah*, on the other side of the *Sacrifice*, has a murderous aura that harmonizes with the new/old identification as the Sacrifice of Cain and Abel, which I am advocating here. David arranges, as it were, the death of Uriah, his beloved Bathsheba's husband, in an act worthy of Cain ("the thing that David had done displeased the Lord," 2 Samuel 12:27). In the tondo composition, the youth on the ground is about to receive blows from a man hovering over him on the right who holds a staff with both hands, and another beside him, while the horse rears up behind the youth, whose left arm is raised. In the left background, rather faintly rendered (unfinished) a Christlike man is kneeling, perhaps in prayer.

These two scenes, along with the other medallions, have been associated with the Ten Commandments by Wind, who on this point has been followed by Dodson: both scholars appear to disregard out of hand Condivi's assertion of connections between the medallions and the subjects in the nearby main field. Dodson does accept the identification of Jehu destroying the idol of Baal as an alternative to several subjects from Maccabees, which in any case she connects to the Second Commandment.[22] For the other

---

21.   Tolnay, *Michelangelo*, 2:73-74, 275. Hartt, "'Lignum vitae'," p. 200, accepts these identifications.
22.   Dotson, "An Augustinian Interpretation," pp. 422, 423-24. For the most part she follows E. Wind, "Maccabean Histories in the Sistine Ceiling," in

theme she accepts the identification as Heliodorus Driven from the Temple in Maccabees, associated with the Eighth Commandment. The subject, of course, was celebrated by Raphael in one of the *stanze* of the Vatican shortly after the ceiling was finished. I see no reason, however, to question the murderous content, as proposed by Tolnay, especially since it conforms not only to Condivi's information, but to Vasari's as well, who said the medallions were related to the Books of Kings. To summarize, the medallions on either side of the *Sacrifice* are perfectly compatible to Cain and Abel's Sacrifice, and indeed provide references to the aftermath, namely the murder of Abel by his brother.

CONCLUSION

Modern criticism has emphatically rejected Condivi's designation of the *Sacrifice*, although Vasari accepted it. Consequently Michelangelo scholarship has left itself open to pitfalls in an ongoing search to explain the entire ceiling. The division of the main scenes into groupings of threes seems sensible and desirable; it has the decided advantage of unifying the design and the subjects into equal groups: Noah scenes, Adam and Eve scenes; and God the Father scenes. Yet this attractive division needs to be abandoned, or at least interpreted somewhat differently when the *Sacrifice* is correctly regarded as the *Sacrifice of Cain and Abel*.

Condivi's life of Michelangelo, written when the master was already old, though still vigorous, is correctly understood as a response to Vasari's *Life* of 1550, offering an opportunity for Michelangelo to make corrections and emendations. That is, Condivi's version has the authority of an official biography. In his second edition of 1568 Vasari somewhat slavishly incorporated Condivi's account, as is the case for the reference to the *Sacrifice*. In the first edition, Vasari identified the scene as the *Sacrifice of Noah;* Condivi corrected Vasari, presumably in consultation with Michelangelo, calling it the *Sacrifice of Cain and Abel*. Vasari, in his second edition, abandons his own earlier identification, an admission that he was convinced by Condivi. The Condivi/Vasari[2] identification has the distinct advantage of removing an obvious chronological inconsistency, one that would have been immediately recognized by Vatican officials, not to mention Michelangelo's enemies. Such an aberration in the highly visible ceiling fresco would undoubtedly have been considered awkward, if not altogether intolerable, at the very center of Christianity.

A complete reinterpretation of the ceiling in the light of the correct identification of the Sacrifice is now required.

Italian Renaissance Studies, ed. E. F. Jacob (London: Faber & Faber, 1960), pp. 312-27.

JAMES BECK

EXCURSUS

We might turn to to the Kabbalah for insights into the
functioning of the Cain and Abel scene in the fresco. In speaking
of the Kabbalah of Isaac Luria (1534-72), Gershom Scholem,
Kabbalah (New York: New American Library, 1974), p. 163, points
to the high rank of the souls of Cain and Abel. These two sons of
Adam were taken to symbolize the restrictive and outgoing
powers of creation. Scholem notes that, paradoxically, many of
the great figures of Jewish history are represented as stemming
from the root of Cain, and as the messianic time approaches the
number of such souls will increase.

Another fascinating connection between Kabbalah and the scene
of Cain and Abel, with the accompanying medallions, may be
raised. See Scholem, *Kabbalah*, p. 348: "In the Kabbalistic commentaries on the Bible many events were explained by [such]
hidden history of the transmigration of various souls which
return in a later gilgul to situations similar to those of an earlier
state, in order to repair damage which they had previously
caused. The early Kabbalah provides the basis of this idea:
there[fore] Moses and Jethro, for example, are considered the
reincarnations of Abel and Cain; David, Bathsheba, and Uriah of
Adam and Eve, and the serpent...."

1. Michelangelo. *The Sacrifice of Cain and Abel*. Sistine Chapel, Vatican, Rome. (Also called *The Sacrifice of Noah*.)

2. Ghiberti. *Noah* scenes. The Doors of Paradise, Baptistry, Florence.

3. Jacopo della Quercia. *Noah Giving Thanks.* Portal, San Petronio, Bologna.

4. Jacopo della Quercia. *Sacrifice of Cain and Abel.* Portal, San Petronio, Bologna.

III

Raising Capital and Funding the Pope's Debt

MELISSA MERIAM BULLARD

The recent surge of interest in the local Florentine church in the fifteenth century has emphasized two related trends: the marked control over local church offices and incomes by laity and secular government, and the tendency for wealthy families to tighten their hold over local benefices, what Roberto Bizzocchi has called the "aristocratization of the *ius patronandi*."[1] To these two observations could be added a third, namely, that lay involvement in the administration and finances of local churches fostered an attitude toward the church as property to be utilized for gain, much like a juicy plum ripe for picking. This proprietary, sometimes predatory, mentality might manifest itself subtly when neighborhoods exercised prerogatives in the appointment of local parish officials[2] or more crassly when patricians eagerly accumulated rights to incomes from ecclesiastical benefices.[3] To what extent can these three observations about trends at the local level help us understand other spheres of church life? Do they hold true for papal finance, another area where laymen were becoming increasingly enmeshed in church property in the fifteenth century?

---

1.   Roberto Bizzocchi, *Chiesa e potere nella Toscana del Quattrocento* (Bologna: il Mulino, 1987), p. 53. See also his "Chiesa e aristocrazia nella Firenze del Quattrocento," *Archivio storico italiano* 142 (1984): 191-282.
2.   Gene Brucker, "Urban Parishes and Their Clergy in Quattrocento Florence. A Preliminary 'Sondage'," in *Renaissance Studies in Honor of Craig Hugh Smyth*, ed. Andrew Morrogh et al., 2 vols. (Florence: Giunti Barbèra, 1985), 1:17-28. See also Dale and Francis Kent, *Neighbours and Neighbourhood in Renaissance Florence: the District of the Red Lion in the Fifteenth Century* (Locust Valley, NY: J. J. Augustin, 1982).
3.   One such example is the case of the Pandolfini family. In 1487, Pier Filippo Pandolfini, the Florentine ambassador, successfully petitioned the pope on behalf of his nephews to obtain a brief putting the church of S. Martino de' Galandi in the diocese of Florence under their protection. Income from the church was valued at 400 *ducati auri di Camera*. See Archivio Segreto Vaticano (hereafter, ASV), Registri Vaticani, 722, fols. 221v-223r.

At the beginning of the century the Schism had decimated the papal fisc by as much as two-thirds,[4] and popes from Martin V on began to rely more and more heavily upon bankers and wealthy investors to provide short-term credit and needed financial services. Cadres of bankers and financiers designated *mercatores romanam curiam sequentes* established themselves in the Rione of Ponte, the Wall Street of Rome, immediately across the Ponte S. Angelo from the Vatican. Sizable fortunes could be made from serving the papacy with loans and administering ecclesiastical tax and revenue farms in exchange for credit. According to De Roover, under Cosimo the Elder in the first half of the fifteenth century, the Medici bank in Rome returned more than half the profits from the family's network of enterprises all over Europe.[5] By the late fifteenth century lay financiers even found their way into the prior preserves of clerics in papal administration. Under Innocent VIII in the 1480s agents of the Sauli bank were keeping accounts inside the *Camera Apostolica* alongside the clerks of the Chamber;[6] and in the early sixteenth century, Clement VII went so far as to appoint one of his lay bankers, Francesco del Nero, as his treasurer general, the highest financial officer under the chamberlain at the Vatican.[7] There is no question that our first observation, namely that in the fifteenth century laymen involved themselves increasingly in local church affairs, holds true for the realm of papal finance as well. But it remains to be seen whether the heightened visibility of papal bankers correlated with growing profits.

The second point, about the "aristocratization" or tightening control over ecclesiastical incomes by a selected few families, would also seem to find a parallel among papal bankers. If we consider the large, well-capitalized banks with international connections to be the "aristocrats" among bankers, these giants dominated the financial services to the papacy, and their relative numbers did not fluctuate very much even into the mid-sixteenth century.[8] Although there was some variation among the fortunes of individual banks under particular popes, such firms as the Spannocchi from Siena, the Sauli from Genova, and the Medici from Florence maintained a steady presence at the papal court throughout much of the century. There is some evidence that in

4. Peter Partner, "Papal Financial Policy in the Renaissance and Counter-Reformation," *Past and Present* 88 (1980): 20.
5. Raymond De Roover, *The Rise and Decline of the Medici Bank, 1397-1494* (New York: W.W. Norton, 1966), pp. 47, 202. See also George Holmes, "How the Medici Became the Pope's Bankers," in *Florentine Studies*, ed. Nicolai Rubinstein, (London: Faber & Faber, 1968), pp. 357-80.
6. ASV, Diversa Cameralia (hereafter, DC), 49, fol. 125r.
7. Melissa M. Bullard, *Filippo Strozzi and the Medici. Favor and Finance in Sixteenth-Century Florence and Rome* (Cambridge: Cambridge University Press, 1980), pp. 132n., 170.
8. Melissa M. Bullard, *"Mercatores Florentini Romanam Curiam Sequentes* in the Early Sixteenth Century," *Journal of Medieval and Renaissance Studies* 6 (1976): 51-71.

the course of the late fifteenth and early sixteenth centuries, a further recognized hierarchy developed within the ranks of papal bankers, such that selected firms that enjoyed special patronage at court controlled a larger share of the papal fisc than their less-favored cohorts. Under the Medici popes, papal in-laws Filippo Strozzi and Jacopo Salviati enjoyed this choice status. Although most of the big papal financiers were not native to Rome, by the late sixteenth century some of their families had been so successful in acquiring estates and incomes, often in repayment of credits with the Vatican, that they formed a new oligarchy and took their place in high society alongside the older Roman baronial families.[9]

Evidence also exists for the spread of an increasingly exploitative mentality towards the church within the Renaissance banking community, especially in the second half of the fifteenth century. In 1486 the new ambassador expressed the collective sentiment of the Florentine community in Rome when he gushed with eagerness to *"godere questo Papa ancora noi,"*[10] that is, for us Florentines to enjoy this pope. After an official visit to Rome, Bernardo Rucellai commented to Lorenzo de' Medici that "the business of the court at Rome would proceed best if it passed through the hands of priests as little as possible."[11] The conceptual framework within which contemporaries approached their dealings with the pope or with each other is expressed in the oft-repeated phrase, *"onore e utile,"* seeking honor and profit. Whether a grain sale to Venice or the position of Depositor to the College of Cardinals was at stake, Lorenzo de' Medici's agents recommended deals to him *"perché importa honore et utile."*[12]

But towards the end of the fifteenth century evidence in Vatican records and in business and diplomatic correspondence around the papal court raises the question of whether the

---

9.   Jean Delumeau, *Vie économique et sociale de Rome dans la seconde moitié du XVIe siècle*, 2 vols. (Paris: E. de Boccard, 1957-59), 2:462-64, 481-85; Peter Partner, "Papal Financial Policy," p. 62.
10.   P. F. Pandolfini in Rome to N. Michelozzi, 25 November 1486, Biblioteca Nazionale di Firenze (hereafter BNF), Ginori Conti, 29.103, fol. 24r.
11.   B. Rucellai to Lorenzo de' Medici, 26 October 1486, ASF, Archivio Mediceo avanti il Principato (hereafter MAP), 49, 53: "E a volere dire el vero che le pratiche di corte di Roma vorrebbono andare per mano de' preti el manco che si potessi."
12.   G. Lanfredini in Rome to L. de' Medici, 2 October 1488, ASF, MAP, 58, 45. Similarly, "Questo caso mi pare al utile et honore vostro di tanta importantia et di tanto benefitio che ho desiderato et confortato Nofri venga fin costì...," idem, 28 April 1489, MAP, 58, 70; and "Potete tirare la cosa inanzi che mi pare honorevole et utile...," Lorenzo de' Medici to G. Lanfredini, 3 September 1488, MAP 59, 218. That the pursuit of *utile* had become so entwined with the older concept of honor is perhaps demonstrated by the negative proof seen in the ironic overstress Piero Capponi placed on the latter in connection with the settling of certain accounts, namely that he regarded one ounce of *honore* to be worth more than a hundred of *utile*, "Perchè stimo più uno onza d'honore che cento d'utile," Piero Capponi to the Dieci, 26 October 1486, ASF, Dieci, Carteggi Responsive 37, fol. 187r.

financial opportunities at the Vatican weren't getting longer on honor than on profit. From the 1470s on, financial prospects in Rome were looking considerably less rosy than before. Despite Lorenzo de' Medici's intimate connections by marriage with Pope Innocent VIII, it was difficult for him to earn the sizable returns that his grandfather Cosimo had made at Eugenius IV's court. Raymond De Roover blamed the declining fortunes of the Medici bank on inattention and poor management,[13] but Lorenzo's letters belie that simple an explanation and lead us to wonder whether there weren't other contributing factors, such as changes in the structure of papal finances that made quick and easy fortunes harder to make later in the century. Just to cite one example, when the contract to farm the alum mines at Tolfa, a monopoly that the Medici bank had been so eager to acquire in the 1460s, was again offered in 1488, Lorenzo expressed considerable doubts whether the bank could do more than barely recoup some of its old credits. Since the pope had encumbered the alum revenue with so many other debt obligations, profit would be hard to turn.[14]

To understand these changes, one must switch perspectives momentarily from that of the bankers who sought personal gain from the papal fisc to that of the Vatican officials inside the Apostolic Chamber who were struggling with ways to cope with worsening problems of credit and debt. As Bauer, Delumeau and Partner have shown, Renaissance popes exploited the tax revenues and incomes of the Papal States mercilessly to pay the mounting costs of papal government and to provide funds for building projects and personal largesse.[15] Incomes from provincial and Roman city taxes paid the interest on loans and supported the pensions for venal offices. But as papal needs increased during

13. De Roover, "Lorenzo il Magnifico e il tramonto del Banco dei Medici," *Archivio storico italiano* 107 (1949): 177-85; idem, *Rise and Decline*, pp. 358-75. In addition, R. Goldthwaite points to the bad mixture of business and politics as contributing to a decline, "The Medici Bank and the World of Florentine Capitalism," *Past and Present* 114 (1987): 3-31, esp. 8, 29-31.
14. "Circa gl'allumi, per quanto scriva Nofri a Giovanni, ogni dì costì vanno facciendo la cosa più scarsa et introducendo nuove cose a nostro danno tanto che a me parrebbe meglo potendo noi valerci del nostro credito delli alumi lasciare lo appalto ad altri <et> usare de' fastidi di cotesti Genovesi. Dispiacemi maximamente che intendo voglono smembrare una parte degli'allumi <dal de>positario, che sarebbe la ruina del tucto, et con quello conditione, io per me non gli voglo,..." Lorenzo de' Medici to G. Lanfredini, s.d. November 1488, ASF, MAP, 137, 504. On the Medici monopoly of papal alum in the 1460s and early 1470s see De Roover, *Rise and Decline*, pp. 152-64; and Jean Delumeau, *L'alun de Rome, XVe-XIXe siècle* (Paris: S.E.V.P.E.N., 1962).
15. Clemens Bauer, "Die Epochen der Papstfinanz," *Historische Zeitschrift* 138 (1927): 457-503; idem, "Studi per la storia delle finanze papali durante il pontificato di Sisto IV," *Archivio della R. Società Romana di Storia Patria* 1 (1927): 319-400; Delumeau, *Vie économique et sociale de Rome*, 2:751-82; P. Partner, *The Lands of St. Peter. The Papal State in the Middle Ages and the Early Renaissance* (Berkeley and Los Angeles: University of California Press, 1972); idem, "Papal Financial Policy," pp. 40-46.

the century, temporal revenues could not keep pace. The costs of a burgeoning bureaucracy made a steady drain on church coffers, but the heaviest burden came from the frequent wars that demanded extraordinary fund-raising measures and consumed an estimated nearly fifty percent of papal revenues in the fifteenth and early sixteenth centuries.[16] Increasingly burdened with debt and in desperate need for new credit, popes kept resorting to short-term bank loans at high interest, often pawning papal jewels or even the precious miter and *bottone* as security.[17]

Willing bankers reaped the highest returns from these short-term loans, frequently arranged at twenty percent or more interest, but such commitments were also the most costly to the church. Beginning with Sixtus IV and continuing under Innocent VIII, Cameral officials began to regularize papal finances and explore new avenues of cheaper, long-term debt. Budgets forecasting receipts and outlays, the creation of annuities in the form of new colleges of venal offices and of tax farms sold for an anticipation of their revenues, all constituted ways of expanding credit, but more importantly, of getting it more cheaply and of lengthening out the debt. Theoretically at least, these measures should have also loosened the stranglehold of the papal bankers and their high interest charges by making the pope less dependent upon short-term credit. The patterns of papal borrowing in the late fifteenth century indicate this to have been the case, except in times of war.

One of the most innovative, but overlooked, attempts to address the problem of papal debt occurred under the reign of Innocent VIII and consisted of a plan to farm the anticipated revenues from annates and common services to a consortium of investors for a period of five years. This *appalto degli spirituali*, as it was referred to, was an early experiment that helped pave the way to the establishment of a regular funded debt, the *Monte della Fede*, under Clement VII in the sixteenth century. Necessity occasioned the invention, in this case, the Barons' War against Ferrante I of Naples that had so exhausted Innocent's resources that estimates placed his total disposable cash in 1486 at a mere 25,000 to 30,000 ducats. And Vatican watchers calculated it would take the pope several years to emerge from under the burden of his war debt.[18]

Spiritual revenues were an important, but sporadic, source of income to Rome, since they flowed in from all over Christendom and were in part dependent on individual benefices being vacated.

16. Partner, "Papal Financial Policy," p. 52.
17. M. Eugène Müntz, *Les arts à la cour des papes: Innocent VIII, Alexandre VI, Pie III (1484-1503)* (Paris: E. Lerous, 1898).
18. "Circa al termine in che si ritruovi el papa di questa guerra, io comprendo che in due anni egl'arà fatica di uscire di debito; e danari contanti ha pochi, che ancora si dica per alcuni di 60 in 70 milla ducati, intendo che non sono più di 25 in 30, e quali si ha sempre voluti reservare per uno extremo bisogno." Bernardo Rucellai a L. de' Medici, 26 October 1486, ASF, MAP, 49, 53. Similarly, P. F. Pandolfini a L. de' Medici, 16 December 1486, MAP, 51, 403, noting the disorder and lack of funds in the Camera.

Their estimated yearly value ran from 40,000 ducats under Sixtus IV to 50,000 ducats under Clement VII.[19] The *appalto* attempted to consolidate these revenues and give the pope early access to them by farming them for loans at regular installments for five years. The idea behind the *appalto* constituted an important step away from the haphazard, hand-to-mouth money-raising tactics that had heretofore characterized fifteenth-century papal finance and that had made the Vatican such a bountiful hunting ground for eager papal bankers. The farm was initially valued at 54,000 ducats a year but had to be renegotiated at a lower rate after the first year's receipts fell below anticipated levels.[20] It was originally sold to a group of nine participants in 1486, but over the eight-year period of its existence the consortium expanded to a total of 46 investors. Eight of the original group were papal bankers and one a close relative of the pope; but of the final, larger group, less than a third were papal bankers, the result of shares having been divided, traded and discounted to a wider pool of participants.[21]

The importance of the farm on spirituals for our present purposes lies in the unusually extensive set of records that survives for individual investors over the eight-year period in which payments to and from it were being made. By analyzing hundreds of individual entries listed in cameral accounts, one can follow investment patterns and assess the farm's profitability both to its individual shareholders and to the papacy. The unusual opportunity for detailed analysis afforded by the *appalto* records stems in large part from the fact that the cameral clerks treated it as a financial entity within, but apart, from other notations in the *Introitus et Exitus* and *Mandati Camerali* series. They specified which individual entries belonged to the *appalto* and even began making consolidated entries both for the total periodic investments by, and repayments to, participants by grouping *appalto* accounts under single headings.[22] This new style of record keeping reveals an attempt to rationalize and discipline the papal accounts. Individual payments of Annates and Common Services that had previously been mixed at random into the general pool of *Introitus*

19. P. Partner, "The 'Budget' of the Roman Church in the Renaissance Period," in *Italian Renaissance Studies*, ed. E. F. Jacob (London: Faber & Faber, 1960), pp. 256-78, esp. 262-67. On the unevenness of spiritual revenues, see A. V. Antonovics, "A Late Fifteenth Century Division Register of the College of Cardinals," *Papers of the British School at Rome* 35 (1967): 94-96.
20. The twenty-two page contract, dated 19 December 1486, is in ASV, DC, 49, fols. 123r-133r. For a fuller description of the terms, see Melissa M. Bullard, "Farming Spiritual Revenues: Innocent VIII's 'Appalto' of 1486," in Morrogh, *Renaissance Studies*, 1:29-42. The contract was amended in July 1487, when receipts came to less than 44,000 ducats as provided in the original contract, ASV, DC, 49, fols. 130v-131r.
21. The 1492 list of creditors is in ASV, DC, 48, fol. 155r-v.
22. Examples of these consolidated entries can be found in the Archivio di Stato di Roma (hereafter ASR), Mandati Camerali, 852-854, passim; and ASV, Introitus et Exitus (hereafter IE), 504, 517-522, passim.

et Exitus accounts were now being differentiated from the rest and grouped together for the *appalto*.[23]

The chief investor and manager of the revenue farm was the Genoese firm of the Cicero and Sauli, which promised to make annual loans of 19,500 ducats. The other participants, with shares ranging in value from 3,000 to 6,000 ducats, put in an annual total of 34,500 ducats, part in cash and part in the value of textiles. One of their number, Alessandro della Casa, handled most of the textile payments for the consortium,[24] evidence of the close cooperation among its members.

What follows is a summary of the *appalto* investments of eight different participants during the period 1487-1494. Three are Genoese: the Centurioni, the Cicero-Sauli, and Lionardo Cibo, a papal relative, all original investors. Four are Florentine: the Capponi, Della Casa, Martelli-Ricasoli, and Medici, of which the Martelli-Ricasoli were late-comers, having bought out the Bini in 1488. The last member studied is Gabriele da Bergamo, the Master of papal couriers, who represents a small investor with no pretensions to papal banking. Information on their investments is based on entries in the *Introitus et Exitus* accounts, which have been checked against the *Mandati Camerali* records where possible.

TABLE 1

RETURN ON INVESTMENTS IN SPIRITUALS COMPARED TO OTHER CAMERAL INVESTMENTS, 1/87-4/94. (All figures are in cameral ducats.)

NAME	DARE A	APPALTO AVERE B	% RETURN C	DARE D	OTHER AVERE E	% RETURN F
CENTURIONI	9,530.0	33,405.0	+250.5	113,177.5	100,530.0	-11.2
CICERO-SAULI	208,960.0	164,024.0	-21.5	96,264.0	101,281.0	+05.2
L. CIBO	23,491.0	11,676.0	-50.3	48,710.0	36,340.0	-25.4
CAPPONI	20,993.0	22,182.5	+.05.7	4,761.0	4,751.0	-0.03
DELLA CASA	42,498.0	44,843.0	+05.5	40,538.0	10,553.0	-74.0
MARTELLI/RICASOLI*	23,449.0	17,290.0	-26.3	38,361.0	44,055.0	+14.8
MEDICI	30,480.5	50,561.0	+66.0	279,696.0	169,749.0	-39.3
G. DA BERGAMO	2,261.0	2,047.0	-09.5			

*Figures beginning 11/88

TABLE 2

TOTAL INVESTMENTS AND PERCENTAGE RETURNS

NAME	DARE A + D	AVERE B + E	% RETURN
CENTURIONI	122,707.5	133,935.0	+09.1
CICERO-SAULI	305,224.0	265,305.0	-13.1
L. CIBO	72,201.0	48,016.0	-33.5
CAPPONI	25,754.0	26,933.5	+04.6
DELLA CASA	83,036.0	55,396.0	-33.3
MARTELLI/RICASOLI	61,810.0	61,345.0	-0.08
MEDICI	310,176.5	220,310.0	-29.0

23. After the five years for investors' loans had elapsed, records of new credits guaranteed in spiritual incomes, *finito appaltu*, reverted to the old style; although repayments to *appalto* creditors continued to be made and identified as such.

24. ASV, DC, 49, fols. 124r, 131v-132r.

Column C, Table 1, which tabulates the percentage payback on capital invested in spiritual incomes, shows how widely returns to different investors ranged, from -50.3% to Leonardo Cibo to +250% to the Centurioni bank, one of the smallest *appalto* investors. The Cicero-Sauli, who were the most heavily committed and who actually controlled the disbursement of funds through the Camera, received less than 80% of their money back. Even the smallest investor, Gabriele da Bergamo, master of the couriers, lost almost ten percent. The Capponi and Della Casa, who received more than 100% of their money back, still made only a slim profit over a long period of time. Of the sample, only the Centurioni and the Medici earned a decent return.

But the *appalto* figures taken in isolation can be misleading. When the handsome profits of the Centurioni and Medici are compared to their other investments with the Camera (Column F) their reimbursements dip to considerably less than 100%. And when we calculate the return on the grand total of their *appalto* credits plus other loans (Table 2), the rate of return falls off even more precipitously. Of our group of investors, only the Centurioni and the Capponi show a slight total profit beyond the restitution of their principal. The Medici, who even surpassed the Cicero-Sauli in total credits with the Camera, and who enjoyed special favor with the pope stemming from the marriage alliance between Lorenzo's daughter and the pope's son, still received only 71% of the money they extended.

From the looks of the data, the farm on spirituals was a dismal investment. Giovanni Tornabuoni, manager of the Medici bank in Rome, had already become wary in the summer of 1487, judging that the *appalto* was divided among too many hands to be profitable.[25] In fact, Vatican records show that by 1493 the farm was so much in arrears that the Camera decided to pay off remaining *appalto* credits at only 45% of their face value,[26] which fact helps account for the gloomy picture revealed in Table 1. No wonder the initial investors were anxious to sell their interests at deep discounts, thus enlarging the pool of creditors to 46, five times the original size.[27]

The financial view of the *appalto* presented in the *Introitus et Exitus* books begs further interpretation, however, and fortunately for the bankers, they were probably not doing quite so badly as the figures indicate. For one thing, the portions of their yearly loans due in textiles were most likely being listed at highly inflated

25. "Sendo questo spirituale apaltato et in molti mani, pensarei et farei ogni opera che avessi a passare tutto per vostre mani et che di questo si fussi depositario...," Giovanni Tornabuoni to L. de' Medici, 11 August 1487, ASF, MAP 40, 116.
26. ASV, IE, 524, fol. 105v.
27. Already in January 1488 the Usumari sold their interest to Antonio Palatio for only 5,000 ducats. By November of that year the Bini were willing to sell their share to the Martelli and Ricasoli for about a twenty-three percent discount on principal, ASV, IE, 517, fols. 41v, 147v.

values, perhaps to disguise interest, as evidenced by the fact that in 1490 the pope's Depositor General took more than a 50% loss on textiles with a declared worth of 78,000 ducats but a real value of only 34,000 ducats.[28] If not his bank, at least Lorenzo de' Medici was receiving extra compensation through the lucrative benefices Innocent was awarding his son Giovanni, the future cardinal and pope. Big investors in the farm were permitted to write off other debts onto the *appalto*, perhaps at inflated values. Much of the Centurioni's spectacular rate of return undoubtedly derives from the fact that they were being reimbursed from *appalto* assets for their outstanding credits in the papal alum mines.[29] The Capponi recouped operating expenses from the papal mint from the consortium,[30] and even the pope's Genoese jeweler, Paolo Poliastra, was permitted to write off the cost of gems onto the *appalto*.[31] These extra debt obligations to particular creditors helped destroy the security of the farm for the rest of the consortium, thus making Innocent's tax farm on his spiritual revenues less than successful overall for its investors. The extra debt heaped upon the *appalto* also illustrates the extent to which various aspects of the papal economy were tightly intertwined and the near impossibility at that time of insulating any single tax farm from the larger weight of papal debt.

The farm, like the Apostolic Chamber, was too heavily burdened with debt to keep ahead of interest payments it owed. Although Vatican records show that during the period the *appalto* loans were being made, Innocent contracted relatively few short-term loans at high interest, he was unable to emerge from beneath the mountain of debt or use farm monies to reduce his deficit. But judged from the longer perspective of the development of papal finance, the *appalto* was at least a partial success. The farm had provided Innocent with steady income and longer-term credit at a much lower cost than straight bank loans. Of the cases studied, a total of 361,000 ducats in credits were even repaid at slightly better than 95% over eight years, including those final credits that the Camera settled at a reduced rate of 45%.[32]

Innocent VIII's *appalto* on annates and common services is but one example of a pope's strategy to meet the rising costs of government debt in the fifteenth century. But the detailed records of its transactions that have survived reveal much about the character of papal finance in the late fifteenth century not just for the *Camera Apostolica* but for investors as well. For them the

---

28.   ASV, IE, 520, fol. 192r; DC, 47, fols. 163r-65r.
29.   The IE accounts reveal that during the period of the *appalto* the Centurioni had over 45,000 ducats in credits from the papal alum mines.
30.   As early as December 1487, the Capponi were being reimbursed for mint expenses with *appalto* funds. See ASV, IE, 517, fol. 35r; IE, 518, fol. 112r; IE, 520, fol. 53v.
31.   ASV, IE, 520, fols. 18v, 140r; DC, 46, fols. 182r-185v.
32.   See above, Table 1, figured from the total of column B divided by the total of column A , or 346,628.5 / 361,662.5 = 95.7%.

outcome of the *appalto* carried more ominous implications. An overly debt-laden papal economy spelled diminished returns from tax farms and investments, a situation that is becoming increasingly familiar to us today.

Bearing this in mind, let us return briefly to our original remarks about the growing involvement of secular bankers in the financial affairs of the church in our period. Although our three observations about the changing relations between laymen and the church on the local level hold true in the realm of papal finance, the common perception that papal bankers reaped easy gains needs to be modified with the understanding that by the end of the fifteenth century the heavy burden of debt accumulated by the papacy made it harder and harder for them to net fat profits. Mounting debt obligated future revenues and diminished the popes' ability to finance new credit. It forced the Apostolic Chamber to search for cheaper, longer-term credit and decrease the cost of debt with schemes, such as the *appalto* on spirituals, which had resulted in loans being paid off at a fraction of their value. Within a generation the Camera would find ways to tap a much wider investing public via funded debts with publicly traded shares, which would have the effect of gradually loosening the big bankers' tight grip on the papal fisc. As bankers' returns began to diminish or disappear, as in the case of Innocent VIII's *appalto*, competition among them increased. If a predatory mentality towards church property was becoming more pronounced by the end of the century, it can be attributed in part to this stiffening competition and to the fact that financial success was coming more and more to depend upon jockeying for special favor with the pope and even less than before upon the workings of the marketplace. Thus, little wonder that Lorenzo de' Medici's agents relied so heavily upon his personal ties with the pope to secure them a competitive edge. The same trend would continue in the sixteenth century.

IV

Church Patronage in France on the
Eve of the Reformation

MARILYN MANERA EDELSTEIN

Although historians have given a great deal of attention to the Concordat of Bologna of 1516 and the controversies that necessitated its enactment, very little work has been done on the implementation of its key provision, namely the right of royal nomination to benefices in France. This provision invested the French king with the control of appointments to 800 abbatial and 114 archiepiscopal and episcopal seats – an enormous power that promoted the centralization of the state and touched not only the religious life of the kingdom but also vast financial resources. Yet no one has studied in any detail how the French monarchy used this authority or, more specifically, how it recruited France's highest ecclesiastical personnel.

Since the Concordat was negotiated by Francis I, his policies governing recruitment are of particular interest and importance. Moreover, his reign marks the advent of Protestantism in France, which placed the church in a state of crisis. This factor should have influenced his ecclesiastical appointments, particularly by the latter part of the reign. But, did it? How, in fact, did Francis I use his right of nomination to benefices? How did ecclesiastical candidates come to his attention, and why did he appoint them? Did he have any specific policies in mind? Was he concerned with religious reform in the age of Reformation? Was it his intention to find and select pious, competent, and qualified men for these high ecclesiastical offices, or did he simply use this power for his own purposes and interests, indulging personal favorites and the aristocracy in general, as he did in so many other ways?

There are obvious obstacles to pursuing these questions. First, in this vast arena of church patronage, many requests and lobbying efforts were doubtlessly verbal, leaving indirect or, more than likely, no documentation at all. Furthermore, neither Francis I nor his chancellor, Antoine Duprat, who negotiated the Concordat, ever explicitly stated their conceptions of the Concordat or its application. Consequently, the only way to investigate this issue is to find out about the candidates themselves and trace their links to the king. I have focused on Francis I's episcopal appointments as a manageable test case. Of the 182 men he named bishops from 1516 to the end of his reign in 1547, I have been able to assemble relevant materials on 167, the overwhelming majority.[1]

It is clear from the evidence that Francis I followed no consistent policy of ecclesiastical recruitment but rather turned the right of royal nomination to benefices into a vast patronage system involving the interests of the most powerful figures of the period. Studying the implementation of the Concordat of Bologna under Francis I reveals the power elite of the reign, the men – and women – from the highest social strata and government offices, who controlled both church and state in Renaissance France.

⚜

Before beginning our study of the recruitment practices of Francis I, we must examine the Concordat of Bologna, which was supposed to regulate these practices.[2] The purpose of the Concordat was to end the electoral system of the Pragmatic Sanction of Bourges of 1438, which had created interminable contested elections, bringing considerable political instability to the kingdom. The Concordat was desirable and advantageous for both the papacy and the French monarchy. For the pope, it meant the end of conciliar claims and the restoration of papal financial rights, specifically the annates and other pontifical taxes. By securing papal good will, the Concordat obviously made a significant contribution to Francis I's Italian policy, which always preoccupied him. For the French monarchy, the Concordat's greatest advantage was the royal right of nomination to benefices. Its terms were carefully delineated in the text of the Concordat.[3] The king alone was to name candidates to benefices within six months after they had become vacant. The qualifications imposed on the king's nominee were the same that had existed under the Pragmatic Sanction: the candidate had to be at least twenty-seven years old and a doctor or licentiate in canon or civil law or a master or licentiate in theology. The Concordat did not oblige the candidate to have received holy orders, but he had to take them

1.   The bishops of this reign are listed in C. Eubel, ed., *Hierarchia Catholica Medii Aevi*, vol. 3 (Münster: Library Regensberg, 1910). Biographical and genealogical information on them were derived from a number of sources. Particularly important were D. Sammarthanus, ed., *Gallia Christiana*, 16 vols. (Paris: J. Coignard, 1715-1865); P. de la Chesnaye-Desbois, ed., *Dictionnaire de la Noblesse*, 19 vols. (Paris: Schlesinger, 1863-1876); and H. Fisquet, *La France pontificale*, 16 vols. (Paris: Repos, 1864-1873).
2.   For the Concordat of Bologna, see J. Thomas, *Le Concordat de 1516*, 3 vols. (Paris: A. Picard, 1910); A. Renaudet, *Préréforme et Humanisme à Paris* (Paris: Librairie d'Argences, 1953); and R. Doucet, *Les Institutions de la France au xvie siècle*, 2 vols. (Paris: A. & J. Picard, 1948).
3.   The entire text of the Concordat in both its Latin and French editions can be found in Thomas, *Concordat*, 2:409-13.

before he could assume his seat. The pope had to confirm the king's nomination and to provide the candidate canonically. If he refused to do so, the king was to present a new name within three months. Past this delay, the nomination went to the pope.[4]

The actual procedure of royal nomination to benefices involved the assembling of a dossier for each candidate of anywhere from three to fourteen documents.[5] These were intended to present the royal candidate to the pope and give evidence of his qualifications and competency for the vacant seat. However, this process turned into a meaningless formality, filled with trite formulas, presenting to the pope and his inquest panel nothing more than the will of the king. These dossiers clearly reveal that, from the outset, Francis I was scarcely concerned with a candidate's religious qualifications. Instead, what he emphasized in his letters of recommendation was loyalty and service – either from the candidate, members of his family, or both – as the essential criteria for ecclesiastical appointments. In a letter introducing Thomas Duprat to the pope, for example, Francis I recommended his worthiness for the episcopacy chiefly "in contemplation of the very great and virtuous services that my chancellor, his brother, has previously made and continues to make to me."[6] In asking for the nomination of Claude de Longwy, the uncle of the powerful Admiral Chabot, to the bishopric of Langres, the king's reason was "in favor and for the consideration of the good, agreeable, and recommendable services that he and some of his close relations, our special servants, have done previously and still ordinarily do each day."[7]

If personal qualifications were mentioned, they were usually worded in meaningless clichés, as in the king's letter of recommendation for Guillaume d'Aydie, presenting him as "a man very knowledgeable, full of good manners, virtue, and

---

4.   This provision fueled the opposition of the Gallican church to the Concordat, for it seemed to enable the pope to block any royal candidate and thus institute his own. However, the papal right to refuse a king's candidate was tightly circumscribed: only if the nominee was unqualified in terms of age, university training, or notorious character could the pope exercise this right. As matters turned out, the pope rarely refused to confirm the king's first choice, although many of the candidates were unqualified. If the pope was not completely satisfied with a candidate, he would content himself by delaying the publication of the bull of investiture.

5.   The best sources on this topic are F. Welter, "Le Choix des Évêques en France depuis le Concordat de Bologne," *Revue ecclésiastique de Metz* (1936): 158-68, 192-98; and above all, M. Madelin, "Les premières applications du Concordat de 1516," *Mélanges d'Archéologie et d'Histoire* 17 (1897): 323-85.

6.   Ibid., pp. 332-33: "en contemplacion des très grans et vertueulx services que mondit chancelier, sondit frère, ma parcidevant faiz et fait continuellement."

7.   L. E. Marcel, *Le Cardinal de Givry* (Dijon: M. Darantière, 1926), pp. 460-61: "en faveur et pour considéracion des bons, agréables et recommandables services que luy et aucuns de ses proches parents, nos espéciaulz serviteurs ont aussy par ci devant faiz et font encore ordinairement par chascun jour."

science."[8]   Almost these same words were used to recommend every royal candidate, with scant attention given to specific religious qualifications and experience.   Sometimes letters of personal recommendation were joined to the king's to further promote the candidate's case.   Most often they were similar to that of the Cardinal de Boisy and his brother, Bonnivet, two of Francis I's most powerful ministers, who wrote to the pope on behalf of one of their younger brothers.   Their letter quickly came to the point by promising the pope "services and satisfactions of all sorts"[9] if he would invest their brother – which the pope did.

The papacy itself participated in the sham that was made of adhering to the stipulations of the Concordat.   Instead of really investigating a candidate's qualifications, the papal inquest summoned incompetent witnesses, usually young French priests studying in Rome, who had not lived in France for several years. They were to testify not on the candidate, but rather on the state of the vacant benefice.   Detailed testimony was heard on its geographical and historical background and especially on the physical condition of the cathedral church and its revenues.   The inquest's chief concerns with the candidate were that he was from a good family, the issue of a legitimate union – and not a cripple. Thus the processing of royal nominations was not used to check or certify a candidate's religious qualifications, but rather to register the will of the king.   By allowing the right of royal nomination to function virtually unbridled, the papacy itself shared the responsibility for any abuses it engendered.

$$\uparrow$$

The Concordat's major asset for the king was astutely noted by the Venetian ambassador to the court of Francis I.   In his view, "This law insures him the obedience and fidelity of the clergy and of the laymen who also aspire to benefices."[10]   By obtaining the right of nomination to benefices, unbridled by any papal criticism or checks, the French monarchy accomplished a major objective in solidifying the sovereignty of the state: advancement in the church now came to rest solely on one factor – the favor of the king, which was, in turn, the reward for loyalty and service.   The church was now a part of the clientage system.

This fact reflects the actual functioning of the Renaissance state and verifies its intensely personal character.   To a large extent, the characteristics of the Renaissance monarchy in France determined how the powers of the Concordat were interpreted and used. Under Francis I, the French state continued to evolve toward administrative centralization and control over various auto-

8.   Madelin, pp. 332-33: "homme très sçavant, rempli de bonnes meurs, vertus et science."
9.   Ibid., p. 334: "services et satisfactions de toutes sortes."
10.   N. Tommaseo, ed., *Relations des ambassadeurs vénitiens sur les affaires de France au xvie siècle*, 2 vols. (Paris: Imprimerie Royale, 1838), 1:49.

nomous centers of power within the state. The Concordat intensified these trends: prior to its enactment, the Gallican church
constituted an independent, self-governing corporation; the
Concordat ended this by putting the French church – or at least its
major offices – under the sole control of the monarch.

Nevertheless, although the state under Francis I grew
increasingly powerful, it lacked an impersonal, rational, and
efficient bureaucracy in the modern sense. Instead, power rested
with the king and an elite group that had close personal ties to the
king. This is not to deny the reality of a bureaucracy that was
actively working for the interests of the king and that constituted
the structure of the state. However, power did not yet lie with this
bureaucracy but, rather, with the king and an elite whose
members were overwhelmingly aristocratic.

The influence of this elite and the personal nature of the
monarchy of Francis I can be well illustrated by our findings of the
king's recruitment practices for the church. Although the king
alone named to all benefices, he was, in fact, pressured in his
selections by a number of powerful interest groups that had
several common characteristics: they all had personal access and
close personal bonds to the king; and they functioned through a
network of patron-client relationships that they sought to
strengthen and preserve.

The importance of personal contact with the monarch in
obtaining appointments should not be surprising and was, in fact,
frankly admitted much later by Louis XIV in his *Mémoires*. On the
matter of government appointments, he wrote:

> Neither you nor I, my son, are going to seek out for these posts
> those who have been kept from our sight by their distance from
> us or by their obscurity. One has to settle upon a small number
> put before us by chance, that is to say, those who are already in
> their charges or whose birth or bent have attached them inti-
> mately to us.[11]

Certainly the impersonal criteria that Louis XIV could not
achieve in government with the superior administrative
machinery he had available, were totally inconceivable to the
monarchy of Francis I. These two kings, one representing the
beginning of absolute monarchy in France, and the other, its
culmination, faced the same limiting circumstances in the
recruitment of their major offices for both church and state.

§

In studying Francis I's episcopal appointments, it is evident that
they originated from three major sources: the royal family, the
royal favorites, and members of the royal households. All shared
direct personal access to the king, which obviously enabled these

---

11.   Louis XIV, *Mémoires pour les années 1661 et 1666*, ed. J. Longnon (Paris:
Bossard, 1923), p. 71.

men and women to promote themselves, family members, or their own favorites to high church offices.

It is hardly surprising that among the most powerful and influential people at the court of Francis I were members of the king's own family, notably his mother, Louise of Savoy, and his sister, Marguerite of Navarre. Each wielded considerable power in the political, religious, and intellectual life of the kingdom and clearly influenced ecclesiastical appointments. Louise of Savoy[12] actually governed France as regent during her son's first campaign in Italy (1515-1516) and later, during his captivity in Spain (1523-1527). It was during the second regency that the Concordat was in effect and that Louise of Savoy personally made forty-three episcopal appointments. They strongly illustrate a pattern of preferment for her personal favorites and protégés. To the rich archbishopric of Sens, for example, she appointed the chancellor, Antoine Duprat, over the intense opposition of the cathedral canons. Duprat, she claimed, was "her very dear and beloved cousin,"[13] who had actually won her affection as early as 1504 when he helped to prosecute and ruin one of her archenemies at court. During her regencies, Duprat was her closest adviser and doubtlessly sponsored his brother, Claude Duprat's, nomination to the bishopric of Mende, also made during her regency. Most of her nominations to episcopal seats went to such loyalists and favorites, and a few went to household members of her brother, René of Savoy, and her daughter, Marguerite of Navarre. Louise of Savoy did not ignore broader issues, however: almost one-fifth of her appointments went to Italians whose families served the king in the Italian wars.[14] Louise of Savoy could be pragmatic as well as loyal.

Louise of Savoy's influence at court remained strong until her death in 1531. In the ensuing years between her regencies and demise, six of her personal chaplains were appointed to the episcopacy.[15] As her chaplains, these men were in daily contact with the queen mother, serving her as priests, confessors, and councillors. Unlike many episcopal nominees in this reign, most of these men were university-educated and generally respected as prelates. Indeed, it is generally acknowledged that their religious and intellectual qualifications procured their appointments as royal chaplains. However, even in this select group, we find two examples of the intrusion of secular interests. Louise of Savoy's First Chaplain during the early part of the reign was Martin de

12. A good source on Louise of Savoy is D. M. Mayer, *The Great Regent: Louise of Savoy* (London: Weidenfeld & Nicolson, 1966). Also available and helpful is Louise of Savoy's *Journal* in *Collection complète des mémoires relatifs à l'histoire de France*, ed. M. Petitot (Paris: Foucault, 1826), ser. 2, 16:383-408.
13. A. Buisson, *Le Chancelier Antoine Duprat* (Paris: Hachette, 1935), p. 357: "nostre très cher et amé cousin."
14. For details, see M. Edelstein, "Foreign Episcopal Appointments During the Reign of Francis I," *Church History* 44 (1975): 1-10.
15. The list is available in A. Lefranc and J. Boulenger, eds., *Comptes de Louise de Savoie et de Marguerite d'Angoulême* (Paris: H. Champion, 1905).

Semblançay, the son of the renowned finance minister, Jacques de Semblançay, who had begun his career as one of Louise of Savoy's protégés.[16] For many years, he directed her personal finances as well as those of the state – sometimes, evidently, confusing the two. Martin de Semblançay was made archbishop of Tours by Francis I a few years after his appointment as First Chaplain. He died, however, soon after his father's trial and execution for embezzlement in 1527. Undaunted, evidently, in her faith – and need – of finance ministers, she appointed the following year as her next First Chaplain, Jacques Babou, the son of the new finance minister.[17] Francis I named Jacques Babou concurrently bishop of Angoulême, where he was succeeded by a younger brother. Aside from these examples of self-interest and opportunism, Louise of Savoy's chaplains who were promoted to the episcopacy were generally devout and qualified men. Most remarkable of all, one was a commoner who had risen in the church hierarchy with no noble or personal connections, but solely on the basis of his scholarly and religious merits.[18]

Next to the queen mother, the most influential member of the king's family was his sister, Marguerite of Navarre. An intelligent and well-educated woman, pious and committed to religious reform, she was a close confidante of Francis I, who was entirely devoted to her. Many contemporaries felt that the king made no important decision without first consulting her. Indeed, her reputation was such that she was popularly referred to as the king's "good spirit."[19] For a considerable part of the reign, both she and her husband, Henri d'Albret, sat on the all-powerful Conseil des Affaires, that small group of the king's closest advisers that deliberated on foreign as well as domestic affairs.

Although Marguerite of Navarre spent many years away from court after her marriage to d'Albret, she kept in close contact with her brother through letters. Fortunately, most of this correspondence has been preserved[20] and clearly reveals the influence she

16.   Louise of Savoy's patronage of Jacques de Semblançay is well documented in A. Spont, Semblançay, la bourgeoisie financière au debut du xvie siècle (Paris: Th. de Lettres, 1895).
17.   The new finance minister, Philibert Babou, was described by a contemporary as "strong in the favor of Madame the Regent." See P. Loutard, ed., Journal d'un bourgeois de Paris sous François Ier (Paris: Union générale d'Éditions, 1963), p. 57: "fort à la grâce de Madame la Regente."
18.   This man was Robert Cenalis, who had a distinguished religious and intellectual career. For details, see Renaudet, pp. 658-59 and Gallia Christiana, 1:408 and 2:497-99.
19.   A. L. Herminjard, ed., Correspondance des Réformateurs, 2d ed., 9 vols. (Geneva: H. Georg, 1878), 1:65-66: "bon genie." The best biography of Marguerite of Navarre remains P. Jourda, Marguerite d'Angoulême, 2 vols. (Paris: H. Champion, 1930).
20.   These letters are compiled in two major sources: Marguerite d'Angoulême, Lettres, ed. F. Genin (Paris: J. Renouard, 1841); and Marguerite de Navarre, Nouvelles lettres de la Reine de Navarre adressées au Roi François I, ed. F. Genin (Paris: J. Renouard, 1842). Some of her correspondance is also available in Correspondance des Réformateurs.

had on his church appointments. As she wrote in a letter to Francis I in 1527, her motives for these recommendations were loyal and selfless:

> And please pardon me if I write you on behalf of your affectionate subjects; but the position where you put us makes me dare to speak to you about those whom I consider useful to your service; because, believe me, Sire, that...I well know those who serve you for their own interests or because they love you.[21]

Based on this relationship of trust and respect, Marguerite of Navarre wrote many letters to her brother recommending various protégés for the episcopacy. She wrote, for example, on behalf of Georges d'Armagnac, whom she had known since he was ten and considered "as my own son," and secured for him the bishopric of Rodez.[22] In another letter, she asked for a personal favorite, Gabriel de Grammont, to be made bishop of Albi. Beginning with a clever apologia, "Sire, I well know that your goodness ought not to be solicited to benefit your servants, for the number of those who claim to be such is so great that it is not possible to satisfy everyone," she went on to plead Grammont's case:

> I am sure that he asks no recompense other than your good grace...that he will solicit from you nothing other than what he hopes will come from your liberality. However, if it is true that M. d'Albi has died, as they so often say, will you please remember M. de Tarbes [Gabriel de Grammont was then bishop of Tarbes]; and what made me take the boldness to write to you about this is that never have I seen him tire of taking pains to serve you.[23]

Albi went to Duprat, but Grammont was soon recompensed with the bishopric of Poitiers (1532), the archbishopric of Toulouse (1533), and ultimately the cardinalate. The close relationship between Marguerite of Navarre and Francis I created one of the most successful routes to church advancement in this reign.

There is perhaps no better proof of this than the religiously suspect, pro-reform candidates that she managed to get named bishops. The most enduring reputation of Marguerite of Navarre

---

21. *Nouvelles Lettres,* pp. 91-92: "Et vous plera me pardonner si pour vos subjets affectionnés je vous escrips; mais le lieu ou vous nous mettez me fait prendre hardiesse de vous parler de ceux que je voy untiles à votre service; car croyez, Monseigneur, que depuis que je suis par dessa, j'ay bien congnu ceux qui pour eux seulement ou pour l'amour de vous vous servent."

22. Ibid., pp. 252-54: "je luy porte telle affecsion que s'il estoit mon propre filz;" "et à ma requeste luy donnastes l'esveché de Rhodez."

23. Ibid., p. 100: "Monseigneur, je say bien que votre bonté ne doit estre sollicité de faire du bien à vos serviteurs, mais pour ce que le nombre de ceux qui se disent tels est si grand qu'il n'est possible a tous satisfaire...je suis seure qu'il ne demande nulle récompense que vostre bonne grâce...qu'il ne vous sollicitera point de ce qu'il espère venir de votre libéralité. Toutesfois, si ainsy est que M. d'Albi soit trépassé, comme si souvent l'on dit, il vous plaira avoir souvenance de M. de Tarbes; et ce qui m'a fait prendre la hardiesse de vous en escripvre est que jamais je ne l'ai veu lassé de prendre peine à vous servir."

has come, of course, from her religious and intellectual interests, specifically as a poet and author. Her sympathy and close relationship with the Meaux reformers was reflected in the fact that two of them, Gérard Roussel and Michel d'Arande, became her personal chaplains and were protected and promoted to the episcopacy through her influence. The religious doctrines of both men created controversy and were frequently labeled heretical, but Marguerite of Navarre always used her influence with the king to protect and defend them. When Roussel was implicated in the Affair of the Placards, she successfully intervened to save him, pleading with the powerful Connétable de Montmorency:

> the king will find that he is worthy of more than being burned, and that he has never held an opinion to merit it, nor anything which seems heretical. I have known him for five years, and believe me, that if I had seen in him anything dubious, I would not have wanted to suffer such a poison so long.[24]

Her arguments were obviously successful, because Roussel was not persecuted; and, indeed, two years later Francis I named him bishop of Oloron. Michel d'Arande had a similarly controversial career, but as Marguerite of Navarre's personal chaplain and confessor received the bishopric of St. Paul-Trois-Châteaux. Of course, neither Roussel nor d'Arande obtained particularly prominent or lucrative benefices. However, their general immunity from persecution, and the fact that they received any ecclesiastical appointments at all, testifies to Marguerite of Navarre's influence with the king. It is also important to note that, although the religious beliefs of Roussel and d'Arande engendered considerable controversy, both men were pious and enthusiastic reformers and gained a reputation as excellent bishops. D'Arande was described by a contemporary as "of such a serious eloquence, of a piety so remarkable, of a fidelity so scrupulous as to harmonize his title and duties as bishop."[25] Such praise rarely fell on other bishops of the reign, a fact that in itself justifies Marguerite of Navarre's unwavering support and patronage of these men.

Aside from Marguerite of Navarre and Louise of Savoy, the only other woman in this reign who exerted some influence on ecclesiastical appointments was Anne de Pisseleu,[26] the king's official mistress for fifteen years. Close to both Louise of Savoy and Marguerite of Navarre, she was much more powerful than either of Francis I's two queens, Claude and, then, Eleanor. Anne de

---

24. *Lettres*, p. 299: "le Roy trouvera qu'il est digne de mieulx que du feu, et qu'il n'a jamais tenu opinion pour le mériter, ny quy sente nulle chose hérétique. Il y a cinq ans que je le congnois et croyés que sy je y eusse veu une chose doubteuse, je n'eusse poiny voulu souffrir sy longuement une telle poison."
25. *Correspondance des Réformateurs*, 2:120: "d'une si sérieuse éloquence, d'une piété si remarquable, d'une fidélité si scrupuleuse à mettre d'accord son titre et ses devoirs d'évêque."
26. Biographical information on Anne de Pisseleu can be found in P. Paris, *Études sur François Ier* (Paris: L. Techener, 1885), 2:204-325.

Pisseleu concentrated on promoting her own interests and those of her numerous family. It is not surprising, therefore, that four members of her family – two brothers, an uncle, and a nephew – with little else to recommend them, received a total of ten ecclesiastical appointments from Francis I.

There were others outside the royal family who also had strong personal ties to the king and consequently acquired considerable power in church and state. These men were the king's personal favorites. They constituted a homogeneous group in that they all came from the nobility of the sword, were raised as children with the future king at Amboise, pursued military careers and fought beside Francis I in the Italian wars. Once king, he appointed them to some of the most important positions in his administration. Through their powerful noble families, their close friendship with the king, their political and military positions, and their voice in key deliberative councils, these royal favorites were among the most powerful people in the kingdom.

This group of royal favorites was dominated by four men: Artus Gouffier and his brother, known popularly as Bonnivet; and then, after their deaths early in the reign, Philippe de Chabot and Anne de Montmorency. The role of these men in securing church benefices is evident in correspondence relating to ecclesiastical appointments. For example, when Aymar Gouffier, the brother of Bonnivet and Artus Gouffier, was nominated to the rich abbeys of St. Denis and Cluny, Francis I wrote to the pope presenting him as

> brother of our very dear and beloved cousins, the Grand Maître [Artus Gouffier] and Admiral [Bonnivet], who are the persons that Your Holiness knows are the closest to us and have the principal charge and conduct of our deeds and affairs.[27]

Bonnivet accompanied this letter with one addressed to the pope's cousin and closest adviser, Giulio de' Medici, promising that "in whatever it pleases you to employ me, you will find me and my house ready to serve you in any way we possibly can."[28] Reminders and promises of loyalty and service were evidently all that mattered: Aymar Gouffier received both abbeys and seven years later was made bishop of Albi.

Of all the royal favorites, however, the one who clearly controlled church appointments for most of the reign was Anne de Montmorency. Although the others secured benefices for relatives and clients, it was Anne de Montmorency who was consistently perceived by his peers as the most powerful figure at court in the matter of ecclesiastical appointments. Members of the

27. Madelin, p. 361: "frère de noz très chiers et améz cousins le grant maistre et admiral, qui sont tels personaiges que V.S. congnoist prouchains de nous et ayans le principalle charge et conduicte de noz faitz et affaires."
28. Ibid., p. 357: "en ce qu'il vous plairoit m'amployer vous trouverez moy et ma maison, prestz à vous faire tout le service qu'il nous seroit possible."

royal family – as well as the king's favorites – all contacted Montmorency to intercede with the king in procuring benefices.[29]

Montmorency's impressive career and close relationship with the king were largely the result of birth and circumstance. He came from an old and powerful noble house and, along with his cousins Bonnivet and Artus Gouffier, was a childhood friend of the king. He fought in the Italian wars and quickly made a reputation as a great military leader. In 1522 he was made a marshal of France, a position that gained him entrance into the king's councils. It was largely a result of the disaster at Pavia that Anne de Montmorency emerged as the most powerful man at court. With so many outstanding military leaders killed there, a tremendous vacuum arose in the military and administrative hierarchy. Moreover, Francis I lost at Pavia his closest friend, Bonnivet. Montmorency's relationship to the king grew as he accompanied him into captivity in Spain, where he faithfully served him and acted as chief negotiator in the king's release.

When the king returned to France, Montmorency became virtually his first minister and closest adviser. Named Grand Maître of France and later, Connétable, he further solidified his favor and power with the royal family by leaving his fiancée to marry the niece of Louise of Savoy, thus becoming her "nephew."[30] For fifteen years, from 1526 to his disgrace in 1541, Anne de Montmorency was the most influential person at the court of Francis I, enjoying the king's complete confidence and invested with the direction of affairs. Francis I wrote of their relationship with effusive trust and warmth, praising:

> his military experience and the sincere, pure, and ardent good will, love, and affection that for a long time he has always had and devoted to our service. From this, since his young and early years, he has taken continual sustenance near and around our person, which gave us true and loyal evidence...of these stated manners, virtues, integrity, judgment, prudence, sufficiency, loyalty and diligence. For these we are disposed to rest entirely on him all of our greatest secrets and arduous affairs that he has so well and so prudently conducted, guided, and administered in times of war and peace.[31]

Montmorency strengthened this bond of loyalty and service by hard work and diligence, which clearly distinguished him from

29. The best source on Anne de Montmorency is F. Decrue, *Anne de Montmorency, Grand Maître et Connétable de France* (Paris: Firmin-Didot, 1885). Its appendix contains much of Montmorency's correspondence.
30. Ibid., p. 71.
31. Ibid., p. 340: "l'expérience qu'il a au faict des armes et la bonne, sincère, pure et ardente voulenté, amour et affection que de longtemps il a toujours eu et porté à nostre service, auquel de ses jeunes et premiers ans il a prins continuelle nourriture près et à l'entour de nostre personne, qui nous a donné vray et loyal tesmoignaige...de ses dicts meurs, vertuz, intégrité, sens, prudence, suffisance, loyaulté et dilligence pour lesquelz nous nous sommes despièça entièrement reposez sur luy de tous noz plus grants secretz et arduz affaires qu'il a si bien et si prudemment conduitz, guydez et administrez en temps de paix et de guerre."

other favorites and courtiers. The Venetian ambassador's succinct remark was undeniably accurate: "The Connétable administers all affairs."[32]

Obviously, anyone who wanted news of the king's intentions or who wanted to gain the king's favor addressed himself to Montmorency. Princes, foreign ministers, ambassadors, governors, even members of the king's own family – all turned to Montmorency for advice, help, and also for ecclesiastical offices. Marguerite of Navarre wrote letter after letter to Montmorency from her husband's court on behalf of several of her ecclesiastical candidates. She contacted him because she recognized "the love that I know he [Francis I] carries for you and the desire he has to please you and your friends."[33] Jean du Bellay, bishop and ambassador to England, constantly wrote to Montmorency, pleading for a lucrative benefice to defray the costs of his embassies:

> [my] being absent, there will be no one to plead my case. That I entrust, my lord, to your discretion for the well being that you appear to wish for me; and if you see that it is not unreasonable for me to change my bishopric for a better one, when they are vacant, and if you make me this advancement, I will not say another thing to you about it.[34]

Even Montmorency's rival at court, Philippe de Chabot, knew he had to ask Montmorency to secure a bishopric for his cousin, Claude de Longwy and to:

> help on your part and make this request for the love of me and for him that he be provided with the bishopric of Auxerre and the abbey of Montier. And for what he holds he will do whatever will please the lord [Francis I] and ladies [Louise of Savoy and Marguerite of Navarre] to order and command of him.... I pray you, Sire, my companion, as much as I possibly can, to employ yourself in this affair.[35]

After receiving Chabot's unending stream of petitions, Montmorency got benefices for Claude de Longwy and several other of Chabot's relatives. Another rival at court, the Marshal Claude d'Annebaut, turned to Montmorency to obtain a cardinalate for his brother. In a revealing letter to Montmorency

32. *Relations des ambassadeurs vénitiens*, 1:173.
33. *Lettres*, pp. 243-44: "l'amour que je sçay qu'il vous porte et l'envye qu'il a de vous faire plaisir et à vos amis."
34. V. L. Bourrilly, ed., *Ambassades en Angleterre de Jean du Bellay* (Paris: A. Picard & Sons, 1905), pp. 290-91: "estant absent, il n'y aura personne qui advertisse et qui demande pour moy. Je remectz, Monseigneur, cela en vostre discretion pour le bien que monstrez me vouloir; et si voyez que ne fust chose desraisonnable de me faire changer mon évesché à une meilleure quant elles vaquent, et me fissiez ceste avance, je ne vous en diz aultre chose."
35. Marcel, p. 455: "aider de vostre part et faire requeste pour l'amour de moy et deluy qu'il soit pourveu de l'Évesché d'Auxerre et de l'abbaye de Monstierender. Et il fera de ce qu'il tient ce qu'il plaira à icellui sr. et dames den ordonner et commander.... Je vous prie, M. mon compaignon tant que m'est poussible vous vouloir employer en cete affaire...."

announcing the nomination, the papacy wrote not of d'Annebaut's influence, but rather of Montmorency's:

> His Holiness, in responding to it, showed much esteem first for the supplication of the king; then for your intercession, to which he promises to always have such respect that if you employ him in something of which he can dispose, you know that he has good care to please you.[36]

Montmorency also saw to it that his own relatives and protégés received episcopal seats. Included in this coterie were several of the most disreputable bishops of the reign. Odet de Coligny, for example, was Montmorency's nephew and ward after his father's death at Pavia. Forced by his uncle to enter the church, he received an archbishopric, a bishopric, several abbeys, and the cardinalate by the age of eighteen. He never bothered to take holy orders and in his later years, of course, supported Protestant doctrines. Montmorency's concerns, as evident from many of his ecclesiastical appointments, were to aggrandize his own power and reinforce his network of clientage relationships. Religious interests were never a priority. Yet, from the available documentation, there is no doubt that for most of the reign of Francis I, it was Anne de Montmorency who most frequently dispensed the major offices of the French church. The victim of court intrigue and the machinations of Anne de Pisseleu, Anne de Montmorency was disgraced and left court in 1541. No one ever replaced him in power, influence, or stature for the rest of the reign. It is important to note, however, that Montmorency's enormous power at court, in ecclesiastical as well as other matters, rested not so much with his office – the position of Connétable was, after all, strictly a military one – but rather with his close relationship with the king. The fact that this relationship could be undermined and destroyed by a jealous mistress illustrates not only the precarious nature of royal favor and power in this reign, but also the very personal character of the Renaissance monarchy.

Aside from the king's favorites and the royal family, the final source of ecclesiastical appointments under Francis I was the royal household.[37] Unlike the first two groups, the household members held no political authority or influence, and generally came from the lower nobility. What they all shared, however, was a close association with Francis I based chiefly on the circumstances of daily access and service to him.

---

36. G. Ribier, *Lettres et mémoires d'Estat*, 2 vols. (Paris, 1666), 1:549-50. "S.S. en luy faisant réponse a monstré faire beaucoup d'estime premièrement à la prière de Roy; puis de vostre intercession à laquelle elle promet avoir toujours tel respect que si vous l'employez en chose dont elle puisse disposé, vous connoistrez qu'elle a bonne enuie de vous faire plaisir...."

37. A list of the officers in the household of Francis I can be found in *Catalogue des actes de François Ier*, 10 vols. (Paris: Imprimerie nationale, 1887-1908), 10:304. Their functions are well described in Doucet, *Institutions*, 2:123-27.

Francis I always maintained a large household. As a young prince of eighteen, he startled the economical Louis XII by bringing with him to Paris an entourage of 222 household members. Once king, Francis I extended his household to include over 700 persons whose maintenance, according to the Venetian ambassador, cost him 1,500,000 livres a year.[38] The king's household was composed of a multitude of officials and servants of all social ranks whose functions were to meet the daily needs of the king's private life.

Francis I had a familial relationship with many members of his household staff. His concern for their welfare ranged from buying a horse for each of his eight court musicians[39] to giving the widow of his hatmaker 45 livres for a silk praying mantle she had embroidered as a gift for him.[40] It was quite natural, therefore, for members of the royal household to approach the king for an episcopal appointment for some member of their family or for themselves. We find, for example, the son of the king's long-serving maitre d'hôtel given a bishopric;[41] the tutors of the king's children,[42] and the reader to the king[43] all rewarded with bishoprics and abbeys. These ecclesiastical appointments were added to other royal gifts they received, such as money, pensions, and houses, all given, according to the king, "in recompense of services."[44] Church appointments were simply another form of Francis I's famous largess used to reward favored members of his personal staff.

Most of the household officers who received episcopal appointments from the king came, as one would expect, from the royal chapel, where they functioned as chaplains to the royal family. In addition to these duties, they were charged with the distribution of royal alms to the poor; and they also served as councillors to members of the royal family, which gave them considerable influence at court. Thirty-four royal chaplains were made bishops by Francis I.[45] Many were well-educated, with degrees in either theology or law, and more than a few were

38.   *Relations des ambassadeurs vénitiens*, 1:195.
39.   *Catalogue*, 2:448.
40.   Ibid., 8:260.
41.   Pierre de Beaujeu, the only surviving child of Francis I's maître d'hôtel, Antoine de Beaujeu, was made bishop of Senez. For details, see *Gallia Christiana*, 3:1261-62.
42.   Benoit Taillecarne and Pierre Duval received numerous gifts from the king, in addition to the bishoprics of Grasse and Séez, respectively. For details of their careers, see P. Jourda, "Un Humaniste italien en France: Theocrenus," *Revue du seizième siècle* 16 (1929): 40-58.
43.   Pierre du Chastel accumulated from Francis I three abbeys and two bishoprics. For details of his career, see R. Doucet, "Pierre du Chastel, Grand Aumônier de France," *Revue Historique* 134 (1920): 1-57; and idem, "La Mort de François Ier," *Revue Historique* 113 (1913): 309-17.
44.   For details, see *Catalogue des actes de François Ier*.
45.   The best source on this topic is A. Archon, *Histoire de la Chapelle des Rois de France*, 2 vols. (Paris, 1704-1711).

outstanding humanists who distinguished themselves as writers, teachers, and bibliophiles. However, although they were well-qualified episcopal nominees, it is a striking, but hardly surprising fact, that most of them never resided in their dioceses. They chose to remain at court, near the king, because due to the Concordat, that circumstance, more than anything else, furthered their ecclesiastical careers.

$

According to the Venetian ambassador, Francis I's use of the Concordat opened the door to Protestantism in France. He wrote:

> All hope was lost for good and lettered priests to receive a recompense for their work.... Incompetent priests, appointed by the king at the whim of ladies and courtiers and motivated only by greed and self-interest, took over the French church. [They] troubled the faith of the innocent people and dampened the fervent piety of the old times. It is by this door...that heresy entered France.[46]

This condemnation of the Concordat clergy under Francis I was reiterated by others. Naturally, the Gallicanists opposed the Concordat, initially on its concessions to papal rights, but as time passed their attacks focused more and more on the caliber of royal nominees. The Parlement of Paris complained of Concordat bishops who were "unworthy people."[47] Later, the Estates of Orleans, the Assembly of Melun, and the councils of Rouen, Rheims, and Bordeaux all echoed the Venetian ambassador's allegation that the decadence of the French church and the consequent spread of Protestantism began with the Concordat of Bologna and its system of royal nominations.[48]

Were these charges true or were they largely expressions of anger and resentment on the part of institutions losing authority and control to an increasingly centralized state? There is simply not enough available evidence to maintain that Francis I's ecclesiastical appointments were any worse than those that came out of the electoral system in previous reigns. We are able to ascertain that the abuse of pluralism flourished under Francis I: almost two-thirds of his bishops were pluralists, usually holding one or more abbeys in addition to their episcopal seats.[49] However, until such studies are done for previous reigns, it is difficult to put this fact in its proper perspective.

It is also apparent that the abuses of pluralism and, consequently, nonresidency never concerned Francis I or influenced his church appointments, even after Protestantism widened its grip

46. *Relations des ambassadeurs vénitiens*, 2:129.
47. R. Doucet, *Étude sur le gouvernement de François Ier dans ses rapports avec le Parlement de Paris* (Paris: H. Champion, 1921), p. 357: "gens indignes."
48. R. Guettée, *Histoire de l'Église de France*, 12 vols. (Paris: Admin. de l'histoire de l'Église, 1856), 8:139.
49. Statistics were compiled from *Gallia Christiana*, 16 vols., passim.

on the kingdom. The king never saw the Concordat as a weapon for religious reform. Indeed, he displayed an almost total indifference to the religious and educational qualifications of his candidates. This attitude was evident from the very inception of the Concordat when, in its first draft, the king exempted princes of the blood from the requirements of age and university degrees. In the margin, next to qualifications for candidacy, was written: "The king can name non-qualified candidates, however, but of royal blood only."[50] In the final text of the Concordat, the exemption from education requirements was expanded to include members of the "great families." The text read: "Dispensation from having a university degree can apply to the great families as well as to relatives of the king."[51] From the inception of the Concordat, then, this social elite had the easiest access to church careers. Since most of Francis I's episcopal appointments went to members of the "great families,"[52] a disregard for religious and educational qualifications for the highest church offices would indeed characterize his reign. More specifically, we can establish from the available documentation that at least one-third of Francis I's bishops were never university-educated,[53] but again, until comparable studies are done for other reigns, this fact cannot be used judgmentally.

For the king, such objective criteria as age and university degrees were obviously secondary and often irrelevant compared to personal criteria. If the route to an ecclesiastical career in this reign could be void of religious and educational credentials, it most definitely had to be paved with personal contacts. Any churchman who wanted to promote his career needed access to the king, either personally or through a powerful patron at court, particularly Montmorency, Louise of Savoy or Marguerite of Navarre. It is hardly surprising that such an ambitious prelate as Claude de Longwy had letters written to all three of these patrons whenever he wanted an ecclesiastical appointment.[54]

Once such contact with the king was established, the qualification that impressed Francis I most – as he so often stated in his letters of recommendation to the pope – was that the candidate and/or members of his family served him "loyally and well." Again and again, in the correspondence of those promoting episcopal candidates to the king's attention, the word most frequently used to describe the candidate or members of his family is *serviteur* – servant. What the word implies is total devotion and unlimited service on the part of the servant who, in turn, is

---

50.   Thomas, 1:334-35: "Le roi pourra cependant nommer des non qualifiés, mais de sang royal seulement."
51.   Ibid.: "La dispense des grades en faveur des parents du roi pourra s'appliquer aux grandes familles."
52.   For details, see M. Edelstein, "The Social Origins of the Episcopacy in the Reign of Francis I," *French Historical Studies* 8 (1974): 377-92.
53.   Statistics were compiled from *Gallia Christiana*, 16 vols., passim.
54.   Marcel, pp. 455-58.

seeking protection and advancement from the king. The inference was clear that in performing his duties, the servant would always first serve the king's interests. As Philippe de Chabot wrote on behalf of his cousin's episcopal candidacy: "He will do for what he holds whatever will please the king."[55]

For Francis I, this personal bond of loyalty and service was paramount in his ecclesiastical appointments. Since most of his nominees came from the nobility of the sword,[56] it is clear that he used the hugh system of patronage provided by the Concordat to reward and bind to him this powerful clientele. As Brantôme noted, the king, deeply in debt because of the Italian wars, yet wanting to reward "the good services that his nobility usually made to him...found it better to recompense those who had served him well with some abbeys and goods of the church."[57] This deliberate confusion of church revenues with public and personal ones to reward *serviteurs* highlights Francis I's real use of the Concordat of Bologna. For the king, the Concordat served personal and political interests, not religious ones. With a hard-pressed treasury, pensions, gifts, favors, and even salaries could now take the form of an ecclesiastical benefice. This drew the nobility of the sword closer to the king because it helped make the rewards of royal service more prestigious, powerful, and financially lucrative.

Francis I thus used the Concordat to secure the loyalty and support of the strongest group in French society and to bind it to an increasingly centralized and powerful state. These goals were achieved, in some measure, at the expense of the church and the religious life of the kingdom. However, their success was ephemeral, as the anarchy and destruction of the religious wars would soon reveal.

55. Ibid., p. 455: "Et il fera de ce qu'il tient ce qu'il plaira a icellui sr. et dames [Louise of Savoy and Marguerite of Navarre] den ordonner et commander."
56. Seventy-six percent of the identifiable French bishops named by Francis I came from the nobility of the sword. For details, see Edelstein, "Social Origins."
57. Brantôme, *Grands capitaines français*, in *Oeuvres completes*, vols. 3, 4, 5 (Paris: J. Renouard, 1877), 3:107.

V

The "Lord God's" Sun
in Pico and Newton

EDWARD A. GOSSELIN

> I TREMBLE TO PRAISE THE WISDOM OF
> THOSE MEN WHO WERE THE FIRST
> TO FIX THE SYMBOLICAL IMAGES
> OF THE ARTS AND SCIENCES.*

It is not uncommon for contemporary pundits to raise the question of the ethics of science. While no one can dispute the good science has achieved in this half century – especially in the realm of medical science – the role of science and technology in creating the nuclear age with all its real and potential destruction has legitimately raised the issue of scientific ethics. To be sure, some of the giants of the modern scientific age – Einstein, Oppenheimer, Sakharov, to name but three – have issued warnings that science must not lose its ethical rootings. Yet how easily this happens in a world where contemporary knowledge is so fragmented and one field of learning is disassociated from others.

In light of this prologemenon, I want in this essay to return to an age when knowledge was thought to be, and probably indeed still was, encyclopedic. At this time, when *paideia* was possible – i.e., culture and encyclopedic learning and the broader perspectives they induced – the religious, philosophical, and scientific perspective of the late Renaissance promoted an essentially *ethical* understanding of nature.[1] The period to which I refer can be denoted in various ways: the late Renaissance; the age of encyclopedic humanism; or, as I shall prefer to use here, "the Solar Age."

This solar age commences in the fifteenth century with the publication of Marsilio Ficino's discourses on light, *De lumine* and

---

*   Christophoro Giarda (1595-1649), *Bibliothecae Alexandrinae Icones Symbolicae* (Milan, 1626/28), quoted in E. H. Gombrich, *Symbolic Images: Studies in the Art of the Renaissance* (London: Phaidon, 1978), p. 180.
1.   See Frances A. Yates, *The French Academies of the Sixteenth Century* (London: Warburg Institute, 1947).

De sole.[2] We can end the solar age with Sir Isaac Newton's great achievement – the law of universal attraction, or gravity.[3] The literature on the Sun, on light, on gravity during this period between 1480 and 1700 can be categorized, to use the phrase of Eugenio Garin, as "solar literature."[4]

In this paper, I want to discuss the texts of two different thinkers: Giovanni Pico della Mirandola and Isaac Newton. These men differ in many ways: Giovanni Pico was not a "scientist," was not an astronomer, was not a Copernican. He believed in a bounded, finite universe, as had most of those who preceded him in Antiquity and the Middle Ages. Isaac Newton was a "scientist" (whatever that meant in the seventeenth century), was an astronomer, and was a Copernican, although he much transcended Copernicus' thought. He believed in an unbounded, infinite universe as had Giordano Bruno. Despite the differences in their cosmological outlooks, Pico and Newton did share intense religious sensitivities, a belief in the sovereignty and active role of God, and a partiality to the Hermetic lore of the Renaissance. I shall argue that Pico and Newton rooted their visions of the cosmos in an ethical core – not the ethical core of "civic humanism" – but one derived from Plato's *Republic* and the marriage of religion and nature.

When Nicolaus Copernicus introduced his heliocentric model of the universe in *De revolutionibus,* he quoted various ancient authorities on the Sun's place in the cosmos. He ended by saying, "Indeed, in the middle [of all this] sits the Sun…. Tri[s]megistus calls it a visible god."[5] This statement relates to a passage in the *Asclepius:*

2.   Cf. Paul Oskar Kristeller, *The Philosophy of Marsilio Ficino,* Virginia Conant, trans. (Gloucester, MA: Peter Smith, 1964), pp. 95, 98; idem, *Supplementum Ficinianum,* 2 vols. (Florence: Olschki, 1937/73), 1:72-77.
3.   Isaac Newton, *Philosophiae naturalis principia mathematica* (London: Joseph Streater, 1687).
4.   Cf. Eugenio Garin, *Studi sul platonismo medievale* (Florence: Felice Le Monnier, 1958), pp. 190-215. Garin includes Campanella and Galileo among the authors of solar literature. It makes sense to include Newton as well. Interesting essays on the Renaissance perceptions of the Sun can be found in *Le soleil à la Renaissance: sciences et mythes* (Brussels: Presses Universitaires de Bruxelles; Paris: Presses Universitaires de France, 1965).
5.   Nicolaus Copernicus, *De revolutionibus orbium caelestium* (Thorn, 1873), pp. 16-17: "In medio vero omnium sol. Quis enim in hoc pulcherrimo templo lampadem hanc in alio vel meliori loco poneret, quam unde totum simul possit illuminare? Siquidem non inepte quidam lucernam mundi, alii mentem, alii rectorem vocant. Tri[s]megistus visibilem deum." Lynn Thorndike, *A History of Magic and Experimental Science,* 8 vols. (New York: Columbia University Press, 1941/66), 5:425, dismisses this passage as "a rhetorical relic of ancient sun-worship." Much more perceptive, I believe, is Alexandre Koyré, *La révolution astronomique* (Paris: Hermann, 1961), pp. 63, 65. There, Koyré says: "Car la fonction attribuée au Soleil, fonction d'illuminer et d'éclairer l'Univers est, pour Copernic, d'une extrême et suprême importance. C'est cette fonction qui explique et assure la place qu'il tient dans le Monde: la première en dignité et centrale en position…. Les vieilles traditions, la tradition de la Métaphysique de la lumière…réminiscence platonicienne et renaissance néoplatonicienne et

the Sun illuminates the other stars not so much by the power of its light, as by its divinity and holiness. And you should hold him, O Asclepius, to be the second god, governing all things and spreading his light on all the living beings of the world, both those which have soul and those which have not.[6]

When the hermetic texts refer to the Sun as divine and holy, they are describing it ethically: the Sun can be compared to the Good. And when this comparison is made, they are ultimately drawing upon Book 7 of Plato's *Republic*. There, the Sun is the source of visible light, the idea of the Good, of invisible light. It is to this rich religio-ethical tradition that both Giovanni Pico and Isaac Newton adhere in their visions of the qualities and role of the Sun.[7]

To understand Pico della Mirandola's views of the Sun, it will be useful to look first at his *Heptaplus* (1489) and then his *Commentary on Psalm 18*. In the *Heptaplus* we find the Sun in the service of Pico's intensely pious philosophical mysticism. He gently berates the blindness of those who wait for the Sun. Perhaps directing his remarks to the Jews, though they would also be applicable (from Pico's Savanarolan perspective) to Christians whose religious fervor had cooled, Pico says that "the Sun is here and shines, but it shines in darkness and your darkness does not comprehend it." The Sun to which Pico refers is Christ: "Through no other way can we better imagine Christ than through the Sun." Christ, "the solar animal," is the "true light *[lumen]* which illuminates all mentality." In this way, the physical Sun is His perfect image in that it "illuminates all bodies." Finally, Pico compares the Sun, which dispels the darkness and allows the previously sterile waters to produce nutritious fruits, with Christ who dispelled the uncomprehending darkness of unbelievers and fulfilled the Law with Grace.[8]

Certainly Giovanni Pico draws here on that rich philosophical and religious tradition that had been passed on to him from pagan Antiquity and the Christian Middle Ages. Yet, when we compare

---

néopythagoricienne (le Soleil visible représentant le Soleil invisible, le Soleil, maître et roi du monde visible et donc un symbôle de Dieu, conception dont Marsilio Ficino nous donne, dans son hymne au Soleil, une expression si parfaite), peuvent seules expliquer l'émotion avec laquelle Copernic parle du Soleil. Il l'adore et presque le divinise."

6.   *Corpus Hermeticum*, A. D. Nock, ed., A.-J. Festugière, trans., 4 vols. (Paris: Société d'Édition «Les Belles Lettres», 1973), 2:336-37.

7.   Ernst Cassirer, *The Individual and the Cosmos in Renaissance Philosophy*, Mario Domandi, trans. and ed. (Philadelphia: University of Pennsylvania Press, 1972), pp. 118, 134 and passim, has suggestive ideas on the relation of ethics to Renaissance philosophy of nature.

8.   Giovanni Pico della Mirandola, *Heptaplus*, in *Opera omnia* (Hildesheim: Georg Olms, 1969), 1:55. For a discussion of the philosophical content and of the relationship between Pico's discussion of the Sun as it relates to the spatial center of the text of the *Heptaplus*, see Raymond B. Waddington, "The Sun at the Center: Structure as Meaning in Pico della Mirandola's *Heptaplus*," *The Journal of Medieval and Renaissance Studies* 3 (1973): 69-86.

these comments on the Sun in the *Heptaplus* with his comments in his *Commentary on Psalm 18*, we can see that at stake was a deep psychological appreciation of the Sun's power and, with it, a yearning and straining for a way to make the Sun's power an even more powerful image and agent of Divinity.

Commenting on Psalm 18:4 ("In them [the heavens] he hath set a tabernacle for the Sun"), Pico discusses the "geographical" or spatial location of the Sun. His stress is always on the Sun's middle position:

> If we follow those who compute the Sun to be the fourth among the seven planets, or if we wish to follow the opinion which was pleasing to Plato and Aristotle, we might place it immediately after the moon. For Plato indeed reckoned the elementary spheres in the order of orbs, whereby [the Sun] was placed, here, fourth among seven; there, sixth among eleven; in both cases [it was placed] in the middle. Whereby it was judged as the center, as the arbiter, as the bond of those things which are below its dwelling place [and those things which are above].[9]

Note how the spatial placement of the Sun is crucial to Pico because of the ethical implications of its position in the elementary world. It is the "arbiter" and the "bond," terms that remind us of Marsilio Ficino's discussions of the ontological status of the human soul.[10] Given this physico-ethical orientation, it should not surprise us when Pico goes on to argue that the middle position of the Sun fills the celestial spheres with all its vigor, motion and light. The planets turn and bow in homage to the Sun, he tells us, as does the moon in its quarter, half and full stages.[11] The Sun, planets and moon of which Pico speaks are, trivially, in the natural heavens; the motions that he describes are those that all can see. However, Pico – as he had done in the *Heptaplus* – indicates that his interest is not in the shadows that we observe in the heavens but in the intelligible world whose "intellects stand in awe of the Sun and whose souls are charged by the Light to the degree that they are turned to the Sun or turned away from it." Again, as he had intimated in *Heptaplus*, the Sun begets all and nourishes all as it performs its life-giving activity.[12]

Up to this point, Giovanni Pico's exposition has seemingly made a careful distinction between *lumen* and *lux*, supercelestial light and its shadow, celestial light. However, toward the end of his disquisition this traditional distinction becomes blurred, or at least the shadow seems to be given much the same divine power as its source. Having spoken about the highest light of Mind "which illuminates everything with intelligible Light," he continues by saying:

9.   Giovanni Pico della Mirandola, *Expositio secunda Psalmi XVIII* (Ferrara, Biblioteca Communale Ariostea, Cod. II 26, fols. 65r-86r). The other *expositiones* are missing. The reference here is to fol. 69r-v.
10.   Cf. Kristeller, *Ficino*, pp. 119-20 and passim.
11.   Pico, *Expositio secunda*, fol. 70r-v.
12.   Ibid., fols. 69r-70v.

> In the same way the Sun illuminates all men with intelligible Light [lumen]. This is the true Sun, this is the Sun which illuminates and warms. It illuminates that it might be known.... Nor is there anyone who hides himself from its warmth, for who does not desire the Good?... Thus, love of mortal things dissipates, the love of the intellectual Sun vivifies and regenerates, while the lover is turned into the loved.[13]

Here the Sun, as in *Heptaplus*, becomes the "image of Christ," which "illuminates all mentality." Thus, our Sun gains in prestige by its equation with the Good and loses something of its traditional umbral character.

Whether or not Pico deliberately intended to blur the line between the supercelestial and celestial Suns, his comments show that he believes that the Sun is a powerful and nutritive celestial body and intelligence whose power, on the one hand, is the redeeming power of Christ and, on the other, is that which obliterates the distinction between subject and object, lover and loved, and perceiver and perceived. It is clear that Pico's religion of the Sun is pietistic and mystical. We can see that the salvational role of the Sun is linked in his mind with the Sun's *middle* place in the spiritual and natural cosmology. Pico is no Copernican but, by stressing the scale of heavenly hierarchies, he is able to twist the world picture so that the Sun, if not at the center, enjoys the middle place, a place most suitable for its dignity and for its power to act upon the spiritual life of man. The Sun's role for Giovanni Pico is, *au fond*, located in the ethical dimension, as it is a static engine of moral change.

Sir Isaac Newton's Copernicanism was second-, perhaps third-generation, influenced by Bruno and subsequent proponents of an infinitely extended and "worlded" universe. Thus, the Sun that had been "in the middle" to the pre-Copernican Pico and central to the Polish canon was but one of an infinite number of Suns in Newton's universe. Or was it? The argument to be spun here rests on the conclusion that something of the same ethical power persisted for Newton as it had for Pico in our solar system's Sun, which made it a governing force for the entire universe. To see this in Newton's case, we need not go through lengthy texts in Latin; rather, we need only consider the development of the formula for Newton's law of universal attraction or gravity.

Newton's law of attraction was at first worked out only in the context of our own solar system. According to this formulation, the law of attraction for our solar system is:

$$F = \left[\frac{4\Pi^2 K}{M_s} \right] \frac{M_s m}{D^2}$$

This law stipulates, then, that the attraction between any planet in our solar system is directly proportional to the product

13. Ibid., fols. 76v-77r.

of the mass of that planet and the mass of the Sun, and inversely proportional to the square of the distance between the planet and the Sun.

Newton's law mathematically answered the question of how our solar system "holds together," i.e., how and why planets revolve about the Sun and moons about their planets. Rather than go off in inertial straight lines into chaos, these planetary bodies "fall inward" and revolve in tidy elliptical orbits.

What actually *caused* the solar system to stay together in this manner had long been a question of some moment. William Gilbert, the Elizabethan scientist, opined that objects remained on the earth and that the planets circled the Sun because these objects were "great magnets." This answer did not prove satisfactory, and it was not until Newton in the mid-1680s developed his law of attraction that a measurable force could be worked out.[14]

However, when asked exactly what attraction or gravity was, Newton could give no precise answer:

> But hitherto I have not been able to discover the cause of those properties of gravity from phenomena, and I frame no hypotheses.[15]

However, Newton did believe and assert, quoting again from his General Scholium to the second edition of the *Principia* (1713), that

> This most beautiful system of the Sun, planets, and comets could only proceed from the counsel and dominion of an intelligent and powerful Being, [and that] this Being governs all things, not as the soul of the world, but as Lord over all; and on account of his dominion he is wont to be called "Lord God"...or "Universal Ruler."[16]

Newton believed that the "Lord God" governed the universe by means of "Active Principles." The most important of these principles was gravity or attraction, that force that we have just seen he could not precisely define. What I want to argue is that the Sun in our solar system was the Piconian-type representative of the "Lord God" that kept a right order, i.e., an ethical order in the entire universe. I say this for the following reasons.

14. William Gilbert, Queen Elizabeth's physician, published *De magnete* in 1600. The idea that the earth, sun and planets were magnets influenced Kepler. However, this idea's probative powers were limited and did not long survive Kepler's death. See Thomas Kuhn, *The Copernican Revolution: Planetary Astronomy in the Development of Western Thought* (Cambridge, MA: Harvard University Press, 1957), pp. 246-47; and I. Bernard Cohen, *The Birth of a New Physics* (New York: W.W. Norton, 1985), pp. 141-42.

15. H. S. Thayer, ed., *Newton's Philosophy of Nature: Selections from His Writings*, with an introduction by John Herman Randall, Jr. (New York: Hafner Press, 1953/74), p. 45. This quotation is from the General Scholium written for the second edition (1713) of Newton's *Principia*.

16. Ibid., p. 42.

Newton "universalized" his solar law of attraction and applied it to the attraction of any two objects, anywhere in the universe, by rewriting his gravitational formula to read:

$$F = G\frac{mm'}{D^2}$$

where "m" and "m'" are the masses of any two objects at any distance from each other in his infinite universe. "G" is a universal constant, which is the same as

$$\frac{4\Pi^2 K}{M_S}$$

in the original gravitational formula for our solar system. "K" is the Kepler constant from Kepler's third (harmonic) law; "M_S" is the mass of our solar system's Sun.

The historian of science I. Bernard Cohen says that "there is no mathematics – whether algebra, geometry, or the calculus – to justify [Newton's] bold step," that is, the application of the law of attraction to any and every pair of objects anywhere in the limitless universe. Professor Cohen asserts that this "bold step" is the result of Newton's "genius."[17] This may be the case, although I dislike the use of that essentially nineteenth-century Romantic term and prefer to find a more tangible link.

I believe the link is the very nature of the Sun, as we have seen it develop in Pico's thought. The solar age believed that the Sun was a powerful engine of change – witness Pico, Bruno, Fludd and others. Newton's vision of the Sun is but the last in this age of the Sun. Always seeking God's "active principles" to show how God keeps the unruly universe from flying apart into inertial chaos, he was able to make his leap of "genius" because he, too, must have seen the Sun as the agent that "reformed" the cosmos daily through its powers. No longer the physical centerpiece of the universe, Newton's Sun still played an ethical role in the universe, not on the individual salvational level, as in the case of Pico della Mirandola, but on the level of right governance of the world system. There it sits, embedded in the universal gravitational constant "G," inexplicably present but for the claims of "genius" or, more likely, those of the Piconian-Neoplatonic past and the tradition of the solar literature of the Renaissance. For certainly, to refer back to the Hermetic text I quoted above,[18] Newton could not have encapsulated our solar sun in the universal constant because of the "power of its light;" it must have had something to do with its "divinity and holiness." As Stephen Jay Gould has written, "Theories... are not inexorable inductions from facts. The most creative theories are often

17. Cohen, *Birth of a New Physics*, p. 167.
18. See n. 6, above.

imaginative visions imposed upon facts; the source of imagination is also strongly cultural."[19]

In the same way that the Florentine populace, viewing the statue of the Virgin carried into the city from San Miniato in times of danger to the commune, cried out, "Here comes the Virgin. There *she* is;" in the same way that we can imagine that Ficino and Pico took seriously the astral powers incorporated in the golden and other solar colors of a solar painting, such as Botticelli's *Primavera;* so we can reliably imagine that Newton, at the end of the Solar Age, still saw our Sun not as a drossy object but as the Lord God's guarantor of order in the Universe, and for basically the same reasons.[20] Only after the Enlightenment had broken the sacral ties that the older religio-philosophical tradition had maintained – in the decades following Newton's death in 1727 – would the ethical dimension of the Sun be forgotten and the ethics of science, the study of nature, become a problematic.

19.   Stephen Jay Gould, *The Mismeasure of Man* (New York: W.W. Norton, 1981), p. 22.
20.   Cf. Richard C. Trexler, "Florentine Religious Experience: The Sacred Image," *Studies in the Renaissance* 19 (1972): 7-41 (my italics); Frances A. Yates, *Giordano Bruno and the Hermetic Tradition* (Chicago: University of Chicago Press, 1964), pp. 76-78, discusses how the "Primavera" would have been seen as channeling the *Spiritus mundi* to the viewer; E. H. Gombrich, "Icones Symbolicae: Philosophies of Symbolism and their Bearing on Art," in *Symbolic Images*, pp. 123-95. See, for example, p. 173, where, in reference to Ficino, Gombrich writes: "These images, then, are not to be regarded as mere symbols of the planets nor are they simply representations of demonic beings. They represent the essence of the power embodied in the star."

VI

The Humanist,
The Banker and the Condottiere:
An Unpublished Letter of
Cosimo and Lorenzo de' Medici
Written by Leonardo Bruni*

JAMES HANKINS

The relationship between Leonardo Bruni and Cosimo de' Medici is something of a mystery. Bruni today is usually seen as the spokesman of Florentine republicanism, the last defender of liberty and equality in a land being engulfed by signory.[1] Cosimo de' Medici is known as the man who put an end to Florentine political liberties, who exercised in secret a personal rule concealed under the forms of traditional communal institutions. The two men ought to have been enemies. Instead, they were friends and allies. Cosimo repeatedly acted as Bruni's patron. Bruni, far from attacking Cosimo, dedicated several of his works to him and (in effect) allowed himself to be used as republican window-dressing during the early stages of Cosimo's regime.

Bruni and Cosimo were no doubt acquainted with each other already in the first decade of the century. They had common friends in Poggio and Niccolò Niccoli; and Cosimo's cousin, Nicola di Vieri de' Medici, was a correspondent of Bruni as early as 1406.[2] Their intimacy probably dated from the Council of

* Research for this article was supported by the Harvard University Center for Italian Renaissance Studies (Villa I Tatti) and the American Council of Learned Societies.

1. This view of Bruni was popularized by Hans Baron, first in *Leonardo Bruni Aretino: Humanistisch-philosophischen Schriften mit einer Chronologie seiner Werke und Briefe* (Leipzig: Teubner, 1928; repr. Wiesbaden, 1969), and later in *The Crisis of the Early Italian Renaissance: Civic Humanism and Republican Liberty in an Age of Classicism and Tyranny*, 2 vols. (Princeton: Princeton University Press, 1955); revised edition, 1 vol. (Princeton, NJ: Princeton University Press, 1966). The *reductio ad absurdum* of Baron may be found in Frederick Hartt's *History of Italian Renaissance Art*, 3d ed. (Englewood Cliffs, NJ: Prentice-Hall, 1987), p. 243, where Bruni is described as "a sort of Quattrocento Churchill."

2. For Bruni's friendship with Nicola di Vieri de' Medici, see F. P. Luiso, *Studi su l'epistolario di Leonardo Bruni*, ed. L. Gualdo Rosa (Rome: Istituto storico per il Medio Evo, 1980), pp. 21, 33, 42, 57, 59, 120.

Constance, where Bruni acted as Pope John XXIII's secretary and Cosimo and his father were bankers following the court. When Bruni returned to Florence in 1415 he began to write his history of Florence, in recognition of which he was awarded Florentine citizenship and a tax exemption; both were probably arranged by Cosimo.[3] During Bruni's period of literary *otium*, from 1415 to 1427, he dedicated two works to Cosimo, his translation of Aristotle's *Economics* (1420) and a version of (Pseudo) Plato's *Letters* (1427).[4] He took his first steps in Florentine public life as an ambassador to the Holy See (1426); and business arising from his legation obliged him to work closely with Cosimo.[5] When in 1427 the Medici party succeeded in ousting the pro-Albizzi chancellor, Paolo Fortini, from his post, Bruni succeeded him, probably as a compromise candidate.[6] He remained serenely in office throughout the 1430s, despite the violent political upheavals of the earlier part of that decade. Eventually, in the later 1430s Bruni came to hold some of the highest offices in the state, including posts on the Ten of War and in the Signoria.[7] It is impossible that he could have held these posts without the support or at least the acquiescence of Cosimo.

Attempts have not been lacking to resolve the apparent contradiction between Bruni's supposed political convictions and his political career. The best known is that of Jerrold Seigel, who sees Bruni as a "mere rhetorician," a hollow man, his head stuffed with Cicero. His "civic humanism" does not represent deep personal conviction, but is simply a rhetorician's attempt to dress up medieval communal institutions in classical garb. Rhetoric being a form of hypocrisy, it is no surprise that Bruni was able to modify his views to suit the times.[8]

---

3. The documents are published and discussed by E. Santini, *Leonardo Bruni Aretino e i suoi "Historiarum Florentini populi libri XII"* (Pisa: Scuola Normale Superiore, 1910), pp. 133-42.

4. See Baron, *Schriften*, p. 165. Baron prints the preface and argument on pp. 120-22. There is no good printed edition of the rest of the text. Some excerpts will be edited from the dedication copy (Florence, Biblioteca Laurenziana LXXIX, 19, with autograph corrections) in G. Griffiths, J. Hankins, D. Thompson, eds., *L'umanesimo di Leonardo Bruni*, Testi latini a cura di L. Gualdo Rosa e J. Hankins (Bologna: Pátron, forthcoming). This is an Italian translation (but with Latin texts in place of English versions) of the book cited in note 10. On Bruni's translation of the Pseudo-Platonic *Letters*, see my *Plato in the Italian Renaissance*, 2 vols. (Leiden: E. J. Brill, 1990), 1:74-80, 2:384-87.

5. The documents from Bruni's legation are printed by C. Monzani, "Di Leonardo Bruni Aretino: Discorso," *Archivio storico italiano*, ser. 2, 5.2 (1857): 3-34 at 25-34. For Bruni's dealings with Cosimo over this legation see my *Plato in the Italian Renaissance*, 2:385-96 n. 22.

6. D. Kent, *The Rise of the Medici: Faction in Florence, 1426-1434* (Oxford: Oxford University Press, 1978), p. 227.

7. For Bruni's offices see L. Martines, *The Social World of the Florentine Humanists* (Princeton, NJ: Princeton University Press, 1963), pp. 165-178.

8. J. Seigel, "'Civic Humanism' or Ciceronian Rhetoric? The Culture of Petrarch and Bruni," *Past and Present* 34 (1966): 3-48, esp. 25 ff.

Seigel's position is a crude one, and my summary of it cruder still. It has an element of truth. But a broader perspective is necessary to resolve the problem, or rather to see that the problem is a false one. There is room here only to make a few suggestions.

I. It is true that Bruni was a rhetorician. It was his job to compose letters espousing a point of view that was not necessarily his own. Anyone who has read through the volumes of *missive* from Bruni's chancery preserved in the Archivio di Stato will find letters praising people Bruni had contempt for, letters espousing policies Bruni disagreed with, letters calling for the torture and extradition of Bruni's friends, letters eulogizing the duke of Milan, letters of one Signoria reversing the policies of previous Signorie.[9] Bruni's outlook was that of the permanent civil servant who is obliged to carry out the policies of successive political masters. No one thought less of him for writing such letters.

II. This raises a second point. The culture of Bruni's place and time was more rhetorical and more feudal than our own. The high estimation of sincerity and ideological consistency is largely a modern (and Anglo-Saxon) phenomenon; Bruni's culture was far more tolerant of rhetorical insincerity than modern democratic culture. It was more important that words be appropriate than that they be strictly true. His age also placed a far higher value on loyalty to persons than on loyalty to political ideologies. Ideological loyalties were reserved for religious faith. Civic politics were a practical matter, and Bruni was a practical man. Cosimo was obviously a much better leader and enjoyed broader support than Rinaldo degli Albizzi. Cosimo's regime, at least at first, was difficult to distinguish from Albizzi's. And the ascendency of Cosimo, bringing as it did a measure of stability to Florentine political life, was probably for most contemporaries a condition preferable to the upheavals of the period 1426-1434.[10]

III. Bruni did have some consistent political convictions, but the level of ideological heat in his writings is rather low. Most of his political beliefs were generalized enough to enable him to serve different kinds of regime without suffering serious ideological qualms. He approved of republican constitutions, but he also approved of monarchies; nor did he see any inconsistency in

9. Bruni's *missive* are preserved in Florence, Archivio di Stato, Miscellanea Repubblicana Busta III 88 (a. 1411); Signori, Missive Ia Cancelleria vol. 29, fols. lr-3v (a. 1411); vols. 32-35 (a. 1428-37); Carte Strozziane III 80 (a. 1429-32); Florence, Biblioteca Nazionale Centrale, Panciatichi 148 (a. 1436-44). About 170 additional *missive* are preserved in scattered manuscripts, of which the most important are Florence, Biblioteca Mediceo-Laurenziana XC sup. 34, fols. 15lr-281r; Biblioteca Apostolica Vaticana, Barb. lat. 1927, fols. 2r-51v and Chigi J IV 119, fols. 156r-288v; New Haven, Connecticut, Yale University Library Marston 60, fols. 95r-129v; and Florence, Biblioteca Nazionale Centrale, Magl. VI 189, fols. 75r-127r.
10. A point made by Gordon Griffiths in G. Griffiths, J. Hankins, D. Thompson, eds., *The Humanism of Leonardo Bruni* (Binghamton, New York: Center for Medieval and Early Renaissance Studies, 1987), p. 20.

this. Like Aristotle he believed the legitimacy of a regime derived not from its constitutional form, but from its willingness to rule in the interests of all, not part, of the citizen body. Like Aristotle he believed that the best form of constitution for a country depended on geography and the collective virtue (what moderns might call the "political culture") of its people. He himself preferred a free republic. But, as papal secretary, he saw nothing wrong with helping to put down the liberties of the city of Rome after her citizens had forfeited their liberty by vicious behavior; nor later, as Florentine chancellor, did he show any sympathy for the attempts of Volterra and Arezzo to escape the Florentine yoke.[11]

IV. Bruni's "civic humanism" can be read as a draping of medieval communal traditions in the toga of classical republicanism. But only in part. His classical republicanism also, covertly, reinterpreted certain important features of Florentine political tradition. For Bruni, as for Salutati, the legitimacy of Florence's foreign policy was no longer necessarily linked to the papacy or to Guelfism. The defense of liberty was in itself valuable, quite apart from its sanction by prescriptive right or by the pope. In describing the spirit of Florence's constitution, Bruni placed more emphasis on equality of *opportunity* to participate than on the equal right of all guildsmen to participate.[12] He also insisted on virtue as a qualification for office, and wealth as a precondition for exercising virtue.[13] Such descriptions may properly be read as oligarchic in tendency. Bruni's "civic humanism" was much more attuned to the oligarchic values of the post-1382 regime than to the popular regimes of the 1290s, the 1340s, or of 1378-1382.

‡

11. For Bruni's views on the relative merits of different constitutions, see the prefaces and letters of transmission accompanying his Latin version of Aristotle's *Politics*, in *The Humanism of Leonardo Bruni*, pp. 154-70. For his attitude to the revolt of the Roman people against Innocent VII see his letters (I.4, I.5) to Salutati of 1405 in L. Mehus, ed., *Leonardi Bruni Arretini Epistularum libri VIII* (Florence: B. Paperinius, 1741), 1:6-11. His attitude to the revolt of the Volterran people in 1431 is reflected in a *littera patens* (not a *missive*) he wrote to them in his capacity of Florentine chancellor, entitled *La presente lettera mandarono i nostri magnifici signiori al popolo della citta di Volterra tornati che furono alla divotione del comune, composto per messer Lionardo Bruni Darezzo nostro Kancelliere, inc. Nobiles viri amici karissime. Le chose humane secondo che ne mostra la experienza* – Data Florentie die XXX Octobris MCCCCXXXI. The work is not recorded in the bibliographical studies of either Baron or Bertalot but is preserved in at least eighteen manuscripts and has been unsatisfactorily printed in L. A. Cecina and F. Dal Borgo, *Notizie istoriche della città di Volterra* (Pisa, 1758), 229n. I am preparing a new edition of the text.
12. See the funeral oration for Nanni Strozzi, in *The Humanism of Leonardo Bruni*, pp. 121-27, esp. 124.
13. See the preface to Bruni's translation of the pseudo-Aristotelian *Economics* (above, note 4; translated in ibid, pp. 305-6) and his letter (V.2) to Tommaso Cambiatore in Mehus, *Leonardi Bruni...Epistularum libri*, 2:8-15.

All of these points obviously require further development and proof, and I hope to do so on another occasion.[14] Here my aim is simply to throw more light on the relationship between Cosimo de' Medici and Bruni by discussing Bruni's role as Cosimo's occasional Latin secretary. The role is revealed in a letter written by Cosimo and his brother Lorenzo to the condottiere Carlo Malatesta after the death of Cosimo's father, Giovanni di Bicci, on 20 February 1429 (Appendix A). The epistle had some circulation as a literary model, surviving in at least six manuscripts. In one of these (Milan, Biblioteca Ambrosiana C 145 inf.) the composition of the letter is attributed to Bruni. False attributions of texts to Bruni are, to be sure, extremely common phenomena in the fifteenth century, but in this case the ascription is convincing. Neither Cosimo's nor Lorenzo's powers as Latinists were equal to the task of writing such a letter.[15] On the other hand, the language of the letter is perfectly consistent with Bruni's style. Moreover, the letter shows parallels in language and themes with another letter written by Bruni, this time in his capacity as Florentine chancellor. This was a letter written by the Florentine Signoria to Carlo Malatesta's wife and children when, six months later, Carlo himself died; in it Bruni uses some of the same commonplaces to praise Carlo as had appeared in the earlier letter written under the names of Cosimo and Lorenzo.[16]

The letter from Cosimo and Lorenzo to the famous general and *signore* of Rimini provides a vivid example of the role of literature in international politics. Every Florentine politician who hoped to exercise influence in the councils or as a diplomat needed to maintain good relations with condottieri, those powerful and independent military entrepreneurs. Malatesta, though famous as an opponent of pagan poetry, was in other respects a remarkably cultivated man – a forerunner, it could be said, of Federigo d'Urbino.[17] Bruni had spent some months with him at Rimini in 1409 after leaving the service of Gregory XII and had come away with an impression it is not too much to call hero-worship: Malatesta, that *Pulcherrimum priscae antiquitatis specimen*, was not only a citadel of military virtue, but a power in the realms

14.   I am preparing a biography of Bruni to be published by Cambridge University Press.
15.   I discuss Cosimo's knowledge of Latin in "Cosimo de'Medici as a Patron of Humanistic Literature," in *Cosimo de' Medici, Pater Patriae, 1389-1464: Essays for the Sexcentenary of His Birth*, ed. F. Ames-Lewis (Oxford: Oxford University Press, forthcoming).
16.   The letter, dated 20 September 1429, is preserved in Florence, Archivio di Stato, Signori, Missive Ia Cancelleria vol. 32, fols. 128v-129v, and in Biblioteca Apostolica Vaticana, MS Chigi J IV 119, fols. 261r-262r. A copy of the letter was kindly made for me by Dr. Ursula Jaitner-Hahner.
17.   For Malatesta's role in the controversy about the destruction of a statue of Virgil, see D. J. B. Robey, "Virgil's Statue at Mantua and the Defense of Poetry: An Unpublished Letter of 1397," *Rinascimento*, ser. 2, 9 (1969): 191-203. On Malatesta, see further M. Mallett, *Mercenaries and Their Masters: Warfare in Renaissance Italy* (London: Bodley Head, 1974), pp. 60-65.

of learning and literature.[18]   Years later Bruni dedicated his famous *De studiis et literis* to Malatesta's learned daughter, Battista. Such a man would plainly be susceptible to flattering appeals dressed in antique garb. So when Giovanni di Bicci died, Cosimo and Lorenzo immediately sent an elegant Latin epistle to the man, reminding him of their father's long devotion to him, appealing to the values implicit in the ancient concept of *amicitia* to request his favor, and generally laying it on with a trowel.

A reply to the Medici letter in the name of Carlo Malatesta was composed by Pier Candido Decembrio and is preserved in the two manuscripts containing the first *sylloge* of his *epistolario*.[19] We do not know how Decembrio, secretary to the duke of Milan, came to write a letter for Carlo Malatesta. It may be that Decembrio met Malatesta on one of the numerous legations he undertook for Filippo Maria Visconti during this period.[20]

If the attribution of the Medici letter to Bruni is accepted, it is plain that the rest of Cosimo's Latin correspondence ought to be reexamined for signs of Bruni's activity. Seven Latin letters are known to have circulated under Cosimo's name. Three were written after Bruni's death.[21] Of the three remaining letters (subtracting the letter to Malatesta), one is very likely, on the basis of linguistic evidence, to have been written by Bruni. It is a letter to Romeo Foscari written in Cosimo's name, and, like the Malatesta letter, informs him of the death of Giovanni di Bicci de' Medici. It uses some of the same phrases as the Malatesta letter and so was probably composed about the same time.[22]

The two remaining letters may well also have been written by Bruni. One is a note from Cosimo to Anastasio Vespucci, returning a copy of Frontinus' *Strategemata* given him by the notary. It contains the Brunian phrase *mirum in modum* – also used of course by Cicero, but in Bruni something of a stylistic tic – and displays the mania for chiastic figures that is a characteristic of

---

18.   Bruni, *Ep.*. III.9, ed. Mehus, 1:76-83. Bruni also praises Malatesta in *Ep.* VI.7, ed. Mehus, 2:51-52 and in his *Rerum suo tempore gestarum commentarius*, ed. C. di Pierro, in *Rerum italicarum scriptores*, n.s., 19, 4 (Bologna: Zanichelli, 1926), p. 439.

19.   Decembrio's letter is in B, fols. 75v-78r, and Br, fols. 53v-55v (see Appendix A, below). Vittore Zaccaria announced his intention of preparing an edition of Decembrio's correspondence in 1952. What appears to be a different letter of reply from Malatesta to Cosimo and Lorenzo (*inc.* Quantum morte optimi viri parentis vestri) is preserved in R, fols. 259v-260v.

20.   For Decembrio's career, see M. Borsa, "Pier Candido Decembrio e l'umanesimo in Lombardia," *Archivio storico lombardo* 20 (1893): 5-75, 358-441.

21.   The letters are listed and discussed in my "Cosimo de' Medici as a Patron of Humanistic Literature."

22.   The letter, dated 10 May [1429], is preserved in Florence, Archivio di Stato, Mediceo avanti il Principato XI 568 and has been published in A. Fabroni, *Magni Cosmi Medicei vita* (Pisa, 1788-89), 2:18; the letter has some of the same phrases as appear in the letter to Malatesta, e.g., "non ea sapientia sum, ut tam gravi casu non movear," "si quid amicitia, gratia aut opibus valemus," which may be compared to Appendix A, lines 13-15 and 75-76.

Bruni's style.[23] The other letter is a patronage request directed by Cosimo to Berto di Antonio Berti, the chancellor of Siena (Appendix B). Cosimo asks Berti to appoint Pier Marino Brancadori as *praetor* (i.e., podestà) of Siena. Berti, as it happened, was also a good friend of Bruni; Bruni dedicated his treatise *De recta interpretatione* (1424/26) to him.[24] The letter to Berti displays less individuality, but it too could easily be Bruni's work. Neither letter is written in Bruni's or Cosimo's hand, so orthography provides little guidance in making an attribution.

In short, at least two and possibly four or more of Cosimo's surviving Latin letters were actually composed for him by Leonardo Bruni. What we can conclude about their relationship based on this information is another question. If Bruni did write the letter to Berti, it argues a certain level of political confidence between the two men. Otherwise, we can only say that political frictions between them, if they did exist, were not so heated as to prevent Bruni from performing small literary favors for Cosimo.

APPENDIX A

A Letter of Cosimo and Lorenzo de' Medici to Carlo Malatesta (1429)

The work survives in the following six manuscripts:

A - Milan, Biblioteca Ambrosiana C 145 inf., fols. 271r-272v. Humanist miscellany, including some works of Leonardo Bruni. Humanistic cursive, s. XV 3/4. See P. O. Kristeller, *Iter Italicum* (Leiden: Brill, 1963-89), 1:320.
a - Milan, Biblioteca Ambrosiana M 40 sup., fols. 3r-5r. Humanist miscellany, including many works of Leonardo Bruni. Semihumanistic script, written in Northern Italy, s. XV 2/4. See ibid., 1:334. A later hand has added some stylistic improvements that cannot be authorial.
Bo - Bologna, Biblioteca Universitaria MS 2387, fols. 73v-75v. First *sylloge* of Pier Candido Decembrio's *Epistolario*. Humanistic cursive, written between 1443 and 1447. See V. Zaccaria,

---

23.   The undated letter to the notary Anastasio Vespucci is printed in its entirety in A. M. Bandini, *Catalogus codicum latinorum Bibliothecae Mediceae Laurentianae* (Florence: Typographia Regia, 1774-78), 3:552: "Frontini librum de re militari nuper a te mihi dono missum, quum voluptati meae satis fuerit eius ordinem ac disciplinam cognovisse, ad te nunc honesta de caussa remitto. Satis tibi gratiarum habeo, si tanti viri, quod mirum in modum cupiebam, de ipsa militia tuo munere sententiam cognoverim; nec sane tua apud me benevolentia ullo munerum testimonio eget; nihil enim aut auctoritatis aut facultatis apud me est quod a te alienum esse velim."
24.   L. Bertalot, *Studien zum italienischen und deutschen Humanismus*, ed. P. O. Kristeller, Storia e letteratura, Raccolta di studi e testi, vols. 129-130 (Rome: Edizioni di Storia e letteratura, 1975), 2:379. On Berto di Antonio Berti see G. Fioravanti, "Alcuni aspetti della cultura umanistica senese nel '400," *Rinascimento*, ser. 2, 19 (1979): 117-67, at 126n., 142-45, 154.

"L'epistolario di Pier Candido Decembrio," *Rinascimento*, ser. 1, 3 (1952): 85-118, esp. 87n., 96.

Br - Milan, Biblioteca Braidense MS A H 1216, fols. 52r-53v. First *sylloge* of Pier Candido Decembrio's *Epistolario*. Semihumanistic script, written in Lombardy. s. XV 2/4. See ibid.

O - Oxford, Bodleian Library MS Canonici misc. 360, fols. 57v-59r. Humanist miscellany. Written at Pavia in 1453 by Michael de Vellate, semi-humanistic script. See H. O. Coxe, *Cat. codd. mss. Bibl. Bodl. Pars Tertia, codd. graec. et lat. Canonicianos complectens* (Oxford, 1854), p. 704.

R - Florence, Biblioteca Riccardiana MS 407, fols. 256v-258r. Humanist letter collection, mostly of Milanese provenance, but including seven letters of Bruni. Gothic cursive script, written s. XV med. See Kristeller, *Iter*, 1:191.

The variants permit the following stemma to be constructed:

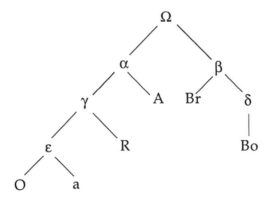

The variants of "O" are based on a collation kindly supplied by Dr. Richard Gyug of the Pontifical Institute of Mediaeval Studies. In editing Bruni's letter I follow the "Brunian" orthography reconstructed by Lucia Gualdo Rosa for the Italian edition of *The Humanism of Leonardo Bruni* (see note 4, above). Punctuation and capitalization have been modernized.

Cosmus et Laurentius Medices illustri Carolo Malateste salutem.

Vellemus, prestantissime atque optime princeps, ut nostre lit-
tere tibi aliquid iocundum afferrent et non id quod nos sine lacrimis
scribere non possumus et te non sine molestia lecturum arbitramur.
Sed quoniam nature repugnare nec possumus nec debemus, non alienum   5
a nostro officio uisum est de tam graui nostri casu te certiorem
facere. Noster parens, qui tecum usque ad extremum uite tempus
summa beneuolentia atque incredibili caritate iunctus fuit, nono
Kalendas Martias, cum nichil pretermisisset quod ad sacra
religionemque pertineret, cessit e uita. Quanto autem luctu suique   10
desiderio nos reliquerit, tibi facile existimandum censemus qui
cognoris quam grauem iacturam perpessi sumus. Neque enim ea
sapientia sumus ut mortem tam optimi, tam cari ac benefici parentis
sine moerore et lachrimis ferre possimus. Nam si unquam summo amore
immortalibus in filios beneficiis aliquis pater lugendus fuit,   15
nemini mirum uideri debet si tam cari genitoris obitu moueamur. Is
etenim in nos amor, ea et in nos merita fuere, ut his nullo officio,
nulla pietate satisfacere ualeamus. Qua consuetudine domestica
fuerit famulorum moerore, qui eius decessum non secus ac parentis
luxerunt, intelligi licet. Neque uero eum senectus morosum ac   20
difficilem reddiderat, non uires animi debilitauerat, sed ea
grauitate, ea iocunditate erat, ut eum tota domus summa caritate
complecteretur. De uigore autem animi dicere pretermittimus: in
promptu enim omnibus est quo consilio, qua cura, qua integritate
omnia rei publice obiret munera. Quanto uero officio amicis   25
nauaret operam, moerore funeris indicatum est. Sed quid commemorando eum qui uita nobis carior erat uulnus nostri doloris
attrectamus? Quid luctus innouamus nostros, presertim cum
nec hoc nobis propositum sit et tuas aures quam minima molestia

---

1 *tit. sic Br*: Cosmus et Laurentius fratres de Medicis Florentini illustri
Carolo Malateste genitoris sui Iohannis obitum significant *B*: Cosma et
Laurentius de Medicis illustrissimo principi Karulo Malateste s. p. d. *A*:
Cosmas et Laurentius de Medicis domino Carolo de Malateste (!) *R*: Ad
illustrem dominum Karolum Malatestas C. et L. de Medicis *a*: Illustri domino
Karulo Malateste Cosmus et Laurentius de Medicis salutem *O* 3 aliquid] aliud
BoBr 5 nec *prius*] non *aO* 6 est *om.* R nostro *aOR* facere certiorem *BoBr* 8
coniunctus *Bo* nono] viij° *A* 9 sacram *AaOR* 10 -que *om.* *AaO* 11 reliquit *aOR*
extimandum *a* 12 enim] in *A* 13 atque *post* tam *aOR* ac] et *aO* 14 possemus *A*:
possumus *R* atque *post* amore *AaOR* 16 nemini] non *A* mirum] nimirum *R* obitu
genitoris *A* 17 etenim] enim *aOR* ea *om.* *aOR* 19 discessum *aOR* 20 parentes *R*
20 uero] enim *aOR* senectus eum *A* atque *AaOR* 21 difficiliorem *aO* 22 ea] et
aO summe *post* summa caritate *Br* 23 uigore] ingenio *aO(R?)* 26 iudicatum *O*
26-27 commemorando eum] commerciorandorum (!) *R* 27 uulnus nostri doloris]
uidemus non dolores *aOR* 28 ita *post* nostros *aOR* 29 nec] ne *A* prepositum *Br*

onerare uelimus? Sed pietas nos traxit inuitos ut Tuam Dignitatem   30
nostri luctus participem faceremus. Nunc uero ne modum excedamus,
dolori finem imponimus, et ad reliqua pergimus.

Non obscurum est nobis, iustissime princeps, quanta noster
genitor dum uixit necessitudine, beneuolentia, amore tecum fuerit
astrictus. Nam tuum nomen semper in ore habebat et tui   35
recordatione miram capiebat uoluptatem, nec tuis preclaris uirtu-
tibus narrandis satis animum explere poterat. Etenim quanta in
subditos iusticia, quanta innocentia, quanta in omnibus rebus tem-
perantia esses, eum sepe narrare audiuimus, qui tam iustis legibus,
tam preclaris institutis, tanta humanitate et amore populos tuos te   40
gubernare asserebat, ut ab his merito et optimus princeps et
carissimus pater appellari posses. Non te, ut idem dicebat, ad
bona ciuium diripienda auaricia impellit, non libido ad uoluptatem
inflammat, non crudelitas ad cedem tuorum prouocat, sed publice
utilitati consulis, modestiam seruas, patrio amore ciuitates tuas   45
complecteris. Quod nobis profecto non mirum uidetur. Didicisti
enim a philosophia, cui te mirifice deditum semper esse cognouimus,
honestatem rebus omnibus humanis esse anteponendam. Quapropter
tutelam potius quam imperium tuorum populorum tibi datum esse
arbitraris, bonumque publicum semper tuo preuertendum putasti.   50
Iam uero tanta humanitate es, tam faciles ad te aditus, tanta
patientia querelis omnium aures prebes, ut non in aliqua dignitate
constitutus, sed priuatus esse uideare. Tuam uero fortitudinem,
industriam, consilium, fidem multis exemplis que a parente
accepimus cognitam perspectamque habemus. Nichil enim a te ges-   55
tum quod Tue Dignitati ornamento esset, ipse obliuioni tradidit,
sed tuas singulares uirtutes tuaque facta egregia tenebat memoria,
et maiori semper cum desiderio narrabat multaque alia de tua
dignitate ab eo audiuimus que dicenda forent, nisi epistolaris
angustia nos prohiberet.   60

Que omnia argumento esse possent qua obseruantia, qua amicitia
Tuam Dignitatem amarit, coluerit. Quantam uero spem in Tua
Dignitate et amicitia haberet, si minus in uita, certe in morte
declaratum est. Nam cum iam mors aduentaret, primum disseruit

30 ennarrare *AR* 32 finem dolori *B* 34 uixerit *R* beneuolentia...tecum] nec
non tecum beneuolentia *A BoBr* 35 in ore semper *O* 39 eum] cum *Br, post corr.
Bo* ennare (!) sepe *a*: enumerare sepe *R, O post corr.* quia *aOR* 40 tanta] tam *R*
preclara *post* tanta *aOR* et amore *om. BoBr* tuos populus *aAOR* 42 clarissimus
aBoBr 43 impulit 44 ad] ac *R* 45 modestiam consulis *a* patrie *Bo* 46 mirum
non *Aa* 47 mirifice *om. O* esse *om. A* 48 omnibus rebus *aOR* humanis esse *om.
aOR* apponenda *R* 48-49 Quam propter (*et* propter *ante* imperium) *R* 49 potius
om. A 50 preponendum *A*: pretermittendum *a*: premittendum *O*: promittendum
R 51 uero] non *O, ut uid.* 53 uidearis *Aa* et *post* fort. *A* 55 prospectamque *Bo*
haberemus *Bo* 56 esse *A* tradit *BoBr* 58-59 ab eo *post* alia *A* audiuimus]
habuimus *a* que] quam *A* 60 angusta *Br* nos] non *Bo* 63 et] atque *aOR* habeat
R pater *post* haberet *s.s. a²* 64 certe *post* Nam *s.s. a²*

quantis beneficiis a te honestatus fuerit, nec pretermisit quam 65
honorifice, quam amice domi tue nos tempore pestis acceperis,
postremo nobis imperauit, iniunxit, ut Tuam Dignitatem eadem
caritate et beneuolentia qua semper erga te fuerit prosequeremur,
te non secus ac sui memoriam coleremus ac nos nostraque Tue
traderemus Dignitati, asseuerans in tua amicitia magnum momentum 70
nobis in omni fortuna uel prospera uel aduersa esse futurum. Tam
iustis ergo parentis preceptis, optime princeps, obtemperantes nos
totos ac nostra tibi permittimus nobis fortuna filiis demum atque
amicis tuo arbitratu utere, et si quid amicis, opibus, gratia
ualemus, id promptum atque paratum Tue Dignitati pollicemur. Nam 75
si aliqua in re Prestantie Tue usui aut honori esse poterimus,
experieris profecto quanti tuam beneuolentiam atque amicitiam
faciamus.

Postremo te maiorem in modum oramus atque obsecramus ut nos ob
memoriam nostri cari parentis summamque erga te beneuolentiam inter 80
humiles tue dignitatis amicos habere uelis. Nam si nos tuo
presidio tuoque amore non destitutos uidebimus, magnum profecto
solatium atque leuamen acerbi doloris erit, nec penitus orbatos nos
esse rebimur. Te faustum atque felicem optamus. Kalendis Martii,
Florentie. 85
*Leonardus Aretinus: De morte Patris Cosmae et Laurentii nunciatio
Karolo Malateste et de laudibus Karoli.*

65 te *post* nec *a* quam] uel *A* 66 honorifice] mirifice *A* nos *om. aO* 67
nobis... iniunxit] imperauit et nobis commisit *A* 68 quae *A* fuit *R* prosequamur
aO 69 collectemur *A* ac] et *s.s. corr. a*^{2} 70 asseuerans] affirmans *s.s. corr. a*^{2} 71
nobis *om. a* omni] ea *aOR* Tam] Iam *A* 72 iustis] in istis *A* 73 ac] atque *AaOR*
promittimus *R* demumque atque *R* 74 quid] quis *A* opibus amicis *AaOR* 75
ualeremus *R* certe *post* Nam *s.s. a*^{2} 76 re] te *A(?)Br* Presencie *A* aut] atque *O*
77 pretii *post* quanti *s.s. a*^{2} 79 Postremum *aO* oramus] rogamus *aOR* 80 et *post*
parentis *s.s. a*^{2} -que *om. aOR* 82 destinatos *aO* 83 nostri *post* leuamen *A* 84
rebimur] uidebimus *A* Te...optamus *om. aOR* Cosmas et Laurentii de Medicis
humiles Tue Dignitatis serui *post* rebimur *aO* Kalendis Martii *om. aBoBrOR*
85 Florentie *om. aOR* 86-87 *sic A: om. aBoBrOR*

APPENDIX B

A Letter of Cosimo de' Medici
to Berto di Antonio Berti, Chancellor of Siena

The text is preserved in Florence, Archivio di Stato, Mediceo avanti il Principato XI 652. I preserve the original orthography, but modernize punctuation and capitalization.

Cosmus de Medicis Berto uiro doctissimo plurimam salutem dicit.

Alias meis litteris te certiorem feci quam gratum mihi esset si tua opera dominus Petrus Marinus, uir preclarus ex Branchadorum familia, pretor vestrae reipublicae eligeretur. Nunc uero cum acceperim tibi pretorem deligendi ius omne mandatum esse, uide quantum mihi de tua humanitate tuaque erga me beniuolentia policeatur; iam confectum negotium esse arbitror.

Est enim uir integer summa iustitia, incredibili fide quemque nemo pretio uel gratia uel amicitia ab eo quod honestum uidetur deducere ualeat. Quamobrem sperans eum tibi honori uestraeque reipublicae usui atque ornamento fore, maiorem in modum tibi commendo teque oro atque obsecro ut tuo studio tuaque opera uir ille ad id munus deligatur, quod cum feceris mihi spera fore gratissimum. Vale, et si qua in re tibi tuisque familiaribus conferre ualeo, me commonefacias.

Florentie VIIII Kalendas Februarias.

VII

Why Did the Codex
Supplant the Book-Roll?

WILLIAM V. HARRIS

In the decades around 300 A.D. the book in codex form massively
supplanted the book-roll, which had been the dominant form for
literary texts throughout classical antiquity. In the second century
some 98.4 percent of the Greek literary texts that now survive –
practically all of which were of course written in Egypt – were in
book-roll form, and in the third century 81.4 percent still were; but
in the fourth and fifth centuries the numbers sink to 26.7 percent
and 11.1 percent. These statistics are derived from C. H. Roberts
and T. C. Skeat, *The Birth of the Codex*,[1] and neither rival views
about the dates of certain manuscripts[2] nor alternative ways of
compiling the statistics make any serious difference as far as the
subject of this study is concerned. As for the Latin literary codex,
the only surviving one that is earlier than the third century is the
anonymous fragment *De bellis Macedonicis*[3] of roughly 100 A.D.[4]
Thus Martial's enthusiasm for the codex form evidently did not
prove contagious; the silence of second-century Greek and Latin
authors on the subject of codex books[5] coincides with the papyro-
logical evidence to make the fact itself fairly definite. An apparent
mention of a batch of literary codices in a letter that has been dated
to the second century, *P.Petaus* 30,[6] must, if it has been correctly
understood, be untypical of that period.

---

1.   London, 1983, pp. 36-37.
2.   See especially G. Cavallo, *Studi italiani di filologia classica (SIFC)* ser. 3,
3 (1985): 120-21; and in A. Blanchard, ed., *Les Débuts du codex* (Turnhout, 1989),
pp. 171-72.
3.   *P.Oxy.* [= B. P. Grenfell & A. S. Hunt et al., eds., *The Oxyrhynchus Papyri*
(London, 1898-)], vol. 1, no. 30; R. A. Pack, *The Greek and Latin Literary Texts
from Greco-Roman Egypt*, 2d ed. (Ann Arbor, 1965), no. 3000; E. G. Turner, *The
Typology of the Early Codex* (Philadelphia, 1977), no. 498.
4.   For its date see J. Mallon, *Emerita* 17 (1949): 1-8, reprinted in *De l'Écriture*
(Paris, 1982), pp. 208-12.
5.   Roberts and Skeat, *Birth of the Codex*, p. 28.
6.   U. Hagedorn, D. Hagedorn, et al., eds., *Das Archiv des Petaus* (Cologne,
1969), no. 30.

The reason for the change from book-roll to codex is an old problem, still unsettled.[7] A fully satisfactory solution must explain why the change took place *when it did*. The codex has a number of advantages over the book-roll, and it was indubitably in use for some literary texts at least as early as the 80s of the first century A.D. Our task, however, is to decide which were the most important advantages (and disadvantages) of the codex form in the specific context of the late third and fourth centuries. What was it about the codex form that appealed to the book-users of late antiquity?

Older scholars, such as C. R. Gregory, had many useful things to say on this subject. An account particularly worth reading, though it is outdated in some respects, is that of F. G. Kenyon.[8] But C. H. Roberts' paper of 1954[9] put scholarly understanding of the material evidence on a much firmer basis. At the same time, unfortunately, Roberts advanced a theory about the special predilection of the early Christians for the codex form that seems to have convinced no one, and scarcely deserved to do so. It may be said that no balanced account of the whole matter has appeared in the recent literature. The latest theories of Roberts, Skeat, Cavallo and others all appear to have fatal flaws, and we need something to put in their place. This paper depends heavily on the work of others, but seeks to provide a somewhat novel synthesis by way of a solution.[10]

The Christians already had the firmly established habit of putting their biblical texts in codex form by the second century; the reason for this preference of theirs is linked to, but also separate from, the problem of the change that affects secular writing. Every one of the eleven Christian biblical papyri to which Roberts and Skeat assign a second-century date is from a codex,[11] and the same is true for the great majority of biblical texts in succeeding centuries.[12] Christian texts of the second and third centuries that are not biblical (the distinction between canonical and non-canonical texts is to a considerable degree anachronistic, but this problem need not be discussed in the present context) are less strictly confined to codices, but still show a very marked preference for the codex.[13]

The material evidence for all this comes practically without exception from Egypt, from Egypt outside Alexandria at that, and

7.   See P. J. Parsons, *Classical Review* 37 (1987): 84.
8.   *Books and Readers in Ancient Greece and Rome*, 2d ed. (Oxford, 1951), pp. 87-120.
9.   *Proceedings of the British Academy (PBA)* 40 (1954): 169-204.
10.   Compare my *Ancient Literacy* (Cambridge, MA, 1989), pp. 294-97, where there was only room for summary remarks.
11.   *Birth of the Codex*, pp. 40-41.
12.   However, Roberts and Skeat, ibid., pp. 39-40, use some excessively special pleading to dispose of the exceptions; K. Aland, *Repertorium der griechischen christlichen Papyri*, I. *Biblische Papyri* (Berlin and New York, 1976), esp. p. 429, is more dispassionate.
13.   Roberts and Skeat, *Birth of the Codex*, p. 43.

it would be safer not to assume that Christian practice was identical in this respect throughout the empire – compare the warning of Roberts and Skeat,[14] which they later[15] decide to disregard on wholly inadequate grounds. Iconographic evidence from Rome itself that will be brought in later ought to make us hesitate before supposing that the codex was dominant among the Christians of the capital city at an early date. What is said by some to be the earliest surviving text of a gospel, a papyrus fragment from Qumran, was written on a roll, and in any case we have textual evidence that adds to the likelihood that the Christians had more than a few sacred writings in roll form.[16] Nonetheless, it can be taken as probable that in the second century the Christians in large regions of the empire were already demonstrating their preference for having their Old and New Testament texts in codex form. Our problem is in any case to know why the codex eventually came to be the preferred form for non-Christian texts too. Recent discussions have led in the main to explanations of the former change which, whatever their validity, do not really apply to the latter.

Another change in book production that took place for the most part in late antiquity was the transition from papyrus to parchment. This change was quite independent of the change from book-roll to codex[17] – or at least, it is now the unanimous belief of scholars that the problems are separate ones, since there exist papyrus codices as well as papyrus book-rolls, and parchment book-rolls as well as parchment codices; and since, furthermore, no one has been able to establish whether parchment cost less than papyrus, still less how the relationship of parchment prices to papyrus prices changed over time. It is possible to doubt whether the change from papyrus to parchment was as independent from the change from book-roll to codex as convention now insists, but no attempt will be made here to disturb the consensus on this point.

Once craftsmen have mastered the technique of making codices, the codex very clearly has a considerable cost advantage over the book-roll, and that might be practically the end of the story. According to Skeat's calculations, a 44 percent saving of paper results from the use of the codex form (because both sides of the paper are used), which he thinks, more speculatively, would mean a 26 percent cost saving if the cost of the copyist's labor were taken into account.[18] These figures can be accepted as rough approximations.

This cost advantage probably did play a significant part in bringing about the conversion to the codex, but it is unlikely to be

14.   Ibid., p. 3.
15.   Ibid., p. 35.
16.   See *Acta Petri* 20 (written c.180); Theodoret on 2 Timothy 4:13 = *Patrologia Graeca* 82:453D; and various martyr acts.
17.   Roberts and Skeat, *Birth of the Codex*, p. 5.
18.   T. C. Skeat, *Zeitschrift für Papyrologie und Epigraphik* 45 (1982): 173-75.

the sole explanation. For a long time the cost advantage had very little effect on ordinary non-Christian book-users. Initially, when copyists and craftsmen lacked experience with codices, those concerned may have found it difficult to realize, in either sense of the word, the full savings that were possible. The documentary codex, incidentally, seems to have come in only in the fourth century,[19] so it was no help to the first makers of literary codices. In any case, part of the demand for new copies of books came from those who were so well-to-do that they are not likely to have been very interested in such economies, and may indeed have preferred to engage in conspicuous expenditure. It can also be agreed – though the subject is a complex and controversial one – that in antiquity technological innovations that were profitable or potentially profitable often spread slowly.[20]

Furthermore, while most second- and third-century Christians who wanted to own parts of the holy writings may well have been people of modest resources, it cannot plausibly be supposed that they were vastly more cost-conscious than non-Christians, or that they were especially so when it came to copying parts of the Bible. (Roberts and Skeat even argue,[21] with a touch of special pleading, that early Christian codices show no signs of a desire to economize. Contrast the judgment of Turner,[22] according to whom the handwriting of papyrus codices of the second and third centuries is "often of an informal and workaday type." After citing some examples he adds that they "give the impression of being 'utility' books; margins are small, lines usually long.") Nor is it likely to be a coincidence that the large-scale extension of the codex form to pagan texts took place in a period when the numbers and the respectability of the Christians were strongly increasing. The price of papyrus in relation to people's incomes, always very high by most standards,[23] may admittedly have risen in the period of the tetrarchs and Constantine (we have no information on this point), making bookbuyers more sensitive to prices. But it looks as if something that the Christians believed about the codex form now at last came to be believed by great numbers of non-Christian book users too.

Cost advantage is not even mentioned by Roberts and Skeat when they seek to explain why the codex supplanted the book-roll for non-Christian texts.[24] Yet unlike most of the other practical advantages of the codex form, this one, during the crucial period,

19. See J. Gascou, in Blanchard, *Les Débuts du codex*, pp. 71-101. But the very earliest documentary codex known is *P.Col.* inv.544, recently studied by J. Sheridan in her "Roman Military Clothing Requisitions in Egypt" (Ph.D. diss., Columbia University, 1990), and dated by her to the period 324-327.
20. See, for instance, L. Cracco Ruggini, in *Tecnologia, economia e società nel mondo romano. Atti del Convegno di Como 27/28/29 settembre 1979* (Como, 1980), pp. 45-66.
21. *Birth of the Codex*, pp. 45-47.
22. *Typology of the Codex*, p. 37.
23. Harris, *Ancient Literacy*, pp. 194-195.
24. *Birth of the Codex*, pp. 67-74.

may well have grown more pronounced. It certainly may have helped to persuade people that the codex form was to be preferred.

⁂

Before we examine the other practical advantages, it is worth considering the aberrant behavior of the Christians in more detail. A number of theories have been advanced to explain their precocious devotion to the codex. Cavallo, for instance, has argued that it was a matter of social class. Not being members of the social elite, the earliest Christians were unaccustomed to books-rolls but familiar with codices.[25] Now it is no doubt true that many first- and second-century Christians lacked direct personal experience of book-rolls. But at the time when Christians were first expressing their preference for the codex, those who possessed any education will all have known books in roll form, regardless of whether their background was Jewish, Greek or Roman. And Cavallo's theory depends on the presumption, which Roberts and Skeat have shown to be incorrect,[26] that what passes for "popular literature" in the high Roman Empire – romances, the *Sortes* of Astrampsychos, and so on – tended to be written in codex form; on the contrary, when such texts survive they are almost always on rolls, the surviving manuscript of Lollianus' *Phoenicica* being exceptional though not unique in this regard.[27] A more fundamental point is that the whole concept of "popular literature" is inapplicable to the ancient world, if the expression means a literature that truly reaches a mass audience in written form.[28]

The determination of the Christians to have their biblical texts in codex form inevitably leads to the conjecture that the reason must in some way, and at least to some extent, have been religious. C. H. Roberts formerly argued[29] that since the codex form was, to judge from its name, of Latin origin, the innovation came from Rome itself, and spread to the eastern Christians through the medium of Mark's gospel, which *may have been* written in Rome, *may have been* produced in codex form – a dubious proposition indeed[30] – and *may have* lent prestige to the codex form. This gossamer theory was later rejected by Roberts

---

25.   G. Cavallo, in Cavallo, ed., *Libri, editori e pubblico nel mondo antico* (Rome and Bari, 1975), pp. 83-85; and in *SIFC* ser. 3, 3 (1985): 118-21.

26.   *Birth of the Codex*, pp. 69-70.

27.   Cavallo's reply to this, *SIFC* ser. 3, 3 (1985): 120, carries little conviction; see further Harris, *Ancient Literacy*, p. 295 n. 41.

28.   Harris, *Ancient Literacy*, pp. 227-28.

29.   *PBA* 40 (1954): 187-89.

30.   Cf. E. Schönbauer, *Iura* 12 (1961): 133. But note that Clement of Alexandria, if M. Smith's Clementine letter is genuine, says that Mark brought his gospel from Rome to Alexandria in the form of *hupomnemata*. See Smith, *Clement of Alexandria and a Secret Gospel of Mark* (Cambridge, MA, 1973), p. 448, fol. lr, lines 19-20.

himself.[31] It is worth remembering that, to judge from the papyri, Mark's gospel, far from enjoying great prestige, was the one in which the early Christians of the Egyptian *chora* were least interested.[32]

Skeat's variant of Roberts' theory, to the effect that "some leading figure in the early church" succeeded in "imposing" the use of the codex form[33] makes no more sense. What can the motive of this leading figure have been? How did he impose his wishes? The first-century Christians did not make up a disciplined hierarchy, such as the modern Catholic church aspires to be. As for the proposal of Roberts and Skeat[34] that the Christian predilection for the codex stemmed from Antioch or Jerusalem (on the grounds that another peculiarity of Christian manuscripts, the taste for contracted forms of certain sacred words, may have done so), it is tenuous in the extreme, and open to the objections just mentioned and others that it would be tedious to set forth.[35] Even a hardened scholar may raise an eyebrow on reading that "the claims of Antioch for at least some part in the origin of...the codex are strong."[36] Both forms of this theory are the merest fantasies without much in the way of historical plausibility. They seem to stem from a desire to find some motive for the Christians' preference for the codex form that is in some way above the material and the quotidian.

McCormick has charitably attempted to rescue the theory that the Christians preferred the codex form for a religious or cultic reason, suggesting that it enjoyed prestige among them because it was associated with very early copies of their holy books.[37] To establish this, he relies heavily on the controversial passage in 2 Timothy 4:13, where the writer refers to certain "*biblia,* especially the *membranai.*" McCormick argues[38] that since the letter is pseudepigraphic (it was written c.100 A.D.), in other words an imposture, the unusual word *membranai* may have been intended to help make it seem authentic and in fact "apostolic." And it does seem probable that although *membranai* is a term that refers to material, not form, the writer meant codices; that is what *membrana* apparently means in almost contemporary verses by Martial (xiv.186.1, quoted below).[39] If, however, *membranai* were so characteristically Christian, is it not strange that they are

31. In Roberts and Skeat, *Birth of the Codex,* pp. 54-57. See also the critique by J. van Haelst, in Blanchard, *Les Débuts du codex,* pp. 29-31.
32. See C. H. Roberts' own investigation in his *Manuscript, Society and Belief in Early Christian Egypt* (London, 1979), p. 61.
33. *Cambridge History of the Bible,* vol. 2 (Cambridge, 1969), p. 72.
34. *Birth of the Codex,* pp. 57-61.
35. See also van Haelst, in Blanchard, *Les Débuts du codex,* pp. 31-32.
36. *Birth of the Codex,* p. 58.
37. *Scriptorium* 39 (1985): 154.
38. Ibid., p. 155.
39. It could be argued that τὰ βίβλια, μάλιστα τὰς μεμβράνας means "the documents, especially the parchment notebooks," but this possibility will not be followed up here.

mentioned nowhere else in early Christian literature? Using a non-Pauline term is a peculiar way of trying to establish Pauline authenticity. In fact, the entire theory that the codex form had some unexplained prestige among early Christians is extremely tenuous. In the end, no doubt, it became a matter of Christian tradition, but we still do not have an explanation for the powerful preference felt by those early Christians who might seem to have had some choice in the matter.

Recent work by the New Testament scholar C. P. Thiede makes it less likely that the earliest versions of the gospels were in codex form.[40] Following a proposal by J. O'Callaghan[41] but improving on his arguments, Thiede has attempted to show that the Qumran papyrus fragment 7Q5 contains parts of Mark 6:52-53; and since the verso is blank, it was very probably part of a book-roll. The date must, according to the usual ideas about Qumran, be prior to 68 A.D. O'Callaghan's original proposal was not very well received – there were weaknesses in his argument, and in any case Qumran is not meant to have been Christian, even in part – but the case in favor of the identification now seems somewhat stronger.[42]

Incidentally, it is worth remarking that if the Christians all held the codex form in higher religious esteem than the book-roll, those who lived in Rome had ceased to do so by the third century. When Jesus is represented holding a book in paintings of this period,[43] it is a book-roll, as is most commonly the case on early sarcophagi.[44] Roberts and Skeat note[45] that the painting of a young man in the catacomb of Saints Peter and Marcellinus that they illustrate in their book (plate VI)[46] is quite exceptional in that he is carrying a codex rather than a book-roll, but they fail to draw any conclusion about the supposed religious authority of the codex form.

40. *Die älteste Evangelien-Handschrift? Das Markus-Fragment von Qumran und die Anfänge der schriftlichen Überlieferung des Neuen Testaments* (Wuppertal, 1986; 2d ed., 1990). I have not seen his new book, *The Earliest Gospel Manuscript?* (Exeter, 1990).
41. *Biblica* 53 (1972): 91-100.
42. Thiede has received significant support from, among others, H. Hunger, *Tyche* 2 (1987): 279. Strongly against: S. R. Pickering and R. R. E. Cook, *Has a Fragment of the Gospel of Mark Been Found at Qumran?* Papyrology and Historical Perspectives, Macquarie University, no. 1 (Sydney, 1989). I thank Professor G. H. R. Horsley for sending me a copy of this pamphlet.
43. See J. Kollwitz, *Das Christusbild des Dritten Jahrhunderts* (Münster, 1953), esp. p. 12 and pl. 3, the Viale Manzoni catacomb.
44. See, for instance, F. Gerke, *Christus in der spätantiken Plastik*, 3d ed. (Mainz, 1948), figs. 48, 49, 52, 53 (also illustrated in Harris, *Ancient Literacy*, figure 8), 61, 70, 71; and A. Grabar, *Christian Iconography. A Study of its Origins* (Princeton, 1968), pl. 22; R. Vielliard, *Rivista di archeologia cristiana* 17 (1940): 143-48, was quite misleading on this subject.
45. *Birth of the Codex*, p. ix.
46. Also in Vielliard, *Riv.arch.cr.* 17 (1940): 144, and in Roberts, *PBA* 40 (1954), as plate XII. See now J. G. Deckers et al., *Die Katakombe "Santi Marcellino e Pietro:" Repertorium der Malereien* (Rome and Münster, 1987), no. 59, with color plate 38, where the painting is in any case down-dated from the third century to the period 320-340 (p. 302).

✸

When it comes to explaining why the codex supplanted the book-roll among the book-using public at large, Roberts and Skeat have nothing to say about its economic advantages. They also reject[47] the notion that Christian influence can have had anything to do with it. It is strange that they are so dogmatic on this point, since they believe that the codex had practical advantages, and in fact attribute the changed attitude of the non-Christians to these characteristics of the codex. Might it not be reasonable to guess that the educated non-Christians of the late third century may have learned a lot about the positive qualities of the codex from the Christians with whom they now had much more frequent contact? And there were now, of course, quite a number of educated people who were or had been Christians themselves (more on this point later).

The "comprehensiveness and convenience" which Roberts and Skeat believe to have been the cause of the pagan conversion to the codex[48] are credible enough up to a point. By convenience they mean the convenience in exposition that a teacher might experience if he possessed a grammatical manual in codex form, such as Pack no. 2145 or 2155 (each of the second or third century). The difficulty is to see why these advantages should at last have come to possess such a widespread appeal.

Discussing the monograph of Roberts and Skeat, Cavallo, who rejects their theories about the Christians' preference for the codex, nonetheless congratulates them on refusing to countenance any practical explanation of the victory of the codex form, such as its superior capacity or handiness or the greater ease with which a codex can be consulted.[49] This curious attitude[50] may partly stem from the realization, correct in itself, that although the practical advantages of the codex were there from the beginning, they failed for some two centuries to make the codex form the preferred one. The codex did not somehow become more capacious, more handy or easier to consult about 300 A.D.

An obvious advantage of the codex form is that it enables the reader to possess a much longer text within a single physical book. Until the codex came into use, it was quite impossible to have the entire *Iliad* or *Aeneid* in a single unit; you needed at least six rolls. Martial lays heavy stress on the remarkable capacity of the new kind of book. "Quam brevis immensum cepit membrana Maronem..." (xiv.186.1). "Pellibus exiguis artatur Livius ingens/ quem mea non totum bibliotheca capit" (xiv.190).[51] Incidentally,

47. *Birth of the Codex*, p. 67.
48. Ibid., p. 73.
49. *SIFC* ser. 3, 3 (1985): 121.
50. Not fully maintained by its author in his remarks in A. Giardina, ed., *Società romana e impero tardoantico* (Rome and Bari, 1986), 4:87.
51. These and the other relevant texts of Martial, who does not, in fact, use the term *codex*, are reviewed by Roberts and Skeat, *Birth of the Codex*, pp. 24-29.

the fact that in Martial xiv.184-192 the poet treats codex books as expensive presents, as he definitely does,[52] detracts not at all from the argument that the codex was among other things a money-saving device; the codex books Martial was thinking of were extremely long ones. The capaciousness of the codex may not be an unmitigated advantage; it means that if you lend me your copy of *Iliad* I, you have to lend me your copy of the rest of the poem as well. But the advantages of such "miniaturization" are plain. And a significant number of the early literary codices did in fact contain texts, Plato's *Republic* for example,[53] that are so long that they could not be contained in a single roll. But why, if sheer capacity was the attraction of the codex form, did it take so long to gain the upper hand?

A refinement on the theory that the capacity of the codex was its key attraction is the notion that both Christians and pagans were initially attracted to the codex by its portability.[54] Martial claims that the codex suits travellers, and it can be argued – with some strain – that Christians were characteristically itinerant, and teachers too (some of the earliest codices are the kinds of texts that teachers might own, such as the grammatical manuals mentioned above, or aids to the study of classical texts, such as Homer [the lexicon in *P.Oxy.* xxx.2517] or Demosthenes [a commentary, Pack no. 311]). But why should the portability of books come to seem so much more important in the decades around the year 300? The reading public had not become vastly more mobile.

The literary book-roll, commonly ten to twelve feet long but sometimes much longer[55] is a more cumbersome object to use than a codex, and Skeat's experiment with rolls of wallpaper[56] have not shown otherwise. A specific advantage of the codex is that it enables the user to find a passage, and especially a series of passages, much more handily.[57]

It should not be difficult to see why ease of consultation made the codex popular with, in fact almost indispensable to, the early Christians. We have only to ask what they used the Bible for. One use was liturgical:[58] passages were read out to the faithful. If a few long passages were read, the codex was perhaps only a minor advantage, but other uses involved reference to one short passage

52. See L. Friedländer's commentary (Leipzig, 1886).
53. *P.Oxy.* xliv.3157.
54. Roberts and Skeat, *Birth of the Codex*, p. 27; McCormick, pp. 157-58.
55. Cf. J. van Sickle, *Arethusa* 13 (1980): 7-12.
56. *Scritti in onore di Orsolina Montevecchi* (Bologna, 1981), pp. 373-76: he concluded that a long roll could be re-rolled in forty-five seconds if the right method was used.
57. Cf. C. R. Gregory, *Canon and Text of the New Testament* (New York, 1912), pp. 322-23; Kenyon, *Books and Readers*, pp. 114-15.
58. Cf. J. Leipoldt in *Reallexikon für Antike und Christentum* (Stuttgart) s.v. Buch II (1954), cols. 713-14; J. A. Jungmann, *Liturgie der christlichen Frühzeit bis auf Gregor den Grossen* (Freiburg, 1967), pp. 56-57; M. Hengel, *Die Evangelienüberschriften (Sitzungsberichte Heid.Ak.Wiss.*, 1984, no. 3), pp. 33-37 (= *Studies in the Gospel of Mark*, trans. J. Bowden, London, 1985, pp. 75-77).

after another. The New Testament itself, including its earliest parts, makes it clear that the Christian style of addressing the faithful already relied on frequent quotation (which, needless to say, will often have been from memory). It was not so much that the Christians were concerned with the precise wording of the holy texts for its own sake, as McCormick implies in a brief and tentative defence of the notion that it was ease of reference that made the Christians like the codex form.[59] Rather, it was their intellectual style to rely on the words of the canonical or soon-to-be-canonical texts, intentionally emphasizing that the "proof" they needed came from written sources. This manner of arguing is, of course, ubiquitous in patristic texts. An oral version of the technique in question is vividly illustrated in a letter of Augustine's:

> mihi praeparatae lectiones suggerendae tenebantur...quae cum dicerem, codicem etiam accepi et recitavi totum illum locum [from *Exodus*]. Tunc reddito exodi codice crimen ebrietatis, quantum tempus sinebat, exaggerans sumpsi apostolum Paulum et...ostendi legens illum locum, etc. (Ep. 29.4-10).

The frequency of reading aids in early Christian manuscripts led Roberts to the belief that most of them were intended for church use.[60]

If ease of reference was a vitally important factor, we at once have an explanation of the otherwise rather odd fact that the Christians put their biblical texts in the less expensive codex form while sometimes putting such texts as Irenaeus' *Adversus Haereses*, on rolls (*P.Oxy.* iii.405). The latter was not needed for prompt reference.[61]

Skeat objected to the view that ease of reference was the vital factor on the grounds that without chapter divisions in the text it would have been as hard to find a passage in a codex as in a roll.[62] But there is an obvious and crucial difference: you can put markers between the pages of a codex. In antiquity, so the objections continue,[63] there was generally no means of giving an absolutely precise reference to a literary text, except for the rather little-used system of verse stichometry. This consideration, far from being a good objection, accentuates the need that must have been felt for books in which one could readily find specific texts, once such a need had become an important reason for possessing books. With the Christians this need was early and powerful.

Furthermore, although the columns of book-rolls had seldom been numbered, some codices very soon began to have numbered pages or leaves, certainly by the third century. Turner, who gives

59. *Scriptorium* 39 (1985): 156.
60. *Manuscript, Society and Belief in Early Christian Egypt*, pp. 21-22.
61. For the other Christian book-rolls of the pre-Constantinian era see J. van Haelst, *Catalogue des papyrus littéraires juifs et chrétiens* (Paris, 1976), pp. 409-13.
62. *Cambridge History of the Bible*, 2:70.
63. Roberts and Skeat, *Birth of the Codex*, p. 50.

the best account of Roman pagination, suggests that it may have been invented as early as the codex form itself.[64] In any case, it seems highly probable – although this is not an essential feature of the present argument – that pagination was intended to make reference easier. The fact that literary texts do not begin to refer to books by page numbers is beside the point: they obviously could not do so, since the pagination of a given text would always vary from manuscript to manuscript. The person most likely to be helped by pagination was the man who needed to return quickly to particular passages in a book that he had already consulted.

We might find some clue in the list of the earliest non-Christian texts that are known to have been produced in codex form (leaving aside those that are mentioned by Martial). Roberts and Skeat drew up a list of seventeen such manuscripts which they believe to have been written in the second century[65] and judged them to be a very mixed group. Cavallo holds that no more than eight of these texts have good claims to date from the second century (see Table 1).[66] The sample is in any case perilously small, and not by any means likely to be typical of the books that were written in codex form in, say, Rome in the same period. Of the seventeen it may be noted that at least seven are suitable for consultation rather than continuous reading (the two grammatical manuals already mentioned, the Homer lexicon and the commentary on Demosthenes also mentioned above, the Homeromanteion, and two medical texts), and three others at least are texts of schoolroom classics (two *Iliad* books and a *Cyropaedia*). But the proportions in question are perhaps too small to prove much, and lists of third-century codices[67] lend themselves even less readily to simplistic conclusions.

So far we have been arguing that cost and ease of reference were the vital advantages of the codex form. The capacity of the codex book was also of some significance. Such a conclusion amounts to a refinement of earlier views.[68] However, there may be more to say.

We have seen why ease of reference must have seemed a special advantage to the Christians, especially with regard to biblical texts. Is there any reason to think that this characteristic of the codex book can have become more attractive to the users of

---

64. *Typology of the Early Codex*, p. 75.
65. *Birth of the Codex*, p. 71; another list is to be found in Turner, *Typology of the Early Codex*, pp. 89-90, 93.
66. See most recently his comments in Blanchard, *Les Débuts du codex*, pp. 171-72.
67. Such as the one in Turner, *Typology of the Early Codex*, pp. 91-94.
68. Compare the brief statement of K. Büchner, in H. Hunger, etc., *Geschichte der Textüberlieferung der antiken und mittelalterlichen Literatur*, vol. 1 (Zurich, 1961), p. 347.

TABLE 1

PARTLY SURVIVING GREEK LITERARY CODICES OF II OR II/III CENTURY

A restrictive list (Cavallo 1989)

1. Homeric lexicon, *P.Oxy.* xxx.2517
2. Lollianus, *Phoenicica*, *P.Köln* inv.3328, ed. A. Henrichs
3. Achilles Tatius, Pack no. 3
4. Homeromanteion, Pack nos. 645, 1801
5. Homer, *Iliad* v, Pack no. 747
6. Pindar, Pack no. 1362
7. Xenophon, *Cyropaedia*, Pack no. 1546
8. Plato, *Republic*, *P.Oxy.* xliv.3157
9. Homer, *Iliad* ii-iv, Pack no. 634; and Tryphon, *Ars grammatica*, Pack no. 1539.

A less restrictive list (Roberts and Skeat 1983)

Nos. 1 to 8 above, plus
10. Grammatical manual, Pack no. 2145
11. Grammatical manual, Pack no. 2155
12. Comm. on Demosthenes, Pack no. 311
13. Medical text, Pack no. 2340
14. Medical text, Pack no. 2355
15. Demosthenes, *De falsa legatione*, Pack no. 293
16. Euripides, *Cretans*, Pack no. 437
17. Homer, *Iliad* xi, Pack no. 868
18. Plato, *Parmenides*, *P. Duke* inv. 5 (dated by Cavallo to fifth century or later)

non-Christian books in the late third or early fourth century? A clear answer to this question is difficult to formulate. It has been suggested that books in codex form were symptomatic of a mentality that relied more and more on authority, especially written authority.[69] Still more vaguely, F. Wieacker claimed to detect something of the inner life of the late-antique *Geist*, as well as practical advantages, in the change to the codex.[70] It is very probably true that increased deference to the authority of the written word was a genuine feature of fourth-century culture,[71] but why should this make the owners of books prefer one physical format to another? Some new works of reference, in particular the new law codes of the 290s, the *codex Gregorianus* and the *codex Hermogenianus*,[72] depended for some or much of their effective-

69. C. H. Roberts, *PBA* 40 (1954): 196, 203.
70. *Textstufen klassischer Juristen* (= *Abhandlungen Göttingen* ser. 3 no. 45, 1960), p. 94.
71. Cf. Harris, *Ancient Literacy*, esp. pp. 303-6.
72. Basic information in L. Wenger, *Die Quellen des römischen Rechts* (Vienna, 1953), pp. 534-36.

ness on the existence of the codex form of book. More generally, one may say that some of the impetus for the change to the codex is likely to have come from the desire on the part of people who worked with books, such as lawyers, *grammatici* and doctors, to have them in a more readily usable form. But we should be looking for some factor that could have a still wider effect.

In the fourth and even the fifth century there were still, of course, people who possessed a wide knowledge of classical literature, men like Gregory of Nazianzus whose own writing was formed by their classical reading, and men like Servius and Macrobius who could quote from a remarkable range of texts.[73] Nonetheless, the reproduction and reading of classical literature declined: a census of manuscript production shows some 636 literary papyri said to date from the third century, but only 204 from the fourth.[74] And literacy was in retreat, at least over the long term. Against this background, we must try to understand the mentalities of the third- and fourth-century book-owners who now, for the most part, had their copies of Homer (by far the most commonly copied author) or of Demosthenes or Callimachus in codex form. Such books were valuable possessions of a tiny educated minority. This minority held on with some fervor to the texts that were the emblems of its *paideia,* and commonly, we may suppose, regarded them with the awe appropriate to the classics. Some at least of the devotees of the traditional *paideia* were as passionately attached to their texts as many Christians were to theirs: hence it was not absurd to think of *Ciceronianus* and *Christianus* as comparable categories.

When the codex form of the literary book originally became known in the first century, many of the texts being copied were classics; but many others were recent or contemporary works that a person might read once but that were not constantly mined for quotations and allusions. In the decades around 300 A.D., by contrast, most of what was being copied, and presumably most of what was being read, was either on the one hand technical or theological, in which case ease of reference favoured the codex form, or on the other hand a literary classic of long ago (this was probably as true in the western empire as it was in Egypt) – which it might also be convenient to own in the form that allowed easy consultation. It would no doubt be exaggerated to say that those – those few – who now read Homer or Demosthenes or Callimachus read these authors in a different way, and the prime evidence that they did so is precisely the conversion to the codex. To some extent, however, fourth-century writers do show a tendency to rely on a relatively small canon of classical texts which they refer to fairly or very frequently. Terence, Sallust, Cicero and Virgil are not the only Latin authors referred to, but

73. But for a sceptical view of the learning of the latter pair see Alan Cameron, *Entretiens de la Fondation Hardt* 23 (1977): 29.
74. W. H. Willis, *Greek, Roman, and Byzantine Studies* 9 (1968): 210.

they predominate, and they are needed over and over again.[75] Many a passage could be drawn from memory, but the apposite quotation might need to be checked, and that could be done more easily in a codex book than in a book-roll.

Those who consulted texts of secular literature would now much more often be Christians. By the end of the third century no simple contrast can be drawn between the culture of the Christians and the pagans. It was now possible to be both a Christian and an ardent lover of the classics without any great strain. This was not unheard of in earlier times,[76] and one of the consequences can be seen in a few surviving book-rolls that preserve pagan and Christian texts side by side, or rather on recto and verso; *P.Oxy.* iv.657 + 668, for instance, has an epitome of Livy on the recto and *Hebrews* on the verso, and it seems that the owner wanted to possess both texts.[77] However, in the early decades of the fourth century the number of such people must have increased greatly.[78] For a considerable time now scholars have been emphasizing the classical tastes of some of the major Christian publicists of the fourth century, from Methodius of Olympus to Gregory Nazianzenus.[79] Some of the fourth-century codices that contained pagan literary texts must have been the property of Christians. One may wonder how many fourth-century Christians who were prosperous enough to own books resembled the famous Cappadocian fathers in their devotion to the classics (even they, as Ševčenko remarks,[80] "speak out of both sides of their mouths"). However a certain proportion of the surviving fourth-century codices of the classical authors can be accounted for in this way. Christians, who were well aware of the

---

75.   H. Hagendahl, *Von Tertullian zu Cassiodor. Die profane literarische Tradition in dem lateinischen christlichen Schrifttum* (Göteborg, 1983), esp. pp. 74-83.
76.   On the very varied attitudes of the earlier fathers see, for instance, G. Glockmann, *Homer in der frühchristlichen Literatur bis Justinus* (Berlin, 1968), esp. pp. 3-17, 30-44.
77.   See Roberts, *Manuscript, Society and Belief in Early Christian Egypt*, p. 10, who dates these texts to the third century. He cites as a parallel *P.Lond.Lit.* [= H. J. M. Milne, ed., *Catalogue of the Literary Papyri in the British Museum* (London, 1927)], no. 207, which has *Psalms* on the recto and Isocrates, *Ad Demonicum* on the verso.
78.   As to how quickly the inhabitants of the Egyptian *chora*, the source of our material evidence, converted to Christianity after 312, there are different views. For recent debate see R. S. Bagnall, *Bulletin of the American Society of Papyrologists* 19 (1982): 105-24 (rapid change); E. Wipszycka, *Zeitschrift für Papyrologie und Epigraphik* 62 (1986): 173-81 (less rapid); with Bagnall's reply, *ZPE* 69 (1987): 243-50.
79.   For a good statement of this position see I. Ševčenko in K. Weitzmann, ed., *Age of Spirituality: a Symposium* (New York, 1980), esp. pp. 56-57. On Christian attitudes towards the pagan classics see now R. A. Kaster, *Guardians of Language: the Grammarian and Society in Late Antiquity* (Berkeley, 1988), pp. 70-95; and E. Heck, *Museum Helveticum* 47 (1990): 102-20 (concerning the appropriation of Vergil).
80.   In Weitzmann, *Age of Spirituality*, p. 60.

practical advantages of the codex form, became a larger and larger part of the clientele – which in absolute terms was shrinking – for new copies of the pagan classics. There being nothing especially sacred about the codex form in their eyes, they also used it for their copies of works of secular literature.

VIII

"Love Conquers All"
The Conversion, Asceticism and Altruism
of St. Caterina of Genoa*

KENNETH JORGENSEN, S.J.

Caterina Fieschi Adorno (St. Catherine of Genoa) has generated unusual interest because of her ability to combine contemplation with action, i.e. private prayer, asceticism, and even mystical experience united to extensive and at times exceptional deeds of charity. After an intense conversion experience, she nursed the sick and plague-stricken in private homes, on the street, and in hospitals. Her life uniquely blended such an appealing spirituality with a heroic commitment to perform the scriptural works of mercy that two important and interconnected sixteenth-century religious groups, the Oratories of Divine Love and the Theatines, used her as a model in defining their piety. The uniqueness and significance of Caterina's life are specifically the result of her religious conversion, her devout and extreme practices of fasting, her eucharistic devotion and independent spirituality, and her extraordinary altruism. This aristocratic woman of the late fifteenth century, who asserted her religious independence against the normative modes of the society, became a catalyst for subsequent Catholic reform and renewal.

Since Caterina allegedly wrote accounts of her life, activities, and spiritual experiences,[1] any discussion or interpretation of her

* I would like to thank Eugene F. Rice, Jr. and Prof. Jerome H. Delamater of Hofstra University for assistance in the original preparation of this essay.
1. The texts traditionally assigned to Caterina include the *Libro de la vita mirabile et dottrina santa de la beata Caterinetta da Genoa; nel quale si contiene una utile e catholica dimostratione et dechiaratione del Purgatorio; Trattato del Purgatorio della detta Beata Madonna Catarinetta Adorna;* and the *Dialogo della detta Madonna Catarinetta tra l'anima et il corpo insieme con l'amor propio, reduto poi al spirito et la humanità.* These titles (with spelling inconsistencies) are taken from the *editio princeps* edited by Antonio Bellono at Genoa, 1551. See Umile Bonzi, *S. Caterina Fieschi Adorno,* vol 2: *Edizione critica dei manoscritti Cateriniani* (Turin: Marietti, 1962), pp. 25-26, hereafter cited as *Edizione critica.* Apart from biographical material, the *Vita* contains numerous sayings, reflections and mystical teachings attributed to Caterina. The *Trattato,* by contrast, examines the state of souls in purgatory, their pains and purification. Due to the condemnation of Luther's teaching on purgatory (1520) and the later

history is dependent on the textual complexity of the multiple
sources from which biographers and hagiographers derived their
information.[2] In spite of their disparate theories, the two chief
students of the saint, Umile Bonzi and Baron Frederic Von Hügel,
recognized the need to use the *Vita Biografia* and the first part of
the *Dialogo* for any biographical examination of Caterina's life.
They both determined that much of the *Opus Catharinianum* came
either from Caterina or from within a circle of close followers
who desired to protect and assure the unambiguous transmission
of her example, sayings, and doctrine. Lacking any comparable,
dependable source and on the basis of Bonzi's arguments that it is
simpler, fresher, and more vividly Genoese than its later relative,
the Bellono MS A, I have employed the Bonzi MS D* throughout
this essay.[3]

The veracity of the *Opus Catharinianum* must be considered
within the overall purpose of her followers' efforts – to present in
written form the story of a married laywoman whom they viewed
as extraordinarily charitable, mystically gifted, and probably approaching saintliness. Since those who had known her personally
and could actually speak of her would not live much longer, they
wanted the tradition and episodes of her life recorded for
posterity. However, it took almost forty years for this material to
be compiled and published, and in the meantime others became
aware of her only through an oral tradition.

Many of these individuals asked for a fuller account of
Caterina's actions. The writers and compilers accordingly must
have accepted the duty as her friends to recount the story of
Caterina, but they were also hagiographers, recording what they
believed God had miraculously performed in her life. That they
may have polished some of the roughness off Caterina's life or

---

controversies of the Reformation period, the *Trattato* was widely read and
studied. The *Dialogo* can be best characterized as Caterina's spiritual biography – although clearly not her autobiography. The editions of the *Vita* (up
to 1800), most of which included the *Trattato* and the *Dialogo*, were, in Italian:
Genoa 1551, 1640, 1667, 1681, 1712, 1737, 1743, 1755; Florence 1568,'1580, 1589;
Venice 1590, 1601, 1615; Naples 1645; Rome 1737; Padua 1743; in French: Paris
1598, 1627, 1646, 1647, 1660, 1661, 1662, 1663; Douai 1599; Lyons 1610, 1616;
Amsterdam 1691; and in Latin: Fribourg 1626, which Urbano Sticker employed
as the text for the *Acta Sanctorum Sept.* (Antwerp: Apud Joannem Meursium,
1755), 5:123-95. See P. Debongnie, "Catherine de Gênes," in *Dictionnaire
d'histoire et de géographie ecclésiastique* 11 (1949): 1514; Bonzi, *Edizione critica*, pp.
27-29; and Frederic Von Hügel, *The Mystical Element of Religion As Studied in
Saint Catherine of Genoa and Her Friends*, 2 vols., 1st ed. (London: J. M. Dent,
1908); 2nd ed. (London: J. M. Dent, 1923). The second edition, used throughout,
is hereafter cited as *The Mystical Element*.
2.   For a discussion see the Excursus at the end of this essay.
3.   The text will refer to the material found in the *Edizione critica* and titled
either *Biografia* or *Dialogo*. For the *Dialogo*, I use the Hughes' translation
based on the Bonzi D* manuscript. See B. Groeschel, *Catherine of Genoa:
Purgation and Purgatory; The Spiritual Dialogue*, trans. Serge Hughes (New
York: Paulist Press, 1979). Because of its specialized theological content, the
Trattato has not been used in this biographical essay.

writings (but clearly not the extremism of her actions) is possible. Because they viewed her as so privileged, they wanted to introduce to a wider audience what they knew and now recorded of Caterina's life and spiritual teachings. These individuals transferred the oral tradition and their reminiscences into writing just as most of them also attempted to imitate the expansive charity that their writings demonstrated about Caterina's life. They presented a story – appealing and heroic – of a dynamic, independent woman who could in fact be quite stubborn once she had reached a decision; they wanted Caterina's story of the importance of charity toward all to reach beyond the limited influence of the oral tradition.

Caterina[4] was born in 1447 into the aristocratic Fieschi family, the youngest child of Giacomo, at one time viceroy of Naples and descendant of Roberto Fieschi, brother of Pope Innocent IV (1234-54).[5] Indeed, the Fieschi were the greatest of the Guelf families of Genoa. In the political maneuvering that followed Giacomo Fieschi's death in 1461, Caterina's family attempted to protect itself amid the complex uncertainties and intrigues of Genoa by astutely negotiating the marriage of Caterina to a major rival family. The chosen groom, Giuliano Adorno (1450-1494), was the descendant of an equally aristocratic Genoese lineage.[6]

Because Caterina's family was Guelf while Giuliano's was Ghibelline, the arranged marriage attempted reconciliation of two families divided by politics who united only when confronted by still other political rivals. Her family's course of action was decided without consulting Caterina. Oblivious to her feelings, her family, because of their position and needs, forced her into obeying, and the marriage took place against her wishes in 1463; she was sixteen years old, and Giuliano was thirteen.

The *Biografia* describes Giuliano as "molto stranio et di mala natura."[7] According to Von Hügel, the marriage united "two mutually indifferent and profoundly unsuited young people."[8] Giuliano was so undisciplined and impatient that his extravagance led him to waste "his time, money, health, and affec-

---

4. The publications on Caterina Fieschi Adorno are extensive. In addition to the works by Von Hügel and Debongnie cited above, see U. Bonzi and M. Viller, "Catherine de Gênes (sainte)," *Dictionnaire de Spiritualité* 2 (1953): 290-325; U. Bonzi, *S. Caterina Fieschi Adorno*, vol. 1: *Teologia Mistica di S. Caterina da Genova* (Turin: Marietti, 1961), hereafter cited as *Teologia*; G. D. Gordini, "Caterina da Genova," in *Bibliotheca Sanctorum* 3 (Rome: Istituto Giovanni XXIII, 1963): 984-89; Groeschel, *Purgation and Purgatory*, pp. 1-43; and S. Pezzella, "Caterina Fieschi Adorno," in *Dizionario biografico degli italiani* 22 (1979): 343-45.

5. The family had also produced one other pope, Adrian V (1276), and several cardinals. Her mother, Francesca de Negro, was also an aristocrat. For the De Negro or Di Negro family, see Bonzi, *Teologia*, p. 20 n. 1.

6. For his family and life, consult G. Oreste, "Adorno, Giuliano," in *Dizionario biografico degli italiani* 1 (1960): 301-2.

7. Page 230.

8. *The Mystical Element*, 1:101; *Biografia*, p. 230.

tions."[9] Later he exhausted Caterina's wealth until they were on the verge of poverty. Presumably, the combined effect of being forced into marriage by her parents and being married to an immature, difficult adolescent contributed significantly to the pronounced unhappiness that characterized Caterina's childless marriage. Caterina spent the first five years of this marriage in loneliness and self-imposed isolation.

If anything, her spiritual impulses turned inward. During the next five years, Caterina attempted (at the urgings of her family) to return to social life by seeking to fill her days with various diversions and amusements, such as attending festivals and banquets, and wearing colorful clothes and cosmetics.[10] However, neither solitude nor compulsive external activity satisfied her, and after these ten years "her life was filled with so much sadness of heart...that she could not find any respite from it."[11] Desperate, she sought help from a priest-confessor at the Genoese convent of S. Maria delle Grazie, where her older sister, Limbania, was an Augustinian Canoness.

According to the *Biografia*, while beginning to make her confession to this priest in March 1473 and at the moment when she was on her knees before him, "suddenly her heart was pierced by an immense love of God, accompanied by a view of her misery and sins and of the goodness of God."[12] She added that this love carried her away from herself and the despondency of the world; and she kept crying out within herself: "No more world, no more sins!"[13] She proclaimed that if she had in her possession a thousand worlds, she would have cast them all away for that flame of burning love she felt.[14] She was incapable of speech and almost senseless.

The *Biografia* does not record that the priest noticed anything amiss but indicates that "he was called away and got up. He returned almost immediately; she however could not speak of her intimate sorrow and immense love."[15] Instead, Caterina could only request a postponement of the confession. "Having returned home, she went into a secluded room, wept and sighed with great passion."[16] She prayed: "Love, is it possible that you have called me with so much love and made known to me in an instant what I cannot express with my tongue?"[17] The intensity of this

9. *The Mystical Element*, 1:102.
10. *Biografia*, pp. 112-13. As both Von Hügel, *The Mystical Element*, 1:104; and Bonzi and Viller, *DS*, col. 291, maintain, Caterina never sinned gravely during this period. To her contemporaries her actions would probably have seemed quite normal behavior, while the converted Caterina judged them much more severely and bitterly regretted them.
11. *Biografia*, p. 113.
12. Ibid., p. 114. Concerning the identity of her confessor, see p. 114 n. 3.
13. "Non più mondo non più peccati." Ibid., p. 115.
14. Ibid.
15. Ibid., p. 116.
16. Ibid.
17. Ibid.

experience continued for several days and caused her to continue secluding herself.

Caterina reported that the mystical encounter concluded with a vision of the Christ, who appeared to her "in spirit, dripping with Blood, with His cross upon His shoulder, so that the entire house seemed to be full of streams of that precious Blood, which she saw to have all been shed because of love."[18] As she later indicated, she immediately interpreted the experience as a powerful gift from God. After this vision and filled with self-disgust, she proclaimed: "Love, if necessary, I am prepared to confess my sins in public."[19] Subsequently, she made a general confession to a priest "with such contrition and compunction as to pierce her soul, because He had interiorly revealed to her whom she had offended and how important her offense."[20] Caterina's desperate search for assistance began with her confessor and finally concluded with confession. However, the actual catalyst for change was an interior vision, as the *Biografia* described it, a deeply personal experience that initiated the transformation of her unhappy life.[21]

Although throughout Caterina's life the only recorded vision or image of the Passion, even of a voluntary, meditational kind, occurred during her conversion crisis, Caterina's traditional meditation on the Passion contained echoes of the earlier visions of such mystics as Birgitta of Sweden and Caterina of Siena.[22]

18. "Se ge mostroe in spirito con la croce in spala, piovendo tuto sangue, immodo che li parea che tuta la casa fuse piena di rogij di quello precioso sangue, et lo vedeiva tuto sparso per amore." Ibid., p. 117.
19. Ibid.
20. Ibid.
21. There is another account of her conversion in the *Dialogo*, pp. 400-405, which reversed the sequence of events, showed no intrinsic link between them, and clearly portrayed a transformed Christ-vision: "Cioè che uno giorno essendo in caza, li aparve in vista interiore Jesù Christo Incarnato, Crucifixo, tuto insanguinato da capo a pedi, che pareiva che da quello corpo piovese sangue per tuta la terra dove andava" (pp. 400-401). Here Jesus is affixed to the cross, with His blood staining the ground. Von Hügel compared these visions in *The Mystical Element*, 1:403-10; 458-62.
22. These, for example, often focused on the image of Christ crucified, lingering in their visions on the bloody details. Birgitta saw "Christ's bloodshot eyes...his face pale and blood-stained...his feet curled like door hinges around the nails that fixed him to the cross, his tender body bloodied from over five thousand wounds, splinters, and cuts." Based on *Revelationes Stae. Birgittae*, 2 vols. (Rome: Ludovicus Grignanus, 1628), 1:414; 2:215-17, cited in Eugene F. Rice, Jr., *St. Jerome in the Renaissance* (Baltimore: Johns Hopkins University Press, 1985), p. 79. Caterina of Siena commonly meditated on Christ crucified and in particular on the thought of His blood, for her the supreme sign and pledge of divine love: "As I say, unless you are drowned in his [Jesus'] blood, you can never acquire the little virtue of true humility born of self-hatred...." See Kenelm Foster and Mary John Ronayne, eds. and trans., *I, Catherine: Selected Writings of St. Catherine of Siena* (London: Collins, 1980), pp. 71-72. She continues: "There the sweet bride reclines on the bed of blood and fire, and the secret of the heart of God's Son is laid bare." Ibid., p. 72. On the positive associations of the fixation on Christ's blood, see Caroline W. Bynum, "The Body of Christ in the Later Middle Ages: A Reply to Leo Steinberg," *Renaissance Quarterly* 39 (1986): 407, 421-22 and 427-28.

Caterina of Genoa's vision of the bleeding Jesus (either carrying His cross on His shoulder or affixed to it) included the imagery of fountains sending forth burning blood from the wounds of Christ; "God deeply impressed upon her the fountains of Christ with their bloody drops of love for man."[23]

Attempting to distinguish between the two versions of Caterina's vision, Bonzi proposed that the *Biografia* text described the Crucified as not attached to the cross but walking around with it while bleeding. Accordingly, this scene could not be a visualization of any scriptural passage (as might be inferred of the motionless Christ in the *Dialogo* version), but rather was the product of her imagination, which created a distinctive and personalized Christ, mobile yet bearing all the physical consequences of the crucifixion.[24] The *Biografia* text was also nonscriptural in depicting Christ dripping blood everywhere He went and in stressing the abundance of blood shed to atone for Caterina's sins. This singular vision in Caterina's life contained a "picture" (produced, of course, in spirit) that affected Caterina emotionally because of Christ's protestation that His condition was the result of her sins.

Since Christ seemed to communicate with her personally, Caterina received the vision with a sense of awe, reverence, and repentance that motivated her throughout her life. Even though meditation on the Passion was central and habitual for some mystics, for Caterina it appeared only this once. She never became preoccupied with this aspect of Christ's life; instead Caterina accepted it as a message compelling her to transform her prior existence – unhappy, unproductive and confined – by working to alleviate real physical suffering.[25]

23. Hughes, *Spiritual Dialogue*, p. 119. "Et questo li fu lasato inprecio, cioè tute quelle fontane de Christo, le qualle gitavano gocie de sangue affocate de uno affocato amore verso l'homo." *Dialogo*, p. 404. Caterina's images form part of a developing tradition; she anticipates the further imagery of St. Mary Magdalen de' Pazzi, who claimed to enter the heart of Jesus through the doors of his five sacred wounds.

24. Bonzi discusses Caterina's vision in *Teologia*, pp. 29-30.

25. One means of situating Caterina's vision emerges by relating it to biblical and post-scriptural traditions. There are numerous stories of visions in the Old and New Testaments, such as those of Moses, Jacob, Ezekiel in the Old, and of Peter, Paul and John in the New. Christian history also contains examples of their frequent occurrence, particularly among the saints and mystics. As a result, Christians have repeatedly sought to interpret them theologically. Caterina's experience, for instance, can be elucidated by reference to Augustine's *The Literal Meaning of Genesis* 12.6-11, 32. For a current treatment of this see Wolfgang Riehle, *The Middle English Mystics*, trans. Bernard Standring (London: Routledge and Kegan Paul, 1981), pp. 125-27. This *visio imaginitiva* contains a pattern similar to Caterina's, in which the vision can occur only by employing the imagination. The eyes see nothing of absent physical objects, but "in the soul behold corporeal images: whether true images, representing the bodies that we have seen and still hold in memory, or fictitious images, fashioned by the power of thought." See Augustine, *Literal Meaning*, 12.6.15. Since Caterina, of course, had not claimed actually to have seen Christ, she imagined (or remembered from church art) aspects of the

The use of the term "conversion" to describe this pivotal episode in Caterina's life is conventional but tends to mislead. The usage fails to differentiate between a spiritual experience leading to a change of religion (e.g., pagan to Christian, such as Augustine's conversion) and Caterina's experience, which vivified her previously accepted religious faith. The mystically inspired phenomenon was not just a turning away from definite sins and her past, but was also a resolute, radical adoption of the Christian life.

In her writings she equated the vision to a gift of divine love; her existence subsequently reflected the appreciation and appropriation of this grace. "Divine love" was indeed the central phrase that came to characterize Caterina's experience and would subsequently be identified with her principles.[26] When this awareness of God's love for her began to dominate her life, she found herself "altogether imprisoned in the furnace of divine love, with so much peace and innermost joy that they [her faculties] seem in this life already beatified and brought to their desired haven;" she felt as if the intimate flames of that pure love would consume hell itself.[27] Each individual, she believed, should perceive how pure are the operations of love and that this love does not seek any good from us in return. "Then indeed the soul also desires, in its turn, to love with a pure love...from the motive of love of God, Who alone is worthy of being loved without any other object."[28]

Her new sense of love enkindled an intensified awareness of the possibilities for action that God offered, but at the same time she felt compelled to inquire of God how she could love her neighbor (as commanded in the Christian scriptures) when, as she protested, her love was only for God. She recounts in the *Dialogo* the interior response and command that she received:

> You will have no friendships, no special family ties. You will love everyone without love, rich and poor, friends and relatives. You are not to make friends, not even spiritual or religious friendships, or go to see anyone out of friendship. It is enough

---

crucifixion. She described her vision as a scene from the Passion that she was "shown in spirit" (*mostroe in spirito*), as the *Biografia*, p. 117 describes it; or "saw in inner vision" (*in vista interiore*), as in the *Dialogo*, p. 400. As so graced, she understood herself to be privileged. Both explanations indicate an awareness that the vision's object [Christ] was not tangible.

26. According to the anchoress Julian of Norwich in *The Revelations*, such a vision "is mediated to man in order to awaken and strengthen [the mystic's] love of God." Cited in Riehle, p. 127. This is certainly the effect it had on Caterina.

27. "Ogniuno ha perso la sua naturale occupatione, e sono impregionati in quella fornace divina, con tanta pace et intimo gaudio, che pare siano per fino in questa vita presente beatificati e conducti a lo suo porto, gustando sensa gusto quelle intime fiame di quello puro amore, che faìano consumare lo inferno in quanto a la possansa. Ma arde e non consuma." *Biografia*, p. 206.

28. Ibid., p. 126.

that you go when you are called, as I told you before. This is the way you are to consort with your fellow creatures on earth.[29]

This reply did not contain a scriptural passage, but it certainly captured much of the social thrust of one form of Christian asceticism. Henceforth, Caterina directed her love of God toward love of neighbor, and her conversion assumed its full contour, not in the event itself, but in her subsequent endeavors. Compelled to abjure personal love and motivated, then, by a special sense of the love of God communicated in and through the vision, Caterina henceforth committed herself to radical acts of charity.

In the summer of 1473, after the conversion, Caterina and Giuliano began to live near the Hospital of the Pammatone, spending their days caring for Genoa's sick and poor. The initial move apparently was as much a result of necessity due to Giuliano's mismanagement of their assets as a means of accommodating their increased religious devotion. Having squandered so much of their fortune, he had to rent their palace and sell other properties. Apparently reappraising his former life, Giuliano resolved to assist Caterina in her new commitment to charitable work. He would also become a Tertiary of the Order of St. Francis.[30]

The couple agreed that henceforth they would live a life of continence; the marriage by then had produced no children.[31] It was as if her new relationship to both God and her husband opened possibilities heretofore unseen. In many ways, the conversion provided a new role for Caterina, one which she herself (not society, her husband, or existing church institutions) would create and define. She overcame her earlier period of imposed conventional behavior along with its unhappiness. Having reappraised the desires and possibilities of her life, Caterina rejected any interest she formerly had in becoming a nun, an attitude she maintained until the end of her life.[32] She clearly believed that remaining in the world created no conflict with her avowed love and devotion.

29. Hughes, *Spiritual Dialogue*, p. 129; and *Dialogo*, p. 422.
30. For the discussion of Giuliano in the *Biografia*, see pp. 229-36.
31. The *Biografia*, p. 230, describes the desire to live together as brother and sister as a grace given to Giuliano. "Lo Signore li fece questa gratia, che mise in chore a lo marito di stare insieme como fradelli et sorelle: et così li stetano molti agni [anni] in castitade et puritade."
32. About the age of thirteen, she had felt drawn to the conventual life as she saw it practiced by her sister Limbania, a member of the Augustinian Canonesses of S. Maria delle Grazie in Genoa. When Caterina attempted to gain permission from these nuns to enter their community, they refused at that time, because of her youth. *Biografia*, pp. 109-10. Her marital understanding with Giuliano would have permitted her to take religious vows, if she had so chosen. Caterina's writings offer no explanation for her obvious change of desire regarding entering religious life. "And up to her death, thirty-seven years later, she never wavers on this point." *The Mystical Element*, 1:130.

An anecdote illustrates this determination. One day a friar questioned her state in life by suggesting that he was better fitted for loving than she because he had become a religious and priest, whereas she had remained married to the world;[33] he claimed to be freer to love God and more open to God's grace. After listening to his contention, Caterina, feeling herself seized by a "*certo fuocho de quello necto amore*," stood up, and responded (as if outside herself): "If I believed that your habit could gain for me one single additional spark of love, I would take it from your shoulders piece by piece, if it could not be acquired otherwise."[34] Although conceding that because of the monk's religious renunciations he may be more worthy of God's grace than she, Caterina adamantly disputed his premise. "But that I cannot love Him as much as you is an assertion that you will never be able to lead me to believe!"[35]

Later when at home and speaking to her "Amore," she closed by answering her own question: "O Love, who will impede me from loving You? Though I were, not only in the world as I am, but in a camp of soldiers, I could not be hindered from loving You."[36] In her statements she not only responded to the views of the insulting friar, but also confirmed her own identity and its values without apology by declaring, "I find that love conquers all, and I cannot believe that a love, which is not for itself, can ever be mistaken."[37] Her emphatic belief in the power of love did not at the same time require her to take the vows of the formal religious state.

To atone for her past failings, Caterina began a period of asceticism that continued for four years (1473-77).[38] She walked with her eyes cast down and also spent six hours a day in prayer. Wearing a hair shirt, she fasted and often kept vigil at night, denying herself sleep by putting thorns in her bed. Even though her body suffered and consequently rebelled, she strongly compelled her will to dominate the flesh.[39] The author of the *Biografia* suggests that during this time Caterina embraced such penances because of her inner feelings. "I do not know [why I do them], but

---

33. For discussion of the preacher's probable identity, see *Biografia*, p. 191 n.
25. Some of the suggested candidates are B. Angelo Carletti da Civazzo, Domenico da Panzò, and B. Bernardino da Feltre.
34. *Biografia*, pp. 191-92.
35. Ibid., p. 192. The *Biografia* then states: "Et questo diceiva con talle fervore che tuti li capelli li cadeivano zu per le spale, de modo che pareiva mata, et così ogniuno restò stupefacto et satisfacto." Ibid.
36. Ibid.
37. "Ma io trovo che lo amore vence ogni cosa, et io non posso credere che uno amore, chi non sia proprio, possa mai essere inganato." Ibid.
38. For the penitential practices of this entire period, see *The Mystical Element*, 1:132-37; and the *Biografia*, pp. 127-31.
39. See Caroline W. Bynum, *Holy Feast and Holy Fast: The Religious Significance of Food to Medieval Women* (Berkeley: University of California Press, 1987), p. 182.

I feel intimately drawn to do so, without any goal, and I believe that He wishes it so, but not that I have any objective there."[40]

Perhaps these penitential practices were also supported by her coincidental hearing of a sermon about the conversion of Mary Magdalen in which the preacher tried to explain all the motives, internal and external, of the Magdalen's actions. While listening, Caterina felt that she could say: "'I understand you.' So much [that she heard] corresponded to what she felt that her own conversion was similar to that of the Magdalen."[41]

At the end of the four years, she claimed that God took away from her mind in an instant these severe penances so that, "even had she wished to carry out such mortifications, she would have been unable."[42] No longer focused on trying to atone for past sins, Caterina ceased such ascetic and penitential practices by pursuing new avenues of Christian activity.

Her apparent ability to endure great fasts continued from this propitiatory period for twenty-three more years. "Soon after her conversion [starting in Lent 1476], her Love spoke to her inwardly and said that He wanted her to keep the forty days [Lent] with Him in the desert; and it was then the feast of the Annunciation."[43] Drinking only a mixture of water, vinegar and salt, she repeated the practice of eating nothing during Lent and Advent each year.[44] As might be expected, "The people at home and other persons who knew her deemed it a great wonder to live so long without

---

40.   "Respondeiva: io non lo so, ma mi sento così interiormenti tirata a farle, sensa alcuno obiecto, credo che voglia così, ma non vole che io li habia alcuno obiecto." *Biografia*, p. 130.

41.   Ibid., p. 131.

42.   Ibid., pp. 130-31. This cessation of penances because "tuto li fu levato de la mente" diverges from much traditional asceticism. Although she claimed that her conversion was similar to that of the Magdalen (see above), Caterina's subsequent short-term penances differed from the legends about the penitential St. Mary Magdalen and St. Jerome. Both these penitents, out of remorse for their past sins, were believed to have performed severe ascetical deeds throughout their post-conversion lifetimes and were accordingly emulated as exemplary. For St. Jerome, see Rice, *St. Jerome*, pp. 75-80. Perhaps Caterina's public efforts on behalf of the poor and sick supplanted her desire for such solitary penances.

43.   *Biografia*, p. 122. She adds: "Poi apreso lo advento lo quale successe, fece lo simile." Ibid., p. 123.

44.   Ibid., p. 124. Caterina of Genoa's practice is in contrast to that of Caterina of Siena who, during the last six years of her life, claimed that she did not need food and could not even eat without pain (all of which she undertook for the sins of others). Rudolph Bell, *Holy Anorexia* (Chicago: University of Chicago Press, 1985), p. 29, considers her fasting to be pathological: "None of the efforts of Catherine's friends, confessors, or enemies succeeded in changing her ways and curing her anorexia, and in the end she starved herself to death." For another view of Caterina of Siena, consult David Rampling, "Ascetic Ideals and Anorexia Nervosa," *Journal of Psychiatric Research* 19, 2/3, (1985): 89-94.

eating, but she did not value it as the least thing, because it seemed that it was the operation of God done without her will."[45]

Occasionally fearing some delusion, she would force herself to eat, which induced vomiting. Although she accepted the fasts, she did not view them as penances since they reportedly caused her neither hunger nor discomfort and since they persisted long after she had abandoned her prior penitential actions. Surprisingly, during these biannual periods of fasting "she [claimed that she] slept well, labored more actively than at other times in performing the works of the hospital, and felt stronger than when she ate."[46]

After her conversion Caterina developed a distinctive sacramental pattern. She perceived an intense longing to receive communion daily because "her love infused in her the desire for Holy Communion, which never disappeared during the rest of her life." This longing was supported in a unique way. "Her love arranged that Communion was given to her without her having to do anything about it, and it was always provided in one way or another."[47] Even though mediated by priests, the host produced a direct communication with Christ, and Caterina hungered for Him daily. "O Lord...it seems to me that if I were dead, I should return to life to receive you."[48] She said elsewhere: "Love, why do you draw me to yourself through these savors [such as the *odore* and *suavità* that she experienced when she received communion]. I do not want anything except you."[49]

As a result of this strong yearning, she decided to receive daily communion without a customary consultation with the clergy. She experienced some embarrassment at communicating so often, but she continued the practice nonetheless. Her uneasiness

45. *Biografia*, p. 125. She continued her explanation: "Però vedeva chiaramenti con lo ochio interiore che de tuto quello fa Dio non si dobiamo maravegiare né gloriare, perché a lui sono como niente, et chiaramenti vedeiva che era cosa da niente a conparatione de quello sentiva nel core, cioè de lo focoso divino amore lo quale continuamenti gustava et tuta la ardeiva de modo che la cosa de lo non mangiare li pareiva una cosa da niente." Ibid., pp. 125-26.
46. Ibid., p. 125. According to Bell, *Holy Anorexia*, p. 161, "the sudden beginning and ending of her inability to eat in precise forty-day cycles twice yearly suggests that her condition was not purely somatic." What the cause might be remains unclear inasmuch as she claimed that she had not chosen to fast. Bell noted in conclusion: "Beginning with observers during her lifetime and continuing to the present day, even Catholic scholars concede that Catherine's fasts were of neurological origin, probably an expression of suppressed religious desires blocked by her married condition" (p. 162). The last possibility seems suspect because the beginning of Caterina's fasting coincided with the marital accommodation and continued beyond Giuliano's death. Simultaneously, her formerly thwarted religious impulses developed into positive charitable activity that she claimed was improved – not impeded – by her biannual fasting.
47. *Biografia*, p. 121.
48. "O Signore – è il grido della sua anima innamorata – mi par se fusse morta, che per riceverti, resusciteria." From the *Vita 1551*, cap. 3, fol. 8b as cited in *Teologia*, p. 34.
49. *Biografia*, p. 121.

occurred because at the time "to communicate one time per month was rare, even for elect souls *(anime elette)*."[50] However, to the end of her life, she remained a daily recipient of communion, which was the main (and, during times of fasting, sole) food and nourishment for her body; she found in it "the truly physical, the truly nourishing, the truly fleshly, in the humanity of Christ, chewed and swallowed in the eucharist."[51] Both her physical hunger and her spiritual longings were satisfied by this quotidian reception of the eucharistic wafer. "The day she did not receive Communion she was hungry all day long. It seemed that she could not live without that sacrament."[52]

During the same time that she was receiving daily, she refrained from utilizing any spiritual director or confessor for twenty-five years (i.e., 1474-99) after her conversion. "She was guided by her gentle Love, without the means of any creature, either religious or secular priest; He taught her with His divine and intimate speech all that was necessary."[53] Actually, whether she consciously considered herself superior to ecclesiastical authority and prevalent custom, even if the rationale for such conduct were visionary, remains ambiguous.[54] Eleven years before her death Caterina did select a spiritual director and confessor, under whose influence, by the time of her death,

50. *Teologia*, p. 33. This rareness can be encountered in the rule for the Franciscan Tertiaries that required, rather than limited, communion to at least three times a year. "E tale era in genere la regola per le pie Congregazioni e Compagnie di Misericordia." Page 34 n. 3.

51. Caroline W. Bynum, "Women Mystics and Eucharistic Devotion in the Thirteenth Century," *Women's Studies* 2 (1984): 199, remarks that Caterina's dependence on the eucharist, especially during her biannual fasts, pales before that of the peasant saint, Alpaïs of Cudot, who "survived for forty years on the eucharist [alone] and became a living proof of the efficacy of the sacrament."

52. Hughes, *Spiritual Dialogue*, p. 133; and *Dialogo*, p. 432. For a discussion that places Caterina's desire for receiving the Eucharist daily within her attitudes toward fasting and food, see Bynum, *Holy Feast*, pp. 181-85.

53. "Era guidata de lo suo dolce amore sensa mezo di alcuna creatura, ne religiosa ne seculare; la amaistrava lui solo in lo interiore, con la sua divina et intrisecha alocutione, de tuto quello li era bisogno." *Biografia*, pp. 134-35.

54. Von Hügel, *The Mystical Element*, 1:118, believed that Caterina's statements excluded her utilization of confession and spiritual direction for this entire period. He endeavored to justify this plainly unconventional practice partly by citing her initial severe asceticism, and then the discipline and continuous self-renouncement that "take thus, for a considerable period, the place of the sacramental forms of Penance" (p. 240). His argument does not do justice to the radicalness of Caterina's actions, which were clearly not orthopraxis. Bonzi interprets this statement differently. Although Caterina did not have a designated spiritual director during this long period, this absence did not preclude her occasional use of confession. Also, he notes the frequent references to the presence of the Holy Spirit as the main (but not the only) influence in Caterina's life during this time: "Et per queste et altre molte cose manifestamenti se vedeiva che *talmenti* era guidata da lo Spirito Santo." *Biografia*, p. 131. That the Spirit guided her *talmenti* did not, according to Bonzi, exclude periodic recourse to the spiritual advice of others (as is alluded to in various places in her writings). For his arguments, see *Teologia*, pp. 236-45.

devotional habits more typical of the period predominate. Out of her esteem for the sacraments and fearing death following a night described as painful as a martyrdom, "she asked for Extreme Unction, which was given to her and which she received with great devotion."[55]

In regard to the sacraments of communion and confession, Caterina followed her own path – basically sidestepping ecclesiastical authorities. Her lack of a director may have been more than just a personal quirk; if she had been under the spiritual guidance of a priest, he would surely have restricted her on the basis of contemporary patterns.[56] Monks and nuns, for instance, could not decide this question on their own, and many could not obtain permission for even monthly communion. Caterina's actions reflected the unconventional precept that came to govern her life: inner religious experience Although respecting whatever she appropriated from others and the past, she finally decided on the testimony of her own conscience how she would use the sacraments of the church.[57]

After completing the period of intense penance,[58] Caterina committed herself first to distributing alms and then to nursing. Until his death in 1497, Giuliano also decided to join in both works. This began when "one day the women in a confraternity of mercy [Donne della Misericordia] asked Catherine for assistance, and she answered the call."[59] Supplied by this group with money and food for the indigent, Caterina and Giuliano were zealous in carrying out all the duties entrusted to them.[60] At the same time, some of these Genoese needy were likewise victims of disease, most notably the bubonic plague. The aim of these amateurs to help the poor meant they began to nurse the sick as well.

Because Caterina viewed her nursing efforts done out of obedience as a humble submission to God, she mingled with the sick and poor of Genoa, never refusing to give any form of care.[61]

55. Hughes, *Spiritual Dialogue*, p. 141; and *Dialogo*, p. 448.

56. For Bonzi's discussion of contemporary practice, including several examples, see *Teologia*, pp. 33-35.

57. Although writing of an earlier period and in the context of various eucharistic miracles, Caroline Bynum, "Women Mystics," p. 194, encapsulates what sacramental practices like Caterina's would mean for laywomen. "Women's eucharistic devotion was the devotion of those who receive *rather than* consecrate, those who are lay *rather than* clergy, those whose closeness to God and whose authorization to serve others come through intimacy and direct inspiration *rather than* through office or worldly power."

58. Scholars have differed on the onset of daily communion and the end date of this period of severe fasting; consult among others *The Mystical Element*, 1:109-13, 135-37; and *Teologia*, pp. 30-33.

59. Hughes, *Spiritual Dialogue*, p. 129; and *Dialogo*, p. 422.

60. *Biografia*, pp. 140-41.

61. Faced with the same helplessness as the doctors, Caterina could have been predicted to grow increasingly frustrated. However, as Caroline W. Bynum points out in "Disease and Death in the Middle Ages," *Culture, Medicine and Psychiatry* 9 (1985): 97-102, religious values shaped the medieval

Many of these sick poor (if infected with the plague) had been abandoned by their family and lacked basic attention.[62] "She went to the said sick and poor and would clean all their miseries and uglinesses, and when her stomach was affected by these acts even to nausea, she put what she handled into her mouth in order to conquer these rebellions of sensuality."[63]

She served the sick with devotion "as much in matters of the spirit, reminding them of spiritual concerns, as in corporal needs and never hesitated before their most disgusting diseases."[64] Caterina was determined to nurse even those who despaired of their diseased condition and who "cursed anyone who came to help them."[65] She conducted herself in the spirit of an exhortation by her contemporary, Bernardino da Feltre: "In the book of the sick," he said, "should be written: Patience, patience, patience, and in that of those who help them: Charity, charity, charity."[66] In response to divine love, she embraced nursing the sick, especially the plague-ridden, and the needs of this nursing required her to embody a diligent charity.

Caterina found herself struggling daily with conflicts between her decision and her sensibilities. She strove to overcome a natural repulsion to the misery she witnessed. By an act of her will, the *Dialogo* notes, she was able "to work with human misery as if it were kneading bread, and even, if need be, to taste it a bit."[67] Since dealing with lice almost made Caterina vomit, her inner

---

person's perspective by providing psychic support and direction in the face of real danger and frustration. On page 101 she writes: "Medieval people did not see disease primarily as something to be cured…. Medieval people, in 1500 as in 1350, faced illness and death with the determination to make it mean something rather than the determination to change it." Accordingly, the role of the nurse included not just caring for the physical exigencies, but, more urgently, attending to the victim's spiritual preparation for his or her expected death. Many patients came to cloak the plague in religious ritual and piety, especially the confession of their sins. "They strove less to avert [their] suffering than to give personal and particular meaning to it" (p. 102). Caterina could assist in this effort.

62. A chance remark by the Benedictine Luciano degli Ottoni of Brescia in his translation of John Chrysostom's commentary on St. Paul's letter to the Romans confirmed this deplorable practice of abandonment. In emphasizing that faith required practical deeds in everyday life, Ottoni compared the practices of the early church to those of his day. "Indeed Christians not only cared for other Christians, but also many amongst the heathen who were neglected by their own people, but nowadays if the plague comes to any city, everyone runs away, and they keep away from each other as much as possible, so that often more die by hunger than by plague." *Divi Ioannis Christostomi in Apostoli Pauli Epistolam ad Romanos Commentaria* (Brescia, 1538), fol. 71r; cited in Barry Collett, *Italian Benedictine Scholars and the Reformation. The Congregation of Santa Giustina of Padua* (Oxford: Clarendon Press, 1985), p. 132.
63. *Biografia*, p. 141.
64. Ibid.
65. Hughes, *Spiritual Dialogue*, p. 129; and *Dialogo*, p. 423.
66. Eugène Flornoy, *Le Bienheureux Bernardin de Feltre* (Paris: V. Coffée, 1897), p. 70.
67. Hughes, *Spiritual Dialogue*, p. 130; and *Dialogo*, p. 424.

voice challenged her to overcome this natural revulsion. It commanded her:

> Take a handful of them, put them in your mouth and swallow them. That way you will free yourself of your nausea. She shuddered but did as she was told, learning to handle them as if they were pearls. Dealing with particularly big lice was harder yet, but even then she obeyed. She did this so often that she overcame that repugnance and nausea once and for all.[68]

Likewise, since working with the sick exposed her to the stench that came from their sores, and this smell continued to give her nausea, "she rubbed her nose with the pus until she freed herself of that revulsion."[69] The repetition of these severe deeds marked a settlement of her interior conflict.

This extremism in depicting Caterina's struggle to overcome her revulsion was prominent in the tradition about her and as a result served as an ideal for anyone desiring a life of penance and austere holiness. Even though few would imitate the extremes of Caterina's actions, the striving to achieve a similar degree of mortification of the natural responses, often by performing the same types of revolting actions, formed an essential component in the works of charity undertaken by the Oratories of Divine Love, the lay confraternities first founded in 1497 by her co-worker, Ettore Vernazza. Among the growing circle of her disciples, she was remembered as a woman for whom the demands of charity overcame all natural reservations.

During the central period of her life, from 1477 to 1499, Caterina worked primarily in the Pammatone Hospital in Genoa. Although Giuliano and she continued to care for the poor sick abandoned in the streets, their work henceforth became identified with this institutional setting. In fact, to enable themselves to work more conveniently within the hospital, the couple lived in a little room there and assisted without pay from 1479 until their deaths. In this hospital, they "found 130 sick-beds always occupied by patients, and over 100 foundling girls, who were being trained as silk-workers."[70]

Caterina first worked as a nurse and then as a matron (*rettora*) of the entire facility from 1490 to 1496. "[She] was hardly a fifteenth-century Florence Nightingale, but she did something to promote the technical side of nursing."[71] To Caterina, this promotion was quite probably incidental, since she claimed that while serving the sick, she was never without consciousness of her tender *Amore* nor "did she, because of this consciousness, fail

---

68. Hughes, *Spiritual Dialogue,* p. 131; and *Dialogo,* pp. 425-26.
69. Hughes, *Spiritual Dialogue,* p. 131; and *Dialogo,* p. 426.
70. *The Mystical Element,* 1:130.
71. H. O. Evennett, *The Spirit of the Counter-Reformation* (Notre Dame, IN: Notre Dame University Press, 1975), p. 87.

in any practical matter concerning the Hospital."[72] Growing into the role as a servant of the sick poor, she nursed with constancy, willing to perform any necessary task, no matter how unpleasant.

During 1493 a severe outbreak of the plague befell Genoa.[73] Having struck in the spring, it still raged fiercely in August of 1494; many of those who had remained in the city succumbed. Caterina organized volunteer ambulances to transport plague victims to temporary, open-air wards. There, other volunteers (doctors, nurses, priests, and Franciscan Tertiaries) did whatever possible to minister to the suffering. Among the Tertiaries was Ettore Vernazza, a layperson whose life would prove to be hardly less remarkable than hers.[74] In 1493, he was twenty-three years old, wealthy, and by profession a notary who, like Caterina, was a member of the Genoese nobility.[75] The plague and the nursing provided an opportunity for Vernazza to observe Caterina caring personally for the stricken. Their contact continued after this outbreak in Genoa, and he became one of the primary means for extending her influence.

One familiar story from 1493 portrayed Caterina's heroism in dealing with a female Tertiary who lay dying of the plague, probably contracted while caring for victims. She had lain speechless for eight days. During her daily visits Caterina would urge her: "Call Jesus." In response the sick woman finally moved her lips as best she could. Believing the Tertiary's mouth was filled with Jesus, Caterina could not refrain from kissing her with

---

72. *The Mystical Element*, 1:143. The *Biografia*, p. 142, also notes approvingly: "Et cosa mirabile, fece le speize tanti ani di longo et per le mane sue pasava tanti dinari, che mai al dar conto trovò manchare uno solo denaro." Apparently, Caterina was something of an accountant in addition to being a nurse and administrator.

73. During Caterina's time at the hospital, the plague of 1493 was the worst. "Quella del 1493 fu la più terribile peste del secolo xv, e una tra le più catastrofiche che ricordi la storia ligure. Il morbo durò dall'inizio del 1493 al 15 agosto 1494." Bonzi, *Teologia*, p. 40. The plague would recur in 1499, 1501, 1504, 1505, and 1524. See *Teologia*, p. 40 n. 1. Bonzi, pp. 40-41, also cites evidence that during this 1493 outbreak Caterina directed the communal nursing work for Genoa. The topic of the plague encompasses a vast field of study. Some recent books include: Graham Twigg, *The Black Death: A Biological Reappraisal* (London: Batsford Academic and Educational, 1984); Robert Gottfried, *The Black Death: Natural and Human Disaster in Medieval Europe* (New York: Free Press, 1983); and Daniel Williman, *The Black Death: The Impact of the Fourteenth-Century Plague*, Medieval and Renaissance Texts and Studies 13 (Binghamton, NY: Center for Medieval and Early Renaissance Studies, 1982).

74. The fundamental source for his life was written in 1581 by Suor Battista Vernazza: "Lettera del padre e madre della reverenda madre donna Baptista [Vernazza]," printed in *Opere spirituali della reverenda et divotissima vergine di Christo Donna Battista da Genova*, ed. D. Gaspard de Piacenza, 3 vols. (Venice, 1588); 4 vols. (Verona, 1602), 4:1-11; reprinted in A. Bianconi, *L'Opera delle compagnie del divino amore nella Riforma cattolica* (Città di Castello: S. Lapi, 1914), pp. 63-71. A life of Ettore Vernazza composed by Bianconi is found on pp. 33-43. Another by Von Hügel is included in *The Mystical Element*, 1:316-35.

75. Bonzi and Viller, *DS*, col. 320.

great and tender affection. As a result, Caterina contracted the disease and very nearly died.[76] As soon as she had recovered, however, she resumed nursing the sick with the same attention and diligence. Presumably, Vernazza knew of Caterina's action, for it became widely retold.[77]

During Caterina's last ten years (1500-1510), her health deteriorated to the extent that she could no longer nurse in the Pammatone. As her death approached, her previous reluctance to seek outside ecclesiastical advice gave way to the selection of a personal spiritual director; from 1499 to 1510, Don Cattaneo Marabotto continued to guide her toward more conventional piety, especially in regard to confession.[78] Throughout this time, she also deepened her contact with the various individuals, such as Vernazza and Marabotto, who had shared her work and ideals and whom she had influenced. Therefore, she had sufficient leisure to share intimately her spiritual experiences; moreover, this is probably the period in which she recorded or drafted – in whatever form – the memories of her life and teachings.

The *Biografia* related her desire to express to her friends her inner feelings: "'Would that I could say to you what this heart feels, which burns me with true love!'" And they would say to her, "'O mother, tell us something of it.' She would respond, 'I cannot find words appropriate to so much fiery love.'"[79] After an intense and enigmatic final illness, Caterina died during the night of September 14/15, 1510, surrounded by many of these friends.[80] The *Dialogo* describes her death in this way: "Thus in that very hour, in all peace and tranquillity, she gently left this life and

76. Her recovery indicates that she was infected by the bubonic type of plague, from which a person could recover. This pattern of contact, infection, sickness, and recovery becomes identified with heroic charitable efforts and became expected of the pious and devout. Ettore Vernazza (1524) and St. Aloysius Gonzaga (1591), for example, gave their lives while nursing plague victims.

77. *Vita 1551*, cap. 8, fol. 21a, as cited in *Teologia*, pp. 40-41. Bonzi, p. 41 n. 2, justifies the inclusion of this story into the biographical material about Caterina by noting: "La narrazione di questo episodio manca nei codici, ma credo non le si possa negare fede storica, essendo sostenuta da una rispettabile tradizione scritta e orale."

78. Concerning Marabotto, see *Teologia*, pp. 53-55; and Bonzi and Viller, *DS*, cols. 317-18. He would also succeed her as the director of the Pammatone hospital. Marabotto would administer her will and select the site of her burial. He has also been identified by historians (Bonzi et al.) as the compiler and amanuensis of Caterina's *Biografia*.

79. *Biografia*, p. 290.

80. Vernazza was in Rome on business at the time of her death and accordingly could not attend her funeral. Even though Caterina could not digest anything during this illness, contemporaries were intrigued by the fact that she never experienced trouble swallowing the Eucharist. This strange occurrence enabled her until her death to continue daily Eucharistic reception, her practice since 1474. See *The Mystical Element*, 1:113-14.

went to her sweet love, whom she now sees and takes joy in for all time."[81]

⚶

Caterina's life did not emphasize self-imposed penances, such as fasting, or mystical phenomena, such as visions. Rather, her life came to be identified with the actual suffering of the poor and sick of Genoese society. Caterina responded to widespread and severe problems, ones that necessitated society-wide undertakings, and she influenced the followers who had gathered around her similarly to pursue such efforts. Caterina performed the evangelical acts of mercy, in particular visiting and caring for the sick. Her response – at once merciful and practical – called others to similar personal involvement aimed at alleviating whatever suffering they witnessed.

Caterina's transformation from personal, inwardly directed contemplation to societal, altruistic activity may explain why she abandoned her early practices of traditional penance while embracing certain extreme actions as described by her biographers; eating vermin and kissing the plague-ridden replaced sleepless nights and the discipline. She was not the first to embody this shift, but her distinctive and important quality is that she began a tradition that was bequeathed initially to groups made up predominantly of laypeople, the Oratories of Divine Love; subsequently that gift became incorporated within a new religious community, the Theatines, founded in 1524, a clerical continuation of the Oratories. It is significant of Caterina's appeal that a woman – a married layperson – following her own instincts and mystical instructions could influence a group of reform-minded clerics in the formation and direction of their activities. By emulating Caterina, the Oratories and the Theatines brought her attitudes into the heart of the Catholic Church.

EXCURSUS
THE SOURCES FOR CATERINA OF GENOA'S BIOGRAPHY

The prevailing, early twentieth-century view of Caterina was formed by Baron Fredric Von Hügel, whose detailed analysis of her life, labors, and teachings was undertaken between 1900 and 1908. His complete results were published in *The Mystical Element of Religion As Studied in Saint Catherine of Genoa and Her Friends*, 2 vols., 1st ed. (London: J.M. Dent, 1908); 2d ed. (London: J. M. Dent,

---

81.   Hughes, *Spiritual Dialogue*, p. 148; and *Dialogo*, p. 461. This *devotione* was especially conveyed by her followers, such as Vernazza and Marabotto, wherever they went. Caterina was buried in the church of SS. Annunziata in Portoria. When she was reinterred two years later in an elaborate tomb at the same site, "Il corpo della Santa fu ritrovato intatto nel 1512 e si conserva ancor oggi, integro...esposto alla venerazione dei fedeli." See *Teologia*, p. 58 n. 4. Even four decades before her writings were published, the stories of this phenomenon contributed to the spread of Caterina's reputation and the development of her cult.

1923). He intended a biography but finished "by writing an essay on the philosophy of Mysticism, illustrated by the life of Caterinetta Fiesca Adorna [sic] and her friends." See *The Mystical Element*, Preface to the first edition; reprinted in 2d. ed., 1: xxiii. Von Hügel wanted to locate the driving energy of this kind of religion and especially "to discover in what way such a keen sense of, and absorption in, the Infinite can still find room for the Historical and Institutional elements of Religion." That is, he investigated how for years her mysticism united with benevolent activity toward the sick. The underlying motive, however, that grew to dominate his efforts was the wish to utilize a long, close contact with "a soul of most rare spiritual depth, a soul that presents, with an extraordinary, provocative vividness, the greatness, helps, problems and dangers of the mystical spirit." Ibid., p. xxii. Von Hügel started by tracing the literary transmission of Caterina's writings in order to ascertain how (and by whom) her influence had spread. He suspected that, because of internal differences in style, editing, and thought, the conventional attribution of the *Opus Catharinianum* was erroneous.

For his Italian text, Von Hügel relied on the thirteenth Genoese edition of the *Vita e Dottrina* of 1847 (based on the 1551 *editio princeps*). See *The Mystical Element*, 1:90. He believed that the 1551 edition by A. Bellono contained the most trustworthy text of the saint's writings because it was based on what was then considered to be the earliest manuscript, known as the Bellono MS A, with some additions. Bellono MS A (as designated by Von Hügel) is the University of Genoa, MS B.I.29. See *Edizione critica*, pp. 9-11. After examining MS A and what he thought were later manuscripts and editions, Von Hügel concluded that Caterina was the author of none of them. His arguments can be found in *The Mystical Element*, appendix to part 2, "Chronological account and critical analysis of the materials for the reconstitution of Saint Catherine's life and teaching," 1:371-466; the conclusions are summarized in 1:90-93. He proposed, instead, that the real authors were Vernazza (1470-1524) and Don Cattaneo Marabotto (?-1528), who wrote them sometime between 1512 and 1528.

Later, in the 1530s and 1540s, Von Hügel believed, Vernazza's daughter Tommasa (hereafter Suor Battista) wrote the *Dialogo* and edited the other texts, which she had received from her father. Although she is also often called "Tommasina," her religious name is maintained throughout to differentiate her from a contemporary nun, Tommasina Fieschi, a cousin of Caterina and, likewise, influenced by Caterina's teachings. For the latter see U. Bonzi, "Tommasina Fieschi," in *Dictionnaire de Spiritualité* 5 (1964): 332-36. Von Hügel did not doubt, however, that the biographical facts and doctrine contained in the *Vita* and *Trattato* were accurate and authentic, even if filtered through the understanding of Caterina's close followers.

Although today one must question the objectivity of Caterina's followers, Von Hügel overcame his own skepticism about the congruence of the texts and her actual life. Unfortunately, this led him, at times, to treat her as piously and reverentially as had her early disciples; negative criticism does not appear. The general outlines of her life are clear, but specific details, judgments, and conclusions require careful reexamination. Nevertheless, in the sixteenth century, her followers would have believed uncritically the details of her life, including the miraculous and heroic. Nevertheless, in attempting to ascertain the contours of Caterina's life from the *Vita* and *Dialogo*, he studied the levels of the written tradition and thereby facilitated his analysis of her teaching on mysticism; because Caterina's actions and teachings were likewise passed on in an oral and lived tradition, Von Hügel supplemented the texts by considering other sources for his study.

Writing several decades later, other scholars came to very different conclusions from Von Hügel about the authorship of the Caterina manuscripts. Some of these are M. Viller and G. Joppin, "Les sources italiennes de l'Abrégé de la Perfection, La vie de sainte Catherine de Gênes et les oeuvres de la M. Battista Vernazza," *Revue d'Ascétique et de Mystique* 15 (1934): 381-402; U.

Bonzi, "L'Opus Catharinianum et ses auteurs: Étude critique sur la biographie et les écrits de sainte Catherine de Gênes," *Revue d'Ascétique et de Mystique* 16 (1935): 351-80; and especially "Il problema critico," *Edizione critica*, pp. 77-103. An English summary is included in the introduction by B. Groeschel to *Catherine of Genoa: Purgation and Purgatory; The Spiritual Dialogue*, trans. Serge Hughes (New York: Paulist Press, 1979), pp. 50-56.

In his *S. Caterina Fieschi Adorno*, Umile Bonzi concluded that the earliest extant manuscripts predate Bellono MS A, which was the text Von Hügel followed. Bonzi MS D*, the earliest version, dated from 1522-25, whereas Bonzi MS D, being a later version of D*, dated from 1671. Bonzi, *Edizione critica*, pp. 18-21, concluded that the MS D*, which was unknown to Von Hügel, is a copy of the earliest manuscript. A copy of this MS, used for the process of canonization for Caterina, is Archivio dell' Ospedale di Pammatone, MS 27, fols. 1719b-1930a. It was entitled: "Copia Processus Remissorialis et Compulsorialis Beatae Catharinae Fliscae Adurnae." MS D (labeled by Von Hügel as MS C) is University of Genoa, MS B.VII.7. For the "Capostipite e Famiglie del MSS dell' *Opus Catharinianum*," see *Edizione critica*, p. 46. As the source for the D* Manuscript, Bonzi posits a "MS X," which is the MS *princeps*, dated to 1520-22, and "sino ad oggi non ancora ritrovato." For a full discussion of this question, see Bonzi, "Il problema codicografico," Ibid., pp. 37-61.

In his *Edizione critica*, Bonzi presents MSS D*, D, and Bellono A in parallel columns and demonstrates that the differences between the Bonzi MS D* and Bonzi MS D are negligible. Von Hügel did not know of Bonzi MS D* and believed Bonzi MS D (his MS C) to be much later and consequently of little importance. In addition, the Bonzi MSS D* and D contain numerous Genoese expressions, spare constructions, and rhythms, whereas the Bellono MS A is written in Florentine Italian, tending to be more flowery and verbose, and is filled with explanatory details and background information that would not have been necessary if written for a Genoese audience. The Bonzi MS D* always gives the story without additional comment, whereas the Bellono MS A tries to draw a conclusion from it.

Bonzi claims that Von Hügel did not sufficiently consider these stylistic differences nor the obviously different perspective of the compiler – both of which point to the lateness of the Bellono MS A. See Hughes, *Spiritual Dialogue*, p. 51. On the basis of consistent attribution going back to 1551, Bonzi argued that the *Trattato* is Caterina's own creation. He also concluded that her confessor, Marabotto, rather than Ettore Vernazza, compiled and composed (sometime between his first contact with Caterina and 1522) the *Vita*, now retitled by Bonzi the *Biografia*, which included accounts from many eyewitnesses, such as Vernazza. Also, Suor Battista Vernazza did not write the *Dialogo*, even if she had become the redactor of the manuscript received from her father, who himself had probably only copied it. Bonzi asserted that, in editing this work, Suor Battista modified and amplified aspects of it, sensitive to the changed religious situation of 1551. Bonzi decided, moreover, that the authorship of the first third belonged to Caterina, whereas the remainder was composed by an unknown male disciple, probably a priest. If his attribution is accurate, Umile Bonzi's conclusions indicate that Caterina, aware of the significance of her spiritual experiences, composed a partial testimony to enable her friends to know and understand them.

IX

Disciplina
The Monastic and Clerical Origins
of European Civility*

DILWYN KNOX

INTRODUCTION

A boy should not constantly wiggle his forehead like a hedgehog
or scowl like a bull.... He may take a second drink towards the
end of a meal, drinking in moderation and without gulping or
making a noise like a horse.... Some people become engrossed in
chomping their food and make loud sounds like pigs.... Others
immediately grab food almost before they are properly seated like
a wolf.... A boy should wait a little while before sampling food,
since this will accustom him to restrain his impulses.... It is
unbecoming to look at someone with one eye closed. What else
is this than to make oneself one-eyed? We should leave this
gesture to the tuna and dory.... Boys should take care to keep
their teeth clean, but should not polish them with powder like
girls.

These translations come from Erasmus' *De civilitate morum
puerilium*.[1] The book was written in 1530 for the ten-and-a-half-
year-old Prince Henry of Burgundy and, as the excerpts suggest,
concerns external, physical comportment. The *De civilitate* proved
popular. It was printed at least thirty-nine times in the six years

* I should like to thank Mary Alberi, Richard Andrews, Francesca
Bugliani, David D'Avray, William Clark, Judith Gale, Alastair Hamilton,
Steven Marcus, and particularly Jean-Claude Schmitt and Caroline Bynum for
comments on a first draft of this paper or parts of it. Professor Schmitt also
very kindly sent me an advance copy of his *La raison des gestes dans l'Occident
médiéval* (Paris: Gallimard, 1990), which arrived after I had completed this
paper. I have added a few references to it below, but my comments on
medieval comportment should be modified throughout in the light of what
Professor Schmitt has to say there. I have used the following abbreviations:
CSEL = Corpus scriptorum ecclesiasticorum latinorum; Hakluyt[1] and *Hakluyt*[2] =
Works issued by the Hakluyt Society, First and Second Series repectively; *MGP =
Monumenta Germaniae Paedagogica; MHSI = Monumenta Historica Societatis
Jesu; PL = Patrologiae cursus completus, Series (latina) prima*, ed. J.-P. Migne.
1. *De civilitate morum puerilium*, i, iv, in *Opera omnia*, ed. J. Clericus, 10
vols. in 11 pts. (Leiden: P. Vander Aa, 1703-6 = LB), 1:1034B, C, 1035D, E,
1038F, 1039B, 1040B.

between first publication and Erasmus' death in 1536. By 1600 at least a further sixty or so editions had appeared in Northern Europe, from Stockholm to Leipzig, including translations into English, French, Bohemian, Dutch, German and other languages. And this is not to mention the many paraphrases and plagiarisms of the whole or part of Erasmus' book. Evidently it was a work that caught the mood of the times.

What is the context of Erasmus work? What does it tell us about the customs of its day and of ours? If we are to believe previous interpretations, the *De civilitate* belongs to a rich tradition of manuals on court behavior, the most famous of which is perhaps Castiglione's *Book of the Courtier*. The popularity of Erasmus' book, like that of Castiglione's, is therefore taken as an indication of how court manners trickled down through European society. This interpretation has been buttressed by a considerable body of scholarship.[2] The most formidable and influential account has been Norbert Elias' *Wandlungen des Verhaltens in den weltlichen Oberschichten des Abendlandes*, first published in 1939 as part of Elias' two-volume *Über den Prozess der Zivilization*.[3] Here Elias described how court behavior spread through society and how, by the nineteenth century, in its popularized form, it differentiated European "civilization" from supposedly primitive cultures. Elias' work has generated many critiques, particularly among sociologists.[4] But this literature has discussed his thesis from an anthropological or sociological standpoint without questioning its historical framework. Even among historians it still passes as definitive,[5] or at most in need of modification.[6]

2.   For bibliography, see O. Ranum, "Courtesy, Absolutism, and the Rise of the French State, 1630-1660," *Journal of Modern History* 52 (1980): 428 n. 2.
3.   I have used N. Elias, *The History of Manners*, trans. E. Jephcott, part 1, *The Civilizing Process* (New York: Pantheon, 1978). On Elias' work, see most recently S. Mennell, *Norbert Elias: Civilization and the Human Self-Image* (Oxford: Blackwell, 1989).
4.   For a convenient survey, see S. Mennell, "Time and Taboo, Civilization and Science: The Work of Norbert Elias," *Journal of the Anthropological Society of Oxford* 11 (1980): 83-95.
5.   Elias' thesis is described as authoritative by, e.g., Ranum, "Courtesy," p. 429; and R. Muchembled, "Pour une histoire des gestes (XVe-XVIIIe siècles)," *Revue d'histoire moderne et contemporaine* 34 (1987): 88, 98.
6.   The only fully elaborated historical modification of Elias' thesis that I know of is C. S. Jaeger, *The Origins of Courtliness. Civilizing Trends and the Formation of Courtly Ideals, 939-1210* (Philadelphia: University of Pennsylvania Press, 1985). Jaeger argues persuasively that courtly behavior (understood in a broader sense than I discuss here) was determined by advisors, tutors, servants, and chaplains in medieval German courts. (For Jaeger's comments on Elias' model, see especially ibid., pp. 5-8.) I would suggest provisionally that my model illustrates a parallel and perhaps related development – the simultaneous appearance of *disciplina* as a key concept in the courtly (Jaeger, ibid., pp. 128-33, 140-141) and monastic tradition is suggestive. But whatever the connection, I do not believe that courts provided the model for comportment that became expected of all Europeans by the end of the sixteenth century.

I shall not argue against Elias' thesis in this paper. I should like, instead, to sketch out here an alternative hypothesis, one that Elias excluded,[7] namely, that polite comportment in Western Europe stems not from courts but from Latin Christianity; that like comportment in, say, China, Japan, India and Islam, it derives from religious or cultural, rather than political, circumstances. I do not, of course, deny that courts had codes of manners, but I would suggest that they were hothouse plants that often died outside their artificial environment. They were seen as conventional by contemporaries rather than as codes applicable to all.

I shall make five points. First, that medieval religious and clerics wrote detailed codes of comportment. Second, that their codes inspired secular codes from the thirteenth century onwards, including the key text for Elias' thesis, Erasmus' *De civilitate*. Third, that these secularized rules were based on the authority of reason. Fourth, that this laicization of monastic and clerical theory mirrored, albeit imperfectly, what was happening in practice. Fifth, that monastic and clerical comportment and secular derivatives were recognized as European because Europeans were becoming familiar with the behavior of other, supposedly primitive, peoples.

I. MONASTIC AND CLERICAL *DISCIPLINA*

The notion that outer comportment revealed the inner workings of the soul was staple to medieval and Renaissance Christian doctrine.[8] "For a state of mind is perceived in comportment of the body. Hence a motion of the body is, so to speak, an expression of the soul," wrote St. Ambrose in what proved to be the most detailed patristic discussion of the subject.[9] Similarly Aquinas in a discussion of anger: "interior motions are perceived through exterior effects."[10] Underpinning this interpretation was the most

---

7.   N. Elias, *Power and Civility* (= *The Civilizing Process*, vol. 2), trans. E. Jephcott (New York: Pantheon, 1982), p. 7.

8.   E.g. St. Gregory the Great, *Regulae pastoralis liber*, iii.23 (47) (*PL* 77:92B-C); Pseudo-Isidore of Seville, *Norma vivendi*, 7 (*PL* 83:1248C); [John of Fruttuaria], *De ordine vitae et morum institutione*, ii.4-6, (*PL* 184:563D-564D); [Bernard Silvestris], *Formula honestae vitae*, 4 (*PL* 184:1169B-C); [Thomas of Froidmont (Thomas of Beverley)], *De modo bene vivendi*, ix.26 (*PL* 184:1215B); [Nicolò Maniacoria], *Vita sancti Hieronymi*, *PL* 22:192; [Bernard of Besse], *Speculum disciplinae*, I.xxv.3, II.i.9, in St. Bonaventurae, *Opera omnia*, 10 vols. (Quaracchi: Collegium S. Bonaventura, 1882-1902), 8:608, 616; Humbert of Romans, *Expositio regulae B. Augustini*, 86, in *Opera de vita regulari*, ed. J. J. Berthier, 2 vols. (Torino: Marietti, 1956), 1:267.

9.   *De officiis ministrorum*, I.xviii.71 (*PL* 16:44C): "Habitus enim mentis in corporis statu cernitur.... Itaque vox quaedam est animi corporis motus," quoted, e.g., by Adam of Dryburgh (Adam Scotus), *De ordine, habitu et professione canonicorum ordinis praemonstratensis*, ii.11 (*PL* 198:459B-C); and [John of Fruttuaria], *De ordine*, ii.6, col. 564B.

10.   Aquinas, *Summ. theol.*, IIa IIae, qu. 158, art. 4, §3, in *Opera omnia*, vol. 1- (Rome: S. C. de Propaganda Fide, 1882-), 10:276: "interiores motus diiudicantur secundum exteriores effectus." Similarly on humility, *Summ. theol.*, IIa IIae, qu. 161, art. 6, §5, in *Opera*, 10:307, quoting Ecclus. 19:26 (29), as in n. 11 below.

important of all authorities, the Holy Scriptures, and in particular a commonly cited passage in Ecclesiasticus: "A man is known by his appearance and a wise man by the look on his face on meeting him. A man's attire, his laugh and gait divulge what he is."[11] This conclusion was corroborated by secular sources, particularly from the eleventh century onwards, as Greek and Arabic learning became better known in the Latin West. For example, a rich and largely unexplored literature on physiognomy hinged on the principle of a correspondence of body and soul. Deception was of course possible, but proved the rule. Deception relied on an inability to discern physical manifestations of intent to deceive, rather than an imperfect correspondence of body and soul.

For medieval and Renaissance authors this correspondence between physical expression and inner disposition was stricter than we would nowadays admit. Before the mid-sixteenth century they rarely distinguished between, on the one hand, gestures that are learnt and, on the other, instinctive expressions of emotions, like blushing, horripilation, or pallor from sadness, fear or pain, and other, almost wholly involuntary, cutaneous phenomena. Consequently, what would nowadays be thought conventional gestures often enjoyed the status of natural gestures and were considered accurate indications of the soul. Furthermore, even when a distinction between natural and conventional gesture was drawn, it was drawn very differently from today. Hence among natural gestures were included many that nowadays would be called conventional – for instance, covering one's head as a sign of melancholy, sadness, or shame, nodding one's head to indicate assent and shaking it to indicate denial.[12]

This belief in the correspondence of body and soul had many practical applications. According to the Parisian scholastic Jean Buridan (before 1300 - after 1358), jurists urged that the bodily movements and expressions of someone under examination should be continuously scrutinized.[13] For present purposes, however, its most important application was in religious life. If physical and spiritual disposition were intimately linked, then modification of the one entailed modification of the other. And just as the soul, ideally, disciplined the body, so too the body

11.   Ecclus. 19:26-27 (29-30), cited, e.g., by [Bernard Silvestris], *Formula*, 4, col. 1169B-C; Aquinas, *Summ. theol.*, IIa IIae, qu. 161, art. 6, §5, p. 307; John of Wales in n. 86 below; Bartolomé de Las Casas on pp. 133-34 below.
12.   D. Knox, "Ideas on Gesture and Universal Languages c.1550-1650," in *New Perspectives on Renaissance Thought. Essays in the History of Science, Education and Philosophy in Memory of Charles B. Schmitt*, eds. J. Henry and S. Hutton (London: Duckworth, 1990), pp. 101-36. Some conclusions there are superseded by my comments in the present paper.
13.   Jean Buridan, *Questiones physonomie Aristotilis edite per magistrum Johannem Biridanum*: Oxford, Bodleian Library, MS Canon. misc. 422, fols. 111ra-128rb (s.XV), at fol. 111vb.

might discipline the soul.[14] Hence, the most rigorous discipline of the body was to be expected of those committed to the most rigorous discipline of the soul, that is, those committed to a clerical and especially cenobitic life.[15] This held for everyday conduct as much as for ritual.[16] St. Ambrose[17] and early rules like those of Saints Basil and Benedict and the Rule of St. Augustine gave guidelines for comportment,[18] often drawing on classical ideas and terminology.[19] The Rule of St. Augustine, for example, stipulated that in the cloister: "In gait, posture and all your movements let nothing be done that might offend anyone's gaze; do only what becomes your spirituality."[20] More specifically some early rules instructed religious to keep their heads bowed,[21] a posture approved, sometimes by default, in the Scriptures.[22] Medieval and late medieval biographies, like those of the Brethren of the Common Life at Zwolle, who adhered to the Rule of St. Augustine, often described religious in a way that conforms

---

14.   E.g., Hugh of St. Victor on p. 113 below; Aquinas, *Summ. theol.*, IIa IIae, qu. 161, art. 6, pp. 307-8; and Cajetan's discussion of Aquinas' conclusions, ibid., pp. 308-9.

15.   On clerical comportment, see e.g., St. Ambrose, *De officiis*, I.xviii.67-80, cols. 43B-47B; St. Gregory the Great, *Regulae pastoralis liber*, iii.23 (47), col. 92B-C; Gratian, *Decretum*, pt. 1, dist. 41, [intro.] and c. 7 (8), in *Corpus iuris canonici*, ed. E. A. Friedberg, 2 vols. (Leipzig: B. Tauchnitz, 1879-81), 1:148, 150-51. Gratian was commonly cited; see, e.g., Bonaguida de Aretio, *Summa introductoria super officio advocationis in foro ecclesiae*, in A. Wunderlich, ed., *Anecdota quae processum civilem spectant. Bulgarus, Damasus, Bonaguida* (Göttingen: Vandenhoeck and Ruprecht, 1841), p. 137; A. Trotti, *De vero et perfecto clerico* (Ferrara: Severinus, 1475), sig. [o3r-v]; and G. Bonifacio, *L'arte de' cenni* (Vicenza: F. Grossi, 1616), p. 381. On monastic comportment, see especially J. Nicholls, *The Matter of Courtesy. Medieval Courtesy Books and the Gawain-Poet* (Woodbridge, Suffolk: D. S. Brewer, 1985), pp. 22-44. I came across Nicholls' discussion after completing this paper and have not therefore been able to take full advantage of it. Nicholl's conclusions on monastic comportment, though based mainly on different sources, are similar to mine.

16.   E.g., on ritual, Henricus de Hassia, *Secreta sacerdotum*, ed. M. Lochmayr, (Nürnberg: G. Stuchs, c.1497, Hain *8377), sig. A2v. Also ibid., sig. a2va-vb.

17.   See n. 15 above.

18.   E.g., Basil, *Regula*, viii.26-37 (*CSEL* 86:44-46); Pachomius, *Regulae monasticae*, ed. P.B. Albers, Florilegium patristicum, 16 (Bonn: P. Hanstein, 1923), pp. 34, 57; Eugippius, *Regula*, i.71 (*CSEL* 87:8); Benedict, *Regula*, vii.62-66 (*CSEL* 75, *edito altera emendata*: 55-56).

19.   See, e.g., St. Ambrose, *De officiis ministrorum*, I.xviii.71 following Cicero, *De officiis*, I.xxxv.126; and St. Augustine in n. 20 below.

20.   *La Règle de Saint Augustin*, ed. L. Verheijen, 2 vols. (Paris: Études Augustiniennes, 1967), 1:423 (*Praeceptum*, iv.3): "In incessu, in statu, in omnibus motibus vestris [cf. Cicero, *Brutus*, xxxvii.141] nihil fiat quod cuiusquam offendat aspectum, sed quod vestram decet sanctitatem." So too Eugippius as in n. 18 above.

21.   Ibid., p. 419 (*Praeceptum* i.6); St. Benedict in n. 18 above.

22.   See, e.g., St. Benedict, *Regula*, vii.65-66, pp. 55-56, citing Ps. 37:7 (38:6), Luke 18:13. Also Is. 3:16 cited e.g., by Hugh of St. Victor, *De institutione novitiorum*, 12 (*PL* 176:939B).

to these instructions,[23] or, more generally, emphasized the spiritual maturity of their comportment.[24]

But apart from St. Ambrose, patristic and early monastic authors commented only briefly on comportment. Specific injunctions, for both monks and nuns,[25] became common, as far as surviving sources tell, only from the ninth century onwards.[26] Medieval commentators began amplifying comments in early rules and often corroborated them with quotations from the Vulgate.[27] By the eleventh and twelfth centuries treatises or compilations written for religious and other clerics included detailed discussions of comportment.[28] For example, in a series of sermons on the Premonstratensian rule written in the 1170s or slightly earlier, Adam of Dryburgh (Adam Scotus) quoted and elaborated at length upon comments in the Rule of St. Augustine and St. Ambrose's *De officiis ministrorum*. A canon's manner, he explained, should display his spiritual gravity to all men and women, including those outside the cloister, and be free of uncontrolled movements of the kind described in Proverbs: "An evil man, a worthless man, goes about with his lips curled. He winks, taps his foot and speaks with his finger."[29] By contrast a canon's every movement should be controlled, a discipline that

23. Cf. St. Augustine in n. 21 above, and *De domo clericorum Sancti Gregorii in Civitate Zwollensi*, in Jacobus Traiecti alias de Voecht, *Narratio de inchoatione domus clericorum in Zwollis*, ed. M. Schoengen, Werken uitgegeven door het Historisch Genootschap, 3d series, 13 (Amsterdam: J. Müller, 1908), pp. 237-38.
24. E.g., ibid., p. 237. Jacobus de Voecht, ibid., pp. 76, 147-48, 152, etc., repeatedly refers to *mores*, which include (ibid., p. 185) *incessus, habitus,* and *verba*. Also Vincent of Beauvais, *Speculum historiale*, xxx.27, in idem, *Bibliotheca mundi*, 4 vols. (Douai: B. Bellere, 1624; photostatic reprint: Graz: Akademische Druck- und Verlaganstalt, 1964-65), 4:1244.
25. E.g., [Bernard Silvestris], *Formula*, 4, col. 1169B-C; [Thomas of Froidmont], *De modo*, ix.26, col. 1215B-C. Also St. Bernard, *Epistolae*, cxiii.2, 5 (*PL* 182:257A-B, 258D).
26. For eleventh- and twelfth-century treatises mentioned below, see C. W. Bynum, *Docere Verbo et Exemplo. An Aspect of Twelfth-Century Spirituality*, Harvard Theological Review. Harvard Theological Studies, 31 (Missoula, MT: Scholars Press, 1979).
27. E.g., Smaragdus of Saint-Mihiel, *Commentaria in Regulam Sancti Benedicti*, 7 (*PL* 102:826D-828A); Hildemar, *Expositio Regulae [Sancti Patris Benedicti]*, in R. Mittermüller and E. Schmidt, eds., *Vita et Regula SS. P. Benedicti una cum expositione Regulae a Hildemaro tradita*, 3 vols. (Regensburg: F. Pustet, 1880), 3:264-68; Hugh of St. Victor [?], *Expositio in Regulam Beati Augustini*, 6 (*PL* 176:897D-898D); Humbert of Romans, *Expositio regulae B. Augustini*, 81-86, in *Opera*, 1:248-68.
28. E.g., Gratian in n. 15 above; Philip of Harvengt (of Hainaut), *De institutione clericorum*, I.18 (*PL* 203:688A); Petrus de Honestis, *Regula clericorum*, i.2 (*PL* 163:708D, 709B-C); Bernard Aylier (Abbot of Monte Cassino), *Speculum monachorum* (Freiburg i. Breisgau: Herder, 1901), pp. 56-74 (i.7), citing Ecclus. 19:26-27 (29-30), Rom. 6:19, and St. Benedict, *Regula*, vii.60-61, p. 50, among other commonly cited passages.
29. Prov. 6:12-14, quoted by Adam of Dryburgh (Adam Scotus), *De ordine*, ii.11, col. 459C.

required he shed his former secular habits.[30] This transformation, this external conversion in comportment, as explained more fully by later religious, was the first step in a novice's training and was a precondition of spiritual conversion:

> At first a novice should tend to the body and ordering of the outer man, just as God first formed the body of Adam and afterwards "breathed the breath of life into his countenance" [Gen. 2:7]. And just as the body is first formed in a mother's womb and then infused with the rational soul, so too those who are new to the religious life must first tend to the training and discipline of the body *(informationi et disciplinae corporis)*. "Not what is spiritual is first, but what is animal; what is spiritual is second" [I Cor. 15:46]. The new soldier of Christ, for whom raging war impends, must have a well-trained mount, one that is not unresponsive, unbridled, temperamental or flawed in any other way, but instead one that obeys its rider, endures hardship and goading, and fears no tumult.[31]

The most detailed precepts of religious comportment were therefore spelled out in manuals for novices. For example, a discussion in a manual by the Benedictine John of Fruttuaria (†1050) derives, like much else in the work, from St. Ambrose's *De officiis ministrorum*.[32] His ideas may have inspired a novitiate manual popular among monks and canons following the Rule of St. Augustine, the *De institutione novitiorum*, perhaps composed before 1125 by the canon regular Hugh of St. Victor (†1142).[33] This was the first treatise (as far as known) devoted entirely to comportment, or *disciplina corporis* as it was later called. By adapting Christian conceptions of spiritual *disciplina*, Hugh systematically developed principles mentioned more briefly by Adam of Dryburgh, John of Fruttuaria and others: the necessity of control-

---

30. Ibid., ii.11-12, vi.2-9, x.1, cols. 459A-461A, 489A-494A, 534A-B, quoting, among other sources, St. Ambrose and St. Augustine on p. 111 above and Proverbs as in the text above. For Adam's comments on comportment, see Bynum, *Docere*, pp. 13-14, 26 n. 42, 55, 60-66, 74.

31. [Guillaume Peyraut (Guillelmus Peraldus)], *Speculum religiosorum sive de eruditione eorum libri sex* (misattributed to Humbert de Romans), with other works (Cologne: J. Kinckius, 1616), pp. 56-57 (II.i.2). Also ibid., p. 71 (II.ii.1). Peyraut's notion of *disciplina* here is taken from Hugh of St. Victor; see p. 113 below. Similarly [David of Augsburg], [*De exterioris et interioris hominis compositione*], i.3, in St. Bonaventura, *Opera omnia*, ed. A. C. Peltier, 15 vols. (Paris: L. Vives, 1864-71), 12:293, quoting I Cor. 15:46; Cajetan commenting on Aquinas, *Summ. theol.*, IIa IIae, qu. 161, art. 6, pp. 308-9. Cf. earlier authors, e.g., Hildemar, *Expositio Regulae [S.P. Benedicti]*, 7:264-65, who insist that *compositio exterioris hominis* procedes from *compositio interioris hominis*.

32. Cf. [John of Fruttuaria], *De ordine*, ii.3-9, cols. 562D-566C, and St. Ambrose, *De officiis*, I.xviii.67-xx.89, cols. 43B-50B. For the *De ordine*, see Bynum, *Docere*, pp. 99-101, 119-23.

33. For the attribution of the *De institutione novitiorum* to Hugh of St. Victor and John of Fruttuaria as a possible source, see Bynum, *Docere*, pp. 24 n. 20, 69 n. 80, 109 n. 11. For the *De institutione novitiorum*, see J.-C. Schmitt, *La raison des gestes*, pp. 173-205.

ling all bodily movement *(disciplina)*;[34] the correspondence of
spiritual and physical disposition;[35] control of the body as a means
of disciplining the spirit, and vice versa;[36] the appropriate use of
each part of the body;[37] and so on.

Why Hugh of St. Victor and others should have written down
these rules is not clear. Earlier religious must have had similar
rules but had not felt the need to commit them to parchment.
Perhaps the recent introduction of canonical orders was an
inspiration. Written rules substituted the presumably well-de-
fined but unwritten traditions developed over the centuries in
monastic orders. But whatever the reason, their composition
proved important. It permitted religious codes to spread beyond
the convent. Hugh of St. Victor's *De institutione novitiorum* was
particularly influential. It soon became a standard authority for
religious, being quoted extensively by thirteenth-century
mendicants, like the Franciscans Bernard of Besse[38] and John of
Wales,[39] and the Dominicans Humbert of Romans[40] and
Guillaume Peyraut.[41] And by the late Middle Ages these written
codes were common among not only new cenobitic orders like the
Brigittines[42] and the Devotio Moderna,[43] but also older monastic
orders like the Benedictines[44] and Carthusians.[45]

34. *De institutione novitiorum*, 10, cols. 933A-B, and passim.
35. E.g., ibid., 12, cols. 938B-D, 940D-941A, 942C-D, etc.
36. Ibid., 10, 12, cols. 935B-D, 941B. Similarly Aquinas and Cajetan in n. 14
above.
37. *De institutione novitiorum*, 12, cols. 941C-943B, and passim. Similarly St.
Augustine, *Enarratio in Psalmos*, Ps. 130, §6 (*PL* 37:1707).
38. [Bernard of Besse], *Speculum disciplinae*, pp. 583-622, where Hugh's work
is quoted freely. See especially, pp. 583, 585, 591-92, 600-608, 617-18.
39. John of Wales, *Ordinarium sive alphabetum vite religiose*, i.12, iii.6-7, 11 in
idem, *Summa de regimine vite humane* (Venice: G. Arrivabene, 1496), fols.
285ra, 298rb-vb, 302va-vb, 303rb, etc.
40. E.g., Humbert of Romans, *Epistola*, 54, in *Opera*, 1:39; idem, *Expositio
regulae B. Augustini*, 81, 84, 85, in *Opera*, 1:248, 256-57, 259-60, quoting, with or
without acknowledgement, Hugh of St. Victor, *De institutione novitiorum*, 10,
11, 12, 18, cols. 935A, 936C-D, 938A, 941C-942A, 949D, respectively; Humbert of
Romans, *De officiis ordinis*, v.7, in *Opera*, 2:218-20.
41. [Peyraut], *De eruditione religiosorum*, pp. 54-138 (II.i-iii). Hugh of St.
Victor's ideas (misattributed to Richard of St. Victor) are also cited extensively in the Dominican compilation *Speculum morale*, I.iii.42, in Vincent of
Beauvais, *Bibliotheca*, 3:307D-309C.
42. See T. G. Ahldén, *Nonnenspiegel und Mönchsvorschriften. Mittelnieder-
deutsche Lebensregeln der Danziger Birgittinerkonvente*, Acta Universitatis
Gotoburgensis, 58 (Göteborg: Elanders Boktryckeri Aktiebolag, 1952), pp. 209-
13, 220-23, which is an adaptation of David of Augsburg's *De exterioris et
interioris hominis compositione*; *Le constitutioni overo dichiaratione sopra la regola
di Sancto Salvatore revelata a Sancta Brigida*: Firenze, Biblioteca Nazionale
Centrale, MS Conv. soppr. B III 1696, fols. 37r-77v (s.XV), at fols. 52v-56v.
43. M. Viller, "Le *Speculum monachorum* et la 'Dévotion moderne'," *Revue
d'ascétique et de mystique* 3 (1922): 45-56. The Devotio Moderna used a
shortened version of David's text up to *De exterioris et interioris hominis
compositione*, p. 301 (i.32), with variations, as printed in *PL* 184:1189A-1198D;
see Viller, loc. cit., p. 51 n. 5.
44. Bernard Aylier in n. 28 above.

II. Secular Adaptation of *Disciplina*

Medieval religious and clerics valued their comportment as a distinctive accomplishment. An anonymous Latin treatise called *Facetus*, written presumably by a cleric or monk, gives, among other things, advice on choosing a career as a cleric, soldier, merchant, lawyer or other. Only the cleric's manner is described in detail. It conforms to traditional monastic or clerical rules: he should be tamed *"sub disciplina,"* avoid fidgeting with his feet, walk with a dignified gait, and so on.[46] Others, like John of Wales, insisted that religious and lay comportment differed,[47] and medieval clerics regularly condemned actors, clowns and similar social misfits for their lewd and undisciplined gesticulation.[48] This distinctive manner corresponded to the clerics' or religious' special spiritual and temporal status. If, then, it were to be adopted in a modified form by laity, it should be adopted preeminently by the nobility, who similarly believed themselves distinct and had no wish to conform to demotic standards. Hence the Dominicans Vincent of Beauvais[49] and Guillaume Peyraut,[50] and the Augustinian Egidio Colonna,[51] quoted or paraphrased in their "mirrors for princes" monastic or clerical rules, particularly those based on the Scriptures, St. Ambrose's *De officiis ministrorum,* and Hugh of St. Victor's *De institutione novitiorum.* These first steps of monastic or clerical *disciplina corporis* into the lay world were matched in humbler tracts and poems. The seminal treatise was a second, quite distinct, treatise called *Facetus*, attributed in some manuscripts to a monastic author and composed sometime before 1192. This poem, and Latin derivatives, like the *Stans puer ad mensam*, sometimes attributed to Grosseteste, originated in "the monastery, the school, and the university." They drew precepts from the Bible, were used in clerical and monastic schools or houses, and were sources, rather than derivatives, of vernacular

---

45. See the copy of David of Augsburg's *De exterioris et interioris hominis compositione*, in Venezia, Biblioteca Nazionale Marciana, MS Lat. Cl. III 138 (2907), fols. 60r-73v (s. XV). On the last written folio of the MS, which is in the same hand throughout, two lines of verse read (79v): "Libelus iste Cartusiensium dicitur esse/ Prope papiam de gratia sancte marie."
46. A. Morel-Fatio, "Mélanges de littérature catalane. III. Le livre de courtoisie," *Romania* 15 (1886): 225.
47. See p. 122 below.
48. C. Casagrande and S. Vecchio, "Clercs et jongleurs dans la société médiévale (XIIe-XIIIe siècles)," *Annales E.S.C.* 34 (1979): 913-28, especially, pp. 916-17, 921-22.
49. Vincent of Beauvais, *De eruditione filiorum nobilium*, ed. A. Steiner, The Mediaeval Academy of America, Publication 32 (Cambridge, MA: The Mediaeval Academy of America, 1938), pp. 118-22, 132-33, 142 (ch. 31, 34, 36).
50. *De eruditione principum*, in Aquinas, *Opera omnia*, 25 vols. (Parma: P. Fiaccadorus, 1852-72), 16:418, 435-42 (iii.5, v.12-25).
51. Egidio Colonna, *Liber de regimine principum* (Venice: S. Bevilacqua, 1498), sigs. m1vb-m2ra (II.13). Cf. especially Hugh of St. Victor, *De institutione novitiorum*, cols. 941C-942A.

vulgarizations and doctrine that eventually reached medieval courts.[52]

Erasmus' *De civilitate morum puerilium* is commonly portrayed as developing from this genre[53] and as a treatise that owed its immediate popularity to its systematic and comprehensive exposition of precepts found in slighter works like the *Facetus*. However, both form and content of the *De civilitate* suggest that it derives directly from monastic and clerical precepts of *disciplina corporis*, rather than indirectly through poems like the *Facetus*. Unlike *Facetus* poems, but like the best-known novitiate manuals, the *De civilitate* is in prose. Unlike derivatives of the *Facetus* (though like the *Facetus* itself), the *De civilitate* covers more than table manners and, like manuals for novices, discusses gesture, control of the body, dress, customs on meeting, greeting and conversing with people, gait, leisure, and behavior at meals, in church and on retiring to bed and similar matters. Indeed Erasmus' comments often echo precepts in David of Augsburg's or Bernard of Besse's manuals for novices. The following is David of Augsburg's comment on gait:

> Your gait should be mature. Do not rush about thoughtlessly or needlessly. As you walk, you should not hold your body completely erect but slightly stooped, nor should you let your eyes rove here and there or wave your arms about. Nor should you in any other way walk with a disorderly gait like a layman. Instead, walk humbly and unaffectedly as if you were coming from devout prayer. When sitting do not lounge languidly to one side or stretch your legs right out, especially in company. For outer disorder of the body indicates an undevout mind.[54]

Erasmus comments similarly:

> Your gait should be neither mincing nor impetuous. The former is characteristic of the effeminate [cf. Cicero, *De fin.*, V.xii.35], the latter of madmen. Nor should you reel from side to side as you walk, a gait of which Quintilian [*Inst. orat.*, XI.iii.128] disapproves. A silly lurching gait we should leave to Swiss soldiers and to those who think that sporting feathers in their cap is very distinguished. (Even so I have seen bishops preening themselves with this carriage.) Fidgeting around with one's feet when seated is something that idiots do, just as wild gesticulation with the hands indicates an impaired mind.[55]

These and other similarities suggest that when writing the *De civilitate* Erasmus had in mind doctrine common in manuals for

---

52. M. T. Brentano, *Relationship of the Latin* Facetus *Literature to the Medieval English Courtesy Poems*, Humanistic Studies of the University of Kansas, 5 (Lawrence: The University of Kansas Press, 1936), especially pp. 2, 14-17, 21-22, 25, 49-51. See also Nicholls, *The Matter of Courtesy*, especially pp. 22-44.

53. E.g., Brentano, *Latin* Facetus *Literature*, pp. 23, 106; Elias, *History of Manners*, pp. 70-71, 79.

54. [David of Augsburg], [*De exterioris et interioris hominis compositione*], i.19-20, pp. 298-99.

55. Erasmus, *De civilitate*, i, in LB, 1:1036E-F.

novices, that he was adapting *disciplina corporis* for the laity. He would have been only too familiar with religious *disciplina corporis*, first from contacts with teachers of the Devotio Moderna at the school of St. Lebwin's at Deventer, secondly from his cenobitic education at the hostel of the Devotio Moderna at 's-Hertogenbosch, and finally from his training as a novice before becoming an Augustinian canon regular at Steyn.[56] Moreover, this interpretation of the *De civilitate*, if correct, conforms nicely with one of Erasmus' abiding aspirations. Like the *Enchiridion militis christiani* and other of his works, the *De civilitate* adapted monastic or clerical learning and ideals for the laity. And it is an interpretation that would also illustrate how ideas of comportment followed the dominant cultural development of the thirteenth to sixteenth centuries, namely, the transition from a culture and religion sustained predominantly by clerics and religious institutions to one more secular in organization, transmission and content.

In one important respect, however, Erasmus' treatise differs from its models. Monastic and clerical codes had based their precepts on the authority of the Scriptures, classical or ecclesiastical authors and, less conspicuously, reason.[57] In Erasmus' *De civilitate*, as in his *De pueris instituendis* published less than a year earlier, reason is the most prominent authority. Let us return to Erasmus' hedgehog, tuna fish and pig mentioned at the beginning of this paper. Do not wiggle your forehead like a hedgehog. Do not chomp food like a pig. And so on. A young boy, in other words, should not behave like an irrational animal. The precepts of the *De civilitate* rely on the Graeco-Roman and Christian notion that humankind's peculiar faculty is reason and, therefore, whatever evinces or promotes reason is by nature superior to that which does not. The grounds that Erasmus gives for other precepts confirm this. For instance, a gaping mouth, rolling eyes and similar gestures are characteristic of the insane, idiots and fools,[58] in other words, those who have forsaken reason. Burping every three words is characteristic of babies,[59] that is, those who have not reached the age of reason. Other gestures and actions were dismissed as inappropriate for an educated, rational, person. Peasants have uncombed hair. Peasants wipe their noses on their hats and clothes, and fishmongers on the arm or elbow. This

---

56. For comportment in the *Devotio moderna*, see *Consuetudines domus nostre,* xxxv (*De institucione noviciorum*), in A. Hyma, *The Christian Renaissance. A History of the "Devotio Moderna,"* 2d ed. (Hamden, CT: Archon Books, 1965), p. 462; *Consuetudines Fratrum Vitae Communis,* ed. W. Jappe Alberts, Rijksuniversiteit te Utrecht. Fontes minores Medii Aevi, 8 (Groningen: J. B. Wolters, 1959), p. 11; *Consuetudines domus nostre,* in Jacobus Traiecti, *Narratio,* p. 265.
57. For *disciplina* based on *ratio*, see, e.g., Hugh of St Victor, *De institutione novitiorum,* 12:938c (and see generally Schmitt, *La raison,* pp. 173-205), [Peyraut], *De eruditione religiosorum,* II.i.4, pp. 59-60 and *De eruditione principum,* v.14, p. 435.
58. *De civilitate,* i-v, LB 1:1033D, 1035A, B, 1040C, E, 1042C.
59. Ibid., i, LB 1:1035D.

might seem to be reading too much into a short book intended for young readers were it not that Erasmus cited natural reason as the guiding principle of all gesture and civility.[60] Moreover, Erasmus was adumbrating an approach that was to be fully articulated during the second half of the sixteenth and early seventeenth centuries. How this approach developed is the subject of the following section.

III. *RATIO* AND *DISCIPLINA*

Erasmus was a religious. But he was also the greatest humanist of his age, a man who believed wholeheartedly in the importance of the Graeco-Roman tradition. We might expect, then, the *De civilitate* to reflect this. But the *De civilitate* quotes remarkably few classical ideas and sources, fewer indeed than many medieval treatments.[61] Why did Erasmus deny classical authorities the more prominent place that we might expect? There are two reasons. First, no systematic account of classical comportment survived. Erasmus' work, like the *Facetus* (the second treatise of that name mentioned above) and its derivatives,[62] were conceived precisely to fill this gap in the classical canon. And second, what comments and ideas did survive were often ana-chronistic and inappropriate to contemporary needs.

Erasmus' approach was shared by many medieval and Renaissance authors. Take, for example, the fortunes of the rhetorical doctrine of *pronuntiatio*.[63] Quintilian and the pseudo-Ciceronian *Rhetorica ad Herennium*, to mention two influential classical sources, had divided rhetoric into five departments: *inventio* (the devising of subject matter), *dispositio* (the arrangement of subject matter), *elocutio* (style or embellishment of discourse), *memoria* (memory) and *pronuntiatio* (delivery, i.e., voice and gesture). Medieval and Renaissance authors were well acquainted with this scheme. Furthermore, they knew that *pronuntiatio* might, in principle, be easily converted into doctrine of comportment. Hence, they often retained or adapted the five-fold framework of rhetoric in both rhetorical and pedagogical[64] works. But although they retained the framework, medieval and Renais-

---

60. Ibid., i, LB 1:1036B. S. Ozment, *When Fathers Ruled. Family Life in Reformation Europe* (Cambridge, MA: Harvard University Press, 1983), pp. 132-44, makes this point. I came across Ozment's discussion after completing this paper and have not, therefore, been able to take proper advantage of it.
61. E.g. [Peyraut], *De eruditione religiosorum*, pp. 54-138 (II.i-iii), *De eruditione principum*, iii.5, v.11-25, pp. 418, 434-442.
62. According to an early commentary, the *Facetus* was written to supplement the *Catonis disticha*, a book of gnomic moral precepts dating from Imperial times; *Liber facetus*, with an anonymous commentary (Deventer: R. Pafraet, 1499), sig. a1v.
63. On late medieval and Renaissance authors on *pronuntiatio*, see Knox, "Ideas on Gesture," passim.
64. E.g., L. V. Rossi, *De docendi studendique modo, ac de claris puerorum moribus libellus...* (with works by other authors) (Basel: R. Winter, 1541), pp. 67-74.

sance authors discarded much, if not most, of the content of classical *pronuntiatio* and supplemented it with precepts of their own. This was the procedure followed in thirteenth-century poetics, like Geoffrey of Vinsauf's *Poetria nova*,[65] Otto de Lüneberg's *Compendium poetrie nove*[66] and John of Garland's *Parisiana poetria*.[67] Again, in late medieval treatises on rhetoric or *ars dictaminis*, or in manuals for canon lawyers, Geoffrey of Vinsauf[68] and Gratian[69] were as authoritative for *pronuntiatio* as the *Rhetorica ad Herennium*.[70] Some fifteenth- and sixteenth-century authors explicitly described classical delivery or aspects of it as inappropriate for contemporary oratory. For example, rhetorical treatises summarizing the lore of gesture in the *Rhetorica ad Herennium* qualified individual gestures with comments like *"secundum antiquos"* or *"sed istud ultimum non placet quibusdam modernis."*[71] Some Renaissance rhetoricians, such as Melanchthon, even eliminated *pronuntiatio* entirely. Not that Renaissance authors thought delivery unimportant. Often they quoted Demosthenes' comment that delivery was the first, second and third most important part of oratory. Rather, they were refusing to prescribe rules for a skill that they believed was best acquired by practical instruction and imitation. Some authors thought that delivery was an entirely natural ability that could not be acquired by instruction, whether practical or otherwise.[72]

In contrast, Christian sources remained prescriptive. Geoffrey of Vinsauf opened his discussion of gesture with a typically religious or clerical comment: *"et interiorem/ exterior sequitur motus."*[73] Again, in discussions of *pronuntiatio*, medieval preaching

---

65.   E. Gallo, *The* Poetria nova *and Its Sources in Early Rhetorical Doctrine*, with text and trans., De proprietatibus litterarum, Series maior, 10 (The Hague, Paris: Mouton, 1971), pp. 18, 124, lines 84-86, 2036-70.

66.   Otto de Lüneburg, *Compendium Poetrie Nove*, with a commentary: Munich, Bayerische Staatsbibliothek, MS clm 14958, fols. 13va-24vb, 44va-48va (a. 1450), at fol. 14ra.

67.   *The* Parisiana Poetria *of John of Garland*, ed. and trans. T. Lawler (New Haven: Yale Universitry Press, 1974), pp. 135, 261.

68.   [Vincentius Grüner], [*Conpendium rethorice sciencie*]: Munich, Bayerische Staatsbibliothek, MS clm 11799, fols. 8r-174r (a.1408), at fols. 90v-91r; Johannes de Ratisbona, [*Ars dictaminis*]: Munich, Bayerische Staatsbibliothek, MS clm 5683, fols. 104r-183v (s.XV), at fol. 132r; Henricus Hardekese de Montenaken, *Resolutio rethorice Tulii ad Herenium scripte*: Leipzig, Universitätsbibliothek, ms 1249, fols. 2r-23v (s.XV), at fol. 23v.

69.   Bonaguida de Aretio, *Summa*, p. 137, citing Gratian in n. 15 above and pseudo-Cicero, *Rhetorica ad Herennium*, I.ii.3: "Pronuntiatio...."

70.   Some rhetorical compendia, particularly Italian ones, followed the discussion of *pronuntiatio* in the *Rhetorica ad Herennium*; see Honofrius de Florentia, *Rhetorica*: Milan, Biblioteca Ambrosiana, MS B. 161 Sup., fols. 24r-50r ("edita anno 1372"), at fol. 50r.

71.   [An anonymous rhetorical treatise]: Munich, Bayerische Staats-bibliothek, MS clm 28643, fols. 80r-105r (s.XV), at fol. 100r.

72.   Knox, "Ideas on Gesture," pp. 108-10.

73.   *Poetria nova*, p. 124, lines 2050-51; and cf., e.g., Hugh of St. Victor, *De institutione novitiorum*, ch. 12, cols. 938B, 941A-B.

manuals cited the Rule of St. Augustine,[74] Hugh of St. Victor's *De institutione novitiorum*,[75] or the Scriptures[76] as their authorities. Even fifteenth- and sixteenth-century humanist treatises on education, for instance those of Enea Silvio Piccolomini,[77] Maffeo Vegio,[78] and Lucio Vitruvio Rossi,[79] adhered to Scriptural and monastic or clerical ideas of comportment, and sometimes at the expense of classical ones. Like thirteenth-century authors of "mirrors for princes," Vegio, Rossi and others were adapting for laity the most appropriate code then available, monastic or clerical *disciplina corporis*. For Vegio and Rossi, religious *disciplina* was a particularly accessible source, since both were Augustinian canons regular at the time of writing their works. They and other humanists were not, of course, shy of classical ideas. But neither had been, say, Gratian, John of Wales and Guillaume Peyraut, all of whom had incorporated classical sources into a framework of monastic or clerical ideals.[80] Indeed, many biblical, classical, and patristic sources cited by Renaissance humanists were common in earlier monastic or clerical discussions.[81]

In one important respect, however, Renaissance humanists did lay the foundations for something new.[82] Their fascination with Antiquity led them to scour Greek and Roman literature for references to comportment. By the end of the sixteenth century and beginning of the seventeenth, scholars were compiling entire works on how the ancients clapped their hands, ate at table, wore

74. Thomas Waleys in Th.-M. Charland, *Artes praedicandi*, Publications de l'Institut d'Études Médiévales d'Ottawa, 7 (Paris: J. Vrin; Ottawa: Institut d'Études Médiévales, 1936), p. 332.
75. Robertus de Basevorn in Charland, *Artes praedicandi*, p. 320 (cited by Schmitt, *La raison*, pp. 281-82).
76. Thomas de Chobham, *Summa de arte praedicandi*, ed. F. Morenzoni, Corpus Christianorum. Continuatio Mediaevalis, 82 (Turnhout: Brepols, 1988), pp. 301-3 (vii.2.5); [*Ars praedicandi*]: Munich, Bayerische Staatsbibliothek, MS clm 3590, fols. 93r-99r (s.XV), at fols. 93v-94r.
77. Cf. e.g., Peyraut on p. 113 above (and similarly idem, *De eruditione principum*, v.13, 14, pp. 435-36) and Piccolomini, *De liberorum educatione*, in E. Garin, ed., *Il pensiero pedagogico dello umanesimo* (Firenze: Giuntine, Sansoni, 1958), p. 204. Piccolomini's comments on gesture, ibid., pp. 208-10: "Cumque... omisit," despite their classical references, are, I believe, similarly monastic or clerical in inspiration.
78. *De educatione liberorum et eorum claris moribus libri sex*, bks. 4-6, ed. A. S. Sullivan, The Catholic University of America Studies in Medieval and Renaissance Latin, vol. 1, fasc. 2 (Washington, DC: The Catholic University of America Press, 1936), pp. 176-204.
79. *De docendi studendique modo*, pp. 67-74.
80. Cf., e.g., John of Wales in n. 86 below; Gratian and Trotti in n. 15 above, citing Sallust, *Catilina*, xv.5: "citus...inerat," [Peyraut], *De eruditione principum*, V.16, pp. 436-37.
81. E.g., Vegio, *De educatione*, v.3, pp. 175-77, 187-88 quotes from, e.g., St. Ambrose, *De officiis*, I.xviii.71-75, cols. 44C-45C, Ecclesiasticus in n. 11 above, Sallust in n. 80 above. Similarly Rossi, *De docendi studendique modo*, pp. 67-74, citing from St. Ambrose, *De officiis*, I.xviii.75, col. 45B-C: "Est etiam...correctio," Seneca in n. 86 below.
82. For the remaining comments in this section, see Knox, "Ideas on Gesture," pp. 109-36.

their toga, and similar minutiae of classical life. The same procedure was also explored for biblical Antiquity. In the hands of many humanists this was an antiquarian indulgence. The methodical collation of ancient sources required no other justification than that it revealed more about Antiquity. But other authors employed this approach more purposefully. For them the collation of classical and biblical sources was the equivalent of a modern-day anthropologist's field-research. By collating passages they believed that they could discover "archetypes." If an aspect of comportment proved consistent throughout Antiquity, they concluded that it must be universal to all humankind. And if universal, it must be natural. And if natural to the rational human, it must itself be rational. By contrast, other aspects, those that obviously differed from place to place and time to time, were conventional.

This recourse to reason was abetted by other developments. Most important was sixteenth-century obsession with "method," particularly Ramist method. All disciplines and sub-disciplines, including comportment, could supposedly be reduced to coherent logical schemes that proceeded from general principles to particulars through definition and dichotomy. For instance, one common distinction was precisely that between conventional and natural gestures. Some authors, for example, the Calvinist Johann Althusen, combined this Ramist method with the collation of Judeo-Christian and Graeco-Roman sources. He opened his work on comportment by explicitly invoking reason as the touchstone: "Civility may be defined as the art of employing appropriate behavior, or as the art of making behavior conform to propriety and right reason."[83]

IV. *DISCIPLINA* FOR THE LAITY

By calling these rules rational, Renaissance authors implied that they were applicable to all humankind, irrespective of individual circumstance. They were also following a pattern established in monastic or clerical codes, and notably those for novices, which deliberately ignored social and geographical distinctions. Again, Erasmus' *De civilitate* is representative. In his peroration he insisted that his precepts applied to all boys, all the more to *"plebeios, humiles, aut etiam rurestres"* in that *elegantia morum* would compensate for the lowly station that fortune had allotted them. Indeed, far from advertising court behavior, the *De civilitate* snipes at it.[84]

Did practice match these aspirations? Had good lay comportment by the sixteenth and early seventeenth centuries come to approximate formerly monastic or clerical standards? The honest answer must be that we shall never know. But there are at

83.   *Civilis conversationis libri duo*, ed. P. Althusius (Hanover: G. Antonius, 1611), p. 1.
84.   Erasmus, *De civilitate*, i, iv, vii, LB 1:1033B, C-D, 1038C, E, 1043B.

least indications that, imperfectly and unevenly, it had – or, more cautiously, that monastic or clerical rules had, in modified form, spread sufficiently for religious, clerics and laity to assume that previously monastic or clerical rules applied to laity as well as to religious and clerics. One way of testing this hypothesis might be to compare thirteenth- and sixteenth-century attitudes towards lay comportment. If sixteenth- and seventeenth-century lay norms had come to approximate monastic and clerical norms, we should expect contemporary religious and clerics, unlike their medieval predecessors, to liken their comportment to that of the laity. What evidence I have – incomplete but suggestive – indicates that this did happen. Medieval and late medieval religious and clerics saw their manner not as a model to be imitated by laity as a whole, but as roots that nourished lay discipline. Good *disciplina corporis* among laity depended on good *disciplina corporis* among the priesthood, but the two were distinct.[85] Again, a thirteenth-century author like the Franciscan John of Wales subscribed to the traditional notion that religious should be deliberate in gesture and dignified in gait. This restrained manner would, he added, distinguish religious from laity.[86] These monastic and clerical rules remained unchanged into the seventeenth century – but they were no longer distinctively religious or clerical. For rather than evince a distinctive status, this restrained manner was recommended to, say, secular priests of the Oratory of St. Philip Neri[87] so that they did not appear distinct from ordinary, morally upright laity in gesture, gait and speech.[88] Similarly, Jesuits and Jesuit pupils were required to conform to traditional monastic or clerical rules of comportment. Thereby they would be not only spiritually edifying,[89] like earlier clerics and religious, but also an example to be imitated by all.[90]

Certainly four related circumstances favoured diffusion of monastic or clerical rules and lay derivatives from the thirteenth to the sixteenth century. First, the spread of the paper book in the thirteenth century and the invention of movable-type printing in the fifteenth century spread and fixed codes that for the most part

---

85.   Anon., *Instructio virorum ecclesiasticorum* (Caen: M. Anger, [1520?]), fol. 13r.

86.   John of Wales, *Ordinarium*, fol. 303rb-va (iii.11): "Item debet esse gravitate morum et gestu maturus, ut sit diformis a secularibus: ...," quoting Rom. 12:2, Phil. 3:20, Hugh of St. Victor, *De institutione novitiorum*, 12, col. 943C: "Gestus hominis...severus," Ecclus. 19:26-27 (29-30), Seneca, *Epist.*, lii.12, (Teubner, p. 148): "Argumentum ...," Ps. 34:18 (35:18). See also Adam of Dryburg, *De ordine*, vi.2, col. 489C-D; David of Augsburg in n. 139 below; [Bernard of Besse], *Speculum disciplinae*, I.xxx.3, p. 611.

87.   M. Borrelli, *Le Costituzioni dell'Oratorio Napoletano* (Naples: La Congregazione dell'Oratorio, 1968), pp. 257, 230.

88.   *Constitutiones Congregationum Instituti Oratorii S. Philippi Nerii a Paolo V. per Breve 'Christifidelium' (24 feb. 1612) approbatae*, i.155-56, in *Institutum Oratorii S. Philippi Nerii. Constitutiones et statuta generalia* (Rome: [Institutum Oratorii S. Philippi Nerii?], 1962), p. 68.

89.   *MHSI* 71:525, 527, 528, 549; 92:12, 201, 210, 334; 107:228; 108:157, 266.

90.   *MHSI* 71:518-22; 92:70, 71, 125; 107:48, 300, 377-78.

had previously been transmitted locally and orally. The success of Erasmus' *De civilitate* is just one example of how printing facilitated the spread of these written codes. Second, the spread of lay literacy, particularly in Protestant Europe with its aspiration to universal literacy, gave laity unprecedented access to written manuals of comportment. Third, education of laity, whether rich or poor, included instruction in comportment, usually by clerics or according to monastic or clerical rules. Medieval and Renaissance nobility were commonly educated by clerics or monks.[91] Similarly, in the ascetic surroundings and discipline of his school, Casa Giocosa, deliberately situated far from the court,[92] Vittorino da Feltre monitored his pupils' every movement and gesture meticulously. He would censure those who bit their lip, twisted their mouth, sniffled rather than blew their nose, fidgeted with their hands concealed beneath their clothing and wore gloves in winter. If he saw a pupil lolling about indecorously, he would become incensed and, drawing a circle around his feet, threaten punishment of he moved outside it before a given time.[93] Again, at a sixteenth-century *collège* in Auch, masters were instructed to correct *les incivilités* of pupils.[94] And so on.

These three factors converge in the fourth circumstance that promoted lay civility, namely, the Protestant and Catholic Reformation. In Protestant Europe good *disciplina* was seen as an indispensable concomitant of piety;[95] dissolute comportment, by contrast, betrayed spiritual, moral and political decay.[96] Comportment therefore became a very conspicuous part of Protestant education for girls,[97] as well as for boys, though with what success is debatable. It was thought no less important than scholastic achievement and promoted as a subject that appropriately followed religious instruction. A proposal dated 1557 for a school at Augsburg suggested that Erasmus' *De civilitate* should be taught after a catechism, since piety rightly leads onto *disciplina*.[98] School regulations, catechisms, pedagogical manuals, and other sources

91. *MGP* 41:150; H. T. Riley, ed., *Gesta abbatum monasterii Sancti Albani, a Thoma Walsingham...compilata*, 3 vols., Rerum Britannicarum Medii Aevi Scriptores, 28, 4 (London: Longmans, Green and Co., 1867-69), 1:397. David D'Avray kindly supplied this reference.
92. For Vittorino's almost monastic pedagogical ideals, see R. C. Trexler, "Ritual in Florence: Adolescence and Salvation in the Renaissance," in *The Pursuit of Holiness in Late Medieval and Renaissance Religion*, ed. C. Trinkaus and H. A. Oberman, Studies in Medieval and Reformation Thought, 10 (Leiden: Brill, 1974), pp. 200-264, at pp. 239-44.
93. Platina, *De vita Victorini Feltrensis*, in Garin, *Pensiero*, p. 690.
94. P. Bénétrix, *Les Origines du Collège d'Auch (1540-1590)* (Paris: H. Champion, 1908), p. 84.
95. *MGP* 49:42.
96. J. Camerarius (the elder), Παραινέσεις sive admonitiones ad praecipuae familiae adolescentem quendam, in *Opuscula quaedam moralia*, by J. Camerarius and others, ed. J. Camerarius (the younger) (Frankfurt: heirs of A. Wechel, 1583), pp. 210-11.
97. *MGP* 38:307-15.
98. *MGP* 60:328 (Augsburg, a. 1557). Also ibid., p. 323.

instructed school teachers and parents to enforce good conduct.[99] Hence comportment was continuously monitored, for example, at mealtimes at some schools[100] and frequently taught in the classroom throughout the sixteenth and early seventeenth centuries. In the town of Braunschweig, according to a school curriculum dated 1535, Erasmus' *De civilitate* was read to all students from nine o'clock to ten o'clock on Thursdays.[101] Part of another such curriculum is shown in Figure 1.

The comportment required of the fledgling Protestant was emphatically not that of the court. It was underwritten by the Scriptures, classical authors, or reason. The young should walk upright, not leaning to the right or left. The Book of Proverbs was the authority: "For why," added Christoph Hegendorff (1500-40), "should I not form the habits of the young from Solomon rather than any other author?"[102] Just for good measure Hegendorff added a passage from Cicero's *De officiis* to the same effect.[103] Others, like Melanchthon, invoked reason. Good comportment was comprehensible to reason, the reason planted in humankind by God, and was therefore required of everyone.[104] As Protestant authors noticed, reason had also been the principle preferred by Erasmus. For example, Reinhard Lorich (†1556 or 1564) rewrote the *De civilitate* as a catechism, including Erasmus' comments on reason there. Schools in Protestant Germany must have rung regularly –or so I like to think – with the following question from the teacher and reply from his pupils: "Which elegant and becoming gestures of the body are acceptable? Not those that please fools and foppish courtiers, but those that conform to nature and reason."[105] For manners, therefore, the important

---

99. G. Strauss, *Luther's House of Learning. Indoctrination of the Young in the German Reformation* (Baltimore: The Johns Hopkins University Press, 1978), pp. 151-52, 207-8, 238-39, 369 n. 48.
100. *MGP* 49:167.
101. *MGP* 1:50. Similarly *MGP* 1:54, 158, 159; 42:407; 49:6, 341, 407.
102. *MGP* 22:406, citing Prov. 4:27.
103. *De officiis* I.xxxvi.131.
104. *MGP* 21:254: "Es ist zweierley frömkeit, davon geschrieben stehet, eine heist Göttlich, die andere weltlich. Weltliche frömkeit nennet Paulus zu den Colossern [Col. 2:8] Elementa mundi, der welt ordnung. Diese stehet yn eusserlicher zucht, erberkeit, geberden, sitten und breuchen. Und die vernunfft mag diese begreiffen, ia sie ist der vernunfft eingepflantzt von Got, wie dem baum eingepflantzt ist, das er diese odder andere frucht trag. Also ist dem menschen eingepflantzt dieser verstand, das er helt, man sol niemand beschedigen, man sol gemeynen fried erhalten, man sol zucht erzeygen fur yderman." Likewise S. Fröschel, *Catechismus, wie der in der Kirchen zu Witteberg nu viel jar, auch bey leben D. Martini Lutheri ist gepredigt worden* (Wittenberg: [printer unknown], 1559), sigs. B4v-B5r.
105. [R. Lorich], *Civilitas morum Erasmi, in succinctas quaestiones digesti*, in Erasmus, *Libellus de civilitate morum puerilium*, with works by other authors (Frankfurt: heirs of C. Egenolff, 1584), fol. 24v.

ANTEMERIDIANA III Claſsis STVDIA.

Hora	Die ☽ ♂ ☿	♃	♀	♄
6	Ediſcunt ſequentibus horis recitanda.	Diſcunt Argumenta componere.	Ediſcunt ſequentibus horis recitanda.	Ediſcunt ſequẽtibus horis recitanda.
7	Recitant Nomenclaturas latinas, & Grammaticæ quæſtiones audiunt	Interſunt ſacræ concioni,	Recitant memoriter Syntaxin.	Recitant Nomenclaturas & Syntaxin.
8	Audiunt Elegantias Fabricii.	Diſcunt argumenta componere	Græ. Nomenclatu. memoriter recitant, & diſcunt græca legere & ſcribere.	Audiunt Catechiſmum Lutheri latinum.
9	Hac hora audita eunt domum.		Recitant germanicum Lutheri Catechiſmum.	Eunt domum.

POMERIDIANA EIVSDEM STVDIA.

Hora	Die ☽ & ♂	☿	♃ & ♀	♄
12	Scribunt & ediſcunt Catonem	Habent ferias	Arithmeticam audiunt & ſcribunt.	
1	Catonem audiunt.		Audiunt fabulas AEſopi.	Audiunt latinum Euangelium.
2	Audiunt Civilitatem morum.		Vt die Lunæ.	Interſunt concioni.
3	Poſt veſpertinas preces dimittuntur domum.			

OECONOMIA SCHOLAE CREMS:

ANTEMERIDIANA II CLASSIS STVDIA

Hora	Die ☽ ♂ ☿	♃	♀	♄
6	Ediſcunt ſequentibus horis recitanda.	Emendantur argumenta.	Ediſcunt horis	ſequentibus recitanda.
7	Audiunt Gram: Philippi Melanch: majorem	Interſunt ſacræ concioni	Audiunt Syntaxin.	Audiunt Syntaxin.
8	Audiunt Epiſtolas ſelectas Ciceronis.	Continuatur emendatio.	Recitant græcas Nomenclat. Et primã part. gr. Gram. audiunt.	Audiunt græcum Lutheri Catechiſmum.
9	Audiunt Theologicam lectionem.	Continuatur emendatio.	Recitant Catechiſmum lat. & germanicum.	Theologicã audiunt lectionem.

POMERIDIANA EIVSDEM STVDIA.

Hora	Die ☽ & ♂	☿	♃ & ♀	♄
12	Audiunt Arithmeticam.	Habent ferias	Audiunt & exercent Muſicam	
1	Audiunt Bucolica Virgilii & Proſodiam		Audiunt Dialogos ſacros Caſtalionis.	Audiunt Euangelium Græcum.
2	Audiunt Civilitatem morum		Audiunt Civilitatem morum.	Interſunt Veſpertinæ concioni.
3	Poſt preces veſpertinas eunt domum.			

OECONOMIA SCHOLAE CREMS:

From: *Scholae Cremsensis in Austria descripta formula. Nunc demum in novorum paedagogorum gratiam, qui ad scholas aperiendas vel regendas vocantur, edita, a Johanne Matthaeo Smalcaldensi, Theologiae Doctore & Professore publico in celeberrima Vitebergensium Academia.* Wittenberg, 1581.

distinction for Protestants, as for Erasmus, was not between court and inferiors anxious to scale a social ladder. It was, instead, the distinction between humans and those lower down the chain of being, the irrational animals – very much more familiar companions of all Europeans in the sixteenth century than today – or those, like peasants, whose comportment differed little from that of the beasts with whom they lived.[106]

Since they were based on the Scriptures and reason, these rules applied to all Protestants indiscriminately. Hence works by Joachim Camerarius, especially his *Praecepta morum puerilium*, Otto Brunfels' *Disciplina et institutio puerorum* and, by far the most popular, Erasmus' *De civilitate,* were read alike by Protestant princes with private tutors[107] and by pupils in town or village schools.[108] The following is a complete list of teaching materials required at a school for poor and orphaned boys at Darmstadt in 1594:

> Hereto and for further promotion of such studies the following books should be prescribed in the school and be purchased for the students, namely:
>
> The ABC book
> Luther's *Catechismus*
> The Bible
> The *De civilitate morum [puerilium* by Erasmus]
> The Grobianus [by Dedekind, also on conduct]
> The *Cosmographia* [presumably Ptolemy's *Geography*]
> Arithmetic books and, as need arises, whatever else might be deemed necessary for the students and their courses
> *item* writing implements
> paper as necessary, quills and inks.[109]

Catholic Europe replied in kind. Here lay confraternities and the new religious orders may have been particularly instrumental in the spread of a uniform code of good comportment. Jesuit practice was probably a methodical application of what was happening more haphazardly elsewhere. Their rules applied indiscriminately to members of the order, novices, and students of all kinds, whether destined for the priesthood or not, of high or humble social station, and whether inside or outside the

---

106. H. Osius (Regensburg, a. 1567), in *MGP* 42:416.
107. For Camerarius', Brunfels', and Erasmus' works studied by Protestant princes, see respectively: *MGP* 52:55, 68; *MGP* 52:68; *MGP* 19:274, 328 (cf. pp. lvii-lviii), 334; 52:55, 68.
108. For Camerarius' *Praecepta morum* used in Protestant schools, see *MGP* 38:206, 240, 242, 439; 49:6; 60:249. For Brunfels' *Disciplina et institutio puerorum* in Protestant schools, see *MGP* 1:127, 166 (cf. p. 560), 175(?); 8:107, 120. (For Brunfels' work, see *MGP* 1:560; 22:194, 197-99, 217-19.) For Erasmus' *De civilitate* in Protestant schools, see this page above; and *MGP* 1:50, 54, 127, 158, 159, 162; 4:336-37; 8:157; 38:206, 240, 242, 287, 332, 335, 439; 41:318; 42:416; 49:6, 341, 371, 407; 60:35, 66, 128, 178, 249, 262, 263, 323, 328; etc.
109. *MGP* 33:208. Cf. ibid., p. 8 for this school regulation.

seminary, college or school.[110] All alike had to follow the same rules listed in the *Regulae modestiae* compiled by St. Ignatius and in many later Jesuit adaptations.[111] In content and even terminology these rules strongly resembled earlier monastic and clerical ones and adaptations like Erasmus' *De civilitate*.[112] The *regulae modestiae* issued in 1563 for poor students at a school in Vienna, which were taken almost verbatim from two rules for Jesuits, are an example.[113] Pupils should stand upright, but keep their head slightly bowed; not gesticulate or "speak" with gestures and nods when conversing with someone, walk at a composed pace, keep their hands and feet still at table, not keep looking around them at table or elsewhere, not drink with their mouth full, and so on. By observing these and other rules, pupils would ensure that their bodily motions would reveal the inner serenity of their souls.[114] The *regulae* were to be encouraged solicitously and enforced by fear and discipline, by punishment and reward, by shaming and praising, and, for good measure, group discussion.[115] Among Jesuits themselves the *regulae modestiae* were taught and monitored by other members reporting to the father superior in confidence or by a member of the order appointed for the purpose.[116] Novices were taught by the novice master[117] and students by a specially appointed *prefetto de costumi* from the order.[118] Lapses among students were to be reported by their companions and, according to some regulations, noted down by secretly designated *syndici*.[119] The last measure understandably caused ill-will among students, and modifications were sometimes proposed.[120] Nor did other measures prove wholly successful, to judge by Jesuits' complaints about their charges' conduct.[121] But one and all show how seriously Jesuits took civility.

These *regulae modestiae* were quite distinct from court manners. Writing of the Collegio Germanico shortly before or during 1570, Father Giuseppe Cortesono distinguished three types of *buoni costumi*, namely, *modestia, costumi politici* and *costumi cristiani*. The first to be learnt should be the *regulae modestiae*, which covered comportment and were required of all pupils, novices, and

110. *MHSI* 71:70, 71, 397, 477; 92:70, 71, 125, 201, 210, 334; 107:202, 228, 362, 383, 392, 495, 858, 859, 1031-33; 108:218.
111. *MHSI* 71:518-29; 107:300-309, 312-14, 355-56, 373-74, 415-16; *MGP* 2:424-31.
112. Also *MGP* 2:424, 426-27 (§1-14), 428-30, citing Ecclesiasticus and St. Augustine on pp. 110, 111 above; deriving precepts directly or indirectly from Hugh of St. Victor, *De institutione novitiorum*, 12, col. 941C-942A; and possibly also from Erasmus' *De civilitate*.
113. Cf. *MHSI* 107:300-301; and *MHSI* 71:520-21, 549.
114. *MHSI* 107:300-314.
115. *MHSI* 107:910, 915-17, 950.
116. *MHSI* 71:200-203, 476-77; 107:858.
117. *MHSI* 71:397.
118. *MHSI* 107:902, 910, 917, 941. Similarly ibid., pp. 859, 950.
119. *MHSI* 92:12, 22, 70, 71, 158; 107:333, 356-58, 809, 903, 910.
120. *MHSI* 92:22 n. 19. See also, more generally, e.g., *MHSI* 107:1015-25.
121. *MHSI* 107:823, 856, 859, 966-70, 1026.

members alike. For the young *modestia* was all the more essential for the control of emotions. Second to be learnt were "social customs, like certain outward gallantries of the kind that courtiers customarily use" *(costumi politici, come certe galanterie esteriori che sogliono usare gli corteggiani)*. These depended on social station and, unlike *modestia* and *costumi christiani*, were not essential accomplishments. If *costumi politici* could be taught, so much the better. But they were best learnt at court rather than from religious. Finally came *costumi christiani*, physical manifestations of obedience, patience and other Christian virtues, which similarly helped control emotions.[122] Like *modestia*, *costumi christiani* were required of all.[123] And these two, rather than courtly gallantries, were the standards that the Jesuits hoped students would spread on returning home. This was one of the grounds on which Father Michele Lauretano (1537-87), reporting on the Collegio Germanico in 1572, defended the education of not only those for whom the Collegio was originally intended, that is, the future ecclesiastics of Northern Europe, particularly Germany, but also those destined for positions of power and influence. These young men, who had to be at least fourteen years old on entering the college,[124] came from towns and cities all over Europe. Eventually they would return home and by their authority and example would reform behavior and preserve Catholic doctrine and piety.[125] The Collegio Germanico was, therefore, a true seminary, a seminary for all Christians, lay and religious alike:

> And the Collegio all the more deserves to be called a seminary in that it embraces persons from not one, two or three dioceses, but from every diocese. For boys come to the Collegio Germanico from every region of the Christendom of Europe as if to a universal seminary of good conduct in life, good doctrine and good comportment *(un seminario universale del buona vita, buona dottrina et buona creanza)*. I say "universal" because other seminaries provide only for those destined for ecclesiastical office. But the Collegio Germanico provides for the benefit of all walks of life, since of boys educated at the collegio some will fill positions in governments of their home cities and states, others will become fathers of families, gentlemen of princes, prelates or pursue still other professions.[126]

Both Protestants and Catholics, then, accommodated comportment as a prominent part of schooling. It was part of the education of the whole Christian, body as well as soul. This emphasis on formal schooling may sound odd. What was the contribution of parents and other adults with whom children

122. *Regulae modestiae* sometimes include rules covering control of emotions; e.g., *MHSI* 107:301.
123. *MHSI* 107:916-17. Cf. also Cortesono, ibid., pp. 876, 878-89. Also ibid., p. 948, on teaching "alcune creanze de nobili."
124. *MHSI* 107:936-38.
125. *MHSI* 107:995-96.
126. *MHSI* 107:995. Similarly ibid., pp. 935-38.

mixed? Were they putting up with children who did not go to school chomping like pigs, slurping like horses, wiggling their foreheads like hedgehogs, and doing all the other beastly things that Erasmus was telling children not to do? The evidence is too patchy to draw firm conclusions. But what evidence there is suggests that the contribution of parents was not deemed as important as that of schools. Teachers, predictably, lamented the comportment of children.[127] Again, according to regulations dated 1594, pupils at a Latin school in Protestant Speyer were to appear quite distinct in comportment from the ill-mannered and unruly children who did not attend the school.[128] And this interpretation, if accurate, does at least sit tolerably well with what Ariès described in his *Centuries of Childhood*. That is, first, that before the fifteenth or sixteenth century, the family was not, as today, the predominant influence in the formation of a child's sensibility. And second, that the beginnings of modern education, well under way by the sixteenth century, identified childhood as a distinct period, during which boys and girls had to be educated before making their way into the world at large. And so too for comportment, school bore more of the burden than did the family. Indeed, sixteenth-century sources say so explicitly. The *De civilitate* was taught in school specifically as a remedy for poor *disciplina domestica*.[129] Again, in a school regulation dated 1580 the head teacher of a Latin school in Rostock, Nathan Chytrus, harshly criticized what he described as a common opinion that teachers alone could teach elegant manners and a minimum scholastic proficiency. Parents too must play a part.[130]

Nor, indeed, could Elias quibble over this point. His model accommodated the conspicuous fact that children were being taught good manners by schoolteachers and that these schoolteachers were, as they had always been, clerics or religious, men or women of God of some kind.[131] But whereas Elias portrayed religious and clerics as passive disseminators of courtly norms, I would suggest, instead, that as might be expected, clerics and religious promoted rules rooted in their own traditions.

V. *Disciplina* and European Comportment

By the sixteenth or early seventeenth century Europeans identified this normative comportment as European. It was, or should be, they assumed, not only characteristic of all laity, irrespective of social circumstance, but also different from that of other peoples. This self-perception germinated as Europeans encountered supposedly primitive, distant peoples of whom they had

---

127. E.g. *MGP* 22:406-7.
128. *MGP* 49:395-98.
129. *MGP* 42:407.
130. *MGP* 38:379, 388-89. Similarly *MPG* 41:231, 304.
131. Elias, *History of Manners*, pp. 101-2.

previously known dimly, if at all,[132] or supposedly primitive peoples living within Europe, like the "wild Irish."[133] And it developed during the very same period, from the thirteenth to the sixteenth century, in which monastic and clerical *disciplina* was becoming laicized and diffused through European society. The "oneness" of European comportment took shape simultaneously with, but independently of, awareness of the "other."

Contact with four peoples proved formative: the Mongols, Canary Islanders, African Blacks and Amerindians. In the mid-thirteenth century mendicant emissaries to Tartary began bringing back reports of a bizarre Mongol world. "It felt just as if I had stepped into another world," wrote the Franciscan Willem van Ruysbroeck of his first encounter with Mongols three days out of Sudak in the Crimea.[134] Mongol comportment surprised as much as anything, since it differed greatly from that of mendicants. The Khan, for example, ordered Willem not to sit with his head bowed (i.e., in humility, as required of European religious),[135] possibly because, according to Mongol custom, this posture was ill-omened, especially if the jaw or chin was rested on the hand.[136] Other more disconcerting habits similarly violated mendicant rules. Willem singled out how the escorts on his journey to the Khan would defecate near him and chat to each other while they did so – a liberty expressly denied to contemporary Franciscans.[137] In eating, drinking and other habits, Mongols were deemed equally repellent. In his account of the first Franciscan mission from 1245 to 1247 Giovanni dal Pian del Carpine described how Mongols ate without table napkins and table cloths, wiped their hands on their greaves or on grass or the like, and would even eat mares' afterbirth, lice and mice. They would cut off a piece of food and offer it on the point of a knife to a companion, a large piece for those they esteemed, a small one for those they did not. Only rarely did they rinse dishes and other utensils, and then with meat broth that they poured back into the pot. They never washed their clothes.[138] Nor did Mongols walk with the dignified

---

132. I have found F. Fernández-Armesto, *Before Columbus. Exploration and Colonization from the Mediterranean to the Atlantic, 1229-1492* (Philadelphia: University of Pennsylvania Press, 1987), pp. 223-45, particularly helpful on medieval and Renaissance ethnology .

133. J. Muldoon, "The Indian as Irishman," *Essex Institute Historical Collections* 111 (1975): 267-89.

134. *Itinerarium*, i.14, in A. van den Wyngaert, ed., *Sinica franciscana*, 5 vols. (Florence: Quaracchi, 1929-54), 1:171.

135. Cf. pp. 111-12 above.

136. *Itinerarium*, xix.8, in Wyngaert, *Sinica franciscana*, 1:215.

137. *Itinerarium*, xiii.5, in Wyngaert, *Sinica franciscana*, 1:196. Cf. [Bernard of Besse], *Speculum disciplinae*, I.xxvi.1, p. 609: "ibi [i.e., in privatis] Religiosus cum summo silentio et operto profunde capite debet esse ...," etc.

138. *Ystoria Mongalorum*, iv.6-9, in Wyngaert, *Sinica franciscana*, 1:47-50. Some of Giovanni dal Pian del Carpine's comments were repeated by Vincent of Beauvais, *Bibliotheca mundi*, 4:1287 (*Speculum historiale*, xxxi.4-5). Similarly C. de Bridia, *Hystoria Tartarorum*, ed. A. Önnerfors, Kleine Texte für Vorlesungen und Übungen, 186 (Berlin: W. de Gruyter, 1967), p. 33 (ch. 54);

gait, the *gradus compositus*, required of European religious on the authority of Isaiah.[139]

Similar judgment was passed on the behavior of Canary Islanders, African Blacks and Amerindians from the fourteenth century onward by religious, clerics and literate, and perhaps illiterate, laity alike. A Swiss canon, Felix Hemmerlin (1389-1457/64) recorded what he had been led to believe was the first European encounter with the Canary Islanders. According to his source, the bishop of Tortosa, Oton de Moncada (†1473), a ship or ships of the Aragonese king had discovered five Canary Islands in 1370 when fleeing some pirates. As they approached the first island, the sailors saw the islanders, male and female, wrapped in untreated animal skins, yapping like small dogs at the strange apparition on the water and staring at each other like pigs. Their features were simian. The sailors – possibly not the most delicately mannered Europeans – found the islanders' customs bestial, particularly their eating habits.[140] African Blacks was deemed similarly bestial. Even a generally sympathetic observer of sub-Saharan Africa like the Venetian Alvise da Mosto (c.1429-83), who was impressed by the ceremony, hospitality and splendid retinue of a chief he called Bodumel, could speak only with contempt of what he considered the African Blacks' bestial eating habits.[141] Again, African Blacks were ridiculed in Spanish dances like the Guineo and Zarambeque, that parodied Blacks' supposedly violent and ridiculous gesticulation.[142] Finally, Amerindians were found similarly wanting. When five Tupi from around the mouth of the Santa Cruz in Brazil were entertained one night aboard Cabral's ships, they were provided "both with food and with a bed with mattresses and sheets to tame them better."[143] Even the most imperfect Christian might be a model of civilized conduct for Indians. To "tame and pacify"

Simon of Saint-Quentin, *Histoire des Tartares*, ed. J. Richard, Documents relatifs à l'histoire des Croisades, 8 (Paris: P. Geuthner, 1965), pp. 32, 40-41 (= Vincent of Beauvais, *Bibliotheca mundi*, pp. 1210, 1212, *Speculum historiale*, xxix.71, 78).

139. Simon of Saint-Quentin, *Histoire*, p. 31 (= Vincent of Beauvais, *Bibliotheca mundi*, p. 1210, *Speculum historiale*, xxix.71). Cf. Is. 3:16, [David of Augsburg, *De exterioris et interioris hominis compositione*], I.19, p. 299: "nec aliter more saecularium incomposito ingressu incedas, ..."

140. Felix Hemmerlin (Malleolus), *De nobilitate ac rusticitate dialogus*, with other works by the same author, (Strasbourg: J. Prüss, c. 1493/1500), fols. 105r-106r (ch. 28).

141. T. Gasparrini Leporace, ed., *Le navigazioni atlantiche del veneziano Alvise da Mosto*, Il nuovo Ramusio, 5 (Rome: Istituto Poligrafico dello Stato; Libreria dello Stato, 1966), pp. 46, 49-58 (*Hakluyt*[2] 80:32, 35-41).

142. E. Cotarelo y Mori, *Colección de Entremeses, Loas, Bailes, Jácaras y Mojigangas desde fines del siglo XVI á mediados del XVIII*, Nueva biblioteca de autores españoles, 17-18, 2 vols. (Madrid: Bailly-Bailliére, 1911), 1:ccl-ccli, cclxxi-cclxxiii.

143. Pero Vaz de Caminha, *La 'Carta do achamento' di Pero Vaz de Caminha*, ed. A. Unali (Milano: Istituto Editoriale Cisalpino-La Goliardica, 1984), pp. 112, 74-75 (*Hakluyt*[2] 81:30). Similarly Caminha, *Carta do achamento*, pp. 64, 73, 92, 108 (*Hakluyt*[2] 81:13, 28).

(*amãsar e apaceficar*) and spread the Christian faith among the supposedly timid but bestial Tupi Cabral left with them two convicts, who, as customary on early European voyages of exploration, had been pardoned on condition that they accompany his expedition.[144]   Only rare and uninfluential exceptions like Bernardino de Sahagún and Andrés de Olmos recognized that Amerindians had, in some cases at least, codes of civility rivaling, if not surpassing, that of Europeans.

To Europeans "primitive" comportment seemed not merely repulsive, obscene, or ridiculous. It was unnatural and betrayed imperfect rationality. The Portuguese chronicler Gomes Eanes de Zurara (c.1415-1473/74), for example, noted on the authority of an anonymous source that Black women of Guinea went naked apart from a burnous over their faces. He concluded that the Blacks of Guinea were irrational. They had only to follow the example of nature, which covered with hair those parts of the body that ought to be hidden.   And since such comportment was irrational and unnatural, it was also un-Christian. God had designed a diversity of customs, concluded Zurara in his discussion of Canary Islanders, and Christians should thank Him that they had been chosen to live according to His law rather than bestially like other peoples.[145]

This un-Christian, irrational conduct was interpreted in two ways. Either the benighted primitive was not a rational creature and could not, therefore, be converted to Christianity.   Or the primitive had not realized his or her rational potential.   If the latter, he or she might be saved. But the precondition was that the primitive – like a European novice or his lay equivalent – first learn Christian comportment. The primitive Amerindians, wrote the Jesuit José de Acosta, had to be taught, under duress if necessary, "first to be humans, and then to be Christians."[146] The seventeenth-century Puritan missionary John Eliot, the "Apostle to the Indians," thought similarly of the Indians in Massachusetts: "In this order they have bene taught, they must have visible civility, before they can rightly injoy visible sanctitie in ecclesiastical communion."[147]

This attitude derived from monastic and clerical doctrine of *disciplina corporis*, as some sources acknowledged. For example, the 1546 edition of the standard Franciscan catechism in Mexico

144. Caminha, *Carta do achamento,* pp. 68, 76, 100, 115 (*Hakluyt*[2] 81:19, 32). For the Tupi's supposedly bestial nature and further comments on taming them, see idem, *Carta do achamento,* pp. 70, 103-4 (*Hakluyt*[2] 81:22-23).
145. Zurara, *Crónica,* 76, 79, pp. 339, 351 (*Hakluyt*[1] 100:231-32, 239.) Similarly, e.g., of Amerindians, André Thevet, *Les singularitez de la France Antarctique,* ed. P. Gaffarel (Paris: Maisonneuve, 1878), pp. 134-35.
146. José de Acosta, *Historia natural y moral de las Indias,* ed. E. O'Gorman, 2d, rev. ed., Biblioteca americana. Serie de cronistas de Indias, 38 (Mexico: Fondo de Cultura Económica, 1962), p. 320.
147. In a letter of 19 July 1652, in W. Eames, ed., *John Eliot and the Indians, 1652-1657* (New York: Adams and Press, 1915), p. 7. See also ibid., pp. 21-22; Muldoon, "The Indian as Irishman," pp. 278-83.

included an appendix, probably compiled by the then bishop of Mexico, the Franciscan Juan de Zumárraga. As the colophon explains, the appendix illustrates elementary doctrine *"para los indios menos entendidos y mas rudos, y negros,"* and includes a section on the prerequisite for conversion, that is, religious *disciplina* as defined for novices, albeit tempered – the author added – for laity.[148] Hence, too, the insistent refrain that Canary Islanders, Amerindians and others had learned or must learn not only Christian faith but also *mores boni, policía, buenas costumbres.*[149] For example, Pope Alexander VI's bull, *Inter caetera,* demarcating Spanish and Portuguese zones of exploration, commended the Spanish crown to make every effort at converting the barbarous peoples that it was discovering both to the Catholic faith and to *boni mores.* It was an obligation that Queen Isabella, in a supplement to her *Testament,* claimed to have fulfilled. Phrases like *mores boni, policía, buenas costumbres* admittedly had many connotations for contemporaries, including Christian morality, customs appropriate to town dwelling, practice of "civilized" crafts and trades, and so on. But for religious, to whom the task of "civilizing" indigenous populations largely fell, these phrases must have recalled as well the monastic and clerical *disciplina corporis* that they knew so well from their own training as novices.

Conversely, sixteenth-century champions of Amerindians' rationality, like the Dominican Bartolomé de Las Casas in his *Apologética historia sumaria,* completed probably after 1551, argued that Amerindians' gesture, gait, manners, physique and physiognomy and similar bodily traits showed that they were rational, that they were not natural slaves and, therefore, that they already met the first condition of conversion to Christianity. Las Casas' argument derives, explicitly, from Christian doctrine of *disciplina corporis.* He opens with the passage from Ecclesiasticus quoted above, a standard authority in discussions of the matter:[150]

> And since Ecclesiasticus says, chapter xix [26-27 (29-30)]: "Ex visu cognoscitur vir, et ab occursu faciei cognoscitur sensatus: amictus corporis et risus dentium et ingressus hominis enunciant de illo" (A man, his wisdom and understanding, are revealed by his look, expression, gait and laugh), I say the truth, which many if not all those informed about these regions know, if they care to admit it, that both among children and adults, male and female, but particularly, among men, one sees and encounters such modesty and gentleness, such composure, decorum and decency, such rigorous control and maturity of bodily actions and movements, in their look, laugh, carriage of the head and bow of the

---

148. Anon., *Doctrina cristiana* (Mexico: J. Pablos for Fray J. Zumárraga, 1546), sigs. n2r, n3r.
149. E.g., sources quoted in C. Bayle, *España y la educación popular en América,* Instituto pedagógico F. A. E. Estudios e Investigaciones, 1 (Madrid: F.A.E., 1934), pp. 99, 105-6, 123, 155-56, 160, 170, 185.
150. See p. 110 above. The English translation in the quotation is from Las Casas' own Spanish translation.

forehead and eyes, in gait and especially in speech – out of sheer
reverence and humility they modulate their voice, so that if they
have a sonorous and authoritative voice they attenuate and
lower it when speaking with persons of authority or those to
whom they should show reverence – that it seems that they were
brought up according to the discipline *(disciplina)* and rules of the
finest religious. This is an indication that they have a properly
balanced constitution and also that they do not lack judgment
and sound reason in matters concerning natural principles.[151]

Monastic or clerical *disciplina* tempered for laity was,
therefore, the measure of Amerindian comportment. Moreover,
Las Casas did not doubt that it was a measure intelligible to lay
readers of the *Apologética historia sumaria*. Nor should he have,
given that it had become the standard expected of contemporary
Europeans by the sixteenth century. Las Casas was judging
Amerindian comportment by standards expected of contemporary
European laity. Other religious state what Las Casas implied. In
his chronicle of the Augustinians in New Spain from 1533 to 1592,
the Augustinian prior in Mexico, Juan de Grijalva, singled out the
Augustinian, Franciscan and Dominican accomplishment in
teaching Amerindians of the province of Chilapa not only the
essentials of Christian faith but also how to build towns and live
communally in them. He concluded triumphantly:

> One cannot exaggerate what the three orders have achieved in
> every respect in this kingdom, since not only does one owe to
> them the promulgation of spiritual doctrine but also that they
> taught the Indians moral and civil behavior, in short everything
> necessary for human life. For these people used to be so savage
> that they did not even know how to eat properly, how to cover
> themselves or converse with each other in at least a courteous
> and civil manner. But all this the three orders in this region
> have taught so thoroughly that it now compares favorably in
> religion and civility *(policía)* with the whole of Europe.[152]

‡

Thus familiarity with other peoples determined that monastic
and clerical comportment and lay derivatives became identified as
European. There is, I believe, a final twist to the story. For clerical
and monastic, that is, Christian *disciplina corporis* had flowered into
a code required of all Europeans at a critical moment. From the
Middle Ages to the thirteenth or fourteenth century the Latin
West identified itself mainly as Christian. Other cultures were
pagan or, in the case of Byzantium and Islam, schismatic or
heretical. But from the thirteenth to the sixteenth century this

151. See Bartolomé de Las Casas, *Apologética historia sumaria*, ed. E.
O'Gorman, 2 vols. (Mexico: Universidad Nacional Autónoma de México,
Instituto de Investigaciones Históricas, 1967), 1:180 (ii.34).
152. Juan de Grijalva, *Croníca de la Orden de S. Augustín en las prouincias de la
Nueua España en quatro edadas desde el año de 1533 hasta el de 1592* (Mexico: J.
Ruyz, 1624), fol. 15ra-rb (i.8).

spiritual, doctrinal and ecclesiastical identity was undermined by the Babylonian Captivity, the Great Schism and, most enduringly, the Protestant Reformation. As a focus of identity Christendom was, therefore, supplemented with the notion of Europe, a notion founded on secular common denominators, like technology, commercial expertise and practices, political structures and the visual image of Europe provided by new developments in cartography.[153]

Civility was a further and peculiarly appropriate common denominator for reinforcing this self-identity, perhaps more so than any other.[154] This should not be surprising. Civility was, after all, both "Christian" and "European." First, it was monastic and clerical by origin, but by the sixteenth century it had spread to sufficient laity for it no longer to appear exclusively monastic or clerical. Second, it was rooted in Christian doctrine and practices, but never entangled in doctrinal controversy. And finally, it was Christian or Judeo-Christian by origin and therefore indubitably correct. But by the sixteenth century its rationality and therefore applicability to all humankind was also demonstrable in the secular Graeco-Roman tradition shared by both Protestant and Catholic Europe.

153. D. Hay, *Europe. The Emergence of an Idea*, rev. ed. (Edinburgh, Edinburgh University Press, 1968). (Reference from Caroline Bynum.)
154. Cf. Elias, *History of Manners*, pp. 53, 55, on this point.

X

Alexander of Aphrodisias, Gianfrancesco Beati and the Problem of *Metaphysics* α*

JILL KRAYE

Book α of Aristotle's *Metaphysics* has troubled scholars since Alexander of Aphrodisias composed his commentary in the second century A.D. Doubts as to the authenticity of this unusually short book (less than four columns in the Bekker edition), whose numbering seems to classify it as an afterthought to the far more substantial Book A, must have been circulating even earlier: Alexander felt it necessary to argue that α was indeed written by Aristotle, on grounds of both style and content. He did, however, think that its extreme brevity indicated that it was a fragment rather than an entire book. Furthermore, he could not make up his mind whether α belonged in the *Metaphysics* at all. First, it was unclear if it interrupted the connection between A and B. Discussing the conclusion of A (993a24-28), where Aristotle says "let us return to enumerate the difficulties that might be raised on these same points; for perhaps we may get some help towards our later difficulties,"[1] Alexander first suggests that the difficulties mentioned here are the problems set out in B. But then he immediately adds that Aristotle's statement could refer equally to α, in which problems concerning causes and principles, the subject of A, are examined. He repeats this suggestion at the beginning of his comments on α , where he observes that the discussion of whether there is an infinite regress of causes and principles, which occurs in chapter 2 of α, might be what Aristotle was referring to at the end of A.[2]

* I would like to thank Martin Davies, Charles Lohr, John Monfasani and Philipp Rosemann for reading an earlier version of this paper and offering helpful suggestions.

1. All translations of Aristotle, unless otherwise indicated, are from *The Complete Works*, ed. J. Barnes, 2 vols. (Princeton: Princeton University Press, 1984); I have occasionally made slight modifications.

2. Alexander of Aphrodisias, *In Aristotelis Metaphysica Commentaria*, ed. M. Hayduck, Commentaria in Aristotelem Graeca, 23 vols. (Berlin: G. Reimer, 1891), 1:136.12-17 and 137.5-12. On Alexander's comments on α, see W. D. Ross' edition of Aristotle, Metaphysics, 2 vols. (Oxford: Oxford University Press, 1924), 1:xxiv-xxv and 213; W. H. Crilly, "The Role of *Alpha Minor* in

137

The end of α raised a further problem. There, after distinguishing the methods of mathematics and natural philosophy, Aristotle proceeds: "we must inquire first what nature is; for thus we shall also see what natural philosophy (φυσική) treats of." From this statement it appeared to Alexander that the book might, in reality, be a preface to a treatise on natural philosophy, since it is in that discipline, not metaphysics, that the meaning of nature is treated. What is more, B does *not* give the account of nature promised at the end of α, but rather raises the difficulties announced at the end of α. Therefore, B would seem to follow directly on A.[3]

At this point Alexander appears once again to change gear, now putting forward the notion, on the basis of the first chapter of α, which concerns the investigation of truth, that the fragmentary book is a preface to theoretical philosophy in general.[4] This position, however, is related to his previously stated view that α might be an introduction to natural philosophy; for in his comments on chapter 3, Alexander says that the statement about the need to inquire into nature and thereby learn what natural philosophy treats of, could, if taken in one way, imply that α is "a preface to all of theoretical philosophy, the first part of which in relation to us is natural philosophy." But, as before, Alexander is unwilling to make a definitive judgement on α. He adds that, interpreted in another way, the statement might mean that the person who has thus discovered what natural philosophy treats of will see that reasoning in metaphysics is different from that in natural philosophy. The implication then would be simply that it is necessary to have studied natural philosophy before beginning metaphysics.[5]

Alexander raises a final problem about α, one that gives more grounds for suspecting that it might not really belong where it now is. He maintains that the book actually concludes with clause "we shall also see what natural philosophy treats of;" the words that follow it: "and whether it belongs to one science or to more to investigate the causes and the principles of things" (995a18-20) he

---

Aristotle's Metaphysics: A Study in Aristotelian Methodology" (Ph.D. diss., University of Fribourg in Switzerland, 1962), pp. 6-7; G. Darms' edition of Averroes, *In Aristotelis librum II α Metaphysicorum commentarius* (Fribourg, Switzerland: Paulus Verlag, 1966), p. 9; and P. Moraux, "La Critique d'authenticité chez les commentateurs grecs d'Aristote," in *Mélanges Mansel*, 2 vols. (Ankara: Türk Tarih Kurumu Basimeví, 1974), 1:265-88 at 282-84. That α was unknown to Andronicus of Rhodes, who c.60 B.C. produced the first edition of Aristotle's works, is indicated by the fact that the catalog of Aristotelian writings that survives only in Arabic sources, but which derives from that of Andronicus, lists the *Metaphysics* in thirteen books; α was, however, known to Nicholas of Damascus, a contemporary of Augustus. See H. B. Gottschalk, "The Earliest Aristotelian Commentators," in *Aristotle Transformed: The Ancient Commentators and Their Influence*, ed. R. Sorabji (London: Duckworth, 1990), pp. 55-81, at 67.

3.   Alexander, *In Metaphysica*, pp. 137.20-138.6.
4.   Ibid., p. 138.9-12.
5.   Ibid., pp. 169.23-170.2.

regards as an interpolation inserted to establish a connection between the end of α and the first chapter of B (995b5-6), where we read: "The first problem concerns the subject that we discussed in our prefatory remarks. It is this – whether the investigation of causes belongs to one or to more sciences."[6]

Later Greek commentators advanced no further in resolving the problem of Book α. The fifth-century Neoplatonist Syrianus, in his commentary on *Metaphysics* B, M and N, did not discuss the authenticity or placing of α, but his references to the book indicate that he accepted it as genuine.[7] Asclepius, writing in the sixth century, did little more than rehearse Alexander's arguments. He asserted that the book was authentic but noted that others had been troubled by the reference to nature at the end of chapter 3 and by the fact that the difficulties announced at the end of A seemed to be found in B rather than α. Adopting a position as ambivalent as Alexander's, he argued that α could follow A, since it too dealt with first causes and principles; but suggested, on the other hand, that it might be a preface to the *Metaphysics* as a whole.[8] The commentary on the *Metaphysics* attributed to Philoponus, but now dated to the twelfth century or later, says that according to some, α was written by Pasicrates, the son of Bonaios of Rhodes, who was the brother of Eudemus.[9] This report is a garbled version of the scholion found in a tenth-century manuscript of the *Metaphysics*, Paris. gr. 1853 (E), which states that some believe the book to be by Pasicles of Rhodes, the son of Boethus, who was the brother of Eudemus, although Alexander thought it genuine. The placement of the note in the margin of E makes it unclear whether it refers to the end of A or the beginning of α. Although modern scholars have traditionally assumed it refers to α, a strong argument in favour of A is that Asclepius, whose commentary seems to be closely related to the scholia in E, says that A, and not α, was assigned to Pasicles.[10]

6.   Ibid., p. 174.25-7. See also Ross' ed. of *Metaphysics* (note 2 above), 1:xxiv and 221.
7.   Syrianus, *In Metaphysica commentaria*, ed. W. Kroll, Commentaria in Aristotelem Graeca, 6, 1 (Berlin: G. Reimer, 1902), pp. 1.5, 37.29 and 98.9. See also Ross' ed. of *Metaphysics* (note 2 above), 1:xxv.
8.   Asclepius, *In Aristotelis Metaphysicorum libros A-Z commentaria*, ed. M. Hayduck, Commentaria in Aristotelem Graeca, 6,2 (Berlin: G. Reimer, 1888), pp. 113-14. See also Crilly, "Role of *Alpha Minor*" (note 2 above), p. 7; Darms' ed. of Averroes (note 2 above), p. 9; and Moraux, "Critique d'authenticité" (note 2 above), p. 284.
9.   The passage, cited from MS Vat. Urb. gr. 49, fol. 16r, is quoted by G. Vuillemin-Diem, "Anmerkungen zum Pasikles-Bericht und zu Echtheitszweifeln am grösseren und kleineren Alpha in Handschriften und Kommentaren," in *Zweifelhaftes im Corpus Aristotelicum: Studien zu einigen Dubia*, ed. P. Moraux and J. Wiesner (Berlin and New York: W. de Gruyter, 1983), pp. 157-92 at 171. For the dating of the commentary, see S. Ebbesen, *Commentators and Commentaries on Aristotle's Sophistici elenchi*, 3 vols. (Leiden: E. J. Brill, 1981), 3:86-87.
10.   Asclepius, *In Metaphysicorum libros*, p. 4.20-2. According to Alexander, *In Metaphysica* (note 2 above), p. 196.19-28, A was regarded by many as spurious. See also Vuillemin-Diem, "Anmerkungen" (note 9 above).

According to Albertus Magnus, the Arabs too believed that A was not by Aristotle, but they attributed it to Theophrastus rather than Pasicles. It was because A was considered spurious, he explained, that it was lacking in the Arabic translation of the *Metaphysics*.[11] The Arabic version is, in fact, missing only the first half of A (980a22-987a6); and the most likely explanation for its absence is that it was lacking in the Greek *Vorlage* of the Arabic translator. Averroes in his commentary on the *Metaphysics* placed α at the beginning of the work, preceding the second half of A. This was presumably because he thought, like some of the Greek commentators, that the last sentence of A (993a24-28) was a reference to B; so, by placing α before, rather than after A, the continuity between A and B would not be disrupted.[12] Averroes was not worried by the statement about nature at the end of α, taking it simply to mean that it was necessary to distinguish natural things from those that formed the subject of metaphysics.[13]

For Albertus Magnus, on the other hand, this passage meant that before embarking on metaphysics, we must investigate nature, a task already accomplished in the *Physics*. Although he assumed the difficulties mentioned at the end of A (993a24-28) were those discussed in B, he did not query the placing of α between A and B. This is probably in some measure because, without access to Alexander, he had no reason to suspect the authenticity of the final clause of α (995a18-20), which firmly linked this book to B.[14] Thomas Aquinas, like his teacher Albertus, thought that the end of A referred to B, but he too accepted the authenticity and position of α, which in the Latin tradition went under the less suspicious name of Book II. As for the problematic conclusion of α, in Thomas's opinion it indicated how to determine the method suited to natural philosophy – a method Aristotle himself used in *Physics* II.[15] The scholastic tra-

---

11.   Albertus Magnus, *Opera quae hactenus haberi potuerunt*, 21 vols. (Lyon: C. Prost, 1651), 1:525 (Liber I Posteriorum, Tractatus II, Cap. I). See also F. Ravaisson, *Essai sur la Métaphysique d'Aristote*, 2 vols. (Paris: Imprimerie royale, 1837-46), 1:79; and Crilly, "Role of *Alpha Minor*" (note 2 above), pp. 8-9. Albertus' statement was later repeated by Gianfrancesco Pico della Mirandola, *Examen vanitatis doctrinae gentium* (1520), in *Opera omnia* (Basel: Sebastian Henricpetri, 1573; reprint Hildesheim: Georg Olms, 1969), p. 1031; and Pierre Gassendi, in his 1624 *Exercitationes paradoxicae adversus Aristoteleos*, ed. B. Rochot (Paris: J. Vrin, 1959), p. 99.

12.   See M. Bouyges' "Notice" in his edition of Averroes, *"Grand commentaire" de la Métaphysique*, 2d ed. (Beirut: Imprimerie Catholique, 1973), pp. cxlix-cl; and Darms' ed. of Averroes (note 2 above), pp. 12-13. Some Latin manuscripts preserved Averroes' ordering of the text; the *editio princeps* (Padua: Johannes Philippus Aurelianus et fratres, 1473) sticks to this order but adds the first half of A before α: see Bouyges, "Notice," pp. lxxiv and lxix-lxx.

13.   Darms' ed. of Averroes (note 2 above), p. 80. See also Crilly, "Role of *Alpha Minor*" (note 2 above), p. 9.

14.   Albertus Magnus, *Metaphysicae libri quinque priores*, ed. B. Geyer (Münster i. W: Aschendorff, 1960), pp. 104 (II.13), 90 (I.16) and 107 (III.2).

15.   Thomas Aquinas, *In Metaphysicam Aristotelis commentaria*, ed. M.-R. Cathala (Turin: M. E. Marietti, 1926), pp. 93 (I.272) and 114 (II.337). This interpretation was followed and expanded upon by the early fourteenth-

dition of *quaestiones* on the *Metaphysics*, which developed from the thirteenth to the early sixteenth century, concerned itself with interpreting the text of α as, and where, it stood rather than with debating its genuineness or correct location.[16] The same was true for more humanistic enterprises, such as the introduction to the *Metaphysics* written in dialog form by Jacques Lefèvre d'Étaples.[17]

The situation changed in 1527 when Alexander of Aphrodisias' commentary on the *Metaphysics* became generally available in the Latin translation of Juan Ginés de Sepúlveda.[18] Since the overwhelming majority of Western philosophers had little or no Greek and therefore could not consult the original – which did not appear in print until the nineteenth century – previous knowledge of Alexander's views on the *Metaphysics* had been limited to passages from his commentary on Book Λ quoted by Averroes.[19] In his dedicatory preface to Pope Clement VII, Sepúlveda stressed the significance of this new source for understanding one of Aristotle's most weighty and difficult treatises.[20]

---

century commentator Antonius Andreae, *Scriptum aureum super Metaphysicam Aristotelis* (Venice: Antonius de Strata, 1482), sig. d 2v.

16. See e.g,. *ad librum II*: Roger Bacon, *Questiones supra libros Prime philosophie Aristotelis (Metaphysica I, II, V-X)*, ed. R. Steele et al., in his *Opera hactenus inedita*, 16 fascs. (Oxford: Clarendon Press, 1930), fasc. 10; Joannes Duns Scotus, *Questiones subtilissime in Metaphysicam Aristotelis* (Venice: Octavianus Scotus, 1497); Jean Buridan, *In Metaphysicen Aristotelis quaestiones argutissimae* (Paris: Iodocus Badius Ascensius, 1518); Pierre d'Auvergne, *Quaestiones metaphysicae*, ed. E. Hocedez, in *Archives de philosophie* 9 (1932): 179-234; Jean de Jandun, *Acutissimae quaestiones in duodecim libros Metaphysicae* (Venice: Hieronymus Scotus, 1560); Nicolaus de Orbellis, *Compendiosa et optima expositio duodecim librorum Metaphysice Aristotelis secundum viam Scoti* (Bologna: Henricus de Harlem, 1485); Joannes Versor, *Questiones super Metaphysicam Aristotelis* (Toulouse: Johannes Parix, c.1479-82); Paulus Soncinas, *Quaestiones metaphysicales acutissimae* (Venice: Simon Papiensis dictus Bevilaqua, 1496).

17. J. Lefèvre d'Étaples, *Introductio in Metaphysicorum libros Aristotelis* (Paris: J. Higman, 1493), sigs. C 5r-7v.

18. Alexander of Aphrodisias, *Commentaria in duodecim Aristotelis libros De prima philosophia* (Rome: Marcellus Silber, 1527). The translation was reprinted in Paris in 1536 and in Venice in 1544, 1551 and 1561: see F. E. Cranz, "Alexander of Aphrodisias," in *Catalogus translationum et commentariorum* (Washington DC: The Catholic University of America Press, 1960-), 1:77-135 at 93-5. On Sepúlveda see C. Lohr, *Latin Aristotle Commentaries* (Florence: Olschki, 1988-), 2:419-20.

19. The Greek text was first published by H. Bonitz (Berlin: G. Reimer, 1847). For Averroes, see Aristotle, *Opera cum Averrois commentariis*, 9 vols., 3 suppl. (Venice: Giunta, 1562-74), 8:290-340; the passages quoting Alexander's commentary have been edited, translated and studied by J. Freudenthal and S. Fränkel, "Die durch Averroes erhaltenen Fragmente Alexanders zur Metaphysik des Aristoteles," *Abhandlungen der Königlichen Akademie der Wissenschaften zu Berlin* (Berlin, 1884).

20. Alexander, *Commentaria*, sig. a 3v. Sepúlveda believed the commentary to be entirely written by Alexander and attempted to refute those who thought it was at least partially the work of Michael of Ephesus. Modern scholars regard the first five books as authentic, but for the most part attribute Books E to N to Michael. The relationship between the Greek text of the commentary on Λ and the passages quoted by Averroes remains controversial: see P. Moraux,

Clement himself seems to have recognized the importance of the translation, for in a letter drafted by his Latin secretary, Jacopo Sadoleto, he granted a six-year papal licence for exclusive publication rights to Demetrius Ducas, who was responsible for having the translation printed at his own expense.[21]

The availability of Alexander's commentary made a dramatic difference to the interpretation of *Metaphysics* α. Renaissance scholars, unlike their medieval predecessors, had the testimony of an ancient authority on Aristotelian philosophy that the book was problematic. The change in attitude that this brought about can be clearly seen in the case of Agostino Nifo. His 1511 *Dilucidarium* presents a series of typically scholastic *disputationes* on the text, without a hint of uncertainty as to either the genuineness of the book or its relation to the *Metaphysics*.[22] But in his 1547 *Expositiones* he begins his account of α by stating that "there is considerable doubt concerning this book;" he then rehearses the various issues raised and positions taken by Alexander, clearly relying – although he knew Greek – on Sepúlveda's translation. He repeats Alexander's assertion that the book is genuine but fragmentary, then mentions his explanation of how α could be seen to follow from A's discussion of principles and causes. On the other hand, he notes Alexander's view that the reference to nature at the end of the book seemed to indicate a connection with natural philosophy rather than metaphysics and also made it appear unrelated to B, which presented the problems promised at the end of A. Finally, Nifo records Alexander's statement that α was a sort of preface to theoretical philosophy in general. It is this judgment that Nifo seems to favor, arguing that the discussion of truth in the first chapter was appropriate to all forms of theoretical philosophy.[23]

Another early appearance of Alexander's interpretation of α occurs in Conrad Gesner's *Bibliotheca universalis*, published in 1545. In a section entitled "In Metaphysicorum libros argumenta, praecipue secundum Alexandrum Aphrodiseum," Gesner gives a simplified paraphrase of Alexander's arguments for and against α's disruption of the A-B sequence and reports both the suggestion that it might belong to natural philosophy rather than metaphysics and the counter-suggestion that it was a preface to all theoretical philosophy.[24]

Alexandre d'Aphrodise: Exégéte de la noétique d'Aristote (Liège and Paris: E. Droz, 1942), pp. 14-19.

21. Alexander, *Commentaria*, sig. Z 5r. See also D. J. Geanakoplos, *Greek Scholars in Venice* (Cambridge: Harvard University Press, 1962), pp. 249-51.

22. A. Nifo, *Metaphysicarum disputationum dilucidarium* (Naples: Sigismundus Mayr, 1511), fols. 94v-117v. Nifo was aware that Alexander had written a commentary on the text (fol. 3v), but may have known it only through Averroes' references; he does not cite it at all in his discussion of α.

23. A. Nifo, *Expositiones in Aristotelis libros Metaphysices* (Venice: Hieronymus Scotus, 1547), pp. 103-4; see also p. 121.

24. C. Gesner, *Bibliotheca universalis, sive catalogus omnium scriptorum locupletissimus...*, 2 vols. (Zurich: C. Froschoverus, 1545), 1:90r.

Petrus Ramus began the discussion of α in his *Scholae Metaphysicae* (1566) by mentioning two of Alexander's views: that it was merely a fragment of a book and that its concluding passage gave it the appearance of a preface to natural philosophy. But Ramus himself thought, on the basis of their similar content, that α could be a part of A. Later on, discussing the end of α, Ramus wrote that although in some respects it had the flavor of natural philosophy, as Alexander had pointed out, it nevertheless belonged to metaphysics. To prove this, he used (even though he was aware that Alexander had regarded it as an interpolation) the final phrase in α, about whether it was the province of one science or more to investigate the causes and principles of things; this was in his opinion a metaphysical problem, one moreover that was amply discussed in the following books.[25]

More interesting is the case of Gianfrancesco Beati, who used Alexander's comments, or at any rate some of them, as the basis for a new theory of α. In 1543, Beati, a Dominican professor at the University of Padua, published a treatise in which he attempted to demonstrate that *Metaphysics* α was in reality the preface to *Physics* II.[26] While he claimed to have produced the arguments and proofs by which he made his case, he gave credit for the thesis itself to Cardinal Jacopo Sadoleto, the dedicatee of the treatise.[27] This may have been nothing more than a pro forma gesture towards a powerful patron. There are, however, reasons for taking it somewhat more seriously. First, Sadoleto did have some connection, albeit tenuous, with the publication of Sepúlveda's Latin translation of Alexander's *Metaphysics* commentary, for it was he who drafted the letter granting the work a papal copyright.[28] Second, Sadoleto, heavily involved in delicate and ultimately unsuccessful negotiations between the pope and emperor, took the time in May 1543 to write to Beati to thank him for the treatise. In this letter he says that it was on his advice that Beati had embarked on his examination of *Metaphysics* α and found, as Sadoleto had always believed, that it was actually the preface to *Physics* II.[29] Finally and most importantly, Sadoleto was

---

25. P. Ramus, *Scholarum metaphysicarum libri quatuordecim, in totidem Metaphysicos libros Aristotelis* (Frankfurt: Andreas Wechel, 1583), pp. 38 and 43.
26. G. F. Beati, *In librum secundum Metaphysicae interpretatio, in qua... ostenditur eum librum ad Metaphysicam omnino non pertinere, sed esse prooemium secundi libri De auscultatione physica* (Venice: Bernardinus Bindonius, 1543). The treatise was originally delivered as a lecture in Padua in 1542: see sig. l 3r. On Beati, see Lohr, *Aristotle Commentaries* (note 18 above), 2:36. Beati was at Padua from 1531 to 1543, when he moved to Pisa, where he continued to teach metaphysics with considerable success until his death in 1546: see A. Fabroni, *Historia Academiae Pisanae*, 3 vols. (Pisa: Cajetanus Mugnainius, 1791-95; reprinted Bologna: Forni, 1971), 2:128.
27. Beati, *Interpretatio*, sig. A 2r.
28. See p. 142 above.
29. The letter is printed (after Beati's letter to him) in *Interpretatio*, sig. A 2v. Sadoleto, who was famous for the elegance of his Latin style, praised Beati's Latinity as much as his erudition. On Sadoleto's curial activities in

a scholar in his own right, with a serious interest in philosophy, although he lacked any formal training in the subject.[30] As Eugene Rice has shown, one of Sadoleto's concerns in *De philosophia*, written in 1533 and published in 1538, was to differentiate between *sapientia*, the contemplation of divine and immutable things, and *scientia*, the knowledge of things subject to generation and change, in other words, to map the border between metaphysics and physics.[31] It is therefore not improbable that Sadoleto, having a hunch that α belonged to the *Physics*, rather than the *Metaphysics*, but lacking both the time and the technical competence to prove the point himself, would have asked a professional metaphysician, such as Beati, to fill in the outline that he had sketched.

Whoever first came up with the idea, it could not have been conceived without Alexander's commentary on the *Metaphysics*. Alexander did not, of course, argue that α was the preface to *Physics* II. But the various possibilities he canvassed were suggestive: that α was not a complete book; that it interrupted the sequence between *Metaphysics* A and B; and, finally, that it was a preface to natural philosophy, or to theoretical philosophy in general.[32] These issues were an essential preliminary to the formulation of Beati's theory. Yet while Beati refers to Alexander frequently, he presents a somewhat distorted version of his position on α: he states unequivocally that the Greek commentator regarded the book as a general preface to theoretical philosophy, neglecting to mention that Alexander also said that it might belong to natural philosophy.[33] The reasons for this convenient omission are obvious, since more credit would accrue to him (or to Sadoleto) for discovering a connection that had remained, as Beati claimed, entirely unnoticed since antiquity.[34] And the same motive will have led him to avoid any reference to the fact that in the *Metaphysics* commentary of Thomas Aquinas, which the Dominican Beati must have known, α was associated with *Physics* II.[35]

Beati begins by examining the first and second books of the *Physics* in order to establish how α fitted in between them. In

1543, see R. M. Douglas, *Jacopo Sadoleto 1477-1547: Humanist and Reformer* (Cambridge, MA: Harvard University Press, 1959), pp. 174-76.
30. He studied with Niccolò Leoniceno at the University of Ferrara – see D. Mugnai Carrara, "Profilo di Niccolò Leoniceno," *Interpres* 2 (1979): 169-212 at 188, n. 48 – but his primary interest as a student was Latin literature. See Douglas, *Sadoleto*, 5.
31. J. Sadoleto, *De laudibus philosophiae libri duo* (Lyon: S. Gryphius, 1538). See E. F. Rice, Jr., *The Renaissance Idea of Wisdom* (Cambridge, MA: Harvard University Press, 1958), pp. 78-85. As further evidence of Sadoleto's philosophical interests, see his Latin translation of the pseudo-Aristotelian *De mundo*, ed. W. L. Lorimer, rev. L. Minio-Paluello, Aristoteles Latinus, 11, 1-2 (Bruges and Paris: Descle de Brouwer, 1965), pp. xli-xlii, 83-99.
32. See pp. 137-38 above.
33. Beati, *Interpretatio*, sigs. A 4v-B 1r.
34. Ibid., sig. A 3r.
35. See pp. 140-41 above.

Physics I, he argues, Aristotle discussed natural principles according to the ancient tradition that did not distinguish between immutable things and things subject to change. Accordingly, when he began to set out a method of scientific investigation specific to natural things, that is, those subject to change, he had to put in another preface. Aristotle indicated as much at the end of *Physics* I (192b6), when he stated: "Let us now proceed, making a fresh start."[36] But, according to Beati, no new beginning was to be found in the opening of *Physics* II (192b9-10). It therefore seemed mutilated *(truncus)* without *Metaphysics* α – the fresh start referred to by Aristotle.[37]

Moving now to the *Metaphysics*, Beati argues, following one of Alexander's suggestions, that the beginning of B continued on directly from the end of A. This showed that α was an unwarranted interpolation between the two books, unnaturally dissolving the connection that Aristotle had made between them. He dismissed Alexander's other suggestion that the end of A might in fact refer to the discussion of causes and principles in chapter 2 of α by making a distinction between posing difficulties and presenting proofs. At the end of A, Aristotle had said that he was going to raise certain difficulties. This promise was fullfilled not in α, where it was definitely proved that there was not an infinite regression of causes, but rather in B, where various difficulties were set out without solution.[38]

In Beati's opinion, the demonstration that causes were not infinite in number or kind, far from connecting α to A, was an indication that α was the preface to *Physics* II. Establishing that there was only a limited number of causes served the epistemological purpose of reassuring the student of nature that even though natural things were subject to change (and were therefore not always true, as were immutable things), scientific knowledge of them could still be obtained.[39] Furthermore, Beati maintained that in this chapter Aristotle dealt with the cause of motion. This meant that, *pace* Averroes, the discussion did not belong to the more universal account of causation appropriate to metaphysics, but to the specific concerns of natural philosophy, since natural things were subject to motion and change.[40] Natural things were also material; and, as Aristotle explained in chapter 3 of α, the method of natural philosophy was determined by the fact that "all nature has matter" (995a17). Therefore, in α Aristotle did not treat the primary causes of immaterial things, which was the domain

36.   All quotations from the *Physics* are taken from the translation and commentary by W. Charleton (Oxford: Oxford University Press, 1985).
37.   Beati, *Interpretatio*, sigs. A 3r-4v.
38.   Ibid., sigs. A 3v and 4v.
39.   Ibid., sig. E 2r-v.
40.   Ibid., sig. E 4v. See Darms' ed. of Averroes (note 2 above), p. 63: "consideratio universalis in omnibus causis...est eius scientiae [i.e. Metaphysicae]. Et Aristoteles, quamvis utatur hic demonstrationibus scientiae naturalis, tamen inducit eas universalius; quia quanto universalior, tanto magis erit propria huic scientiae."

of metaphysics. Instead he focused on the causes of natural, material things, thus preparing the way for the more detailed account of causation in *Physics* II.[41]

While he had no shortage of arguments to prove his case, Beati's trump cards were the references to nature at the beginning and end of α. In the second sentence of α (993b1-2), Aristotle claimed that everyone says something true about "the nature of things" (περὶ τῆς φύσεως, *de natura*); as if, Beati maintained, he intended to introduce a discussion of natural philosophy.[42] And in the concluding sentence (995a17-19) Aristotle wrote: "we must first inquire what nature is; for thus we shall also see what natural philosophy treats of and whether it belongs to one science or more to investigate the causes and principles of things." Everything promised here, said Beati, was to be found in *Physics* II. At the very beginning of that book (192b21-23) we are told what nature is: "nature is a sort of cause or source of change and remaining unchanged in that to which it belongs."[43] And in chapter 7 (198a27-29) we are given the explanation that natural philosophy treats of things that are themselves changed in changing other things. Beati did not follow Alexander in regarding the final clause of α as an interpolation. Nor did he think it referred to the beginning of B, arguing instead that, despite the similarity of content, the *form* of the question in α was different from that in B. In α Aristotle predicted that when we had established what nature was, we would have the answer to our question; in B, however, as Beati had already shown, difficulties were raised but not resolved. The answer to the question in α was therefore not to be found in B but rather in *Physics* II (198a22-24), where Aristotle, having explored what nature was, determined that it belonged to the (one) science of natural philosophy to know all four causes. The conclusion was inescapable: α was concerned with natural philosophy, not metaphysics, and was in reality the preface to *Physics* II.[44]

It cannot be said that Beati's treatise had a major impact on the mid-sixteenth-century philosophical scene – the problem of α, like the book itself, was a minor one. His thesis did, however, win a few adherents. The first of these was Mario Nizolio, who welcomed it with open arms, as he welcomed any piece of evidence that allowed him to argue that Aristotle's works had not come down to us in the form in which they were written. In his *De veris principiis et vera ratione philosophandi contra pseudophilosophos*, published in 1553, Nizolio attempted to demonstrate that the true method of philosophy was that of orators, rather than that of

41. Beati, *Interpretatio*, sig. K 2r.
42. Ibid., sig. B 1v.
43. Ibid., sig. K 4v. Beati rejected the view that α might refer to the definition of nature given in *Metaphysics* Δ (1014b16-1015a19), on the grounds that, first, in Δ not only nature but all terms used in metaphysics are defined; and second, Δ does not follow directly after α, nor is nature the first term defined in that book.
44. Ibid., sigs. L 1v-3r.

dialecticians and metaphysicians. Just as Cicero, the orator *par excellence*, attracted Nizolio's adulation, so Aristotle, the arch-dialectician and arch-metaphysician, and hence the Pseudo-Philosopher, was his primary target of attack.[45] In order to weaken the position of Aristotle's latter-day followers, he maintained that the works they slavishly venerated not only contained false, obscure and vacuous doctrines, but were not even the treatises produced by Aristotle.[46] They were rather epitomes and compendia that Aristotle's son Nicomachus had put together with scissors and paste from the genuine works of his father, which no longer survived. Nizolio's main evidence came, naturally, from Cicero, who had written in *De finibus* 5.12 that the *Nicomachean Ethics*, although ascribed to Aristotle, were in fact by Nicomachus.[47] Since no one doubted that all Aristotle's books came from the same hand, on account of their similarity of content and their cross-references, by proving that the *Nicomachean Ethics* was put together by Nicomachus, Nizolio demonstrated to his own satisfaction that he was the compiler of the entire *corpus Aristotelicum*.[48] Nizolio's theory explained why some of the treatises were so badly organized. The verbatim repetition, for instance, of the fourth, fifth and sixth books of the *Eudemian Ethics* as the fifth, sixth and seventh books of the *Nicomachean Ethics* was an ineptitude unworthy of Aristotle but not beyond the incompetence of his son.[49]

A further example of Nicomachus' slapdash editing was his placing of α after *Metaphysics* A; whereas A dealt with metaphysical issues, α was concerned with natural philosophy, as the references to nature at the beginning and end of it indicated. It was clear from these phrases, Nizolio said, that α was the preface to *Physics* II, as Gianfrancesco Beati had demonstrated. Nizolio, like Beati, was amazed that such an egregious error had not been noticed before by the numerous Greek, Latin and Arabic com-

45. M. Nizolio, *De veris principiis*, ed. Q. Breen, 2 vols (Rome: Fratelli Bocca, 1956), 2:166-67. See also Q. Breen, "Marius Nizolius: Ciceronian Lexicographer and Philosopher," *Archiv für Reformationsgeschichte* 46 (1955): 69-87; M. Wesseler, *Die Einheit von Worte und Sache. Der Entwurf einer rhetorischen Philosophie bei Marius Nizolius* (Munich: W. Fink, 1974); and M. Ballestri, *Mario Nizolio 1488-1566* (Milan: Biblioteca Ambrosiana, 1985).
46. Nizolio first developed this line of argument in his *Antapologia pro M. Cicerone et oratoribus contra M. Antonium Maioragium* (Venice: Aldi filii, 1547/48), pp. 23-27, to which Maioragio replied in the thirteenth chapter of his *Reprehensionum libri duo contra Marium Nizolium* (Milan: F. Moschenius?, 1549), pp. 85-104; as proof that the *Metaphysics* was a genuine work of Aristotle, Maioragio mentions the "doctissima commentaria" of Alexander of Aphrodisias: ibid., p. 101.
47. Nizolio, *De veris principiis*, 2:167-68. This evidence was corroborated by Diogenes Laertius, who did not mention the *Nicomachean Ethics* in his supposedly comprehensive list of Aristotle's works (5.22-27) and who ascribed a statement about Eudoxus, found in *EN* X.2, to Nicomachus (8.88); and by the *Suda*, in which it was stated that Nicomachus "ἔγραψεν 'Ηθικῶν βιβλία." See *Suidae lexicon*, ed. A. Adler, 5 vols. (Leipzig: B. G. Teubner, 1928-38), 3:469.
48. Nizolio, *De veris principiis*, 2:174.
49. Ibid., p. 168.

mentators on the *Metaphysics*. With such ignorance and bad judgment on display, it came as no surprise that the Peripatetics considered metaphysics – a fatuous and childish discipline – to be a true science necessary for perfection of the intellect and understanding of the principles of other sciences.[50]

Beati's thesis was also adopted by the sixteenth-century Platonist Francesco Patrizi. Like Nizolio, he used it to undermine Aristotle's authority among contemporary philosophers by questioning the authenticity and integrity of works that circulated under his name.[51] Patrizi does not mention Beati, nor does he go into his arguments in any detail. It may well be that he learned of his views through Nizolio, whose work he certainly knew since he specifically rejects his theory about Nicomachus.[52] According to Patrizi, it was not Aristotle's son but his prize pupil Theophrastus who was responsible for the chaotic condition of many of the works, above all the *Metaphysics*.[53] Embroidering on the account presented by Strabo (13.1.54), he suggested that Aristotle had left the uncorrected text of this, as well as other treatises, to Theophrastus, who, being more concerned with his own reputation than that of his teacher, neither edited nor published them, bequeathing them untouched, along with the rest of Aristotle's library, to his own heir Neleus. If, on the other hand, Aristotle really did put the final touches to the *Metaphysics*, Patrizi claimed that it must have been corrupted by the bungling editorial efforts of the bibliophile Apellicon of Teos, who, much later, purchased Aristotle's books from Neleus' descendants.[54]

Whatever its cause, the confused organization of the *Metaphysics*, which had been noted in antiquity by Nicholas of Damascus and Plutarch,[55] manifested itself primarily in the mixture of disciplines contained in the book: A, B and K to N belonged to "first philosophy," "wisdom" or "theology," that is, the science concerned with the first principles and causes of being, such as God and other separate, unchangeable substances; Γ to I

50. Ibid., p. 171. See also Beati, *Interpretatio*, sig. A 3r.
51. For a bibliography of literature on Patrizi, see C. Vasoli, "'L'amorosa filosofia' di Francesco Patrizi e la dissoluzione del mito platonico dell'amore," *Rivista di storia della filosofia*, n.s. 3 (1988): 419-41 at 421 n. 3 and 441 n. 79.
52. F. Patrizi, *Discussionum peripateticarum tomi primi, libri XIII* (Venice: Dominicus de Franciscis, 1571), fol. 12v.
53. A similar theory has recently been put forward by J. Zürcher, *Aristoteles' Werk und Geist* (Paderborn: F. Schöningh, 1952); see also E. J. Schächer, *Ist das Corpus aristotelicum nach-aristotelisch? Jos. Zürchers Hypothese und ihre Beurteilung in der gelehrten Forschung* (Munich: Anton Pustet, 1963).
54. Patrizi, *Discussiones*, fol. 67v. On the report given by Strabo and other ancient authors on the fate of Aristotle's library, see P. Moraux, *Aristotelismus bei den Griechen*, 2 vols. (Berlin and New York: W. de Gruyter, 1973), 1:3-31; and H. B. Gottschalk, "Aristotelian Philosophy in the Roman World," in *Aufstieg und Niedergang der römischen Welt* (Berlin and New York: W. de Gruyter, 1987), 2: Principat, 36.2:1079-1174 at 1083-97.
55. Patrizi, *Discussiones*, fol. 67v. For Nicholas see Averroes' commentary on *Metaphysics* Λ, in Aristotle, *Opera cum Averrois commentariis* (note 19 above), 8:290; for Plutarch, see his *Life of Alexander* 7.5.

dealt with "philosophy," that is, the general science of being as such, which included all substances: natural, sensible and mathematical as well as separate;[56] and interspersed in Δ, Z, H, Θ and I were various chapters that contained material relevant to logic.[57] On top of all this there was the problem of α, which belonged to none of these three sciences. Alexander of Aphrodisias, according to Patrizi, had realized that this book was not part of the *Metaphysics.* Ignoring Alexander's equivocations, Patrizi repeated his argument that α interrupted the sequence of A to B. He also pointed out that although Aristotle proposed at the end of α to deal with nature, this subject was not treated in B. Patrizi therefore concluded that α did not belong to the *Metaphysics*, but was to be placed after *Physics* I.[58] And in his eight-fold classification of Aristotelian treatises, he assigned it to the category of natural philosophy, which begins with five books on principles: *Physics* I, "and that book that up till now was *Metaphysics* α," followed by *Physics* II to IV.[59] Although Patrizi, perhaps covering his tracks, said that α should be put after *Physics* I, rather than before *Physics* II, it is clear that he picked up this idea, whether directly or indirectly, from Beati.

Patrizi's views on the *Metaphysics* were challenged in 1584 by the physician Teodoro Angelucci. Fortified more by indignation than erudition, Angelucci took it upon himself to defend Aristotle against one of his most hostile and learned opponents.[60] He began by dismissing Patrizi's claim that it was not Aristotle who put the *Metaphysics* together in the form we have it. This notion, he said, was based solely on the obscurity of the work. But, according to the very passage of Plutarch that Patrizi had

56.   The Jesuit Benito Pereira proposed a similar division of metaphysics in his *De communibus omnium rerum naturalium principiis et affectionibus* (Rome: Franciscus Zanettus & Bartholomaeus Tosius, 1576; Paris: Michael Sonnius, 1579), p. 23: "Necesse est esse duas scientias distinctas inter se; unam, quae agat de transcendentibus et universalissimis rebus; alteram, quae de intelligentiis." See also C. H. Lohr, "Metaphysics," in *The Cambridge History of Renaissance Philosophy*, ed. C. B. Schmitt et al. (Cambridge: Cambridge University Press, 1988), pp. 537-638 at 606.
57.   Patrizi, *Discussiones*, fols. 15v and 66r-70v.
58.   Ibid., fols. 15v and 69r-v. Patrizi also used Alexander's testimony, quoted from Sepúlveda's translation, to show that the authenticity of A and Δ had been doubted by some Peripatetics: ibid., fol. 26r; see Alexander, *In Metaphysica commentaria* (note 2 above), pp. 196.19-28 and 344.1-4; and Alexander, *Commentaria* (note 18 above), sigs. l 2r and u 6v.
59.   Patrizi, *Discussiones*, fol. 66r: "is qui hactenus fuit A minus Metaphysicorum." On Patrizi's classification, see M. Muccillo, "La vita e le opere di Aristotele nelle 'Discussiones peripateticae' di Francesco Patrizi da Cherso," *Rinascimento*, 2d series, 21 (1981): 53-119 at 97-100; and A. Antonaci, *Ricerche sul neoplatonismo del Rinascimento: Francesco Patrizi da Cherso* (Bari: Editrice Salentina, 1984-), 1:207-25.
60.   On Angelucci, see G. Mazzuchelli, *Gli scrittori d'Italia*, 2 vols. (Brescia: Giambattista Bossini, 1753-63), 1:70-72; Lohr, *Aristotle Commentaries* (note 18 above), 2:15; F. Purnell, "Francesco Patrizi and the Critics of Hermes Trismegistus," *Journal of Medieval and Renaissance Studies* 6 (1976): 155-78 at 156-59; and Antonaci, *Patrizi* (note 59 above), 1:30 n. 40.

adduced, Aristotle himself predicted that those who were not already trained in the discipline would find the treatise obscure.[61] Having found an Aristotelian justification for the apparent disorganization of the text, Angelucci went on to make his main point: the *Metaphysics* was in reality a more expansive exposition of material that had been treated in a cursory and succinct way in the *Physics*. The title Μετὰ φυσικὰ did not mean, as was generally thought, "concerning those things that come after the *Physics*" – what could be more absurd than to name a treatise after the discipline that precedes it? Rather it meant "concerning those things that are in the *Physics*," because in it Aristotle dealt at length and more generally with everything he had previously mentioned in that book.[62] Aristotle had himself drawn attention to the connection between the two works: in *Metaphysics* A (983a33-b1), for instance, he went out of his way to indicate that causes had already been discussed in the *Physics*, which he would not have done had he regarded the two treatises as totally separate. Moreover, at the end of α (995a14-20), he explained the reason behind the order observed at the beginning of *Physics* II. He did this, according to Angelucci, because the *Metaphysics* followed in the tracks of the *Physics*. As for those recent interpreters who had used this passage in support of the view that α was a preface to *Physics* II, they had simply misunderstood it. Angelucci did not trouble to give arguments to disprove this theory since others – whom we will examine shortly – had already demonstrated that it was without foundation.[63]

Patrizi immediately fired back with a treatise in which he defended his own views and ridiculed those of Angelucci, in particular his notion that the *Metaphysics* was an elaborate reworking of material already presented in the *Physics*. The problem of α, never at the center of the dispute, now received even less attention, being mentioned only in passing among several reasons for doubting the authenticity of the *Metaphysics*. But quite casually Patrizi added a new piece of evidence: he said that according to Philoponus, as well as Alexander, α did not belong to the *Metaphysics*.[64] The year before, in 1583, Patrizi had published his Latin translation of the (Pseudo-) Philoponus commentary on the *Metaphysics*, in which, as we have seen, it was said that some

61. T. Angelucci, *Quod Metaphysica sint eadem quae Physica, nova...sententia* (Venice: Franciscus Zilettus, 1584), fol. 2v. For Patrizi's reference to Plutarch see note 55 above.
62. Ibid., fols. 12v-13r. For a typical statement of the traditional interpretation of the title, see A. Bucci, *In universam Aristotelis philosophiam praefatio* (Pavia: Haeredes Hieronymi Bartoli, 1592), p. 14: "non alia ratione [libri] Metaphysicorum nomine inscripti sunt, quam ut eos post naturalem philosophiam tractandos esse, vel ex ipsa nomenclatura intelligeremus."
63. Angelucci, *Quod Metaphysica*, fol. 50r-v. He does not name Beati or Nizolio in this context; he does, however, criticize Nizolio's attack on the uselessness of the *Metaphysics*: ibid., fol. 5v.
64. F. Patrizi, *Apologia contra calumnias Theodori Angelutii eiusque novae sententiae quod Metaphysica eadem sint quae Physica eversio* (Ferrara: D. Mamarellus, 1584), fol. 9v.

people attributed α to "Pasicrates," the nephew of Aristotle's student Eudemus.[65] This story was rather different from Alexander's, who regarded the book as genuinely Aristotelian, questioning only whether it was a part of the *Metaphysics*. But Patrizi, who never made it clear whether he thought α was spurious or merely misplaced, was in too much of a hurry to make such fine distinctions.

And so was Angelucci, who the next year counter-attacked with another treatise, in which he produced a sentence by sentence rebuttal of Patrizi's arguments. Had he taken the time to check his opponent's sources, he would have discovered that Alexander and Philoponus did not say the same thing about α. Instead, he chose to accept Patrizi's claim, which he interpreted as an assault on the authenticity rather than the placing of α, but to twist it to his own purposes: the fact that Alexander and Philoponus rejected only α meant, he said, that in their view the remaining books were genuine.[66] The debate had now reached such a low intellectual level that even the combative Patrizi lost interest. Nonetheless he allowed Francesco Muti, a disciple of Bernardino Telesio, to continue the battle on his behalf. Muti had little to offer except fierce loyalty to Patrizi, whose position on α he defended by turning Angelucci's argument on its head: the fact that Alexander and Philoponus rejected α as non-Aristotelian, far from guaranteeing the rest of the *Metaphysics*, called it all into doubt.[67]

It is unfortunate, for our purposes, that Angelucci felt it unnecessary to argue against the thesis that α was the preface to *Physics* II, regarding it as already disproved by others. To pursue the debate on this issue we must therefore turn to these others. Whom did Angelucci have in mind? A likely candidate is Antonio Bernardi, one of the less well-known philosophers from Mirandola.[68] He began his career with a work arguing that the *Categories* were part of metaphysics rather than logic and therefore

65. Ioannes Philoponus, *Breves sed apprime doctae et utiles expositiones in omnes XIIII Aristotelis libros eos qui vocantur Metaphysici*, trans. F. Patrizi (Ferrara: D. Mamarellus, 1583), fol. 7r. On this passage, see p. 139 above. On Patrizi's translation, see Ebbesen, *Commentators and Commentaries* (note 9 above), 3:86-87. Pedro Nuñez, in his 1594 commentary on the *Vita Aristotelis* (Helmstedt: Jacobus Mullerus, 1666), pp. 94-95, also noted the testimony of Philoponus and stated: "Quae si vera sententia sit, fuit...is [sc. Pasicrates] sapientissimus."
66. T. Angelucci, *Exercitationum cum Francisco Patritio liber primus, in quo de Metaphysicorum authore, appellatione et dispositione disputatur, et quod Metaphysica sint eadem quae Physica iterum asseritur* (Venice: Franciscus Zilettus, 1585), fol. 16v.
67. F. Muti, *Disceptationum libri V contra calumnias Theodori Angelutii in maximum philosophum Franciscum Patritium* (Ferrara: Vincentius Galduras, 1588), fol. 70r. On Muti see F. Fiorentino, *Bernardino Telesio*, 2 vols. (Florence: Le Monnier, 1872-74), 1:369-70; and E. Garin, *La cultura filosofica del Rinascimento italiano* (Florence: Sansoni, 1961), pp. 428 n. 1 and 433.
68. See the article on Bernardi by P. Zambelli in *Dizionario biografico degli italiani* (Rome: Istituto della Enciclopedia Italiana, 1960-), 9:148-51; and Lohr, *Aristotle Commentaries* (note 18 above), 2:41.

did not belong in the *Organon*.[69]   Through his powerful patron Cardinal Alessandro Farnese, the treatise was circulated among a number of prominent philosophers, whose views on it were solicited. Among those who responded was Gianfrancesco Beati, who was extremely critical of Bernardi's controversial thesis. In his reply, published in 1543 together with his treatise on *Metaphysics* α, Beati defended the traditional classification of the *Categories* as part of Aristotle's logical works with as much vehemence as he had attacked the traditional location of α in the *Metaphysics*.[70]   In 1545 Bernardi published his own treatise, along with responses to the philosophers who had criticized it, identifying all of them by name except Beati, whose critique was presumably sent anonymously.[71]

Apparently unaware that Beati had written against his theory about the *Categories*, Bernardi produced a detailed rebuttal of Beati's theory about *Metaphysics* α. He did this in his reply, not to Beati, but to Marcantonio Genua.   The latter had attacked Bernardi's contention that Aristotelian metaphysics and natural philosophy dealt with the same subject matter, the only difference between them being that metaphysics operated from a universal point of view, natural philosophy from a particular one. So, for Bernardi, both metaphysics and natural philosophy were concerned with nature; but in metaphysics nature was a universal principle of being as such, while in natural philosophy it was a specific principle of natural being.[72]   One of the strongest arguments in favor of this unconventional view was the reference to nature at the end of α, for it showed that Aristotle had considered nature relevant to the study not only of natural philosophy but also of metaphysics.[73]   Bernardi was therefore anxious to refute Alexander of Aphrodisias' claim that α might preface natural philosophy.   Against Alexander, he argued that α could not be a prelude to natural philosophy since the proof in chapter 2 that there was not an infinite regress of causation presupposed knowledge of the four causes, which were not discussed until *Physics* II.   Although, as Alexander had noted, the definition of nature promised in α did not occur in B, it was nonetheless to be found later on in the *Metaphysics*, having been unavoidably postponed – he does not explain why – until Δ (1014b16-1015a19).[74]

69.   There was a long-standing commentary tradition that associated the *Metaphysics* with the *Categories*: see Lohr, "Metaphysics," pp. 598-99.
70.   G. F. Beati, *Praedicamenta in veterem auxiliatricis disciplinae locum servata* (Venice: Bernardinus Bindonius, 1543).
71.   A. Bernardi, *Institutio in universam logicam.... In eandem commentarius.... Apologiae libri VIII* (Basel: J. Hervagius, 1545). In Book 8 of the *Apologia* (401-22) Bernardi replied to Beati's *Praedicamenta in veterem...locum servata*, referring to the author simply as "homo." The other books contain responses to Marcantonio Genua, Vincenzo Maggi, Giacomo Giacomelli and Ubaldino Bandinelli.
72.   Ibid., pp. 149 and 164.
73.   Ibid., p. 161.
74.   Bernardi may have borrowed this argument from Beati, who rejected it: see note 43 above.

As for Alexander's point that the end of A seemed to refer to B rather than α, Bernardi replied (using a suggestion made by Alexander himself) that the difficulties announced by Aristotle at the end of A were to do with causes, amongst which was the question of whether they were infinite in number – a clear reference to chapter 2 of α.[75]

Having dismissed Alexander, Bernardi now moved on to the theory, equally damaging to his eyes, that α was the preface to *Physics* II. Although the supporters of this theory are not identified, the arguments rejected by Bernardi are those that Beati had offered in his treatise two years earlier. For instance, Beati had asserted that although Aristotle said at the end of *Physics* I (192b6): "Let us now proceed, making a fresh start," no such thing occurred at the beginning of *Physics* II. Bernardi disagreed, arguing that the definition of nature found in the first chapter of *Physics* II (192b21-22) signalled the beginning of a new approach to natural philosophy, different from that presented in the previous book. To confirm the point he drew attention to a similar transition at the end of the first chapter of *Rhetoric* I (1355b23-25): "We must make as it were a fresh start, and before going further define what rhetoric is." Bernardi then disputed Beati's description of the opening of *Physics* II (192b9-10) as incomplete unless preceded by α. There was nothing missing from it, in Bernardi's view; rather, the division between those things "due to nature" and those due to "other causes" with which the book began was the necessary preliminary to the definition of nature that shortly followed. He also argued, recycling one of the points he had made against Alexander, that α could not be the preface to *Physics* II since it assumed that the reader was already informed about the four causes, which were not discussed until *Physics* II itself.[76]

Around fifteen years later Bernardi produced a massive work, ostensibly concerned with dueling, but actually treating a rag-bag of issues, many of them philosophical. One of these was his redefinition of Aristotle's three branches of theoretical philosophy – metaphysics, natural philosophy and mathematics – as merely parts of one universal science concerned with all reality.[77] In this new classification, the *Physics* did not come under the rubric of natural philosophy, as one might expect, but of metaphysics. For Bernardi now maintained, building on the ideas put forward in his earlier work, that since the *Physics* and *Metaphysics* dealt with the same subjects and presented the same demonstrations, there was no difference between them.[78] This entailed asserting once

75. Bernardi, *Institutio*, p. 151. For Alexander's views, see pp. 137-38 above.
76. Ibid., pp. 152-53. For Beati's views on these points, see pp. 144-46.
77. A. Bernardi, *Eversionis singularis certaminis libri XL* (Basel: Henricus Petri & Nicolaus Bryling, 1560?), pp. 272-73. For Aristotle's tripartite division of theoretical philosophy, see *Metaphysics* E.1. See also the critique of this theory by Pereira, *De communibus principiis* (note 56 above), pp. 26-29; and Lohr, "Metaphysics" (note 56 above), pp. 605-6.
78. Bernardi *Eversio*, pp. 296-97. This notion was also criticized by Pereira, *De communibus principiis* (note 56 above), pp. 90-91.

again that nature, amongst other things, was treated in metaphysics as well as natural philosophy; and in support of this claim he repeated word for word his attack on the attempts of Alexander and Beati to remove α from the *Metaphysics*.[79]

At this point another ancient Greek commentator on Aristotle re-enters our story, taking his place beside Alexander of Aphrodisias and Philoponus. In 1576 the philosopher Antonio Storella, having managed to get hold of a copy of Asclepius' *Metaphysics* commentary from a passing Cretan, published a Latin translation of the preface, which he had commisioned to serve as an introduction to Alexander's "headless" *(acephalus)* commentary.[80] Storella supplemented the translation with a series of annotations; and in the twenty-fourth of these, he listed four problems that had come up in relation to *Metaphysics* A and α. First, according to Asclepius, some thought that A was by Pasicles, not Aristotle; second, others believed that α was not genuine, as was shown by the fact that both Alexander and Asclepius had felt it necessary to refute this charge; third, Averroes put α before A; and, lastly, there were those who held that α was the preface to *Physics* II.[81] Storella thought the solution to all these problems was to be found in the closing lines of A (993a24-28). According to him, when Aristotle stated, "let us return to enumerate the difficulties that might be raised on these same points," he was referring, as Alexander and Asclepius had suggested, to the questions about causes discussed in α.[82] And when Aristotle continued, "for perhaps we may get some help towards our later difficulties," he meant that the questions dealt with in α would aid us in resolving future difficulties, that is, those in B and later books. Since on this interpretation the end of A referred to α, the latter could not precede the former, as Averroes had thought, but must follow it. Also, since A, α and B were now firmly linked together, the first two books could not be spurious, unless one was prepared to go the absurd length of also doubting the authenticity of the third. Finally, since α now clearly belonged in the opening sequence of the *Metaphysics*, it could not be the preface to *Physics* II.[83]

Asclepius provided Storella with another argument to prove this last point. A crucial piece of textual evidence for the preface theory was that the definition of nature that seemed to be promised in α was found not in B but in *Physics* II (192b22-24). Asclepius explained that the *Metaphysics* was in an extremely disorganized state because Aristotle had not completed it when he

79. Bernardi, *Eversio*, pp. 316-18.
80. Asclepius, *In Metaphysicam Aristotelis praefatio* (Naples: H. Salvianus, 1576), sig. A 2r. See also A. Antonaci, *Francesco Storella, filosofo salentino del Cinquecento* (Galatina: Editrice Salentina, 1966), pp. 195-98. The Greek text of Asclepius' commentary was not published until 1836.
81. Asclepius, *In Metaphysicam*, sig. B 4v. For the first point, see p. 139 above; the second, pp. 137 and 138; the third, p. 140; the fourth, pp. 143-45.
82. For Alexander and Asclepius, see pp. 137-38 and 139 above.
83. Asclepius, *In Metaphysicam*, sig. B 4v.

died.[84]   Since the author's death had caused such substantial lacunae elsewhere, was it surprising, asked Storella, that the final section of α, in which nature would have been defined, was also missing?[85]

Antonio Scaino was the next philosopher to engage in the small war of α. In his commentary on the *Metaphysics*, published in 1587, he opened his discussion of the book by declaring that it was surrounded by the greatest uncertainty – hardly an overstatement. To begin with, according to Philoponus, it was attributed by some to Pasicrates.   Alexander had defended its genuineness on stylistic and methodological grounds.   But he had had doubts as to whether the book belonged in the *Metaphysics* or was rather a preface either to natural philosophy or to theoretical philosophy in general.   Scaino, unlike most earlier writers, emphasized the fact that Alexander was in at least two minds about α.   Nonetheless, he concluded that the Greek commentator inclined more to the view that α was a preface to theoretical philosophy but regarded its content as essentially metaphysical.[86]

Scaino realized that others had drawn different inferences from Alexander's commentary.   The problems raised there had, he recognized, led Beati to think that α was the preface to *Physics* II.   In rehearsing the evidence adduced by Beati, Scaino pointed out (as Beati himself had failed to do) that Thomas Aquinas' interpretation of the concluding sentence of α supported his theory.[87]   But since Scaino himself believed that α belonged where it stood, he went on to produce a series of arguments designed to refute Beati's theory.   He claimed, for instance, that the opening statement of α (993α31-32): "the investigation of truth is in one way hard, in another easy," fitted very well with A, in which Aristotle had explored and evaluated the views of all earlier philosophers, thereby demonstrating in what ways the search for truth was hard and easy.   He also asserted that Aristotle's general discussion in chapter 3 of the sorts of lectures that please or displease different types of listeners – those trained in mathematics, for instance, having unreasonable expectations of accuracy when hearing talks in other fields – was appropriate only to metaphysics, since it alone had the responsibility of prescribing rules for other disciplines.[88]

Borrowing an argument without acknowledgement from Bernardi, Scaino claimed that the definition of nature at the

---

84.   Ibid., sig. A 4r; for the Greek text, see Asclepius, *In Metaphysicorum libros* (note 8 above), p. 4.4-16. What Asclepius, in fact, seems to be saying is that Eudemus, to whom the *Metaphysics* was sent, died before being able to revise it.
85.   Asclepius, *In Metaphysicam*, sig. B 4v.
86.   A. Scaino, *Paraphrasis in XIIII Aristotelis libros De prima philosophia, cum adnotationibus et quaestionibus in loca obscuriora* (Rome: Bartolomeo Grassi, 1587), p. 94. For Philoponus, see p. 139 above; for Alexander, pp. 137-38. On Scaino, see Lohr, *Aristotle Commentaries* (note 18 above), 2:406-7.
87.   Scaino, *Paraphrasis*, p. 94. For Thomas, see pp. 140-41 above.
88.   Ibid., pp. 94-95.

beginning of *Physics* II was the "fresh start" referred to at the end of *Physics* I.[89] He also adopted Alexander's suggestion that Aristotle might have referred to natural philosophy at the end of α in order to distinguish it from metaphysics. Scaino then applied this interpretation to the concluding clause of α, maintaining that on the basis of this distinction it would become clear "whether it belongs to one science, or to more, to investigate the causes and principles of things" (995a19-20), in other words, whether it belongs only to the science of metaphysics or to natural philosophy as well. Scaino did not mention that in Alexander's view this clause was an interpolation; no doubt because he wanted to avoid arousing any suspicion about the words that provided him with another proof that α was directly connected to the beginning of B (995b5-6), where the question was repeated. Scaino did take issue, however, with Alexander's statement that the brevity of α indicated it was merely a part or fragment of a book. The size of α proved nothing; there was, after all, no law that prescribed that a book had to be any particular length.[90]

Further justifications for keeping α in its place within the *Metaphysics* were presented two years later by Pedro Fonseca, a Jesuit philosopher from Portugal. Fonseca's idea was that α had been given its unusual number because the Greeks regarded it as a sort of appendix to A rather than a complete book.[91] He was, of course, aware of Alexander's doubts as to whether α should actually come between A and B. But he overcame this problem by arguing that, although the end of A referred directly to the beginning of B, it was not inappropriate for Aristotle to insert between them a brief digression on the means of investigating truth, such as α provided, since in A questions were treated *pro utraque parte* as a means of finding out the truth about various metaphysical issues. Furthermore, since many of the questions in B were concerned with first principles and causes, it was necessary before posing them to determine whether such first principles and causes really existed, or whether, on the other hand, there was an infinite regress of causation. This was precisely the subject to which the greater part of α was devoted.[92]

Apart from Alexander's qualms, Fonseca had also to confront the view of certain recent scholars, whom he identified in the margin as Sadoleto and Beati, that α was the preface to *Physics* II.[93] He disputed Beati's claim that *Physics* II, without α, was mutilated. In Fonseca's opinion quite the reverse was true: the book would in fact be monstrous *(portentosus)* if α were added to it. What is

89. Ibid., p. 95. Scaino does cite Bernardi's *Eversio*, but in another context: ibid., p. 96
90. Ibid., p. 96. For Alexander's views, see pp. 137-38 above.
91. P. Fonseca, *In libros Metaphysicorum Aristotelis*, 2 vols. (Rome: Giacomo Tornieri, 1577-89), 2:294; this argument is repeated almost verbatim by G. Du Val in his edition of Aristotle, *Opera*, 2 vols. (Paris: Typi Regii, 1619), 2:89.
92. Fonseca, *In libros Metaphysicorum*, 2:293-94. On Fonseca, see Lohr, *Aristotle Commentaries* (note 18 above), 2:150-51.
93. Fonseca, *In libros Metaphysicorum*, 2:293.

more, α presupposed knowledge of the four causes, but this topic was not treated until the third chapter of *Physics* II – an argument taken over directly from Bernardi.[94]

Bernardi, Storella, Scaino and Fonseca took a lively enough interest in the problem of α to search for ways of disproving the accounts presented by Alexander and Beati. But many sixteenth- and seventeenth-century commentators on the *Metaphysics* ignored the issue or were simply unaware that there was a problem with α.[95] Other scholars expressed their own opinions on the book, but did not involve themselves in controversies surrounding it. Felix Accorombonius, for example, merely stated parenthetically that in his view α was not metaphysical in character, without giving reasons for his belief.[96] The Spanish Jesuit Francisco Suárez, in a postscript to his *Disputationes metaphysicae*, first published in 1597, noted that there was much disagreement about α, but declined to go into it. Instead, he put forward his own view that α was a part of or addition to the preface to the *Metaphysics*. The evidence for this was that when, in B (995b4-5), Aristotle referred back to α (that is, to the concluding clause 995a19-20, athetized by Alexander but accepted as genuine by Suárez) he described it as his "prefatory remarks." Suárez explained that in A, Aristotle had identified metaphysics with the investigation of truth and had then shown how earlier philosophers had gone astray. Now, in α, as a sort of appendix to those preliminary observations, he returned to the difficulty of investigating truth and set out the methods and principles that were to be used.[97]

Although Suárez's postscript was conventional enough, the *Disputationes* themselves marked a turning point in the history of metaphysics. It was one of the first treatises – and by far the most influential – to rewrite the *Metaphysics* in the form of systematically arranged disputations based on the philosophical

---

94.   Ibid., p. 377; see also p. 378, where there is a marginal reference to Bernardi's *Eversio*. For Bernardi's use of this argument, see p. 152 above.
95.   See e.g. *ad librum II*: M. A. Zimara's annotations to Jean de Jandun, *Quaestiones* (note 16 above); Crisostomo Javelli, *Quaestiones in Aristotelis Metaphysices libros* (Lyon: C. Pesnot, 1576); J. B. Rubeus, *Commentaria et quaestiones in universam Aristotelis Metaphysicam* (Venice: Ioannes Guerilius, 1618); M. Aquarius, *Dilucidationes in XII. libros primae philosophiae* (Rome: Bartholomaeus Bonfadinus & Titus Dianus, 1584); F. Araujo, *Commentariorum in universam Aristotelis Metaphysicam tomus primus [-secundus]*, 2 vols. (Burgos and Salamanca: Ioannes Baptista Varesius, 1617); M. Zanardus, *Commentaria cum quaestionibus in duodecim libros Metaphysicae Aristotelis* (Cologne: A. Boëtzerus, 1622); P. Barbay, *Commentarius in Aristotelis Metaphysicam*, 3d ed. (Paris: Vidua G. Josse, 1680).
96.   F. Accorombonius, *Interpretatio obscuriorum locorum et sententiarum omnium operum Aristotelis...* (Rome: Sanctius et socii, 1590), p. 754.
97.   F. Suárez, *Metaphysicarum disputationum tomi duo* (Mainz: Balthasarus Lippius, 1605), 2:KKK 2v. On Suárez, see Lohr, *Aristotle Commentaries* (note 18 above), 2:441-45; and J.-F. Coutrine, "Suarez et la tradition aristotelicienne de la métaphysique," in *Aristotelismus und Renaissance*, ed. E. Kessler, C. H. Lohr and W. Sparn (Wiesbaden: O. Harrassowitz, 1988), pp. 101-26.

principles underlying the questions treated by Aristotle.⁹⁸ This new mode of studying metaphysics meant that α won even less attention than before. In a commentary that proceeded book by book through the treatise, there was at least some chance that the various difficulties connected with α would raise a few scholarly eyebrows. But when the contents of the *Metaphysics* were rearranged, sometimes in conjunction with material taken from the *Physics*, there was no longer any need to pay attention to the order of the books or their relationship to each other. The result was that in the numerous systematically organized treatises on metaphysics produced in the seventeenth century the problem of α was entirely neglected.⁹⁹

Nor did the philologists of the time show any interest in it, with the exception of Samuel Petit. Even he was not concerned specifically with α. What he wanted to do was to establish a new arrangement of all the books in the *Metaphysics*. It was his belief that Aristotle had written the various books over a long period and that the present order reflected not Aristotle's intentions but the misguided efforts of some later compiler(s). Attempting to reconstruct the correct organization of the work, Petit argued that since Δ and I were methodological tracts, they should come first.¹⁰⁰ These two introductory pieces were to be followed by α and Γ, which he regarded as in reality one book, dealing with the investigation of truth and scientific inquiry.¹⁰¹

Petit began his defense of his new theory about the placing of α by using the standard argument, deriving ultimately from Alexander, that it did not belong in its present position because it disturbed the otherwise smooth transition from A to B. Then, taking the mention of "prefatory remarks" in B (995b4-5) as a reference to α, he maintained that the combined book α and Γ was the preface to A and B, which together formed a two-book tract on principles.¹⁰² The proper sequence of books in the first half of the *Metaphysics* was thus: Δ and I (methodological introduction); α and Γ (prefatory remarks); A and B (treatise on principles).¹⁰³

98. See Lohr, "Metaphysics" (note 56 above), pp. 608-17.
99. On the treatises of J. and C. Martini, C. Scheibler, R. Goclenius, C. Timpler, B. Keckermann and J. H. Alsted, see Lohr, "Metaphysics" (note 56 above), pp. 628-38. See also C. Bartholinus, *Enchiridion metaphysicum* (London: Ioannes Billius, 1618); and J. Channevelle, *Metaphysica generalis iuxta principia Aristotelis*, 2 vols. (Paris: Vidua E. Martini, 1677).
100. S. Petit, *Miscellaneorum libri novem* (Paris: Carolus Morellus, 1630), sig. EEee 1v-2r. Petit identified both books with Aristotelian works listed by Diogenes Laertius: Δ with περὶ τῶν ποσαχῶς λεγομένων (5.23); and I with περὶ 'εναντίων (5.22). The first identification is now accepted, but not the second: see P. Moraux, *Les listes anciennes des ouvrages d'Aristote* (Louvain: Éditions universitaires de Louvain, 1951), pp. 52 and 73.
101. Petit, *Miscellanea*, sig. EEee 3v. He identified this unified book as περὶ 'επιστημῶν in Diogenes Laertius' list (5.22); see Moraux, *Listes anciennes*, p. 46.
102. Petit, *Miscellanea*, sigs. EEee 3v-4v. He thought A and B were the work περὶ 'αρχῆς mentioned by Diogenes (5.23); see Moraux, *Listes anciennes*, p. 83.
103. Petit, *Miscellanea*, sig. GGgg 2v; Petit's sequence continues: E, Z, H, Θ, M, N, Λ and K.

In the late seventeenth and eighteenth centuries, less attention was paid to problems associated with the Aristotelian corpus than had been in the past and would be in the future.[104] It is not surprising, then, that it was over 150 years before Petit's conclusions received serious consideration. The Göttingen scholar J. G. Buhle, writing in 1788, agreed with Petit that the *Metaphysics* had not been put together by Aristotle himself. He went much further, however, claiming that it was a miscellaneous collection of tracts, some spurious and others not concerned with metaphysics, amalgamated into one treatise by Aristotle's first editor, Andronicus of Rhodes.[105] Buhle also challenged Petit's judgments on individual books. Thus, while Petit had regarded A as the first book of a treatise on principles, Buhle considered it merely a fragment of such a work or, possibly, the beginning of a very late Greek commentary on the second and third chapters of *Physics* I.[106]

No more did Buhle accept Petit's idea that α was linked to Γ, for he found no connection whatever between the end of one book and the beginning of the other. A better idea, in his view, had been put forward by Patrizi, who had said (following Beati, whose treatise Buhle clearly did not know) that α should be placed between *Physics* I and II. But there was a problem with this theory as well. Towards the end of α (995a17-18) Aristotle said: "we must first inquire what nature is." Surely it was not possible that an extremely systematic and methodical writer, such as Aristotle, having already launched into a long discourse on natural philosophy in *Physics* I, would suddenly announce to the reader that it was *now* time to determine what the object of this discipline was. Even to suggest such an absurdity would be to desecrate the Philosopher's ashes. It was therefore necessary to modify the theory somewhat: α was a fragment of what had originally been the first book of the *Physics*, now lost, in which Aristotle had

---

104. See H. Reiner, "Die Entstehung der Lehre vom bibliothekarischen Ursprung des Namens Metaphysik," *Zeitschrift für philosophische Forschung* 9 (1955): 77-99 at 83. One exception is *De mundo*, which continued to generate controversy during this period: see my "Daniel Heinsius and the Author of *De mundo*," in *The Uses of Greek and Latin: Historical Essays*, ed. A. C. Dionisotti, A. Grafton and J. Kraye (London: Warburg Institute, 1988), pp. 171-97; and "Aristotle's God and the Authenticity of *De mundo*: An Early Modern Controversy," *Journal of the History of Philosophy* 28 (1990): 339-58.
105. J. G. Buhle, "Über die Aechtheit der Metaphysik des Aristoteles," *Bibliothek der alten Litteratur und Kunst*, 4 (1788): 1-42 at 41-42. Buhle repeated this theory in his influential article on Aristotle in J. S. Ersch and J. G. Gruber, *Allgemeine Encyclopädie der Wissenschaften und Künste*, 3 Sections (Leipzig: Johann Friedrich Gleditsch, 1818-89), 1.5:273-303 at 278-84. On Buhle, see J. S. Pütter and F. Saalfeld, *Versuch einer academischen Gelehrten-Geschichte von der Georg-Augustus Universität zu Göttingen*, 4 parts (Göttingen and Hannover: Wittwe Vandenhoek, 1765-1838), 2:193-94; 3:195-97; *Allgemeine Deutsche Biographie*, 56 vols. (Leipzig: Duncker und Humblot, 1875-1912), 3:509-10; and Reiner, "Die Entstehung" (note 104 above), pp. 84-86.
106. Buhle, "Über die Aechtheit," p. 29.

explained, as was appropriate at the outset of a work on natural philosophy, what nature was.[107]

With Buhle, this long story about a short book finally draws to a close. Not that the problem of α was solved or forgotten. On the contrary, it continued to be a bone of philosophical contention throughout the nineteenth century and has remained so in the twentieth. Although a computer has now been brought in to play the role of *deus ex machina*, the convoluted plot still seems far from a denouement.[108] But the development of modern, as opposed to early-modern, scholarship on α is another story.[109]

107. Buhle, "Über die Aechtheit," pp. 30-33. He was encouraged to put forward this thesis because he had learned from Patrizi, *Discussiones* (note 52 above), fol. 15v, that Justin Martyr had known nine books of the *Physics*, rather than the eight we now have; see Justin Martyr, *Aristotelis dogmatum confutatio*, in *Patrologia Graeca*, 6:1532: "'εκ τοῦ 'εννάτου λόγου"; the quotation which follows is, however, from *Physics* VIII (251b19-28).

108. See A. Kenny, "A Stylometric Comparison between Five Disputed Works and the Remainder of the Aristotelian Corpus," in *Zweifelhaftes im Corpus Aristotelicum* (note 9 above), pp. 345-66 at 366: "the overall picture of particle usage in Metaph. α appears to be quite different from that in other works." But the other articles on α in this volume do not support this conclusion: see O. Gigon, pp. 193-220, T. A. Szlezák, pp. 221-59, and E. Berti, pp. 260-94. These authors also tend to discount the once influential theory put forward by W. W. Jaeger, *Studien zur Entstehungsgeschichte der Metaphysik des Aristoteles* (Berlin: Weidmannsche Buchhandlung, 1912), pp. 114-18, and accepted by Ross (note 2 above), 1:xxv: viz., that α consists of fragmentary notes by Pasicles on Aristotle's introductory lecture for a course on natural philosophy.

109. For a survey of nineteenth- and twentieth-century views of α, see Crilly, "Role of *Alpha Minor*" (note 2 above), pp. 11-24; and Darms' ed. of Averroes (note 2 above), pp. 5-12. To trace briefly the *fortuna* of Beati's theory in modern times: it was criticized by Ravaisson, *Essai* (note 11 above), 1:87 n. 1, on the ground that it fitted only the final chapter of α; but an attempt to revive it was recently made by A. Jannone, "Il libro A ΕΛΑΤΤΟΝ della *Metaphysica* di Aristotele," in *Atti del XII Congresso internazionale di filosofia*, 12 vols. (Florence: Sansoni, 1958-61), 9:139-45.

XI

The Life of Canons
in Sixteenth-Century Castile

CONSTANCE JONES MATHERS

Canons were familiar figures in sixteenth-century Castile as they sang in the carved wooden choirstalls of the cathedrals during the seven canonical hours every day or as they walked about their city, distinguished by their dark robes and by their tonsures, for which the shaved spot on the head was required to be "as large as the lead seals on apostolic bulls."[1] Less visibly, they were the voting members of the cathedral chapter, which administered the cathedral. In Castile, they played no role in choosing the bishop.

The pages that follow will look at canons in Castile before the Council of Trent, which enacted some reforms directed at them in 1562-63. Imagining a young man whose parents wanted him to enter the church, we may suppose that he would have asked what prospects lay before him if he became a canon. What was the social background of his fellow canons? What income would he have? What duties would be required? What would his daily life be like? And how did a person obtain a position as a canon? To avoid becoming excessively abstract, we will assume that our prospective canon is from the city of Burgos, a prosperous wool-exporting city in northern Castile; but we will also compare its cathedral chapter with those of Avila, León, and Granada.

No two cathedral chapters were exactly alike, but Burgos' chapter was typical. There were forty-four canons. There were also eighteen "dignitaries" attached to the church in Burgos, namely, bishop, dean, precentor, treasurer, prior, six archdeacons, and seven secular abbots, who were the heads of chapters of canons in important churches of the diocese. Some of the dignitaries were canons at the same time. Many were honored with the title *don* and sat above the rest of the canons. Ranking below the canons were twenty *racioneros*, who shared the responsibility of participating in the choir but who had no votes in the cathedral chapter. (A *ración* was a "share" of the cathedral income, that is, a prebend.) In Burgos, the canons and *racioneros*

---

1. Nicolás López Martínez, "Don Luis de Acuña, el Cabildo de Burgos y la reforma (1456-1495)," *Burgense* 2 (1961): 259 (clothes, tonsure).

shared equally in the cathedral income. In addition, Burgos had twenty half-*racioneros*.[2]

Generally, a canonry was a dead end as a career, except when the appointment itself had been a sign of favor by the bishop or the pope. Many canons were therefore local men, who remained in the city where they had been born and where their parents, uncles and aunts, brothers and sisters, nieces, nephews, and cousins still lived. A list of thirty-seven dignitaries and canons who attended chapter meetings in Burgos on July 15 and 21, 1550 includes many locally prominent names, represented both in the merchant guild and on the city council, such as Castro, Quintanadueñas, Cuevas, Díaz de Arceo, Miranda, Salamanca, Torquemada, Pesquera, Mazuelo, Bocanegra, Astudillo, Santa María, Lerma, and (less prominent) Encinas and Carrión.[3] Assuming that our prospective canon was a son of the local elite, he could not only look forward to maintaining family ties but would also probably have some relatives who were fellow canons or dignitaries.

✦

Although a canonry was not likely to lead anywhere, it was a very lucrative dead end. In Burgos, the income of a canon, it has been said, "did not exceed 400 ducats" about 1539.[4] In spite of the phraseology, 400 ducats (150,000 maravedis) was an excellent income, the same as that of a judge in the royal law court at Valladolid and not much less than that of the highest royal official in Burgos, the *corregidor*, who made just under 500 ducats per year. A description of Burgos, written at the end of the sixteenth century, gives an even higher figure: "44 canonries at 500 ducats and 20 *raciones* at the same amount." The incomes of the dignitaries, not counting the bishop, were between 300 and 600 ducats, except for the five highest-paid dignitaries, whose incomes ranged from 1000 to 3000 ducats.[5]

2. "Figura de Burgos," *Boletín de la Institución Fernán González* 177 (1971): 710.
3. Nicolás López Martínez, "El estatuo de limpieza de sangre en la catedral de Burgos," *Hispania* 19 (1959): 73, 75. This list includes some outsiders like Rebenga, Blanquis, Trapaz, Castrillo, Abanza, and Gobantes. Occasionally they are recognizable as newcomers brought in by a new bishop. Otherwise, we may speculate as to whether they might tend to be from the elites of other cities, from families of country gentry, or from the lower echelons of society.
4. Manuel Martínez y Sanz, *Historia del Templo catedral de Burgos* (Burgos: Institución Fernán González, 1983), p. 61.
5. "Figura de Burgos," p. 710. A letter from Juan de Polanco in Rome to Dr. Gerónimo Gallo, on May 21, 1556, about a *ración* for which Dr. Gallo was suing Francisco Pesquera, advises Gallo, "Y quanto a los dineros de los fructos, creo sabrá V. md que non son la 6ª parte de los que se han hecho pagar por vía del fisco, que a lo menos creo serán 3000 [escudos]," which seems to mean that the revenue from the *ración* was 500 escudos, equivalent to 440 ducats. Juan Alonso de Polanco, *Polanci Complementa: Espistolae et Commentaria P. Joannis Alphonsi*

Most prospective canons were probably not aware that, while the duties of the position had remained much the same for centuries, there had been an evolution in the way that canons were paid, as the church tried first to attract canons by increasing their financial independence and then later tried to manipulate the canons financially into performing their duties more conscientiously.

In the early history of Spanish cathedrals, the canons lived a life in common with their bishop and with their fellow canons. However, in the twelfth century, the canons of Spanish cathedrals were freed from restrictions of a common life. In the first place, the finances of the bishops and the cathedral chapters were separated by the creation of the so-called "Episcopal Table" and the "Chapter Table," which were independent of each other. In the second place, the individual canons and *racioneros* were assigned a prebend *(prebenda)* consisting of the income from specific property, for life, thus gaining security and financial independence not only from the bishop but also from their fellow canons.[6]

In the early thirteenth century, more reforms were made to deal with problems that had become evident. Typically, as in the case of León, the number of prebends had been allowed to grow, reducing the average prebend to an inadequate level. Another abuse, associated all too frequently with lifetime tenure, was that the canons too often did not stay in residence or participate in the cathedral choir. It was Pope Honorius III who instituted various reforms at León in 1224.[7] In Burgos, Bishop Don Mauricio took the initiative about the same time. At mid-century, Cardinal Gil Torres, who was influential in the papacy of Innocent IV, helped to make these new reforms general in Spain.[8]

The first of the thirteenth-century reforms fixed the number of canons, *racioneros* and half-*racioneros*, which until then had been at the discretion of the bishop. "The number established [in the various constitutions of the thirteenth century] never varied thereafter in some cathedrals.... The members of the cathedral chapter made every effort not to raise the number of chapter members, thus receiving higher incomes themselves."[9]

The second reform of the thirteenth century was to establish only a base amount of income through property assigned to each position, and then to tie additional income to the individual's record of attendance at choir, with the goal of restoring the

de Polanco, Monumenta Historica Societatis Iesu (annus 23, fasc. 269, Madrid, 1916), 1:134.
6. Tomás Villacorta Rodríguez, *El Cabildo Catedral de León: Estudio histórico-jurídico, siglo XII-XIX* (León: Centro de Estudios e investigación "San Isidro," 1974), pp. 35, 38-40.
7. Ibid., pp. 45-46. Toledo, Salamanca, Avila, Calahorra, and Burgos were similarly reformed (p. 36).
8. Demetrio Mansilla, *Iglesia Castellano-Leonesa y Curia Romana en los tiempos del Rey San Fernando* (Madrid: Consejo Superior de Investigaciones Científicas, 1945), pp. 195-96.
9. Ibid., p. 198.

record of attendance at choir, with the goal of restoring the "dignity of the cult."[10] As will be seen later, there were several refinements made to create a complicated system under which those who were absent from choir without good reason or without permission lost income to which they otherwise would have been entitled.

The effects of this series of reforms were still evident in Burgos in the sixteenth century, even though the number of canons had grown from 30 to 44.[11] The most important effect was that the income of canons had come to consist of several parts: the prebend was presumably still the largest part, but the *horas* (hours) and the *aniversarios* (anniversaries), both being direct rewards for attendance at specific services, had become sizable components of a canon's income.

In the final analysis, the members of the cathedral chapter were supported financially by the income of the Chapter Table, which by the end of the fifteenth century was derived partly from urban real estate but mostly from a share of the tithes, known as *préstamos*.[12] The *préstamos* were a substantial portion of the tithes of the diocese, consisting of "a part or even the whole of the papal third of the tithe."[13] They had been divided evenly between chapter and bishop since the twelth century: the bishop collected the *préstamos* from the northern part of the diocese, and the chapter was entitled to those from the southern part, which included the area around the city.[14]

The basic source of income for canons was the prebend *(prebenda)*, which was known also as the *ración*, the *porción*, or the *gruesa*. It has not proved possible to show whether canons in Burgos in the sixteenth century received their prebends as shares from a common fund, perhaps distributed at the end of the year, or whether they were assigned specific *préstamos* for each position, yielding approximately the correct share of the total income of the Cathedral Table. Hilario Casado Alonso, who has studied the cathedral chapter's finances in the fifteenth century, states that, "The cathedral chapter of Burgos had distributed many of its *préstamos* by assignment among all of its members, so that, by the mere fact of becoming part of the chapter, one would begin to receive for life all these rights, provided that one resided in the diocese."[15] However, the entries in a levy made in 1566 on "all

10.   Villacorta, *El Cabildo Catedral de León*, p. 46.
11.   For the thirteenth century, see Mansilla, *Iglesia Castellano-Leonesa*, pp. 200, 201, 205.
12.   Hilario Casado Alonso, *La Propiedad Eclesiástica en la Ciudad de Burgos en el Siglo XV: el Cabildo catedralicio* (Valladolid: Universidad de Valladolid, 1980), pp. 76-79, 87 *(préstamos)*, 134, and 136 (urban real estate).
13.   Letter from Casado Alonso, February 1987.
14.   Casado Alonso, *La Propiedad Eclesiástica*, pp. 44-45.
15.   Letter from Casado Alonso, February 1987. See also Casado Alonso, *La Propiedad Eclesiástica*, p. 33: "A cada una de éstas hay asignadas una serie de préstamos e ingresos de disfrute individual durante la posesión de cada uno. Junto a esto llevan anejo el derecho al cobro de la parte correspondiente en el

the ecclesiastical revenues and fruits of the said church, city, and bishopric of Burgos" tend to suggest that only the dignitaries had *préstamos* assigned to their position.[16] If so, perhaps the method of distribution to canons was more like Avila's system, in which the amount of each share was calculated at the end of the year by taking the total income of the Cathedral Table, overwhelmingly *préstamos*, subtracting expenses as well as other payments to the members of the chapter, and then dividing the remainder (*residuo*) among those entitled to shares.[17]

The shares were allocated among the dignitaries, canons, *racioneros*, and sometimes the half-*racioneros* in standard proportions, which, however, were not the same in all cathedrals. For instance, in Avila, it can be deduced that the half-*racioneros* each received half a share, the *racioneros* a share, the canons two shares, the dignitaries three shares, and the dean four shares.[18] In León, however, the dignitaries had no share unless they were also canons but, instead, had entirely separate incomes from property assigned to their position, which was no longer considered part of the Cathedral Table; the canons got a share each; the *racioneros*, known as *porcionarios*, got half a share each.[19] In Burgos, the half-*racioneros* apparently did not receive even a part of a share, while the *racioneros* and canons received equal shares; perhaps the dignitaries received no shares, unless they were simultaneously canons.[20]

---

reparto de los ingresos de la mesa capitular, así como a las distribuciones – si se asiste – de rentas asignadas a cada una de las celebraciones litúrgicas." This would be a continuation of the reformed thirteenth-century system, described by Mansilla, *Iglesia Castellano-Leonesa*, p. 208.

16.   Demetrio Mansilla, "Repartimiento o tributo impuesto por el Cardenal Mendoza y cabildo de Burgos para la fundación y sostenimiento del Seminario de San Jerónimo," *Burgense* 2 (1961): 423-24, 426. To reach the range of figures stated in "Figura de Burgos," p. 710, for the dignitaries, one would have to multiply by at least 3; if this multiplication were done for the *prebendas*, it would produce a share worth 512 ducats. (The calculation would be based on the 12 mill levy of 49,188 maravedis on "the Chapter Table of the *señores* dean and chapter, with the *préstamos* annexed to it, which the precentor and canon Rebenga left," converted to the assessed value of 4,099,000 maravedis, or 10930.67 ducats, and divided by 64 prebends.)

17.   Juan Ramón López-Arévalo, *Un Cabildo Catedral de la Vieja Castilla: Avila: Su estructura jurídica, s.XIII-XX* (Madrid: Consejo Superior de Investigaciones Científicas, 1966), pp. 197-99, 218.

18.   Ibid., pp. 197-99.

19.   Villacorta, *El Cabildo Catedral de León*, p. 140. In cases where the dignitaries had "una o dos prebendas anejas," they would receive "ración mayor o gruesa, pero no las distribuciones," to which only the titular canons were entitled. They did not have to "reside;" but, on the other hand, they were not entitled to a voice or vote in the chapter. Ibid., pp. 221, 410-11.

20.   "Figura de Burgos," p. 710. The proportions were not the same as those in the Constitutions of 1250, where the following annual amounts, expressed in *morabutinos*, which was the gold money of the time, were established: the dean, 700; archdeacon of Burgos, 500; other archdeacons, precentor, and treasurer, 400 each; canons, 80 each; *porcionarios mayores*, 40 each; *porcionarios menores*, 20 each; *organista*, 40. See Mansilla, *Iglesia Castellano-Leonesa*, p. 213. For the half-*racioneros*, Bishop Acuña in the 1460s stated, "son veinte medios

The other main sources of income for the dignitaries, canons, *racioneros*, and half-*racioneros* were the "hours" and "anniversaries." These were monies that were paid to them for attending the various services in the cathedral, each one with its own endowment. To generalize from the case of León after 1450, when a series of popes authorized "the incorporation of various *préstamos*" to raise the incomes of canons, the new *préstamos* were added to "the distributions of the hours, *salves*, and some masses and offices."[21] In Burgos too, especially after 1462, the popes greatly increased the total income of the Chapter Table as they annexed various *préstamos* to it for "the distributions for attendance at choir," and further increased the total available for this purpose by suppressing three *raciones* and a canonry.[22] The reward for actual participation in the services was thereby increased. Since part of the endowment was for masses on the anniversaries of deaths, the reward was different from service to service and from day to day.[23] The amount of payment probably also depended on the status of the person: in Burgos, the dignitaries received twice as much as the canons, while in León the dignitaries were not eligible to receive anything.[24]

The relative weight of the different sorts of payments depended on local policy. In Burgos the information is vague: anniversaries ranked behind the payments from *El Libro Redondo*, which was "the distribution according to attendance at the canonical hours and the division of certain items of income," but income from the prebend must have been off-the-books.[25] In Avila in 1558 the average amount earned by canons during the year was 3000 maravedis (8 ducats) for the anniversaries, 17,000 maravedis (over 45 ducats) for the hours, and a distribution of 109,042 maravedis – over five times as much, almost 291 ducats – from the "residue" of the income of the Chapter Table.[26] By contrast, in Granada the canons were paid entirely from "daily

---

racioneros.... Por cuanto los benefiçios de las medias raçiones desta dicha nuestra santa iglesia son tan pobres que, servida la media raçión e con interesençia de todo el año, no rentan quinse ducados...." See López Martínez, "Acuña," p. 215; cf. the separate and very small amount allocated to them in the levy of 1566 (Mansilla, "Repartimiento," p. 426).
21.   Villacorta, *El Cabildo Catedral de León*, pp. 49-50.
22.   Casado Alonso, *La Propiedad Eclesiástica*, p. 82.
23.   Ibid., p. 88 ("adscribiendo determinadas cantidades a cada una de las horas canónicas de los diferentes días del año y a algunas celebraciones litúrgicas, siendo función de los 'puntadores' del cabildo llevar la contabilidad de la asistencia de los capitulares y, conforme a esta, efectuar el reparto.")
24.   Ibid., p. 88. This was a long-lasting rule, for according to the 1250 Constitutions, "En Burgos, la asistencia a maitines tenía asignada al año una renta de seiscientos marabutinos, a dividir proporcionalmente entre todos los asistentes a coro.... Las dignidades debían percibir el doble que los canónigos, e éstos el doble que los porcionarios." See Mansilla, *Iglesia Castellano-Leonesa*, p. 216. For León, see note 19.
25.   Casado Alonso, *La Propiedad Eclesiástica*, p. 92.
26.   López-Arévalo, *Avila*, pp. 197-99 (interesting accounts for the year 1558), 218.

distributions," a system that was established in 1492, when the city was recaptured from the Moslems at the end of the Reconquest and a cathedral was established there. The simple system introduced at Granada marked the culmination of the process of tying income to attendance at choir, and dispensed with the prebend or *gruesa* and paid the canons their salaries entirely through "daily distributions" for day-to-day attendance at the liturgical "hours." Moreover, the canons could lose their offices altogether as the penalty for absences exceeding four months.[27]

❧

Aside from administering the cathedral church, the function of the canons in religious life was to participate in the choir, especially at the seven canonical hours. Their income was structured to reward them for attendance, as a response to the fact that absenteeism was a perpetual problem in most, perhaps all, churches. The prebend had to be earned by the canons. In Burgos and Avila, a canon had to "reside" continuously for an initial period of six months before he was eligible to receive any income from his position; in León at the end of the fifteenth century the new prebendaries had to come to the cathedral daily for eight months, participating every day in one of the hours.[28] Thereafter, in León canons were entitled to four months of vacation, during which they were counted as present. For the rest of the year, they earned their prebend by attending one hour daily. In Avila canons were not entitled to the prebend unless they had "resided" for four months out of the year, "in the choir at the canonical hours of Matins, Terce, and Vespers;" on the other hand, they were entitled to the full share if they had "resided" for eight months. For periods between four and eight months, their stipend was prorated by the day. Thus, canons enjoyed four

---

27.   Antonio Garrido Aranda, *Organización de la Iglesia en el Reino de Granada y su proyección en Indias. Siglo XVI* (Sevilla: Escuela de Estudios Hispano-americanos de Sevilla, 1979), p. 273.

28.   Mansilla, *Iglesia Castellano-Leonesa*, p. 206; Carlos García de las Heras, "Don Jerónimo Pardo de Salamanca, Abad de San Quirce," *Burgense* 17 (1976): 165, for the year 1601; López-Arévalo, *Avila*, pp. 159-60; and Villacorta, *El Cabildo Catedral de León*, p. 222. In 1569, Bishop Pacheco, in Rome, wanted the Burgos chapter to make an exception to the six-months residence requirement: "le había dicho que conforme a derecho él puede tener dos o tres personas de su iglesia en su servicio; y que, habiendo proveído al licenciado Castro el canonicato como saben Vs. Ms. persona tan benemérita, del cual él tiene grande necesidad aquí para su servicio, que no obstante que él lo puede hacer, no quiere sino que sea con la voluntad y consenso de Vs. Ms. Y ansí, que les ruega mucho sean contentos de hacerle presente, no obstante que no haya hecho la primera residencia, pués él por su persona lo merece y a él le harán grandísimo placer y darán gran contento, pues lo hicieron con don Francisco Sarmiento que, aunque lo merezca, no concurren las ocasiones y causas que aquí hay." See Nicolás López Martínez, "Notas documentales sobre el Cardenal D. Francisco Pacheco de Toledo, primer Arzobispo de Burgos (1567-1579)," *Burgense* 9 (1968): 353-54.

months of vacation a year, at least until the Council of Trent set a general standard of three months of vacation.[29]

The payments on a daily basis for participating in hours and anniversaries were an even more obvious method of insuring attendance at the seven daily hours. The Council of Trent, concerned about continuing absenteeism, decided that the relative weight of such payments should be increased by allocating a third of chapter revenue to "the daily distributions of the canonical hours." The canons could be expected to oppose any change, as they did in Avila and León, where they claimed that over a third of the income was already used for the daily distributions.[30] Granada pointed out that it already operated under a system where "there is no *gruesa*, all the income is earned by daily distributions."[31]

Absenteeism was not the only problem a choir might face. A set of rules drawn up by Bishop Fray Alonso de Montúfar in 1570 for the choir in the cathedral of Mexico City illustrates the sorts of problems that might occur anywhere in the Spanish world. Aimed at keeping the canons in order, it has appropriate penalties, as canons may lose "points" and "hours" and "part of the prebend" for various offences. (A chapter would have a recorder of points to keep track of attendance.) Drawn up after the Council of Trent, it announces:

> it is fitting that we desire that our God and, for His honor and glory, men also, regard us as devout and religious men and special servants of God.... The canons cannot earn the *gruesa* or daily distributions [except by saying the hours] and singing them together with the rest, when they are gathered for this purpose – since it for this that their revenue or salary is given to them, and not for saying them in private, and so they are obligated to sing their parts and not to be mute and silent, under penalty of not obtaining the *prebenda*, even though they are attentive and pray what the others are singing.

A second rule is that "No one is to speak from the one choir to the other [in a divided choir], or signal, or send messages, under penalty of a point." The eleventh ordains:

> In the choir, no one is to read letters or books while the hours are being said, under penalty that if the President reminds him and he does not obey, he will be penalized in the hour.

The twenty-eighth:

29. López-Arévalo, *Avila*, pp. 164-65 (attendance), p. 183 (Trent). For León, Villacorta, *El Cabildo Catedral de León*, pp. 244 (attendance), 258 (four months of vacation).
30. López-Arévalo, *Avila*, p. 166. Villacorta, *El Cabildo Catedral de León*, pp. 248-49; L. Cristiani, *L'Église à l'époque du concile de Trente*, Historie de l'Église, 17 (Paris: Bloud and Gay, 1948), pp. 193, 200: Chapter III of the reform decree of June 1562 at Council of Trent, enacted September 1562.
31. Garrido Aranda, *Organización de la Iglesia en el Reino de Granada*, p. 317; cf. p. 314.

No one is to go out of the choir without permission of the President and without giving just cause, under penalty of losing the hour. And we declare that ordinary business that could be deferred until after the hour is not a just cause; but one can leave for necessities of nature, provided that one does not dally in the sacristy or elsewhere, talking or strolling, under penalty of a point.

The fortieth:

All the prebendaries are to know how to sing...; and anyone who does not know how is to learn within a year, and if after a year he still does not know how, he is to lose a tenth of his prebend, with the obligation to learn within the next year, and if then he still has not learned, he is to lose an eighth, and thus it will keep increasing.[32]

🌢

How did a canon spend his time when he was not in choirstalls or, more rarely, in religious processions? An historian of the church in Burgos says:

In the day of many officeholders there was no other occupation than attendance at choir. Even admitting that, as they complained, "the hours are long," there remained enormous room for idleness. There are indications that some studied, but this amounted only to preparing some sermons, and we can guess that this was an occupation of only a few, and on rare occasions.

Someone who was preparing a sermon was excused from choir for ten days, but in fact most of the sermons were preached by Franciscans and Dominicans. "It was, then, normal that their lives tended to become secularized in relaxations, disputes, and business."[33] A noteworthy exception was the archdeacon of Burgos, Don Pedro Fernández de Villegas, who in 1515 published his Castilian verse translation of Dante's *Divine Comedy*.[34] The atmosphere of many a canon's life must be conveyed in this description of the sudden but peaceful death of Doctor Aresti in 1609:

Doctor Aresti, canon *magistral* and preacher in this cathedral,... spent that afternoon at the Chapel of the Visitation of Saint Elizabeth, where he was the head chaplain. Having arranged for the vespers of the next day, which is the principal devotion and feast of the said chapel, after vespers he went, together with the other *señores* prebendaries, to play nine-pins in a garden, where they enjoyed themselves greatly, and they went from there to

32. Fray Alonso de Montúfar, OP, *Ordenanzas para el coro de la catedral mexicana, 1570,* ed. Ernest J. Burrus, SJ (Madrid: Ediciones José Porrua Turanzas, 1964), respectively pp. 34, 36, 42, 52, 60.
33. López Martínez, "Acuña," p. 254.
34. Amancio Blanco Díez, "Los Arcedianos y Abades del Cabildo Catedral de Burgos," *Boletín de la Real Academia de la Historia* 130 (1952): 286.

dine, each one to his own house, and Doctor Aresti to his...
[where he died without warning].[35]

One amusement that canons had enjoyed came under attack by
Burgos' prelate in 1576, as he tried to enforce Pope Pius V's
condemnation of bullfights by forbidding clergymen to attend
them. One member of the cathedral chapter expressed his dismay:

> Today the abbot of Cervatos brought up how the illustrious lord
> Don Francisco Pacecho, cardinal, archbishop of Burgos, had
> issued a certain command, like an edict, with penalty of auto-
> matic major excommunication against the clerics who went to
> see bulls run...which seemed to him was a great hardship for the
> clergy.

The cathedral chapter decided to appeal to their archbishop
(Burgos became an archbishopric in 1574) to reconsider.[36]

In Burgos, there were meetings of the chapter twice a week,
which offered some opportunity for politicking and, if the canon
were able and willing, the chance to undertake many miscellaneous jobs, such as supervising a charitable work of the chapter,
overseeing repairs or construction in the cathedral, or going on
missions to the bishop.[37] There were probably some clerics whose
main source of excitement was the occasional struggle between
the cathedral chapter and the bishop of Burgos. The chapter
claimed that it was exempt from the bishop's control, and that
both it and the bishop were directly under the pope, but this claim
itself was the occasion for heated conflicts. An example of the
extremes to which both sides were willing to go came in 1559,
when in a struggle over whether the bishop could "visit" the
cathedral, the bishop used the weapon of suspension a divinis,
which even prevented the members of the chapter from
participating in Charles V's funeral rites in the cathedral.[38]

Of course, a canon could make his own life even more
exciting. Don Juan de Lerma, archdeacon of Briviesca, was
remembered by people in Burgos because he had killed a servant
of the abbot of Salas, a crime for which he was imprisoned by the
cathedral chapter in its jail.[39] This particular archdeacon was not
especially hampered by personal inhibitions. He had several
illegitimate children. He established his daughters as nuns and
devoted part of his last will and testament in 1538 to dictating the

---

35. Eloy García de Quevedo, *Libros burgaleses de Memorias y Noticias* (Burgos:
Monte Carmelo, 1931), p. 21.
36. López Martínez, "Pacheco," pp. 345-46.
37. Casado Alonso, *La Propiedad Eclesiástica*, p. 30, Wednesday and Friday.
Jobs: García de las Heras, "Pardo," pp. 165-245 passim.
38. Nicolás López Martínez, "El cardenal Mendoza y la Reforma tridentina
en Burgos," *Hispania sacra* 16 (1963): 81-90 *(visita)*.
39. *Memorial ajustado del pleyto de compromiso que se sigue entre el ilustrisimo
señor Don Joseph Xaviér Rodriguez de Arellano, Arzobispo de Burgos y el venerable
dean, y Cabildo de su Santa Iglesia Metropolitana* (Madrid: 1768-1770), pp. 66, 80.

future of his legitimated son, Juan Martínez de Lerma, to whom he left considerable property.[40]

†

How did a boy or man obtain a position as a canon or dignitary? In the case of dignitaries, at least in León in the fifteenth century, the pope filled the positions that fell vacant in the eight "apostolic months;" later, this right was conceded to the kings of Castile. In the other months, it probably was the bishop who named the dignitaries. In the case of canonries in León, the bishop and chapter filled vacant offices.[41] In Burgos the bishop and the chapter alternated in filling vacant canonries.[42]

Actually, however, few positions of either type "fell vacant," because many offices in the cathedral chapter passed from person to person by resignation, confirmed by the pope.[43] For example, in the sixteenth century the office of archdeacon of Burgos passed from one archdeacon to the next by resignation at least half of the time, in several cases to relatives – and even to descendants.[44] The system of resignations reigned supreme for canonries as well. At mid-sixteenth century, the cost of "the bull of resignation of fruits and *regreso* [retaking possession of a benefice]" for a canonry was 250 ducats.[45]

A candid description of this process was provided by the canon Diego de Melgosa in 1566, when he reported to the cathedral

40. Archivo del Colegio de Notarios, Burgos: Prot. 2883, 14 Sept. 1538.
41. Villacorta, *El Cabildo Catedral de León*, pp. 205, 497 (eight months).
42. See note 46. López Martínez, "Acuña," p. 198, refers to this practice: "[In 1466] Otro sobrino por el que [Bishop] don Luis manifestó gran interés fue Martín Vázquez de Acuña. Falló el primer intento de hacerle canónigo, porque su candidatura fue presentada en ocasión que tocaba al cabildo proveer."
43. Studies subtitled "Estudio histórico-jurídico" (Villacorta, *El Cabildo Catedral de León*) or "Estructura jurídica" (López-Arévalo, *Avila*) miss this fact, which is perfectly obvious to a social historian, such as Ruth Pike, *Aristocrats and Traders: Sevillian Society in the Sixteenth Century* (Ithaca, NY: Cornell University Press, 1972), pp. 52-56. Cf. Vicente Beltrán de Heredia, *Cartulario de la Universidad de Salamanca (1218-1600)*, vol. 3 (Salamanca: Universidad de Salamanca, 1971), pp. 571-72: Letter of Burgos' Bishop Mendoza to the canon Andrés Sánchez, from Madrid, July 1563: "Ya sabéis cómo murió en Salamanca el diciembre pasado el abad de Gamonal. Agustín de Torquemada fue a hacelle dar cierto poder para resignar en Diego de Melgosa el abadía y canonicato y su renta, y no lo pudo acabar con él. Es necessario saber lo que en esto pasó entre él y su hermano y después, porque la resignación que se halla en Roma no carece de difecto, y el consensu se extendió a 19 de enero deste año, habiéndose prestado dos o tres años antes."
44. Blanco Díez, "Los Arcedianos y Abades del Cabildo Catedral de Burgos," pp. 285-87. An interesting case was Don Fernando Ruiz de Villegas, who followed his grandfather Don Pedro Ruiz de Villegas, who died in 1536 at the age of 84. He held the position until 1546, when he decided not to pursue an ecclesiastical career; a few years later, he married. For the relationship and his career, see Manuel Martínez Añibarro y Rives, *Intento de un Diccionario Biográfico y Bibliográfico de autores de la Provincia de Burgos* (Madrid: Manuel Tello, 1889), pp. 433-36.
45. Archivo del Colegio de Notarios, Burgos: Prot. 3219, 10 Nov. 1546.

chapter on the proceedings of the provincial church council in Toledo. The bishops were insisting on carrying out the decision of the Council of Trent that half of the canons should have university degrees, but Melgosa refused to become alarmed

> since we can resign the canonries to whom we wish, although the person is not a graduate.... What has probably concerned your graces the most is the matter of the dignities and canonries – which decree does not deprive each one in particular of the ability to resign his dignity or canonry to the person whom His Holiness approves, graduate or not; because it has never crossed their minds to tie the hands of the pope nor, if it ever did, would it do them any good, so that the decree deals with those that are to be filled on account of death, either by the bishops or by the chapters.[46]

Only a few canonries were outside this system. The canonry *magistral* and the canonry *doctoral* were established by Pope Sixtus IV in 1474. The former position was to be held by a licenciate or doctor in theology; the latter office was to be given to a licenciate or doctor in canon law, who was to advise the chapter on legal questions and defend it in court. A third canonry, known as the *lectoral*, was established by the Council of Trent. It carried with it the obligation to lecture for an hour and a half daily, particularly on moral themes. These three offices were to be filled by open oral competition, after being advertised at the universities. The cathedral chapter was the judge.[47] For example, in 1559 the chapter heard seven candidates competing for the new position of *lectoral*. The winner was Dr. Juan Liermo, "who had recently received the doctor's degree in Siguenza." These positions were the most likely to serve as stepping stones to higher positions. Liermo, for example, eventually became the archbishop of Santiago.[48]

There were some potential obstacles in the way of a young man from the upper classes whose goal was to become a canon in the cathedral of Burgos. In the sixteenth century the cathedral chapter at Toledo took the lead in Spain by adopting a statute requiring "purity of blood." Burgos' chapter discussed such a statute in 1550 and again in 1584-1585: it would have required that in the future a prospective member of the cathedral clergy prove that he was not the son, grandson, or great-grandson of a "Jew,

46. See López Martínez, "Mendoza," pp. 108-9.
47. Villacorta, *El Cabildo Catedral de León*, pp. 124-25, 128-30. The *lectoral* had been established by the fifth Lateran Council, and was confirmed by Trent. The Council of Trent also established a *penitenciario*. Ibid., p. 124.
48. López Martínez, "Mendoza," p. 92. There is a reference to the competition for the *canonjía magistral* in 1538 in Martínez y Sanz, *Historia del Templo catedral*, p. 249. García de Quevedo, *Libros burgaleses*, p. 21, has the following description of the competition in 1609 for the same position, after the death of Dr. Aresti: "Pasados dos meses se pusieron edictos en toda España para la oposición del canonicato y vinieron cuatro opositores muy calificados en sangres y letras, haciendo sus actos públicamente. Al fin le llevó el Doctor Gil que le posee el día de hoy."

Moor, or person burned, reconciled, or punished by the Inquisition" on his father's side, or the son or grandson of such an unclean person on his mother's side. However, although the chapter approved the statute, the pope rejected it, probably because of the opposition of the powerful patrons of the chapels in the cathedral, who claimed that the measure infringed upon their freedom of action as patrons.[49]

Illegitimacy was supposed to be an impediment.[50] However, it is obvious that sufficiently high birth could tip the scales in favor of the candidate, even if illegitimacy was in the balance on the negative side. At the end of the fifteenth century, no one in Burgos would have been ignorant of the fact that Bishop Acuña's illegitimate son, Don Antonio de Acuña, was making a career in Burgos' church with his father's support, in spite of initial objections by the cathedral chapter. In 1486, when Don Antonio was probably about 25, Pope Innocent VIII "authorized him to obtain dignities, benefices, or *préstamos* in the dioceses of Burgos and Segovia, conferring upon him an expectative for the first vacant position. He was already a cleric, but he would wait many more years before he received major orders." In 1487 he became a canon in Burgos; he got another canonry there in 1491; in 1492 he became archdeacon of Burgos; three years later, shortly before his father's death, he resigned this position to take over the more lucrative post of archdeacon of Valpuesta, which he continued to hold as late as 1507, even after the pope had named him bishop of Zamora. Don Antonio's activity during his tenure as bishop of Zamora earned him a place in Spain's history books, for he emerged as a warrior prelate and one of the main military leaders of the revolt in Castile against the new monarch, Emperor Charles V, in 1520/21.[51]

It was possible for a person to become a canon or dignitary without being ordained as a priest, deacon, or even as a subdeacon. The Council of Trent opposed this practice,[52] which made it possible for a man to draw a comfortable income from the church for years, without eliminating the possibility that he might

---

49.   López Martínez, "El estatuo de limpieza de sangre," pp. 53-66. At the same time, the pope was approving a similar statute for León. Villacorta, *El Cabildo Catedral de León*, p. 209.

50.   Villacorta, *El Cabildo Catedral de León*, p. 207; in 1466 Bishop Acuña's nephew, Martín de Acuña, had to obtain a dispensation and legitimation in order to become a canon. See López Martínez, "Acuña," p. 199.

51.   López Martínez, "Acuña," pp. 200-206, quotation at p. 203; Blanco Díez, "Dignitarios eclesiásticos burgaleses: Los Arcedianos de Valpuesta," *Boletín de la Real Academia de la Historia* 121 (1947): 469-70.

52.   The Council of Trent required that at least half of the canons and *racioneros* be priests, with the rest being deacons or subdeacons. Villacorta, *El Cabildo Catedral de León*, p. 208. The Tridentine reform decree of September 1562 deprived those canons who were not at least subdeacons of their voice in the chapter. Cristiani, *L'Église*, p. 200. The age requirements established at Trent in 1563 were 21 for a subdeacon, 22 for a deacon, and 24 for a priest. Ibid., pp. 205 ff.

eventually marry. Burgos' bishop, Cardinal Don Francisco de Mendoza y Bobadilla, agreed with the council and made a scene in a chapter meeting in 1561:

> [Bishop Mendoza came to the chapter meeting]...he asked Don Diego Díez de Arceo Miranda, precentor and canon, if he were ordained. And then his illustrious lordship said to the precentor and canon that he required him to be ordained, in accordance with his legal obligation, and that meanwhile he was not to enter the chapter meeting nor to preside. The said precentor and canon replied that, although he was not ordained, he could preside, as he had presided in the chapter many other times....[53]

When the next bishop, Cardinal Don Francisco Pacheco de Toledo, made an issue of this reform in 1570, the chapter replied that "in this holy church, out of 63 prebendaries, 59 are ordained, and the rest have not been, some because they are underage and the others because of just impediments, but they want to be...." The bishop, in Rome, was not prepared to listen to excuses and told the chapter's representative in Rome so:

> The bishop responded to me that His Holiness had told him that in many churches in Spain there were many men who were unordained, and that after they had taken church revenues for a long time, then they got married; and so they are to understand that in order to avoid these problems, he would not change his mind, because though they are few it is just that they be ordained. And that it was not true that there are any who are underage; and that Don Francisco [Sarmiento?] had spoken to him on behalf of Señor Castillo, saying that he is so religious – and that, if he is, why doesn't he want to be ordained? And that the abbot of Castro had likewise spoken to him on behalf of an archdeacon who is over 60 years old and who is waiting for a nephew of his to come of age so that he can resign his benefices to him, and who hasn't wanted to [be ordained] – and that is not a just thing. And so that your graces see that he is not doing this so as to take away their benefices, that he has ordered his vicar to arrange for their ordination even if they are not able or sufficient – just so they be ordained.... It did not do any good to tell him about the high level of religion and goodness that exists in your cathedral....[54]

The educational requirement was vague. A traditional requirement, at least in León, was that the canons "ought to know how to read and write, to compose Latin, and to sing." "For a better musical preparation, they ought to attend the classes that the chapel master has in the cathedral."[55]

The desirability of knowing Latin was fairly obvious, except to some of the canons themselves. The cathedral of Burgos did have

53. López Martínez, "Mendoza," p. 106.
54. López Martínez, "Pacheco," p. 355. The sixty-three *prebendas* were presumably held by the 44 canons and the 20 *racioneros*, with one position being vacant.
55. Villacorta, *El Cabildo Catedral de León*, p. 206.

a grammar school. In 1468, a date when it had been run by the same teacher for twenty-eight years, the chapter commented that "most of them had been his students." Nevertheless, there were complaints in the chapter in 1460 that some "do not even know how to read the lesson well." In 1467, the chapter named some of the know-nothings:

> therefore, it was necessary that they go to learn. And they named Ruy Gomez, and Liaño, and Maluenda, and Francisco Días, and Cuevas Rubias, and Osorio, and Martín de Acuña so that from today until All Saints' Day they go out to the *estudios* [classrooms or schools] that each one prefers.

Similar orders, directed at some of the same men in 1469, proved that they were recalcitrant, as well as being unskilled in Latin.[56]

About the only other way of persuading men in the church to study Latin was to make it a requirement for ordination. Both the cathedral chapter and the bishops used this tactic. In the time of Bishop Acuña, "the chapter required knowledge of grammar by those who were to be ordained as priests, who had to study it at least for a year." At the same time, the bishop required candidates for sacred orders to pass an examination. However, the chapter in Burgos naturally refused to allow the bishop to conduct any examination of its members, and Bishop Acuña (in the late fifteenth century) agreed that the chapter would conduct its own examinations and that he would accept its certifications. Most canons did not go beyond the local grammar school in the second half of the fifteenth century.[57]

Members of the cathedral chapter were encouraged to continue their studies both locally and at the university, mainly by being granted excused absences from the residence requirement, so that their absence did not entail a loss of the *ración*.[58] Nevertheless, of the 37 dignitaries and canons who attended the chapter meetings in Burgos on July 15 and 21, 1550, only four had advanced university degrees.[59] The Council of Trent was in favor of raising

---

56. López Martínez, "Acuña," pp. 251-52. "In 1469, mandan que vayan a estudiar los canónigos Pedro de Covarrubias, Francisco Díaz, Osorio, Martín de Acuña, Puentedura y Francisco de Torquemada, así como el racionero Ruy Gómez. Todos ellos se excusaron en repetidas ocasiones y no fueron." Ibid., p. 252.

57. Ibid., pp. 252-53.

58. Villacorta, *El Cabildo Catedral de León*, pp. 261-64. In Burgos, similar excuses were granted to attend the grammar school: in 1564, "que era statuto y costumbre que a todos los beneficiados que iban al estudio del Sarmental se les daba el punto habiendo ganado prebenda...." The chapter agreed that this policy would cover Bernardino de la Puebla, *racionero*, if he were good enough in Latin to attend the arts course that was being given at the monastery of San Pablo: "que, haciendo primero prebenda en una de las horas que es obligado a hacer residencia para la ganar, le puntasen lo que en oír la dicha lección se ocupase." See López Martínez, "Mendoza," p. 91.

59. Bachelor's degrees were not mentioned. See López Martínez, "El estatuo de limpieza de sangre," pp. 55, 73. Licenciado Don Francisco de Mena, archdeacon of Lara; Lic. Andrés de Astudillo, Dr. Jerónimo de Velasco, and Lic.

the educational level and, therefore, resolved that all of the dignitaries and at least half of the canons should have degrees (*Maestro, Licenciado,* or Doctor) in either theology or canon law.[60] The bishops who attended the Council of Toledo in 1566-1567 agreed. In Burgos, in spite of Canon Melgosa's aplomb regarding the ability of canons to pass their offices on to nongraduates, "the petitions of benefice-holders who wanted to study at the university multiplied."[61]

Although the cathedral chapters in Castile were similar in most ways to each other, it is obvious when we look abroad that a great deal of variety was possible, at least before the Council of Trent attempted to eliminate "abuses." For instance, according to Margaret Bowker,[62] between 1495 and 1520 in Lincoln it was rare for more than five out of fifty-eight canons "to reside" – a great contrast to Burgos, where at least three-fourths, and probably almost all, of the canons were on the scene, attending chapter meetings and choir. On the other hand, Lincoln's canons were highly educated, with the vast majority holding higher university degrees; whereas in Burgos the number of canons with advanced degrees could be counted on one hand. Many of the dignitaries and canons at Lincoln Cathedral were in fact really in the royal service, which was not true in Burgos. Differences in the method of obtaining office and in the amount of income and method of payment also existed.[63]

Andrés Méndez. The last three were among the most recent canons, all being among the last nine names on the list. According to C. Gutiérrez, *Españoles en Trento* (Valladolid: Consejo Superior de Investigaciones Científicas, 1951), pp. 570-71, Dr. Velasco was the *magistral.*
60. Villacorta, *El Cabildo Catedral de León,* pp. 207-8.
61. López Martínez, "Mendoza," pp. 108-9.
62. *The Secular Clergy in the Diocese of Lincoln, 1495-1530* (Cambridge: Cambridge University Press, 1968).
63. Ibid., pp. 155-63.

XII

The Fraticelli and Clerical Wealth in Quattrocento Rome

JOHN MONFASANI

In the late 1460s,[1] Cardinal Jean Jouffroy[2] came across a *libellus* of a Fraticello condemning the worldly pretensions of the Roman Curia.[3] The Fraticello attacked Pope Paul II by name and identified Rome with the whore of Babylon,[4] whose "time of judgment would come."[5] Jouffroy ignored the prophesy, but he took the criticisms of clerical wealth seriously enough to write a refutation.[6] Indeed, he seems to have restructured what was

1.   See Massimo Miglio, *Storiografia pontificia del Quattrocento* (Bologna: Pàtron, 1975), p. 138, who dates Jouffroy's response to 1468. It seems to me that the evidence would allow a date in 1467.
2.   In addition to the literature cited by Miglio, *Storiografia*, p. 136 n. 24; see also Angela Lanconelli, "La biblioteca romana di Jean Jouffroy," in *Scrittura, biblioteche e stampa a Roma nel Quattrocento: Aspetti e problemi*. Littera antiqua, 1.1-2 (Vatican City: Scuola Vaticana di Paleografia, Diplomatica e Archivistica, 1980), 1:275-94; and Laura Onofri, "*Sicut fremitus leonis ita et regis ira*: Temi neoplatonici e culto solare nell'orazione funebre per Niccolò V per Jean Jouffroy," *Humanistica Lovaniensia* 31 (1982): 1-28.
3.   The first to discuss this episode and to identify Jouffroy as the anonymous author in MS Vatican, Ottob. lat. 793 rebutting the (lost) Fraticellian *libellus* was Massimo Miglio, "*Vidi thiaram Pauli pape secundi*," *Bullettino dell'Istituto Storico Italiano per il Medio Evo* 81 (1969): 273-96, reprinted in his *Storiografia*, pp. 119-53. A miniature on fol. 2r in Ottob. lat. 793 depicts Jouffroy sitting with the *libellus* open on the table before him; a Fraticello stands facing him; and in the background three elegant curial figures mull about.
4.   For various strands of apocalypticism and prophesy among the Franciscans and the Fraticelli see Marjorie Reeves, *The Influence of Prophecy in the Later Middle Ages: A Study in Joachimism* (Oxford: Oxford University Press, 1969), pp. 191-228 and 411-14.
5.   MS Ottob. lat. 793, fol. 14r: "Ve, ve, ve, civitas illa magna Babilon et civitas illa fortis quoniam una hora venit iudicium!... Ve, ve, ve civitas illa magna quoniam una hora destitue sunt tante divitie!" Cf. Apoc. 18:10, 16-17.
6.   Jouffroy had a long-standing interest in the Fraticelli *de opinione*. He mentioned them in 1455 in his funeral eulogy of Pope Nicholas V apropos the heresies that the pope had combatted. See Onofri, "Temi neoplatonici," p. 23. In MS Ottob. lat. 793, fol. 5v, he wrote the word "Verum" in the margin next to where he explained that his first impulse was to feed the *libellus* to flames, but the possibility that other copies might exist provoked him to write a refutation.

originally a treatise on the dignity of cardinals in order to take into
account this fresh attack on Curial wealth.[7]
Nor was Jouffroy alone in the effort. In the 1460s treatises on
poverty and clerical wealth became a growth industry at Rome.[8] In
the main, the authors were reacting to the apprehension and trial
of a group of Fraticelli *de opinione* in 1466.[9] But what most
characterized this literary campaign was its orchestration by the
various members of the Curia rather than by the pope. Thus,
Cardinal Jouffroy addressed his treatise to Cardinal Bessarion.
Cardinal Guillaume d'Estouteville commissioned a massive
treatise against the Fraticelli from the Spanish scholar and
apostolic subdeacon Fernando of Cordova.[10] Bothered by the

7.   The space on fol. 2r of MS Ottob. lat. 793 for the title of the treatise was
never filled in. On the facing fol. 1v, a later librarian wrote *Bessarionis
cardinalis Dialogus de dignitate cardinalatus*. This title confuses the dedicatee
with the author, but it does reflect the subject matter of most of the treatise.
After the preface to Bessarion (fols. 2r-5v), Jouffroy refutes the *libellus* of the
Fraticello, in part by quoting passages, but mostly by creating a fictive dialog
between himself and the Fraticello (fols. 5v-38r). The bulk of the treatise,
however, is given over to a dialog between a patriarch and a cardinal
concerning the dignity of the cardinal's office (fols. 38r-116r). The disparity
between the two parts is too large to have been the way Jouffroy originally
conceived the work.
8.   See Ludwig von Pastor, *The History of the Popes from the Close of the
Middle Ages*, trans. F. I. Antrobus, vol. 4 (London: Routledge & Kegan Paul,
1894), pp. 113-16. The only study is the posthumous and somewhat inaccurate
Decima L. Douie, "Some Treatises Against the Fraticelli in the Vatican
Library," *Franciscan Studies*, n.s. 38 (1978): 10-80. See also Livarius Oliger,
"Documenta inedita ad historiam Fraticellorum spectantia (continuatio et
finis)," *Archivum Franciscanum Historicum* 6 (1913): 710-47, at 746-47.
9.   The acts of the *processus* have been edited three times from MS Vatican,
Vat. lat. 4012 (best by Ehrle, though he omitted parts): Albert Dressel, *Vier
Dokumente aus römischen Archiven: Ein Beitrag zur Geschichte des Protestantis-
mus vor, währrend und nach der Reformation* (Leipzig: Hahn, 1843; I cite the
second edition, Berlin: Duncker, 1872, pp. 1-48); Franz Ehrle, "Die Spiritualen,
ihr Verhältnis zum Franciscanerorden und zu den Fraticellen," *Archiv für
Litteratur und Kirchengeschichte* 1 (1885): 609-69, 2 (1886): 106-64, 3 (1887): 553-
623, 4 (1888): 1-190, at 4:111-34; and Mario Mastrocola, *Note storiche circa le
diocesi di Civita C., Orte e Gallese. Parte III. I vescovi dalla unione delle diocesi alla
fine del Concilio di Trento (1437-1564)* (Civita Castellana: Pian Paradisi, 1972),
pp. 253-78. See also Renzo Mosti, "L'eresia dei 'fraticelli' nel territorio di
Tivoli," *Atti e memorie della Società Tiburtina di Storia e d'Arte* 38 (1968): 41-110;
Luigi Fumi, "Eretici in Boemia e fraticelli in Roma nel 1466," *Archivio della
Società Romana di Storia Patria* 34 (1911): 117-30; Michele Canensi, *De vita et
pontificatu Pauli Secundi pontificis maximi*, ed. Giuseppe Zippel, in Rerum Italicarum Scriptores, 2d ed., 3, 16 (Città di Castello: Lapi, 1904), p. 153; and
Giuseppe Cascioli, *Memorie storiche di Poli* (Rome: Della Vera, 1896), pp. 122-28.
10.   For d'Estouteville's commission see Fernando's preface to his *Adversus
hereticos qui Fraterculi de la opinione appellantur* in MS Vatican, Vat. lat. 1127,
fol. 1v: "Deinde tua nos iussa inpulerunt.... Itaque iussibus tuis magis
parentes...." The standard work on Fernando is Adolfo Bonilla y San Martín,
*Fernando de Córdoba (¿1425-1486?) y los orígenes del Renacimento filosófico en
España* (Madrid: V. Suárez, 1911). For literature on d'Estouteville see Anna
Esposito Aliano, "Testamento e inventari per la ricostruzione della biblioteca
del cardinale Gugliemo d'Estouteville," in *Scrittura, biblioteche e stampa* (n. 2
above), 1:309-42.

claims to moral superiority of those who professed poverty, the Curial bishop Alvarus Alfonsi asked another Curial bishop, the theologian Niccolò Palmieri, to write on this issue.[11] Still another (anonymous) Curial bishop asked Palmieri to write on the origins of the mendicant orders and the apparent contradiction between the bulls of Pope Nicholas III and John XXII concerning evangelical poverty.[12] Cardinal Juan Carvajal asked Palmieri for a new treatise on the issue of poverty.[13] Palmieri then combined these treatises with two other items, i.e., a treatise on the history of poverty in the church and a brief address to the leader of the Fraticelli of 1466,[14] to make a corpus of writings on the issue of poverty.[15] He seems initially to have addressed the corpus to

11.　This is the *Adversus pauperes nomine,* edited by Livarius Oliger, "Ein unbekannter Traktat gegen die Mendikanten von Nicolaus Palmerius O.S.A., Bishof von Orte," *Franziskanische Studien. Quartalschrift* 3 (1916): 77-92, from MS Vatican, Vat. lat. 4158. Mastrocola, *Note storiche,* pp. 336-42, made a new edition.

12.　Two treatises were involved, namely, the *De origine mendicantium Predicatorum et Minorum post mille et ducentos annos a Christo. Ante vero nusquam legitur* and the *Tractatus de concordia Nicolai III et Ioannis XXII, quod in veritate summe perdifficile est, stante approbatione regule beati Francisci,* edited in Mastrocola, *Note storiche,* pp. 302-6 and 306-13 respectively, from MS Vatican, Vat. lat. 4158. At the start of the first treatise, Palmieri states: "Petisti a me, suavissime frater, unde contingit quod per mille ducentos annos et plures..." (Mastrocola, p. 302). Palmieri used the title *frater* when referring to a fellow bishop. In the second, he referred back to the prior treatise ("ut supra in tractatu de origine mendicantium plene diximus," ibid., p. 312) and ended, "Vale et ora pro Nicolao, veterano tuo." It is conceivable that the anonymous is Alvarus Alfonsi, to whom Palmieri addressed the *Adversus pauperes nomine* and whom he called his *veteranus amicus* (Oliger, "Ein unbekannter Traktat," p. 84).

13.　Ignored by Lino Gómez Canedo, *Un español al servicio de la santa sede, Don Juan de Carvajal, Cardenal de Sant'Angelo, Legado en Alemania y Hungría (1399?-1469)* (Madrid: Consejo superior de investigaciones cientificas, Instituto Jeronimo Zurita, 1947). The treatise is directed against John Milverton, Provincial of the English Carmelites, and is titled *Tractatus contra illos qui asserunt Christum omnia abdicasse similiter et apostolos. Unde mendicare dicunt omnia, recepisse titulo misericordie, nullo pacto mercede aut debito iustitie,* edited by Mastrocola, *Note storiche,* pp. 313-36, from MS Vatican, Vat. lat. 4158. At the start, Palmieri states that he wrote "mandato tamen prestantissimi patris et domini mei Ioannis Carnaval [sic], cardinalis Sancti Angeli" (MS Vatican, Chig. A IV 113, fol. 71v; inaccurately in Mastrocola, p. 314). A little later on he addresses Carvajal as "dignissime pater" (Mastrocola, p. 317).

14.　This is the opuscule *De triplici statu ecclesie* (edited by Mastrocola, *Note storiche,* pp. 282-301, from MS Vatican, Vat. lat. 4158). As edited in Mastrocola, the treatise against the English Carmelite, John Milverton, the *Tractatus contra illos qui asserunt Christum omnia abdicasse* of the previous note gives the impression of postdating the *De triplici statu* since it refers back to the *De triplici statu:* "quia in prima parte opusculi de triplici statu ecclesie hoc...ostendimus" (MS Vatican, Chig. A IV 113, fols. 115v-116r; cf. Mastrocola, p. 335). But this is a false impression because an earlier redaction of the treatise (MS Genova, Bibl. Franzoniana, Urbani 49, fols 201r-210v) lacks this reference. I am preparing a new edition of the *Tractatus contra illos qui asserunt Christum omnia abdicasse.*

15.　The corpus exists in three manuscripts, two of which (Vatican, Chig. A IV 113; and Florence, Bibl. Nazionale, Magl. XXXIV, 11) contain the

Cardinal Juan Carvajal, then rededicated it to Pope Paul II, and finally, he, or his literary executor, made a new dedication to Cardinal Jean Jouffroy.[16] At about the same time, the castellan of Castel Sant'Angelo, Bishop Rodrigo Sánchez de Arévalo, addressed to Pope Paul II his own lengthy refutation of the Fraticelli.[17] In a subsidiary debate, Cardinal Juan Torquemada and the Master of the Sacred Palace, Jacob Gil, OP, attacked Palmieri on the issue of poverty.[18] So a considerable constellation of leading lights at the Curia took part in the literary campaign that the Fraticelli of 1466 had helped to engender.

The Fraticelli arose from the conflict between the Franciscan Order and Pope John XXII more than a century earlier.[19] In 1322, with the bull *Ad conditorem canonum*, John XXII forced the Franciscans to accept ownership of the property and goods they used, and thereby destroyed the Franciscans' special claim to evangelical poverty.[20] The next year John XXII went further and

---

dedication to Pope Paul II. In its final form, as seen in Magl. XXXIV, 11, the corpus consists of (1) the preface to the Pope, (2) a preface to the reader, (3) a brief *Allocutio in Nicolaum heresiarcham Fraticellorum*, (4) the *De triplici statu ecclesie*, (5-6) the two treatises addressed to the anonymous bishop, *De origine mendicantium* and *De concordia Nicolai III et Ioannis XXII*, (7) the treatise against the English Carmelite John Milverton, *Contra illos qui asserunt Christum omnia abdicasse similiter et apostolos* to Carvajal, and (8) the *Adversus pauperes nomine* to Bishop Alvarus Alfonsi.

16. I take up the complicated question of the dedications in a separate study of Palmieri that will appear in *Analecta Augustiniana*. The dedication to Jouffroy survives in MS Vatican, Vat. lat. 4158, edited in Mastrocola, *Note storiche*, pp. 280-81. The other two manuscripts mentioned in n. 15 above have the dedication to the pope.

17. See Douie, "Some Treatises," pp. 43-65; Teodoro Toni, "Don Rodrigo Sánchez de Arévalo (1404-1470) y uno de sus manuscritos inéditos. El tratado 'De pauperate [sic] Christi et apostolorum'," *Razon y Fe* 105 (1934): 356-73, 507-18; idem, "La Realeza de Jesucristo en un tratado inédito del siglo XV," *Estudios ecclesiásticos* 13 (1934): 369-98; Richard H. Trame, *Rodrigo Sánchez de Arévalo 1404-1470* (Washington, DC: Catholic University of America Press, 1958), pp. 139-43; and Juan Maria Laboa, *Rodrigo Sánchez de Arévalo Alcaide de Sant'Angelo* (Alcala: Fundacion universitaria española, Seminario Nebrija, 1973), pp. 147-65, and 421, num. 16 (for manuscripts of the *Libellus de paupertate Christi et apostolorum*).

18. See *infra*.

19. See Giampaolo Tognetti, "I fraticelli, il principio di povertà e i secolari," *Bullettino dell'Istituto storico italiano per il medio evo e Archivio Muratoriano* 90 (1982-83): 97-145; Clément Schmitt, "Fraticelles," *Dictionnaire d'histoire et de géographie ecclésiastiques* 18 (Paris, 1977): 1063-1108; Malcolm D. Lambert, *Medieval Heresy. Popular Movements from Bogomil to Hus* (New York: Barnes & Noble, 1977), pp. 182-216; Gordon Leff, *Heresy in the Later Middle Ages*, 2 vols. (New York: Barnes & Noble, 1967), 1:51-255, esp. 238-55; and Decima L. Douie, *The Nature and the Effect of the Heresy of the Fraticelli* (Manchester: The University, 1932), pp. 209-47. Indispensable for their data are Oliger, "Documenta inedita;" idem, "Beiträge zur Geschichte der Spiritualen, Fratizellen und Clarener in Mittelitaliens," *Zeitschrift für Kirchengeschichte* 45 (1926): 215-42; and Ehrle, "Die Spiritualen," 4:1-190.

20. He had the papacy retain ownership of the Franciscan places of worship and accoutrements of divine service. See *Bullarium Franciscanum* 5 (Rome: Vatican, 1898), p. 245b. The bull exists in two versions, each dated 8 December

outlawed their notion of evangelical poverty *tout court*. In the bull *Cum inter nonnullos,* he asserted that Christ and the apostles had indeed owned property,[21] even though in 1279, in the bull *Exiit qui seminat,* Pope Nicholas III would seem to have sanctioned the very doctrine which John XXII now abolished.[22] Nonetheless, from 1323 on, it was heresy to deny that Christ and the apostles held property. The doctrine of evangelical poverty that had inspired St. Francis of Assisi was now officially dead.

One of the groups that took life out of the ashes were the Fraticelli. The name "Fraticelli" did not itself necessarily imply heresy. Through the fourteenth and fifteenth centuries, it also meant Franciscans and their lay followers who accepted church authority, but rejected the material comforts of the Franciscan Order and the rest of the clergy.[23] In 1446, the papacy recognized some Fraticelli as constituting the order of Clarenists, named after the fourteenth-century Spiritual Franciscan, Angelo Clareno.[24] Other orthodox Fraticelli were probably absorbed into the Observant Franciscans. The unorthodox Fraticelli, on the other hand, who by the late fourteenth century had received the

---

1322; the definitive second version appeared after 14 January 1323 (the first version: *Bullarium Franciscanum.,* 5:235b-237a, in the apparatus; the second: ibid., 233a-246b, in the main text). On 14 January 1323 the Franciscan procurator, Bonagratia of Bergamo, delivered in consistory a *libellus* (ibid., 237a-246b, apparatus) refuting the first version of the bull. For both versions and Bonagratia's rebuttal see Leff, *Heresy,* 1:164-65, 238-41; and Malcolm Lambert, *Franciscan Poverty: The Doctrine and of the Poverty of Christ and the Apostles in the Franciscan Order* (London: S.P.C.K., 1961), pp. 226, 230-35.

21. Dated 12 Nov. 1323 (*Bullarium Franciscanum,* 5:256-58). For this and the two other doctrinal bulls on poverty (*Quia quorumdam mentes* of 1324 and *Quia vir reprobus* of 1329) see Leff, *Heresy,* 1:241-49. Lambert, *Franciscan Poverty,* overemphasizes the juridical bull *Quia nonnunquam* (see Leff, *Heresy,* 1:164 n. 2 and 165 n. 4), and in *Medieval Heresy,* pp. 200-202, the juridical bull *Quorumdam exigit.*

22. Nicholas III's *Exiit qui seminat* can be read in *Bullarii Franciscani Epitome,* ed. Conrad Eubel (Quaracchi: Collegio S. Bonaventura, 1908), pp. 289-300. The debate over the power to alter prior papal decisions figured in the development of the doctrine of papal infallibility; see Brian Tierney, *Origins of Papal Infallibility, 1150-1350* (Leiden: Brill, 1972).

23. See Ehrle, "Die Spiritualen," 4:168-80; Tognetti, "I fraticelli," pp. 97-110, 132-33; and *Bullarium Franciscanum,* n.s., 3 vols., ed. U. Huntemann (vol. 1) and I. M. Pou y Marti (vols. 2-3) (Quaracchi: Collegio S. Bonaventura, 1929-49), 2:57-58, no. 107.

24. On the Spirituals see Lydia von Auw, *Angelo Clareno et les spirituels italiens* (Rome: Edizioni di storia e letteratura, 1979); and Ronald G. Musto, "Queen Sancia of Naples (1286-1345) and the Spiritual Franciscans," in Julius Kirshner and Suzanne Wemple, eds., *Women of the Medieval World: Essays in Honor of John H. Mundy* (New York: Basil Blackwell, 1985), pp. 179-214; on the Clarenists, Ehrle, "Die Spiritualen," 4:186-87; Paolo Maria Sevesi, "S. Carlo Borromeo e le Congregazioni degli Amadeiti e dei Clareni," *Archivum Franciscanum Historicum* 37 (1947): 104-64, at 107-8; Douie, *Heresy of the Fraticelli,* pp. 223-24; John Moorman, *A History of the Franciscan Order from its Origins to the Year 1517* (Oxford: Oxford University Press, 1968), pp. 496, 582-85.

distinguishing epithet *de opinione*,[25] never accepted John XXII's settlement of the poverty issue.[26] They adhered to the theological position of Michael of Cesena, the general of the Franciscans who had rebelled against John XXII. In their eyes, John XXII was a heretic. Consequently, the pope and clergy of the Roman Church after John XXII were also heretics. Furthermore, simony, concubinage, and the taking of money for the performance of the sacraments had rendered the Roman clergy an abomination. These dissidents therefore undertook to maintain a separate hierarchical church.[27] While only some Fraticelli denied the

25. See Eugenio Dupré Theseider, "Sul *Dialogo contro i fraticelli* di S. Giacomo della Marca," *Italia Sacra* 16 (1970): 577-611, at 600-602. I doubt the validity of the distinction between Fraticelli *de paupere vita* and Fraticelli *de opinione* common in the literature (e.g., Douie, *Heresy of the Fraticelli*, p. 225 n. 9; Leff, *Heresy*, 1:231; Lambert, *Medieval Heresy*, p. 203). I have encountered the former appellation only in fourteenth-century sources, the latter only beginning in the late fourteenth century, and never together as denoting separate sects. Both names are generic labels for heretical Fraticelli. Oliger, "Documenta inedita," 3:254, is confusing on this point since he implies that the label "Fraticelli *de paupere vita*" was used in the fifteenth century when, in fact, the examples he cites refer only to Fraticelli *de opinione*. Felice Tocco, *Studi Francescani* (Naples: F. Perrella, 1909), pp. 455-96, excerpts the Florentine "Statuta Populi et Communis" of 1415, where reference is made to "fratres della povera vita;" but this passage merely repeats a fourteenth-century ordinance; cf. Tognetti, "I Fraticelli," p. 112.

26. In addition to the works cited above, see Raymond Creytens, "Manfred de Verceil O.P. et son traité contre les fraticelles," *Archivum Fratrum Praedicatorum* 11 (1914): 173-208; and for the social climate, John N. Stephens, "Heresy in Medieval and Renaissance Florence," *Past and Present* 54 (1972): 25-60; and "A Rejoinder," ibid., 62 (1974): 162-66, where he answers Marvin B. Becker, "Heresy in Medieval and Renaissance Florence: A Commentary," ibid., 153-61.

27. Any discussion of Fraticellian sacraments must confront the *barilotto*. According to the trial records of 1466 and an interview that John Capistrano had with a female adherent of the Fraticelli c.1450 and that was incorporated into Flavio Biondo, *De Roma triumphante*, Bk. 8: *Picenum sive Marchia Anconitana* (Basel, 1559, pp. 337-38; see Bartolomeo Nogara, *Scritti inediti e rari di Biondo Flavio*, Studi e testi, 48 [Rome: Vatican, 1927], p. 223), the *barilotto* consisted of communal sex after a night mass. A child born of this fornication would be ritually murdered, its corpse burned, and the ashes mixed with wine to be drunk by the community (the rite of *pulveres*). But this description of *barilotto*, even in its language, duplicates a practice long ascribed to the sect of the Free Spirit and other medieval heretics; see Robert Lerner, *The Heresy of the Free Spirit in the Later Middle Ages* (Berkeley: University of California Press, 1972), pp. 26-33; and Giovanni Miccoli, "La storia religiosa," in *Storia d'Italia* 2.1 (Turin: Einaudi, 1974), pp. 431-1079, at pp. 964-65. Thus, while Romana Guarnieri, "Il movimento del Libero Spirito: Testi e documenti," *Archivio italiano per la storia della pietà* 4 (1965): 351-708, at 466-69 and 476-80, identifies the later Fraticelli with the sect of the Free Spirit; and Tognetti, "I fraticelli," p. 140 n. 224, denies any link; Miccoli rejects outright the existence of the *barilotto*; and Lerner doubts that an antinomian sect of the Free Spirit itself ever existed. Interestingly enough, the trial confessions tell a rather nuanced story, which we can divide into four points: first, that "Bishop" Nicolaus de Massaro and Caterina Palumbaria, who, like the other women, confessed without torture, had sex with each other at different *barilotti*; second, none of the other sixteen captives participated in a *barilotto*, though

efficacy of the sacraments administered by the Roman Church,[28] all of them rejected as worthless confession to anyone other than their own priests.[29] By the fifteenth century, the Fraticelli *de opinione* were exclusively an Italian phenomenon found in Tuscany, Umbria, the Marches, Lazio, and Italian communities in Greece.[30] The post-schism papacy vigorously persecuted them. In 1418, even while on his way to Rome from his election at the Council of Constance, Pope Martin V ordered all bishops to suppress the Fraticelli in their dioceses.[31] Once in Rome he ordered further measures against the sect, including the preaching campaigns of John Capistrano and Iacopo della Marca, both of whom continued in this task for thirty years.[32] Martin's successors kept up the persecutions.[33] The policy worked – the

---

one (Franciscus de Maiolati) thirty years earlier, as a boy, had seen adults engage in the rite, and another (Angelus de Poli) had heard the captured friar Bernardus of Pergamo (i.e., Bergamo) bragging of being in many *barilotti* (Ehrle, "Die Spiritualen," 4:118); third, none of the captives was a party to infanticide (the confession of "Bishop" Nicolaus on this point is a misnumbering [Ehrle, "Die Spiritualen," 4:125]; and that of Caterina is really only a confession of fornication [ibid. p. 126]); and, fourth, that "Bishop" Nicolaus, Caterina, and Franciscus de Maiolati drank *pulveres*. Attributing the *pulveres* to fakery and the infanticide myth to the folklore of the religious underground, I still find persuasive the evidence that later Fraticelli practiced sexual rites, especially celibate leaders, such as "Bishop" Nicholas and Friar Bernardus. Pointedly, the bravest of the captives, Antonio de Sacco, after having been broken, later recanted only one item in his confession, namely, participation in *barilotti*, but not because they were fictive, but rather because he had refused to share his "young" wife and "beautiful" daughter (Ehrle, "Die Spiritualen," 4:131).

28.   See Tognetti, "I fraticelli," p. 134. Indicative of the confusion on this issue are the proceedings of 1455 at Foligno published by Mariano d'Alatri, "Il processo di Foligno contro quattro abitanti di Visso, seguaci dei fraticelli," *Picenum Seraphicum* 12 (1975): 223-61, where one Fraticello denied the efficacy of baptism administered by the Church (p. 241), and another accepted it along with the Church-administered Eucharist and marriage (p. 243).

29.   E. g., one of the charges in 1466 was that the Fraticelli held "quod non licet confiteri peccata sacerdotibus nostris [sc., *papal*] quia absolvere non possunt" (Ehrle, "Die Spiritualen," 4:123).

30.   This geographic diffusion is clear from the treatises of Manfred of Vercelli and Iacopo della Marca and from the trial of 1466. For Tuscany see also Sandra Poggi, "I Fraticelli in Toscana," in Domenico Maselli, ed., *Eretici e ribelli del XIII e XIV sec.: Saggi sullo spritualismo francescano in Toscana* (Pistoia: Tellini, 1974), pp. 253-83; Tocco, *Studi francescani*, pp. 406-94; and Stephens, "Heresy." For Umbria see also d'Alatri, "Il processo di Foligno." Even as late as 1466, after the Turkish conquest, there were Fraticelli in Greece (perhaps only Crete was meant); see Ehrle, "Die Spiritualen," 4:115.13 ("frater Egidius nunc moratur in Gressia") and 116.29-31 ("Luisius de Nerociis de Pictis Florentinis est de hac secta, quia natus est in Gressia...et de mense iunii venit de Gressia cum uno fratre, Johanne de Manolacta eiusdem secte").

31.   Dupré Theseider, "Sul *Dialogo contro i fraticelli*," pp. 602-3.

32.   Ibid., pp. 604-5; Luke Wadding, *Annales Minorum*, ed. Jos. Maria Fonseca, 2d ed., 19 vols. (Rome: Rochus Bernabò 1731-45), 10:101-2; D. Lasić in his edition of Iacopo della Marca, *Dialogus contra Fraticellos* (Falconara Marittima: Biblioteca Francescana, 1975), p. 28; Schmitt, "Fraticelles," col. 1104; Creytens, "Manfred de Verceil," pp. 187 and 193.

Roman *processus* of 1466 was the last trial on record against the Fraticelli.[34]

The plethora of treatises on poverty in the 1460s suggests that few anticipated this result. But was the literary onslaught necessary? Certainly not to persuade the captured Fraticelli, who, by worldly standards, were a pretty scruffy lot. Probably not more than two or three of them could have read the Latin of the Curialists.[35] In any case, they all recanted during the trial.[36] What broke the back of the Fraticelli movement in Italy was not the apologetic skill of the Curialists, but rather the persecutions, the preaching campaigns of the Observant Franciscans, prudent accommodation as represented in the recognition of the Clarenists, decreasing societal sympathy for beggary, and a bit of luck. In 1466, when it was learned that the Fraticelli would come together at Assisi to gain the Portiuncula Indulgence (available at the time only on 1-2 August), the authorities were able to apprehend not only some activists, but also the head of one of the very few (if any) remaining bands of Fraticelli in Italy.[37] The reverence for St.

33. For Eugenius IV see Lasić, in Iacopo della Marca, *Dialogus contra fraticellos*, pp. 28, 47-48 n. 111, and 124 n. 68; *Bullarium Franciscanum*, n.s. 3:21-22, no. 29; 39, no. 63; 251, no. 520; Oliger, "Documenta inedita," 6:528-29 and 710-16. For Nicholas V see Jouffroy cited in n. 6 above; *Bullarium Franciscanum*, n.s. 3:544, no. 1076; 731-32, no. 1445; 750-51, no. 1494; Oliger, "Documenta inedita," 6:529-30; and Flavio Biondo, cited in n. 27 above.
34. I am not persuaded by the suggestion of Mosti, "L'eresia dei 'fraticelli'," pp. 99-102; and Schmitt, "Fraticelles," col. 1101, that there might have been another process against the Fraticelli in 1495. The sole source is Wadding, *Annales*, 15:99, who reports that in 1495 the authorities moved against one Fra Mattia (né Pietro Nardi) of the Roman Province, learned in Greek. There is nothing in Wadding's account to suggest that Mattia was anything more than a charismatic rigorist calling for poverty and strict observance of the rule.
35. "Bishop" Nicolaus de Massaro and friar Bernardus de Pergamo (i.e., Bergamo) probably knew Latin. The other prisoners were laity without any apparent literary education. The Fraticello whom Jouffroy refuted possessed some learning, but he seems not to have been one of the captives. On the culture of the later Fraticelli see Tognetti, "I fraticelli," p. 143.
36. According to the trial proceedings, all the apprehended Fraticelli abjured their heresy, and none were burned. This agrees with Canensi, *De vita Pauli Secundi*, p. 153 (see n. 9 above) and is not contradicted by Stefano Infessura [speaking of 1467 sic], *Diario della città di Roma*, ed. Oreste Tommasini, in Fonti per la storia d'Italia 5 (Rome: Forzani, 1890), pp. 69-70, nor the Milanese ambassador Agostino de Rossi, who is sometimes mistakenly read as saying that the Fraticelli were burned, instead of that they *were willing* to be burned ("pregano de essere brusate;" Fumi, "Eretici in Boemia," p. 126).
37. For their capture see the account given at the start of the trial record (Ehrle, "Die Spiritualen," 4:111). The only other group mentioned at the trial was one led by Paulus de Florentia, which separated from the group led by the captured "Bishop" Nicolaus de Massaro (ibid., p. 114). On Paolo da Firenze see d'Alatri, "Il Processo di Foligno," pp. 233-35, who makes a case (p. 236) for "Bishop" Nicolaus de Massaro of 1466 being none other than the "Pontifex" (Pope) Nicolaus de Massaccio mentioned in the 1455 proceedings at Foligno. In the preface to his corpus of writings against the Fraticelli, Niccolò Palmieri gave another variant of Nicolaus' hometown, which Oliger, "Documenta inedita," p. 736 n. 6, also think should be read as Massaccio: "vir quidam

Francis that brought the Fraticelli to accept the indulgences had also led them into the trap.

Nor should we think the treatises of the Curialists were necessary because the assertions of the Fraticelli had gone unanswered in the past. The Fraticelli had been adequately rebutted a number of times since the fourteenth century,[38] and as recently as 1458 by Iacopo della Marca, OFM, the most successful and most knowledgeable of all the preachers against the Fraticelli.[39]

The trial of the Fraticelli clearly had touched upon issues of clerical wealth and power that made the Curia very defensive. However, the immediate cause for the rebuttals were three new Fraticellian texts that came to light in the 1460s. The first was the "small book" mentioned twice in the trial proceedings. It contained the doctrines and the rituals of the sect,[40] and was perhaps the same work to which Niccolò Palmieri, a judge in the proceedings, twice referred in one of his treatises.[41] The second Fraticellian text of the 1460s specifically attacked Pope Paul II. This is the *libellus* Jean Jouffroy answered.[42] The third Fraticellian text was that rebutted by Fernando of Cordova. This last was a scientific work divided into ten tractates, the content, order, and

---

scelestus Nicolaus nomine pro episcopo se ingerebat. Hic ex agro Piceno oppido Mazani [*not* Maçam *as in Oliger*] a vilissimis parentibus originem traxit" (Mastrocolo, *Note storiche*, p. 281; MSS Vatican, Chigi A IV 113, fol. 4v; Vat. lat. 4158, fol. 1v).

38. To the already-cited sources add S. G. Sikes, "Hervaeus Natalis: *De paupertate Christi et apostolorum*," *Archives d'histoire doctrinale et littéraire du moyen âge* 12-13 (1937-38): 209-97.

39. Lasić in Iacopo's *Dialogus contra Fraticellos*, pp. 38-44, corrects the previously accepted date of 1450-52 proposed by Ehrle.

40. "Et in hoc longe melior erat eorum secta, quam vocant inter se veritatem, iuxta tenorem unius parvi libelli" (Ehrle, "Die Spiritualen," 4:114.35-37; Dressel, *Vier Dokumente*, p. 9; Mastrocola, *Note storiche*, p. 257). Later, having described the ritual of the *barilotto*, the text goes on: "pluraque alia turpia, gravia, et enormia crimina et maleficia variasque et diversas haereses nefandissimas faciunt et committunt, que pro magna parte in quodam parvo codice apud quendam prefate secte sacerdotem reperto, quorum tenore scripsimus, continentur, contra omnia tam naturalia quam canonica, civilia quam etiam municipalia..." (not in Ehrle; Dressel, p. 22; Mastrocola, pp. 263-64, ruins the passage, reading "in quemdam prefacte secte" for "in quodam parvo codice apud quendam prefate secte").

41. It is possible that he was referring to the same work as Fernando (see n. 43 below). In the *Tractatus de concordia Nicolai III et Ioannis XXII*, MS Vatican, Chig. A IV 113, fol. 65v-66r: "Heretici qui Fraticelli dela opinione nuncupantur, prout in libro ipsorum aperte percipitur, distingunt Christum et apostolos.... Concedunt etiam isti fraticelli Christum et apostolos iure poli [*ecclesiastical law according to R. E. Latham*, Revised Medieval Latin Word-List from British and Irish Sources (*London: British Academy, 1965), p. 264b*] habuisse; et negare modis supradictis Christum neque apostolos habuisse est hereticum etiam; nec negare Christum et apostolos pro aliquo tempore nihil possedisse audent. Hoc in libello in quo fundamenta ipsorum sunt adnotata videri potest, ex quo videtur quod isti, qui sentiunt cum Nicolao et Ioannem damnant, Christum et apostolos in communi possedisse affirmant;" cf. Mastrocola, *Note storiche*, p. 311.

42. See nn. 6 and 7 above.

JOHN MONFASANI

even some of the wording of which we know because Fernando
specifically tells us that the ten tractates of his own treatise exactly
parallel the ten tractates of the Fraticellian text.[43]
In at least one respect, the text Fernando refuted was unusual.
To be sure, most of it dealt with poverty. Nonetheless, it began
with a different, though related topic, namely, political power, its
first two tractates discussing the earthly kingship of Christ and the
temporal power of the pope.[44] In response, Fernando gave over
more than half of his book to proving Christ's earthly kingship
and the pope's right to temporal dominion. Sánchez de Arévalo's
treatise shares the same imbalance, and, as Decima Douie suggested,[45] may be a response to the same Fraticellian work. Both
Fernando and Arévalo grounded their argument for Christ's

43. See the rubric of the table of contents (MS Vatican, Vat. lat. 1127, fol.
1r: "adversus quorundam errores qui fratricheli dela opinione vulgo
appellantur... liber incipit...qui iuxta horum decem hereses et tractatus quoque
conplexus est") and the *incipit* of Tractate 7 (ibid., fol. 165r: "Huic tractatui
ideo titulum dedimus quod ordinem tractatuum hereticorum secuti sumus"). For
the wording of the titles of the tractates see the title to Tractate 3 ("ut eorum
[*sc., the Fraticelli*] questionis formula utar") and Tractate 4 ("ut eorum verbis
utar"). The titles of Fernando's ten tractates are (I have abbreviated them
somewhat but kept Fernando's orthography):
1. De Christi in assumpta natura inclito principato.
2. De principatu pape et summi pontificis potestate.
3. Utrum Christus, in quantum homo mortalis, dicendus sit dominus habens
proprietatem et dominium omnium rerum temporalium, et, in quantum talis,
possit per temporis successus sibi dominia rerum conquirere que prius essent a
se aliena.
4. Utrum appostoli habuerint in speciali et sigilatim, non solum in comuni
proprietatem et dominium multarum rerum.
5. Utrum Christus imposuerit aliam legem vivendi appostolis quam
quibuscumque aliis discipulis.
6. Utrum litigare in iudicio pro rebus temporalibus diminuat de perfectione
evangelica.
7. Utrum dominus noster Ihesus Christus interdixerit simpliciter et absolute
appostolis ne possiderent aurum et argentum neque pecuniam in zonis vel
solum pro tempore vie, cum irent ad predicandum, ita ut post redditum a
predicacione libere possidere et portare potuissent.
8. Utrum bona primitive ecclesie seu multitudinis credencium, de quibus
Actuum secundo et quarto, ne quisquam eorum que possidebat aliquid suum esse
dicebat, sed erant illis omnia comunia; et an votum religiosorum se extendat
ad illa que necessario eget vita humana.
9. Utrum in rebus usu consumptibilibus usus vel iuris vel facti licite possit a
proprietate et dominio separari; et an in temporalibus rebus ius utendi
separata proprietate rei seu dominio possit constitui vel haberi.
10. Utrum sint Io. 22 excusaciones admittende circa obiectas sibi hereses.
44. 1 have not come across a similar order in Fraticellian texts. Denying the
temporal power of the pope was itself a traditional Fraticellian position, on
which they agreed with secular anti-papal theorists, such as Dante and
Marsilio of Padua.   See W. Kölmel, *Wilhelm Ockham und seine kirchen-
politischen Schriften* (Essen: Ludgerus, 1962).
45. "Some Treatises," pp. 55-56, where she also suggested that Palmieri was
responding to the same Fraticellian work.

temporal kingship on the hypostatic union of his two natures.[46] The Augustinian friar Agostino Favaroni had first formulated this argument thirty years earlier,[47] but neither Fernando nor Arévalo mention him – probably because Favaroni's Christology was under formal censure by the Church.[48]

Jouffroy also discussed the kingship of Christ.[49] However, he was much more concerned with defending curial pomp. His was a defense not of mere evangelical possession of property, but of conspicuous consumption, of ecclesiastical luxury and wealth. He quotes the Fraticello as asking about Paul II's papal tiara, bedecked with diamonds, emeralds, and other jewels: "Is this a spectacle of religion? Or do we call it the fall and ruin of humility and modesty?"[50] Jouffroy's answer was not only to defend the use of the papal tiara, but even more so to justify the jewels of the tiara for their symbolic value and power as talismans.[51] Furthermore, while conceding that Christ and the apostles were poor, Jouffroy argued that times had changed and that a more "ornate," luxurious church was now in order.[52] A splendid illustration of this fact, he contended, was the normally austere Cardinal Niccolò Albergati, who, while legate to the Council of Basel, showed his disdain for the Council's complaints against the pomp of the Rome by arraying himself and his entourage in an especially

46. See Toni, "La Realeza de Jesucristo;" idem, "Don Rodrigo Sánchez de Arévalo," pp. 510-18; Trame, Rodrigo Sánchez de Arévalo, pp. 141-42; Laboa, Rodrigo Sánchez de Arévalo, pp. 162-63. The title De Christi...inclito principatu of Tract. 1 of Fernando's work is an unacknowledged quotation of the title of Favaroni's De Christo capite ecclesiae et eius inclito principatu.

47. See Jean Leclercq, "L'idée de la royauté du Christ pendant le Grand Schisme et la crise conciliaire," Archives d'histoire doctrinale et littéraire de moyen âge 24 (1949): 249-65, at 261-64; cf. also Aldo Vallone, "Favarone de' Favaroni e il suo inedito trattato De principatu papae," in Studi storici in onore di Gabriele Pepe (Bari: Dedalo, 1969), pp. 499-507.

48. Uneasy about his use of Favaroni, Fernando added a disclaimer to the end of the treatise (fol. 166r): "Que in primo huius operis capitulo diximus [see n. 43 above] magis scolasticorum more protulimus quam obstinate pro veris tueri cupiamus; reliqua vero ecclesie sacrosancte determinacioni subicimus." For the censure and for the theology of Favaroni see Karl Binder, Wesen und Eigenschaften der Kirche bei Kardinal Juan de Torquemada O.P. (Innsbruck: Tyrolia, 1955), ad indicem; idem, "Zum Schriftbeweis in der Kirchentheologie des Kardinals Juan de Torquemada O.P.," in L. Scheffczyk, W. Dettloff, and R. Heinzmann, eds., Wahrheit und Verkündigung: Michael Schmaus zum 70. Geburtstag, 2 vols. (Paderborn: Schöningh, 1967), 1:511-50, at 524, 537-38; Gino Ciolini, Agostino da Roma (Favaroni + 1443) e la sua cristologia (Florence: Coppini, 1944); and Thomas Izbicki, Protector of the Faith: Cardinal Johannes de Turrecremata and the Defense of the Institutional Church (Washington, DC: Catholic University of America Press, 1981), pp. 7, 38, 40-41.

49. MS Vatican, Ottob. lat. 793, fols. 26r-28r, 33v-34r.

50. Miglio, Storiografia, p. 139.

51. Ibid., pp. 139-45.

52. E.g., (MS Vatican, Ottob. lat. 793, fol. 22r): "Vis semper secter ordinem constitutum, scilicet, legis divine, iuris nature, moris sanctorum, legis et canonis ut scias quod mores ecclesie translati ex paupertate ad cultus ornatiores probatissimis omnibus legibus? Vis scire predictum divinitus decus ecclesie, quale vides, iubente deo crevisse?"

ornate manner. Even his mules received gold bridles, such being the splendor demanded by the cardinalate's dignity.[53]

Fernando of Cordova put forth an even more extraordinary defense of clerical wealth. Not mincing words, he argued that prelates had a right to enjoy a *vita delicata* out of the goods of the Church, complete with dainty foods, fancy clothing, well-decorated horses, and other household accoutrements suitable to their station.[54] Indeed, he insisted, the opulent lifestyle proper to the dignity of a cardinal no more led to pride than the sandals of the discalced friars led to sanctity. The holier-than-thou attitude of the Fraticelli was mere hypocrisy.[55] With much gusto, he mocked the morose, solemn demeanor of those who criticized the cardinals. Conversely, he praised the jokes and levity enjoyed by the prelates and their entourages.[56]

53. Ibid., fol. 25v: "Sed mihi monastice philosophie princeps, cardinalis sancte Crucis, unicus sufficit. Is aliquando legatus, cum illam sinagogam Basiliensem a processu furoris arceret, audivit isthic quosdam blactratores allatrare ornatus Romane sedis. At gravissimus, sanctus, severus pater atque, etiam si fabriciis, curiis compararetur, moderatissimus omnium rerum humana-rum contemptor, illico et propere familiam vestivit ornatius quam ante fecerat frenosque aureos mule adiecit. Credo patrem illum causas sanctimonie <intellexisse?>, etsi nullus ei dolor privati honoris insideret, tamen fuisse ipsi cogitationem in allatratione cardinalium ceterorum se despectum dignitatemque altissimi ordinis contemptam et abiectam. Nec debuit sanctissimus vir dissimu-lare aut conticuendo firmare ut insulso statuto ducti homines existimarent amplissimos ecclesie et pontificum cultus non modo ad invidiam, sed ad contumeliam superbie natos et institutos."
54. MS Vatican, Vat. lat. 1127, fol. 132v-134v. This is Tract. 1, c. 26, the title of which runs: "Quod falsso [sic] <et> ippocrite fraterculi obiciunt ecclesiasticis viris cum negant licere eis de bonis ecclesie delicatam ducere vitam pro semetipsis delicatos cibos vescentibus et utentibus preciosis vestibus atque equis et ornamentis equorum et ceteris [cetera MS] que per ippocrisim ecclesiasticis viris inpingere soliti sunt."
55. Ibid., fol. 134r: "Cardinalis ad magnificenciam et ospitalitatem et dignitatem servandam et preciosis uti cibis potest et ornatis equis. Quodsi ad superbiam referre possint et ad ambicionem, nihil ad propositum. Nam et idem in asel<l>is vilibus, quibus discalciati fraterculi insidere solent, contin-gere potest, ut id ad sanctitatem per ippocrisum simulandam refferunt. Unde in his nec vicii ratio esse potest neque virtutis nec in eorum usu nisi in abusum convertatis [convertata MS] per corruptas circumstantias, sicut ippocritalium oc<c>ulorum in terram deiectio et obtorta cervix et crebra suspiria et male et bene fieri possunt. Unde hii ippocrite in obstrictionem dei iudicio iudicandi sunt qui suos superiores iudicant."
56. See the previous note for his characterization of the Fraticelli. He gives the same characterization in Tract. 4, c. 39 (ibid., fols. 155r-160v), which has the title (from the table on fol. 104v; the rubric is missing on fol. 155r): "Capitulum 39 contra supercilium ippocritarum disputat cardinales et reliquos apostolicos viros tante opportere esse severitatis afirmancium ut risum et iocos inter confabulandum miscere non possint neque circa iocos atque concitandos risus virtutem esse posse neque artem, ubi nos contra docebimus, scilicet, et esse circa risus et iocos virtutem et circa risus movendos artem versari, cuius quidem artis precepta adhibemus." The chapter begins: "Nichil iam superem [*the subjunc-tive of* supero, *which I cannot construe with* quam *further on*] quod superiores heretici in prelatis ecclesiasticis criminentur quam habitum corporis atque vultus modestiam ut vix eis concedant spuere eis in terra licere, quin pocius

Yet, by his lights, Fernando was no apologist for corruption. He condemned the accumulation of benefices because the pluralist could not fulfill the offices for which he was being paid.[57] But poverty and mendicancy did not exist for him as spiritual values. This is especially clear in the work on annates that he wrote for Pope Sixtus IV. In it Fernando listed the professions that owed the pope material support as universal pastor. One of the professions was that of beggars, who, as becomes clear from Fernando's listing of their names, asserted some sort of spiritual title. These beggars came right after prostitutes and pimps in Fernando's list. Fernando gave beggars the formal Latin title of *questores*, ("importuners"), but he immediately characterized them as charlatans and proceeded to itemize forty different kinds of uncanonical "religious" beggars, each having its own niche in what today we would call the charity market.[58] Fernando was

---

exigant ab eis sibi esse similimos, obtorta cervice incedere et deiectis in terram oculis, negentque eos ullo casu posse ridere vel miscere iocos, sed opportere esse eos tan [sic] obstinate severitatis ut subtristem perpetuo frontem habeant, que morum, ut aiunt, gravitatem indicare possit. Et id quidem tan obstinate defendunt ut heresiarca quidam eorum Guillelmus Anglicus [Ockham?] afirmet opportere cardinales et reliquos ecclesiasticos principes tante esse severitatis ut nec ridere eos liceat."

57. See ibid., Tract. 4, c. 27, fols. 135r-137v. "Utrum sit abusus, ut heretici ecclesiaticis viris obiciunt, vel habere beneficiorum pluralitatem vel ad habendum petere dispensacionem." Fernando defended the principle of dispensations for multiple benefices, but he says on fol. 137r-v that if it is wrong to keep multiple benefices in even one church ("Cum ergo vix sit aliquis qui unicum beneficium in una ecclesia ad plenum deservire suf<f>iciat"), he concludes that: "quare et multo fortius in diversis et maxime episcopatibus aut in diverssis [sic] provinciis, quia quanto magis beneficia sunt distancia tanto minus potest unus in pluribus deservire, quamquam in speciali ratione dispensari solet ut aliquis plura beneficia habeat in diversis ecclesiis, non autem ut in unica. Sic ergo plura beneficia simul tenere non solum malum est quia de iure publico prohibitum, sed potius prohibitum quia malum et vergens in animarum periculum eo quod sibi bona usurpant pro quibus ecclesie deservire non possunt, que aliis debent concedi quia ea possunt deservire.

58. See his *De iure medios exigendi fructus quos vulgo annatos dicunt et Romani pontificis in temporalibus potestate* (Rome: Georgius Herolt, 1481; Hain 5719), fols. 74v, 81v-88r. Fernando divides his beggars by religious types (fol. 74v): "[in the forty-first category of those who owe annates there is a] multitudo questorum, quos vulgo Italorum charratonos [*i.e., Hispanized spelling of* "ciarlatonos"], Hispanorum vero echacuervos [*in modern Spanish a "pimp" or a "fraud," see the Real Academia Española,* Diccionario de la lengua española, 2 *vols. (Madrid, 1984)]* vocant, quos, ut et ex sacris litteris et divis intepretibus constat, certum est in quadraginta genera esse distributos. Itali autem his quadraginta generibus charratanorum aptissima rebus nomina aptaverunt ut nobis sit in animo in eis recensendis Italorum uti nominibus. Sunt itaque quadraginta charratanorum modi. Primus dicuntur angelici; secundus, apostolici; tertius, anime simplices; quartus, balla in Christo; quintus, boca suta; sextus, begardi; septimus, capitorti; octavus, capuceti; nonus, conscientiati; decimus, chinelli; undecimus, devoti; duodecimus, discreti; tredecimus, gabadei; quatuordecimus, girovagi; quindecimus grataceli; sedecimus, humilitosi; decimus septimus, iubilate; decimus octavus, catholici; decimus nonus, laude Christo; vigesimus, mania sancti; vigesimus primus, mania terra; vigesimus secundus, mel in bocca; vigesimus tertius, obedientes; vigesimus quartus, observanciales;

neither the first nor the only one in the period to prepare a taxonomy of beggars. We have a listing from Basel from about 1450.[59] Chapter 63 of Sebastian Brant's *Ship of Fools* (printed in 1494) classified and pilloried beggars. But the prize for the fullest description of different categories of beggars must go to the *Liber Vagatorum*, which became an immediate best-seller upon its publication c.1509.[60] To demonstrate continuity in these matters one may point to the extraordinary division of beggars found in the late sixteenth-century Roman police report that Jean Delumeau put to good purpose in discussing the social and economic life of late Renaissance Rome.[61] Fernando's list differs from all the others in its exclusive concentration on those he viewed as religious charlatans. But it therefore suggests all the more that in fifteenth-century Rome many viewed mendicancy not primarily as an expression of destitution or of spiritual discipline, but as an unsavory economic enterprise with specific sub-specializations.

From the fifteenth century onward, European governments increasingly attempted to cope with beggary by simple prohibition and other means.[62] Rome was not exempt from this phenomenon. In 1581, Pope Gregory XIII tried to solve the problem at Rome by arranging to have beggars housed and fed in the former Dominican monastery of San Sisto. What is remarkable about this episode is that the Roman beggars made their calculations and, as if justifying the later police report, put forward the counter offer of 2,600 écus in return for their liberty.[63]

This perception of beggary as an economic and even criminal problem in the later Middle Ages and Renaissance contrasts with

---

vigesimus quintus, pacientes; vigesimus sextus, pacifici; vigesimus septimus, penitentes; vigesimus octavus, placidi; vigesimus nonus, pizzocati; trigesimus, poverelli; trigesimus primus, querulosi; trigesimus secundus, sanctarelli; trigesimus tertius, stabaite; trigesimus quartus, spiritelli; trigesimus quintus, supersticiosi; trigesimus sextus, scrupulosi; trigesimus septimus, solitarii; trigesimus octavus, timorosi; trigesimus nonus, singulares; quadragesimus, iusti."
59. See Friedrich Kluge, *Rotwelsch. Quellen und Wortschatz der Gaunersprache und der verwandten Geheimsprachen*, vol. 1 (Strassburg: Trübner, 1901), pp. 8-16. Kluge also gathers some earlier German reports of rogues' argot (*Rotwelsch*).
60. See D. B. Thomas, ed. and trans., *The Book of Vagabonds and Beggars with a Vocabulary of their Language and a Preface by Martin Luther First Translated into English by J. C. Hotten* (London: Penguin, 1932). The *Liber Vagatorum* was written in Switzerland and uses many of the same names for classes of beggars found in the earlier Basel list.
61. *Vie économique et sociale de Rome dans la seconde moitié du XVIe siècle*, 2 vols. (Paris: E. De Boccard, 1957), 1:405-7; which is based on A. Massoni, "Gli accattoni in Londra nel secolo XIX e in Roma nel secolo XVI," *Rassegna italiana* 2 (1882): 197-229, at 221-27.
62. A useful survey is Bronislaw Geremek, "La Lutte contre le vagabondage à Paris aux XIVe et XVe siècles," in Luigi de Rosa, ed., *Ricerche storiche ed economiche in memoria di Corrado Barbagallo*, 3 vols. (Naples: Edizioni scientifiche italiane, 1970), 2:211-36.
63. Delumeau, *Vie économique*, 1:412-13, based on the Roman *Avisi*. I wish to thank Prof. Barbara McClung Hallman for calling this episode to my attention.

the acceptance by the Church in the thirteenth century of the Franciscan ideals of mendicancy and absolute poverty involving no ownership whatsoever of property. John XXII's bull *Cum inter nonnullos* of 1323 in effect desacralized these ideals by declaring that Christ and the Apostles had a right to, and actually did own, property. But the ideals still survived not only among the Fraticelli who rejected John XXII's dogmatic settlement, but also as a form of religious idealism among the orthodox who honored voluntary poverty as the high road to sanctity and who were troubled by the worldliness of the contemporary Church. These historical and moral contradictions are well illustrated by the writings of Niccolò Palmieri.

As we have already seen, in the 1460s several Curialists with intellectual and moral qualms concerning poverty and mendicancy asked him to address these issues.[64] As an Augustinian friar who had become bishop of Orte, as a papal theologian, and as an experienced preacher before the papal court, Palmieri understood well the concerns of the Curialists. To one bishop, he explained that poverty is no perfection; our only perfection is our final goal, God himself, to whom we are led most eminently by charity; poverty is merely an aid to charity; in respect to poverty the distinction between use of goods and dominium over goods is silly and leads to hypocrisy. What is useful in turning us from the world to our perfection, God, is not such distinctions but a *voluntas povertatis* involving an abdication of goods in use and dominium, the avoidance of women, and the fleeing of cities and their temptations.[65] Insofar as the pursuit of poverty was a religious value, Palmieri rejected the mendicant ideal and replaced it with the much older eremitic ideal, which, in fact, was still very much alive among Catholics.

To another bishop who asked how it happened that the mendicant orders began only twelve hundred years after Christ, Palmieri explained that St. Augustine had condemned mendicancy in the name of religion; moreover, none of the popes had ever practised it; and only heretics had preached it before the time of Francis and Dominic. The two sainted founders of the mendicant orders appropriated this particular doctrine of the heretics as an expediency to forestall the spreading influence of heretics. Furthermore, Pope John XXII's settlement of the poverty issue did

---

64. These works are summarized by Douie, "Some Treatises," pp. 16-43. The edition of the texts in Mastrocola, *Note storiche*, pp. 280-342, is useful, but not especially reliable. See my forthcoming study of Palmieri in *Analecta Augustiniana*; Mastrocola, *Note storiche*, pp. 23-63; and Paul Oskar Kristeller, *Medieval Aspects of Renaissance Learning*, trans. and ed. Edward P. Mahoney (Durham, NC: Duke University Press, 1974), p. 148; and John W. O'Malley, S.J., *Praise and Blame in Renaissance Rome* (Durham, NC: Duke University Press, 1979), *ad indicem*.
65. See his *Adversus pauperes nomine* in Oliger, "Ein unbekannter Traktat."

not contradict the earlier pronouncements of Pope Nicholas III on the matter.[66]

Palmieri most fully worked out his notion of the historical meaning of mendicancy in the treatise De triplici statu ecclesiae.[67] He accepted the traditional tripartite division of history into the age of nature beginning with Adam, the age of the Law beginning with Moses, and the age of Christ. He then divided the Christian era into three different stages or status. The first was that of Christ's lifetime when Christ used poverty as an instrument to spread the Gospel, though he himself never promoted, let alone practiced, mendicancy. In the second stage, during the great expansion of faith over the face of the earth, the apostles and doctors of the Church possessed gold and other goods, instituted the orders of deacons to handle Church property, and founded monasteries where property was held in common. In the third stage, when princes and temporal governments became subject to the pope, the Church established various forms of religious life to deal with the many different demands laid upon it. Thus it permitted the poverty of mendicancy, the possession of goods in common by communities, and also individual ownership of property by churchmen.

Finally, in the treatise to Cardinal Juan Carvajal,[68] Palmieri rejected the notion that Christ himself was ever a beggar. What Christ received for maintenance from the faithful, he received by reason of justice for his administrations to them, and not because he was a mendicant receiving charity. Indeed, Christ had private property, and the apostles held goods in common.

As far as I know, no Fraticello or even a Franciscan ever tried to refute Palmieri, but two Dominican theologians did precisely that. One was Jacob Gil, OP, a judge in the proceedings against the Fraticelli in 1466, and, as Master of the Sacred Palace, the pope's official theologian.[69] The other was the distinguished theologian and cardinal, Juan de Torquemada.[70] What triggered the controversy between these Curialists concerning poverty was not the trial of the Fraticelli in 1466, but rather the coming to Rome in

---

66. For his De origine mendicantium Predicatorum et Minorum and De concordia Nicolai III et Ioannis XXII see nn. 12 and 15 above.
67. See nn. 14 and 15 above.
68. This is the Contra illos qui asserunt Christum omnia abdicassee; see nn. 13 and 15 above.
69. See Raymond Creytens, "Les Écrits de Jacques Gil O.P.," Archivum Fratrum Praedicatorum 10 (1940): 158-68; and Thomas Kaeppeli, Scriptores Ordinis Praedicatorum Medii Aevi, 3 vols. (Rome: Santa Sabina, 1970-1980), 2:295-97.
70. See Clément Schmitt, "Le Traité du cardinal Jean de Torquemada sur la pauvreté évangélique," Archivum Fratrum Praedicatorum 57 (1987): 103-4; Kaeppeli, Scriptores, 3:30, no. 2713; Izbicki, Protector of the Faith, pp. 27 and 133-34 n. 99; Douie, "Some Treatises," pp. 24-31. Torquemada also attacked Sánchez de Arévalo, but on the issue of papal temporal dominium and not mendicant poverty; see Hubert Jedin, "Juan de Torquemada und das Imperium Romanum," Archivum Fratrum Praedicatorum 12 (1942): 247-78; Trame, Sánchez de Arévalo, pp. 157-58; Izbicki, Protector of the Faith, pp. 28, 110-12, 137 n. 18.

1465 of the English Carmelite John Milverton.[71] Milverton, along with some other Carmelites, had been censured by the bishop of London for having attacked the endowed clergy and having preached that Christ had been a propertyless mendicant who begged from door to door (*mendicare hostiatim*). Milverton eventually ended up in Castel Sant'Angelo with the Fraticelli, and was not released until 1468, when he disavowed his opinions concerning poverty. It was to answer Milverton that Cardinal Carvajal had asked Palmieri to write.[72] The problem was that Gil and Torquemada agreed with much that Milverton preached. In fact, as judge in his first trial, Torquemada had cleared Milverton of all charges of heresy. Gil first wrote in 1465 a treatise against the accusers of Milverton, in which he proved that Christ had indeed been a pauper and had begged as a true mendicant.[73] He followed this treatise with another in 1467 directed explicitly at Palmieri, in which he accused Palmieri of holding a heretical position on the poverty and mendicancy of Christ.[74]

Several scholars have assumed that in his first and largest pamphlet on poverty Torquemada attacked Palmieri.[75] This is false. Rather he refuted the *libellus* of a certain anonymous *hereticus* (William Ive, I suggest, who was the leading English

71. See F. R. H. Du Boulay, "The Quarrel between the Carmelite Friars and the Secular Clergy of London, 1464-1468," *Journal of Ecclesiastical History* 6 (1955): 156-74; *The Historical Collections of a Citizen of London in the Fifteenth Century*, ed. James Gairdner, Camden Series of the Royal Historical Society, Publications, n.s., p. 17 (Westminster: Camden Society, 1876), pp. 228-32; and *Registrum Thome Bourgchier Cantuariensis Archiepiscopi, A. D. 1454-1486*, ed. F. R. H. Du Boulay, The Canterbury and York Society, 44 (Oxford: Oxford University Press, 1957), p. 35. For Milverton and his chief English opponent, William Ive, see also A. B. Emden, *A Biographical Register of the University of Oxford to A.D. 1500*, 3 vols. (Oxford: Oxford University Press, 1957-59), 2:1008-9 and 1284-85.
72. Palmieri called Milverton *ille Anglicus Ioannes* (MS Vatican, Chig. A IV 113, fol. 91v).
73. This treatise, titled *Tractatus Catholice veritatis contra impugnantes paupertatis Christi sacramentum compositus in urbe Rome anno domini millesimo quadringentesimo sexagesimoquinto*, dedicated to Pope Paul II, survives in three manuscripts; see Creytens and Kaeppeli in n. 69 above. In the margin of MS Vatican, Vat. lat. 1000, fol. 1v, the scribe wrote: "Contra quosdam de Anglia" (i.e., those who had rejected Milverton's position on the poverty of Christ). The text at this point runs: "Novo propterea in partibus variis pullulante errore contra Christi paupertatem asserentibus certis Christum non mendicasse nec fuisse pauperem et qui oppositum affirmant errant, hereticant, blasphemant."
74. This is the *Tractatus Catholice veritatis contra prophanas vocum novitates asserti cuiusdam religiosi, olim mendicantis, nunc vero episcopi, circa fidem sacramenti paupertatis Christi altissime excidentis compositus in urbe Rome anno domini MCCCCLXVII*, in MSS Vatican, Vat. lat. 1000, fols. 27r-76r; Chig. A V 159 (the only work in the manuscript); and Pavia, Bibl. Univ., Aldini 438. This treatise was also dedicated to Pope Paul II.
75. See Schmitt, Izbicki, and Douie in n. 70 above. The treatise is the *Libellus velociter compositus et editus...contra certos hereticos noviter impugnantes paupertatem Christi et suorum apostolorum*, extant in MS Vatican, Vat. lat. 974, fols. 55v-62r.

opponent of Milverton),[76] and then the summary of another work that in the mode of Fernando and Arévalo rejected the poverty of Christ on the grounds of his human kingship.[77] Torquemada quotes the arguments and the words of the anonymous *hereticus*, and they are not Palmieri's;[78] but most of the positions he condemns concerning the poverty agree with Palmieri's views.[79] So it is not surprising that soon after this treatise, Torquemada did refute Palmieri in an untitled opuscule which served as an addendum to the main pamphlet.[80] In a separate, third opuscule Torquemada denied that poverty was the essence of perfection, but this piece had nothing to do with Palmieri.[81]

76. See n. 71 above. His *lectiones de mendicitate Christi* are extant in MS Oxford, Bodleian Library, Lat. Theol. e. 25.
77. See Schmitt, "Le Traité," pp. 138-44; cf. Douie, "Some Treatises," pp. 28-29.
78. One will not find in Palmieri's treatise *Contra illos qui asserunt Christum omnia mendicasse*, or in any other of his extant writings, any of the arguments reported by Torquemada in Schmitt, "Le Traité," pp. 122-25, 128, 130-34.
79. Palmieri advocated all but the last two of the six "errors" identified by Torquemada. The six errors of the heretical *libellus* were as follows: 1) "quod Christus non fuit pauper;" 2) "quod Christus nunquam mendicaverit sive quod ex paupertate petierit aliquid ab alio;" 3) "quod apostoli non fuerunt ita pauperes quod aliquando mendicarent;" 4) "quod Christus non mandavit iuste acquisita dimitti ita ut quis facultates suas vendens remaneret actu pauper et mendicus;" 5) "quod mendicitas sit illicita; dicit enim illam pro maledictione poni in Psalmis, 'deus, laudem meam,' et per consequens reprobat statum eorum qui relictis omnibus egere voluerunt;" 6) "quod melius faciunt qui utuntur rebus suis et paulatim fructus possessionum suarum dimidunt pauperibus quam qui possessionibus omnibus venditis simul omnia pauperibus larguntur."
80. MS Vatican, Vat. lat. 974, fols. 62va-63vb. There seems to have been some personal animosity involved. In a harsh remark, apparently directed against the English Carmelites, Palmieri says in the *Contra illos qui asserunt Christum omnia mendicasse* that "quare ridiculum est dicere mendicitate Christi hostiatim nos divites factos fuisse" (MS Vatican, Chig. A IV 113 , fol. 89r; the Carmelites did assert something like this; see Du Boulay, "The Quarrel," p. 173). Nowhere in his extant writings does Palmieri mention Torquemada. Nonetheless, at the start of his own refutation of Palmieri, Torquemada says (fol. 62va) about Palmieri: "Verum primo absolvemus nos ab uno quod false imponit nobis. Dicit enim quod nos diximus Christum mendicum hostiatim fuisse, in quo salva pace non dicit verum." Perhaps, Palmieri orally identified Torquemada with Milverton's position. In any case, the three "puncti" to which Torquemada reduced Palmieri's "errors" do reflect Palmieri's views, namely, "quod negat Christum pauper fuisse inopia rerum terrenarum;" "quod Christus degit paupertatem habitualem, que est in preparatione animi, que potest omnibus convenire, non actualem;" and "quod Christus non mendicavit." We should note that Palmieri possessed a copy of Torquemada's *Summa de ecclesia:* MS Vatican, Vat. lat. 2701, which carries Palmieri's coat of arms, but no marginalia by him; cf. Izbicki, *Protector of the Faith*, pp. 133-34 n. 99.
81. MS Vatican, Vat. lat. 974, fols. 63va-65ra. Izbicki (see n. 70 above) mistakenly connects this opuscule with Palmieri. Douie, "Some Treatises," pp. 30-31, summarizes the piece, but patently misunderstood an abbreviation when she asserted that the dedicatee was a mysterious "R deV." Torquemada seems to be addressing the pope when he begins: "(R)evendissime pater et domine,

Neither Gil nor Torquemada denied that the clergy had a right to property,[82] and as faithful Thomists they did not identify mendicant poverty with perfection. But like the Fraticelli, they cherished the exemplary image of Christ as pauper and beggar. And so, in the midst of the papal court, they fought an odd rearguard action, attacking the defenders of Curial wealth and agreeing with the spirit, if not the principles, of many of the Fraticelli's criticisms. Indeed, only a few years earlier, in the pontificate of Pius II, Cardinal Nicolaus Cusanus and the papal referendarius and bishop Domenico Domenichi had each drawn up programs of reform that attacked Curial wealth and especially the pomp and luxury of the cardinals and their households.[83] One might even argued that Jean Jouffroy and Fernando of Cordova were answering these and other "in-house" critics of cardinalate splendor.

But in the end we have to ask ourselves what good was the criticism of the Curia advanced by the Fraticelli. Their critique was based on a vision of the Church that may have served well as a protest against worldliness, but that could not work even as the basis of the Franciscan Order, let alone of the Church as a whole. Far from being precursors of the Reformation, the Fraticelli were the latter-day representatives of the powerful medieval ideal of absolute poverty.[84] Such an ideal held little attraction for the sixteenth-century magisterial Reformers, but in the 1460s it was still strong enough to prick the collective conscience of the papal court.

---

domine mi singularissime, perlectis r(everende) d(ominationis?) v(estre) litteris, intellexi...."

82.   E.g., towards the end of his treatise against Palmieri, Gil defended the temporal possessions of bishops (MS Vatican, Chig. A IV 159, fols. 54v-58r).

83.   See S. Ehses, "Der Reformentwurf des Kardinals Nikolaus Cusanus," *Historisches Jahrbuch* 32 (1911): 274-97: especially 293-94; and F. Adorno, "Domenico Domenichi: «De reformationibus Romanae Curiae»," in Università degli Studi dell'Aquila, *Annali* an. 1967 (L'Aquila: L. U. Japadre), pp. 89-123, especially 108-11 ("[cap.] 14. Quales debeant esse lecti, tapetia, cortinae, et reliquia supellex cardinalium. [cap.] 15. Quales esse debeant vestes et tonsura clericorum...in Curia Romana. [cap.] 16. De immoderatis conviviis cardinalium et praelatorum..."). See also H. Jedin, *Studien uber Domenico de' Domenichi (1416-1478)* in Akademie der Wissenschaften und der Literatur in Mainz, *Abhandlungen der geistes- und sozialwissenschflichen Klasse*, an. 1957, num. 5:247-50; and R. Haubst, "Der Reformentwurf Pius des Zweiten," *Römische Quartalschrift für christliche Altertumskunde und Kirchengeschiche* 49 (1954): 188-242, especially 211-15 ("De vita et officiis cardinalium"). For the continuity of internal attempts at reform at the Curia, even to the extent of collecting older reform programs, see L. Celier, "Alexandre VI et la réforme de l'Église," *Mélanges d'archéologie et d'histoire* 27 (1907): 65-124.

84.   For a survey, see Michel Mollat, "Pauvreté chrétienne. III. Moyen âge," *Dictionnaire de spiritualité, ascétique et mystique* 12, 1 (1988): 647-58.

XIII

Just Wars and Evil Empires: Erasmus and the Turks

RONALD G. MUSTO

The problem of the "evil empire" and its threat to "good" societies is one that has obsessed the West for centuries, both today and in the sixteenth century. This is the problem of the aggressive attitudes – real or perceived – of certain states, cultures, and individuals at specific times and places that seem to fall outside the scope of "civilized" behavior and beyond the call of reason or the appeal to virtue: the problem of an Adolf Hitler, of the Soviet Union as viewed in the Cold War, or of the demonized Islamic world in the 1980s. For the Renaissance West the evil "other" was the Turkish Ottoman Empire.[1]

The following essay will attempt to analyze one aspect of sixteenth-century thought by tracing the evolution of Desiderius Erasmus' views on the just war called in defense against the Turks.[2] It will focus on works in which Erasmus devoted considerable attention to the question of the "crusade" against the Turks and of the Christian response to Turkish aggression. Secondarily, to illustrate a common humanist theme, it will refer

1.   Useful works consulted include Richard J. Schoeck, "Thomas More's 'Dialogue of Comfort' and the Problem of the Real Grand Turk," *English Miscellany* 20 (1969): 23-37, which offers a good bibliography on pp. 25-26 n. 6; Robert Schwoebel, *The Shadow of the Crescent: The Renaissance Image of the Turk (1493-1517)* (New York: St. Martin's, 1967); and Kenneth M. Setton, "Lutheranism and the Turkish Peril," *Balkan Studies* 3 (1962): 133-68. Older work on the Turkish threat is presented in the excellent bibliography in Myron P. Gilmore, *The World of Humanism 1453-1517* (New York: Harper & Row, 1952), pp. 273-75.
2.   The most important recent works are Pierre Brachin, *"Vox clamantis in deserto:* Réflexions sur le pacifisme d'Erasme," *Colloquia Erasmiana Turonensia,* ed. Jean-Claude Margolin, 2 vols. (Toronto: University of Toronto Press, 1972) 1: 247-76; J. A. Fernandez, "Erasmus on the Just War," *Journal of the History of Ideas* 34 (1973): 209-26; Maria Cytowska, "Erasme et les Turcs," *Eos* 62 (1974): 311-21; Michael J. Heath, "Erasmus and War Against the Turks," in *Acta Conventus Neo-Latini Turonensis,* ed. Jean-Claude Margolin (Paris: Vrin, 1980), pp. 991-99; Jean-Claude Margolin, "Erasme et la guerre contre les Turcs," *Il Pensiero Politico* 13 (1980): 3-38; and John Mulryan, "Erasmus and War: The Adages and Beyond," *Moreana* 89 (Feb. 1986): 15-28.

to some of the works of two other Renaissance humanists who addressed this issue: Thomas More and Juan Luis Vives.

Before proceeding, however, we must first carefully state that we are breaking with much of the past tradition of scholarship[3] in not discussing Erasmus as a "pacifist." This is not because we flee the designation or the implications of the term, but because the labels "pacifism" and "pacifist" are meaningless in any context other than that of the internationalists of the early twentieth century by and for whom they were first coined.[4] Instead, we will

---

3. Roland H. Bainton, *Erasmus of Christendom* (New York: Charles Scribner's, 1969), sees Erasmus as central to the "pacifist tradition." See also his *Christian Attitudes Toward War and Peace* (Nashville, TN: Abington Press, 1979), pp. 131-35; and his "The Querela Pacis of Erasmus, Classical and Christian Sources," *Archiv für Reformation Geschichte* 42 (1951): 32-48; Brachin, "*Vox clamantis in deserto;*" George Chantraine, "*Mysterium et Sacramentum* dans le *'Dulce Bellum',*" in *Colloquium Erasmianum* (Mons: Centre Universitaire de l'État, 1968), pp. 33-45. José Chapiro, *Erasmus and Our Struggle for Peace* (Boston: Beacon Press, 1950), offers a very personal and modern reappraisal, with a translation of the *Querela Pacis* as "Peace Protests." C.-J. Friedrich, "Guerre et paix d'après Erasme et Kant," in *Colloquium Erasmianum* 1:277-83; places him in an ethical tradition. Aloïs Gerlo, "Erasme conciliateur," in *Miscellanea Moreana. Essays for Germain Marc'hadour*, ed. Clare M. Murphy, Henri Gibaud, and Mario A. Di Cesare (Binghamton, NY: Center for Medieval and Early Renaissance Studies, 1989), pp. 381-84, places Erasmus' "pacifisme conciliateur" among his attempts to reconcile Christian and Classical, reformer and conservative, humanity and God. Otto Herding, "Humanistische Friedensideen am Beispiel zweier Friendenklagen," in Herding and Stüpperich, *Die Humanisten*, pp. 7-34, lays out the intellectual tradition that preceded the *Complaint of Peace*. See also *Guerre et paix dans la pensée d'Erasme*, ed. Jean-Claude Margolin (Paris: Aubier Montaigne, 1973), a collection of Erasmus' works on war and peace; the texts are translated into French, this remains a useful guide to his thought. John C. Olin, "The Pacifism of Erasmus," in *Six Essays on Erasmus* (New York: Fordham University Press, 1979), pp. 17-31, offers a revised version of the article in *Thought* 50, 199 (December 1975): 418-31; Rudolf Padberg, "Pax Erasmiana. Das politische Engagement und die 'politische Theologie' des Erasmus von Rotterdam," in *Scrinium Erasmianum*, 2 vols. (Leiden: E.J. Brill, 1969) 2: 301-12, reviews the historiography on Erasmus as a peacemaker and his relevance to the post-World War II world. Somewhat dated, and emphasizing the secular, political nature of this "pacifism," is Ines Thurleman, *Erasmus von Rotterdam und Johannes Vives als Pazifisten* (Freiburg: Sweitz, 1932). On the other hand, James Tracy, *The Politics of Erasmus: A Pacifist Intellectual and His Political Milieu* (Toronto: University of Toronto Press, 1978), is the best analysis of Erasmus as a realistic and evolving peacemaker at work. Roland H. Bainton, "Erasmus and the Persecuted," in *Scrinium Erasmianum*, 2: 197-202, is not on Erasmus' views but on his active efforts to intercede for persecuted individuals. A good reminder that the Humanist writer lived as he wrote.

4. The earliest appearance of the term "pacifism" in English is in a 1902 British press report of the remarks on *pacifisme*, in French, of Emile Arnaud at the 10th Universal Peace Congress. The first appearance of the term *pacifisme* occurs in French in 1845 and *pacifiste* in 1907. The occurrences of the terms in German and Italian also occur only in the first decade of the twentieth century. Their initial uses, and most subsequent ones, have been derogatory, associated with dreamy idealism or the acceptance of "peace at any price." At best "pacifism" is the internationalist approach to the abolition of war through arbitration among sovereign states. As recently as James T. Johnson,

discuss Erasmus' Christian peacemaking,[5] those elements of his "philosophy of Christ," the imitation of the Beatitudes that today describes the life of Christian nonviolence.[6]

Thus, while the term "pacifist" may be useful to distinguish adherents of nonviolence from advocates of the just war in modern times,[7] the question, "Was Erasmus a pacifist?" is mean-

The Quest for Peace: Three Moral Traditions in Western Cultural History (Princeton: Princeton University Press, 1987), it is seen as "withdrawal from the world and all its ills" (p. xi), and as as tradition that "seeks to solve the problem of war and violence not for the world as a whole, but only for particular communities living lives withdrawn from some or all participation in the world wherein these disturbances are manifested" (p. xiii).

For the very recent invention of these terms, see *Oxford English Dictionary* (Oxford: The University Press, 1989), p. 38; Centre National de la Recherche Scientifique, *Trésor de la langue française. Dictionnaire de la langue du XIXe et du XXe siècle 1789-1960*, vol. 12 (Paris: Gallimard, 1986), p. 770,1; Paul Robert, ed., *Le Grand Robert de la Langue Française. Dictionnaire alphabetique et analogique de la langue française*, vol. 7 (Paris: Le Robert, 1985), p. 3, 1; Manilio Cortelazzo and Paolo Zolli, *Dizionario etimologico della lingua italiana*, vol. 4/O-R (Bologna: Zanichelli, 1985), p. 859; Carlo Battisti and Giovanni Alessio, *Dizionario etimologico italiano*, vol. 4 (Florence: G. Barbera, 1954), p. 2716; Salvatore Battaglia, ed., *Grande Dizionario della lingua italiana*, vol. 12 (Torino: Unione Tipografico Editrice, 1984), pp. 329-30; and *Meyers Enzyklopädisches Lexikon*, vol. 18 (Mannheim-Vienna-Zurich, 1976), p. 329, 2.

5. "Peacemaking" can be defined as not only *antiwar* efforts, but also efforts aimed at the positive goals of conversion, reconciliation, and social justice, human realization, and global renewal. Since their origins in the Hebrew Bible and in Greek and Roman concepts of peace these have been, and remain today, the broader meanings of "peace" and "peacemaking." For the development of the terms "peace" and "peacemaking" in the Western tradition see my *The Catholic Peace Tradition* (Maryknoll, NY: Orbis Books, 1986), pp. 7-23, 46-47, 62-63, 188-95, 262-64 et passim; and my *The Peace Tradition in the Catholic Church: An Annotated Bibliography* (New York: Garland Publishers, 1987), pp. xvii-xviii for a Catholic definition that better suits the historical context of the Renaissance Humanists.

6. Current usage prefers the terms "nonviolence" or "peacemaking." This is the method of Gandhi's *satyagraha* and of Martin Luther King's nonviolence. I have previously addressed the issues of Erasmus' peacemaking in my *Catholic Peace Tradition*, pp. 122-35; and my *Annotated Bibliography*, pp. 237-63. On peacemaking in the Renaissance see *Catholic Peace Tradition*, pp. 110-67; and *Annotated Bibliography*, pp. 215-320.

7. The best of the current works on the just-war tradition, with full bibliographies, are Frederick H. Russell, *The Just War in the Middle Ages* (New York: Cambridge University Press, 1975), which emphasizes the legal documents and tradition of the canonists; and James T. Johnson, *Ideology, Reason, and the Limitation of War: Religious and Secular Concepts 1200-1740* (Princeton: Princeton University Press, 1975), which is more useful and comprehensive, also drawing on the courtly literature, scholastic theory, theological writings and the tradition of the *ius gentium* inherited from the Romans. Johnson's latest book, *The Quest for Peace*, offers little new to the historian other than a rehashing of Roland H. Bainton's categories in *Christian Attitudes*. Johnson's work has been criticized for too patently ideo-logical a commitment to the just-war at the expense of more positive peace traditions. See the review by Berenice A. Carroll in *American Historical Review* 94, 3 (June 1989): 717-18. Johnson's approach, like Russell's, is to see the peace tradition as part of the "cultural," i.e., intellectual, history of the West, thus dissociating it from fields of ethics and action, an approach largely

ingless both in the historical misappropriation of the term and in the attempt to apply modern criteria to forms of thought and action that did not exist in the sixteenth century. The following essay will, instead, show that no such distinction existed in either Erasmus' language or polemic and that attempting to determine whether Erasmus was either a proponent of "total pacifism" or of the just war is to frame the study in terms that are bound to be fruitless. Instead, it will examine Erasmus' thought on the Christian attitude toward the Turks and his attempts to square his call for positive peacemaking within Christian Europe with a perceived need to combat the threat of Islamic expansionism.

❧

The notion of Renaissance peacemaking and affirmation of its existence has been well covered in the scholarship on the period.[8] That Erasmus devoted most of his life and many of his works to furthering Christian peace is beyond dispute and has been examined thoroughly by many scholars.[9] The issue of his work

---

abandoned by European researchers. For further bibliography on the just war see my *Catholic Peace Tradition*, p. 277 n. 33; and *Annotated Bibliography*, pp. xxii-xxvi, 80-86, 203-8, 301-10. One might also criticize George Weigel, *Tranquillitas Ordinis. The Present Failure and Future Promise of American Catholic Thought on War and Peace* (Oxford and New York: Oxford University Press, 1987) for the same shortcomings. See the remarks by Phillip Berryman, *Our Unfinished Business. The U.S. Catholic Bishops' Letters on Peace and the Economy* (New York: Pantheon, 1989), pp. 60-63.

8.   See, for example, Robert P. Adams, *The Better Part of Valor: More, Erasmus, Colet, and Vives on Humanism, War and Peace 1496-1535* (Seattle, WA: University of Washington Press, 1962); and his "Pre-Renaissance Courtly Propaganda for Peace in English Literature," *Papers of the Michigan Academy* 32 (1946-48): 431-46; Bainton, *Christian Attitudes Toward War and Peace*, pp. 122-35. Philip C. Dust, *Three Renaissance Pacifists. Essays in the Theories of Erasmus, More and Vives* (New York: Peter Lang, 1987) emphasizes the literary over the religious or political qualities of his writings. Otto Herding and Robert Stüpperich, eds. *Die Humanisten in ihrer politischen und sozialen Umwelt* (Boppard-am-Rhein: Harald Boldt Verlag, 1976); Jack H. Hexter, *The Vision of Politics on the Eve of the Reformation* (New York: Basic Books, 1973) place his thought in broader contexts. Christian Louis Lange, *Histoire de la doctrine pacifique.* (The Hague: Academy of International Law, 1927) provides a survey that includes sections on several Renaissance peacemakers; as does his *Histoire de l'internationalisme*, 3 vols. (Kristiania [Oslo]: H. Aschenhoug, 1919-1963). For the literary topoi of peace employed by the Humanists in their appeals for real peace see James Hutton, *Themes of Peace in Renaissance Poetry*, ed. Rita Guerlac (Ithaca, NY and London: Cornell University Press, 1984).

9.   The texts consulted for Erasmus' attitudes toward war and his pleas for Christian peace are (in chronological order with English editions if available): *The Handbook of the Militant Christian*, in *The Essential Erasmus*, ed. John P. Dolan (New York: Mentor-Omega, 1964), pp. 24-93 (1501); *The Praise of Folly*, trans. with introduction and commentary by Clarence H. MIller (New Haven, CT: Yale University Press, 1979) (1509); *The Julius Exclusus of Erasmus*, trans. Paul Pascal (Bloomington, IN: Indiana University Press, 1968), (written 1513/14, published 1517); *Dulce Bellum Inexpertis (Erasmus Against War; War is Sweet to Those Who Do Not Know It; or Bellum Erasmi)*, in *The Adages of Erasmus*, trans. and ed. Margaret Mann Philips (Cambridge: Cambridge

for peace and his criticism of war and Europe's new war-states[10] therefore need not detain us.

As early as his *Letter to Anthony Bergen* of March 1514[11] and the *Sileni Alcibiades* of 1515[12] Erasmus had attacked appeals to a just war as a mockery, a pretext by princes to rob the people. He uses the just-war notion of proportionality of means to disqualify every known war, repeating a theme of all his works on the subject: the evils that stem from war are far greater than the benefits accrued.[13] The history of the Roman Empire, with all its pretexts of legal grievance and just war and all its conquest in the name of peace, is a case in point.[14] In the final analysis the wars of kings are fought on flimsy pretext, and the welfare of their people has nothing to do with them:

> If you look narrowly into the case, you will find that they are, chiefly, the private, sinister, and selfish motives of princes, which operate as the real causes of war.[15]

University Press, 1968), pp. 308-53 (1515); the *Dulce Bellum* is an expanded version of his *Letter to Anthony of Bergen*, in *The Pacifist Conscience*, ed. Peter Mayer (Harmondsworth: Penguin Books, 1966), pp. 53-59 (1514); *The Grub Pursues the Eagle*, in Philips, *Adages*, pp. 229-65 (1515); *Sileni Alcibiades*, Philips, *Adages*, pp. 269-300 (1515); *You Have Conquered Sparta, Now Govern It*, in Philips, *Adages*, pp. 300-308 (1515); *The Education of a Christian Prince*, ed. Lester K. Born (New York: Columbia University Press, 1968) (1516); *The Complaint of Peace*, Dolan, *Essential Erasmus*, pp. 174-204 (1517); *Letter to Paul Volz*, in *Desiderius Erasmus: Christian Humanism and the Reformation*, ed. and trans. John C. Olin (New York: Harper & Row, 1965), pp. 107-33 (1518); *Military Affairs*, in *The Colloquies of Erasmus*, ed. and trans. Craig R. Thompson (Chicago: University of Chicago Press, 1965), pp. 11-15 (1522); *The Soldier and the Carthusian*, in Thompson, *The Colloquies*, pp. 127-33 (1523); *The Funeral*, in *Erasmus, Ten Colloquies*, ed. Craig R. Thompson (Indianapolis and New York: Bobbs-Merrill, 1957), pp. 92-112 (1526); *The Ignoble Knight*, in Thompson, *The Colloquies*, pp. 424-32 (1529); *Charon*, in Thompson, *Ten Colloquies*, pp. 113-19 (1529); *Cyclops, or the Gospel Bearer*, in Thompson, *Ten Colloquies*, pp. 120-29 (1529); *Ultissima consultatio de bello Turcis inferendo*, in *Desiderii Erasmi Roterodami Opera Omnia*, ed. J. Clericus, 10 vols. (Leiden: P. Vander Aa, 1703-6; reprint Hildesheim: G. Olms, 1961-62) (henceforth LB), 5:345-68 (1530; reissued in 1643, reprinted Athens: Karavia, 1974); *On Mending the Peace of the Church*, in Dolan, *Essential Erasmus*, pp. 327-88 (1533). For other materials see Benjamin G. Kohl, *Renaissance Humanism, 1300-1500. A Bibliography of Materials in English* (New York: Gardland Publishing, 1985), pp. 209-40.

10. On the topic of war and the new nation-states in the sixteenth century see Walter F. Bense, "Paris Theologians on War and Peace, 1521-1529," *Church History* 41 (1972): 168-85; J.R. Hale, "Armies, Navies, and the Art of War," *New Cambridge Modern History*, vol. 2, *The Reformation 1520-1559* (New York: Cambridge University Press, 1975), pp. 481-509; his "Sixteenth-Century Explanations of War and Violence," *Past and Present* 51 (1971): 3-26; and his "War and Public Opinion in the Fifteenth and Sixteenth Centuries," *Past and Present* 22 (1962): 18-35. See also Paul D. Solon, "Popular Response to Standing Military Forces in Fifteenth-Century France," *Studies in the Renaissance* 19 (1972): 78-111.

11. Mayer, p. 55.

12. Philips, *Adages*, pp. 269-96, especially p. 280; Adams, *Valor*, p. 93.

13. *Letter*, Mayer, p. 56.

14. Ibid.

15. Ibid., p. 59.

The *Against War* of 1515, the *Education of the Christian Prince* of 1516, and the *Complaint of Peace* of 1517 amplified this criticism of the just war. Even the theory of war as a punishment for wrong-doers and of the prince's right to defend national sovereignty are mere shams. In a court of law, he reminds his readers in *Against War*, a wrongdoer is convicted in front of judges before he is punished. In war each side prosecutes the other, and the only ones punished are old people, wives, orphans, and young women.[16] Using the notion of proportionality, Erasmus states that it is better to allow a few wrongdoers to go unpunished than to have thousands of innocents die as a result of war.

As for the prince's right to defend his sovereignty, Erasmus reminds his readers that princes' rights stem from the people and that rulers therefore have no right to endanger the people in pursuit of trivial grievances.[17] Even in the clearly recognized danger of Turkish aggression, which we will examine below, he rejects recourse to arms as counterproductive and anti-Christian.[18] Erasmus therefore concludes that all just-war claims are nonsense. "'Just,' indeed – this means any war declared in any way against anybody by any prince."[19]

Men fight, the *Complaint of Peace* declares, because they love it.[20] "All pretense aside," Erasmus asserts, "ambitions, anger, and the desire for plunder are at the base of Christian wars.... The most criminal of all causes of war is, of course, the desire for power."[21] He also attacks the notion of necessity, of unwilling defense:

> The excuses that are made to explain warfare are well-known to me. They protest that their action is not the least voluntary. It is time they threw aside the mask and dropped their pretenses. If they examined their consciences, they would find that the real reasons are anger, ambition, and stupidity. If these constitute necessity, you ought to reevaluate them.[22]

In "On Beginning War," Chapter Eleven of the *Christian Prince*, the humanist offers every reason for the prince not to wage war, unless it is impossible to avoid, he still concedes the possibility of fighting just wars but warns that such wars should be fought with as little bloodshed as possible.[23] He thus appears to admit two of the prime requirements of the classic just-war theory: proper cause in the case of inescapable necessity and proper conduct in the waging of this war.[24] Yet, at the same time, he questions

16. Philips, *Adages*, pp. 339-40.
17. Ibid., pp. 340-43.
18. Ibid., pp. 344-48. See Adams, *Valor*, pp. 106-7.
19. Philips, *Adages*, p. 337.
20. Dolan, p. 184.
21. Ibid., p. 188.
22. Ibid., p. 192.
23. *Christian Prince*, p. 249.
24. See the works by Russell and Johnson cited in n. 7 above.

whether "there really is any war which can be called "just'"[25] and states outright that "we will not attempt to discuss whether war is ever just."[26]

Erasmus repeats his doubts over the just war as late as the popular *Paraphrase of Matthew* in 1522.[27] In fact, his opposition to war, based on his thorough study of scripture, only increased over time.[28] In his colloquy *Charon* of 1529 he mocks those friars and other clerics who preach the false doctrine of just wars:

> To the French they preach that God is on the French side: he who has God to protect him cannot be conquered! To the English and Spanish they declare this war is not the emperor's but God's: only let them show themselves valiant men and victory is certain! But if anyone *does* get killed, he doesn't perish utterly but flies straight up to heaven, armed just as he was.[29]

Yet as early as 1518 Erasmus had come under attack for his apparent attitude of passive nonresistance and had begun to defend himself by asserting that he never said that he absolutely rejected war, a claim he repeated in 1522.[30] In his letter to Francis I in 1523, Erasmus asserts that when he said that Christ had ordered Peter to put up his sword he never intended this prohibition to apply to the prince, but only to Peter as the cleric. Nevertheless, Erasmus adds, the sword mentioned by Paul in Romans 13 is to protect the public peace, and not for the prince's own ambitions.[31] As we shall see below in our discussion of his *Paraphrase* on Romans 13, not all princes are ordained by God, although all authority ultimately derives from God with the consent of the governed.[32] Again, in his 1526 edition of *Against War*, he notes that a Christian doctor should never approve of war, but that he may be forced to "think it permissible, but with reluctance and sorrow."[33]

How, then, are we to interpret these ambiguities and apparent self-contradictions? Erasmus himself complained more than once that he had been misinterpreted. In his *Letter to Paul Volz*,[34] the

---

25. Born, p. 249.
26. Ibid., p. 251.
27. Léon-E. Halkin, "Erasme et la politique des rois," in Herding and Stüpperich, *Die Humanisten*, pp. 109-18 at p. 114; Margaret Mann Philips, *Erasmus and the Northern Renaissance* (London: English Universities Press, 1967), p. 146.
28. Philips, *Adages*, pp. 113-15.
29. Thompson, *Ten Colloquies*, p. 115.
30. Letter to Paul Volz, in P. S. Allen, *Opus epistolarum Des. Erasmi Roterodami*, 12 vols. (Oxford: Clarendon Press, 1906-1958), Epist. 858, 3:371-72. See also Brachin, "Vox clamantis," p. 266,
31. Allen, Epist. 1400, 5:354-55. See Brachin, p. 266.
32. *Christian Prince*, pp. 175-79. See also Richard F. Hardin, "The Literary Conventions of Erasmus' *Education of a Christian Prince*: Advice and Aphorism," *Renaissance Quarterly* 35 (1982): 151-63, at pp. 162-63.
33. Philips, *Adages*, p. 338; Brachin, p. 266.
34. See Olin, *Christian Humanism*, pp. 107-33.

preface to the 1518 edition of the *Handbook of the Militant Christian*, he complains that:

> If anyone should deter men from the wars...he is marked out by the tricksters as if he holds with those who deny that Christians should wage any war. For we have made heretics out of the authors of this opinion because some pope seems to approve of war. He is not censured, however, who, contrary to the teaching of Christ and the Apostles, blows the trumpet to summon men to war for any and every cause.[35]

In his 1526 edition of *Against War* he also complains of those "great doctors" who condemn opposition to war as heresy and then interpret the scriptures to satisfy their own princes' lust for power.[36]

Perhaps the best explanation for this misunderstanding was Erasmus' tendency, shared by other humanists, to examine war both in its abstract and in its very real contexts. Thus, while Erasmus might admit of the possibility of the just war in the ideal, just as Thomas More was willing to see it in *Utopia*,[37] in reality no war that he knew in history, in the present, or in the foreseeable future was just as fought.[38] He thus ironically used the notion of the just war to condemn all wars, for while admitting its possibility along with the very stringent requirements of the theory, he simultaneously rejected all of Europe's present wars as unjust. He thus remained a "determined and passionate" opponent of war in the real world.[39]

≰

Despite this consistent outlook on warfare and Christian peacemaking, there remained one problem that haunted Erasmus, as it did the other humanist peacemakers, for which the just-war restrictions of Christians fighting against Christians did not seem to apply. This was the present danger of Turkish aggression and the Christian response to it. This problem is key for understanding humanist positions on nonviolence and the just war. In the past this has led to the classic question posed to practitioners of nonviolence: "What would you have done about Adolf Hitler?" a question still raised today in the face of other "evil empires." Erasmus' analysis asks many of the same questions and may provide us with some relevant insights.

In his *Letter to Anthony Bergen* of 1514 Erasmus had already dealt with the issue of the crusade against the Turks but reminded his reader that the Apostles and early church had always opposed

---

35. Ibid., p. 123.
36. Philips, *Adages*, p. 338. See Adams, *Valor*, pp. 254-55.
37. See discussion below, pp. 208-9 and n. 67.
38. Philips, *Adages*, pp. 114-15, rephrases this as Erasmus' "consciousness that to be categorical is to be unrealistic."
39. Ibid.

war, even when faced with barbarian invasions.[40] Even before the publication of Leo X's bull for a crusade against the Turks in 1516,[41] Erasmus had written to the pope cautioning that a war against Christian vice was certainly called for, but such a crusade against the Turks was dubious.[42] Again, in letters to Thomas More and John Colet in 1518, the humanist mocked the preparations for the crusade and denounced it as a cynical ploy of papal power politics.[43] In his *Letter to Paul Volz* Erasmus notes preparations in progress for a war against the Turks. Ironically commenting that at least a few Turks will survive the war, he goes on to remark that the disunity among Christian theologians and the ambitions, tyranny, debauchery, avarice, and lust of Christian rulers and people will dissuade even these Turks from converting, which should, after all, be the function of any crusade. "And although...it will happen," Erasmus concludes, "that the pope or his cardinals perhaps may rule more widely, but not Christ, whose kingdom flourishes at last only if piety, charity, peace, and chastity thrive."[44] Erasmus therefore suggests a pamphlet and propaganda campaign against the Turks coupled with the example of simple Christian virtues in an effort to convert them long before any Christian resort to arms.[45] The *Christian Prince*[46] and the *Complaint of Peace*[47] repeat the same message.

In his *Paraphrase on Romans* 12-13[48] Erasmus examines the problem later faced by More in his *Dialogue of Comfort Against Tribulation*,[49] "if persecution by rulers and magistrats should break out against you because of your profession of Christianity." Erasmus first approached Romans with a commentary in 1501, probably began his paraphrase in 1514, and published the final version in November 1517.[50] He reveals a similar concern with external threats and the possibility of Christian life under persecution. A close comparison between Paul's texts of Romans 12 and 13 – even as they appear in Erasmus' Greek New Testament[51] – and Erasmus' paraphrase[52] of the same passages reveal some very

40. Mayer, p. 58. See Brachin, p. 268.
41. *Bulla absolutionis concilii Laterani cum decreto expeditionis in Turcas.* See Cytowska, "Erasme et les Turcs," p. 313.
42. Allen, Epist. 335, 2:83-84. See Brachin, p. 268.
43. Allen, Epist. 785, 3:239; 786, 3:241. See also Adams, *Valor,* p. 171.
44. Olin, *Christian Humanism,* p. 113.
45. Ibid., pp. 114-15. See Adams, *Valor,* pp. 174-75.
46. Born, p. 256.
47. Dolan, p. 196.
48. In *Paraphrases on Romans and Galatians,* ed. Robert D. Sider, *Collected Works of Erasmus,* vol. 42 (Toronto: University of Toronto Press, 1984) *New Testament Scholarship,* pp. 69-77. For the Latin text see LB 7:817-22.
49. See below, pp. 209-10.
50. See the introduction to Sider, *Paraphrases,* pp. xiii-xiv. See also John B. Payne, "Erasmus, Interpreter of Romans," *Sixteenth-Century Essays and Studies* 2 (1971): 1-35.
51. In the 1516 and subsequent editions. See LB 6:632-34 for these passages.
52. On the differences between a translation, a paraphrase, and a commentary for Erasmus see Sider, *Paraphrases,* pp. xi-xiii.

interesting differences. Where Romans 12:14-21 contains the call to "bless your persecutors" and "do not be mastered by evil, but master evil with good," Romans 13:1-7 contains the classic statement that "everyone is to obey the governing authorities." Often used as the classic topoi for both Christian nonviolence and the duty owed by the Christian to the state that precludes such nonviolence, Romans 12 and 13 are treated by Erasmus as flowing naturally into one another, a classic expression of an overall theory of activist nonviolence.

Unlike Paul's text, however, Erasmus' paraphrase continues the themes of persecution and the nonviolent response to it of Romans 12 straight into his introduction to Romans 13, with a conflation of the themes of persecution and nonviolence toward political authority that well matches the historical context of Paul's letter. He begins his paraphrase of chapter 13, "But if persecution by rulers and magistrates should break out against you because of your profession of Christianity, it must be endured even though it did not arise from any fault of yours."[53] That is, Erasmus takes the selection not in the sense of obedience to Christian rulers but in its original historical context as referring to obedience to an authority outside the realm of Christian relations with other Christians, in this case of a pagan Roman Empire. Christians must obey authority, which comes from God in all things, even under persecution, except, as Paul also makes clear, where human laws conflict with divine laws. As Erasmus paraphrases it, obedience is owed in all matters "provided it does not plainly conflict with the righteousness of Christ."[54] His paraphrase then proceeds to expand on, but to otherwise faithfully mirror, Paul's call to obedience.

Two things are of interest here. The first is Erasmus' carrying over the idea of persecution of Christians by the civil authorities, a notion still beyond the realm of probability in 1517. If Christians cannot be expected to suffer persecution as Christians from Christian authority, then from whom can they expect it? A closer look at the linguistic differences between Paul's words and Erasmus' paraphrase may again prove instructive. Where Paul exhorts the love of "persecutors"[55] (Rom. 12:14) and calls on Christians to show the same consideration to "all others" (16)[56] and to be at peace with "everyone" (18),[57] even with the "enemy" (20),[58] Erasmus exhorts Christian love to the "other" (alieni), the

53. *Paraphrase*, p. 73; LB 7:820. Romans 13:1, of course, reads, "Everyone is to obey the governing authorities, because there is no authority except from God and so whatever authorities exist have been appointed by God."
54. *Paraphrase*, p. 74.
55. *Lat.* persequentibus, *Gk.* διώκοντας. Erasmus' Latin New Testament reads "de iis qui vos insectantur." For what follows see LB 6:632-34.
56. *Lat.* idipsum invicem, *Gk.* ἀλλήλους
57. *Lat.* cum omnibus hominibus, *Gk.* μετὰ πάντων ἀνθρώπων. Erasmus further clarifies his point by using the Greek εἰρηνεούντες to complete the phrase.
58. *Lat.* inimicus, *Gk.* ἐχϑρός

"barbarous," the "wild," and the "harsh" and to calls on Christians
to convince the enemy to repent of his "savagery," all the while
making reference to the "heathens."[59] In the world of the early
sixteenth century, before the era of religious wars, such barbaric
savages probably meant the forces of the non-Christian world,
especially the Turks.

What answer to such aggression then? Erasmus' paraphrase
offers a clear-cut solution once again. In his bridging the hermen-
eutical gap between Romans 12 and 13 Erasmus was drawing
upon a long-standing Christian tradition that had found
expression many times from the late Roman Empire to the
sixteenth century.[60] Love of enemies, overcoming evil with good
– the conclusion to Romans 12 – is clearly linked to its existential
and practical correlative: the suffering of persecution for the very
fact of being a Christian "because of your profession of
Christianity," as he introduces Chapter 13. Yet such persecution
comes not from individual encounters with personal violence,
but from the violence of the state, turning nonresistance on a
personal level into political nonviolence: the public response to
unjust political action of governments. Since at this time
Erasmus had just completed his *Education of the Christian Prince,* he
was not writing in the context of seeing any existing Christian
state as unjustly persecuting its subjects. Nevertheless, as he had
deliberately added this passage on persecution by governing
authorities to Paul's exhortation to obey magistrates, Erasmus
must here have had life under a unjust, *non-Christian* rule in
mind as the sixteenth century correlative of Paul's Christian
audience living under Roman pagan rule.

His solution to such life under an unjust empire for his own
time was thus that of practical nonviolence: the expression of
Christian love in all things, overcoming evil with good,
obedience to government – even unjust government – and suffering persecution for living a Christian life rather than violent
rebellion against such tyranny. Having raised the theme of persecution of Christians, he then follows Paul's exhortation to resist,
though nonviolently, even if this involves suffering persecution.

Even in the 1520s, when the Turkish threat was growing more
real every day, Erasmus' basic position changed very little. In his
third edition of *Erasmus Against War* published in 1523, after the
fall of Belgrade and during the siege of Rhodes, and in his 1526
edition published the year of the Turkish victory at Mohacs, he
continued to insist that Christians follow the example of the
primitive church in dealing with the barbarians. If Christians put
away the Christian cross of nonviolence, they themselves become
Turks.[61] Even if the Turk clearly launches the first strike,
Christian war against them must be waged "in the name of Christ,

---

59. All *Paraphrase,* p. 73; LB 7:819.
60. See my *Catholic Peace Tradition,* pp. 31-109.
61. Philips, *Adages,* pp. 344-46.

with Christian means and with Christ's own weapons."[62] Erasmus also defines what these weapons are:

> If we wish to conquer for Christ, let us gird on the sword of the word of the Gospel, let us put on the helmet of salvation and take the shield of faith, and the rest of the truly Apostolic panoply.[63]

Drawing a parallel to the unholy and unjust wars of Pope Julius II, he implies that current plans for a crusade are a farce and a pretext.[64] The preface to his *Paraphrase of Luke* of 1523 repeats his call for nonviolent martyrdom in the face of aggression.[65]

※

Erasmus was not alone in these views about the just war and the Turks. Sharing the same humanist approach to issues of war and justice, Erasmus had joined with Thomas More and Juan Luis Vives in an intellectual circle that combined an outspoken, if prudent, anti-militarism with a call for the implementation of peace and justice based on the Gospel model. Robert P. Adams has used the phrase coined by R. W. Chambers to label this short-lived circle the "London Reformers."[66]

We need not go into a lengthy analysis of More's thoughts on war and peace in *Utopia*, except to note that in Utopian warfare More was essentially describing the state of affairs in a world constructed by human reason unaided by Christian revelation, the state of a pre-Christian or imaginary non-Christian society. Thus using the rhetorical devices of irony, literary parody, and satirically outrageous exaggeration of classical models, More was able to use a comparative hermeneutic tool to strip bare what was specifically Christian in the just-war theory and to demonstrate that the just-war, as ideally practiced by the Utopians, had nothing specifically Christian about it at all.[67] More draws pointed comparisons to contemporary European practice through

---

62. Ibid., p. 348.
63. Ibid., p. 347, quoting Eph. 6:14-17.
64. Ibid., p. 348; Adams, *Valor*, pp. 108, 208-9.
65. Allen, Epist. 1381, 5:312n, 317-21. See also Adams, *Valor*, p. 217
66. Adams, *Valor*, p. 3 et passim.
67. For such analyses of *Utopia* see Fritz Caspari, "Sir Thomas More and *Justum Bellum*," *Ethics* 56 (1946): 303-8; Edward Surtz, SJ, *The Praise of Wisdom: A Commentary on the Religious and Moral Problems and Background of St. Thomas More's Utopia* (Chicago: Loyola University Press, 1957), pp. 270-71; Adams, *Valor*, pp. 127-43; Hexter, *Vision of Politics*, pp. 68-82; Philip C. Dust, "War in *Utopia*: Ironies Between Books I and II," in *Three Renaissance Pacifists*, pp. 73-85; Dust, "War in Utopia: Ironies in Book II," ibid., pp. 87-104; and the introduction by Surtz and Hexter to *Utopia*, vol. 4 of *The Yale Edition of the Complete Works of St. Thomas More* (New Haven, CT: Yale University Press, 1965), esp. pp. li-liv. Schlomo Avineri, "War and Slavery in More's Utopia," *International Review of Social History* 7 (1962): 260-90, calls this the "neo-Catholic" "dialogic" interpretation, which he prefers to traditional, socialist, and realpolitik readings, but which he de-Christianizes as a "sociological" reading of human perfectability.

Hythloday's naively non-judgmental and sometimes contradictory narrative of Utopian customs. His pointed comparisons to the warmongerings of European Christian courts and rulers thus clearly lead the reader to conclude that wars fought between Christians as Christians could never be condoned for their rending the peace of the Mystical Body and their negation of Christian virtues.

Yet if wars between Christians are immoral, what of defensive wars fought for clear-cut preservation of Christian life against the barbarity and tyranny of foreign invaders and evil empires, such as that of the Turks? Compelling and consistent answers come from More's *Dialogue of Comfort Against Tribulation*,[68] composed after his sentence for treason and while awaiting execution in the Tower in 1534. It is an extended meditation on the Christian virtues of Faith, Hope, and Charity in an attempt to alleviate his own fears of death and as an exhortation to patient suffering under persecution. Significantly, More turned his meditation into a dialog between an uncle and nephew living in Hungary between the Turkish victory over the Christians at Mohacs in 1526 and Sultan Suleiman's second invasion and conquest in 1529.[69] The discussion turns to their fears of living under the persecution and tyranny of the infidels and, ultimately, to their determination to follow the example of Christ in defending the truth of the faith even with their lives.

While More's immediate subject was actually the tyranny of Henry VIII and the duty of the Christian to resist this through nonviolence,[70] the Turkish threat was very real both for him and for his intended reading public, who may or may not have understood his oblique references to the English king. As he had done in his *Dialogue Against Heresies*, however, More also identified the Turks with the Protestants, both, in his eyes, persecuting the faithful and destroying the unity of the Mystical Body.[71] As More well knew, there were alternatives to this suffering: one could accede to the wishes of the tyrant, could abandon the faith and thus survive. Yet the imitation of Christ and the knowledge that this must inevitably lead to the scaffold permeates the work. One must resist evil, but without violence.

68. See the text in the Yale edition by Louis L. Martz and Frank Manley, *A Dialogue of Comfort Against Tribulation*, vol. 12 in *The Yale Edition of the Complete Works of Thomas More* (New Haven, CT: Yale University Press, 1976).
69. See Adams, *Valor*, pp. 301-3; Manley, pp. cxxi-cxxxi.
70. For what follows see Manley, pp. cvi-cvii, cxxi-cxxxiii. See also Anne M. O'Donnell, SND, "Cicero, Gregory the Grat, and Thomas More: Three Dialogues of Comfort," in Murphy et al., *Miscellanea Moreana*, pp. 169-97, especially 177-78, 181-83.
71. We are, of course, well aware of the controversy over More's role in the active persecution of Protestants. For a recent review see, for example, Richard Marius, *Thomas More, A Biography* (New York: Alfred A. Knopf, 1985), pp. 325-50, 386-406. Marius is considerably less kind to More than was R. W. Chambers, *Thomas More* (Ann Arbor, MI: University of Michigan Press, 1962), pp. 274-82.

As he concludes, "the Turk is but a shadow"[72] of the evil that all Christians must face: the powers of violent tyranny.

Another example of this approach comes from the work of Juan Luis Vives,[73] the noted Spanish Erasmian and a member of Adams' "London Reformer" circle. By the 1520s Vives had gained a European-wide reputation and used this fame to persuade Europe's rulers to make peace. In his *On the State of Europe and its Upheavals*[74] of 1522, addressed to Pope Adrian VI (1522-1523), and in letters to Emperor Charles V and to Henry VIII, both of 1525, he called on the princes to heed the suffering of the people, to exercise restraint, and to deal honorably with one another. Vives' letter to Henry VIII of October 8, 1525, again stressing the need for a peace policy, was probably the direct cause of his being fired from the Oxford faculty in early 1526.[75]

Francis I's denunciation of the Treaty of Madrid with Charles V and the Turkish victory at Mohacs, both in 1526, moved Vives to publish his *On Europe Divided and the Turkish War*.[76] As the Turks press ever and ever deeper into Christendom, Vives warns, Christian princes and the pope himself are steeped in ever greater hatreds and rivalries. Europeans, he writes, are not really Christians but raving wolves. No war between them can be considered just, all are *latrocinium*, theft. While he recognized the great oppression that the Turks threatened, Vives also warned that there are worse oppressors than even the Turks: those European princes who use force, conquest, and domination as instruments of rule. Only Christian unity and Christian principles of government can bring about the spiritual and material strength needed to overcome the Turks.

⚜

72. Page 317.
73. For an introduction to Vives' life and works see William H. Woodward, *Studies in Education During the Age of the Renaissance, 1400-1600* (New York: Columbia University-Teachers' College, 1967), pp. 180-210; Marian Leona Tobriner, SNJM, *Vives' Introduction to Wisdom: A Renaissance Textbook* (New York: Columbia University-Teachers' College, 1968), especially, pp. 1-36; Carlos Noreña, *Juan Luis Vives* (The Hague: Martinus Nijhoff, 1970); Rafael Gibert, "Lulio y Vives sobre la paz," *Recueils de la Société Jean Bodin* 15 (1961): 125-70; Philip C. Dust, "The Structure of Vives' De Concordia et Discordia," in *Three Renaissance Pacifists*, pp. 135-90; Dust, "Luis Vives' Pacifist Sociology in De pacificatione," in *Three Renaissance Pacifists*, pp. 191-214; Adams, *Valor*, pp. 285-91 et passim. Vives' works are edited in *Joannis Ludovici Vivis Opera Omnia*, ed. Gregorio Majensio, 8 vols. in 7 (Valencia: Benedictus Monfort, 1784).
74. *De Europae statu ac tumultibus. Epistola ad Hadrianum VI* in *Opera Omnia* 5:164-74. See also Adams, *Valor*, p. 207; Gibert, pp. 152-56; Dust, "The Structure of Vives' De Concordia et Discordia."
75. Adams, *Valor*, p. 249.
76. *De Europae dissidiis et bello Turcico* of 1526, in *Opera Omnia* 6:452-81. See also Vives' *De Conditione vitae Christianorum sub Turca* in *Opera Omnia* 5:447-60, which was written in 1529 and which Michael Heath, "Erasmus and War," p. 998 n. 22 suggests, along with the *De Europae dissidiis*, as a possible source for Erasmus' statements about the Turks in the *Consultatio*. See also Adams, *Valor*, pp. 262-64; Gibert, pp. 159-60;

Yet, while Erasmus had allies and collaborators in his writings for peace, his own explicit calls for reconciliation and Christian reform put him in the forefront of humanist efforts and made him the most visible proponent, and most hard-pressed defender, of peacemaking in an era of increasingly bitter polemic and very real conflict. As the optimism of the 1510s drew into the battles of dynastic war and Reformation, Erasmus found himself more and more on the defensive not only over doctrinal issues, but also for his peacemaking efforts. In an age of closing minds, royal aggression and intellectual pogroms, his outspokenness made him an easy target for his enemies.

Within this context two factors became paramount: the renewed victories of the Turks, culminating in the conquest of Hungary in 1529 and in the same year the publication of Noel Beda's *Apologia adversus clandestinos Lutheranos*, linking Erasmus and Jacques Lefèvre d'Étaples with Martin Luther's supposed appeal to Christians to accept Turkish rule passively as a punishment for sin and his condemnation of Rome's call for a crusade as a sham to extort further taxes from Christian Europe.[77] Beda, a syndic of the theology faculty at Paris and a long-time enemy of Erasmus, his methodology, his biblical and patristic translations, his popular works and his reformist tendencies,[78] thus linked Erasmus' calls for peace with clandestine treason to Catholic religion and empire.

In March 1530, therefore, Erasmus published his controversial *Most Timely Consultation on the War Against the Turk*[79] as a letter to

---

77. Luther had already been condemned for his call for nonresistance, which he based on Matthew 5 and Romans 12-13, in the bull *Exsurge Domine* of 1517. On April 15, 1521 the Paris theology faculty condemned two of Luther's proposals that opposed a crusade against the Turks. Luther had called for nonresistance because he both disapproved of the holy war and because he suspected the crusade was a money-making scheme of the papacy. Luther had also continued to link Rome with the Turks as the enemies of Christendom. See Bense, p. 170; and Hans J. Hillerbrand, "Martin Luther and the Bull *Exsurge Domine*," *Theological Studies* 30 (1969): 108-12. In 1523 Josse van Clictove's *De Bello et Pace* rejected Luther's position that the Turks were God's rod and therefore not to be resisted. See Bense, p. 175.
78. See Bainton, *Erasmus of Christendom*, pp. 201-2; and Erika Rummel, "Noel Beda and the Paris Faculty of Theology," in her *Erasmus and His Catholic Critics*, 2 vols. (Nieuwkoop: De Graaf, 1989), 2:29-59; notes, 2:164-71.
79. *Ultissima consultatio de bello Turcis inferendo*, the 1530 edition in LB 5:345-68; also as reprinted in 1643, reissued Karavia, Athens, 1974. Erasmus' *Consultatio* has been the object of some controversy in recent years. Without retracing ground already well covered, we can say that interpretations tend to fall into two camps: those who stress the importance of the just-war and condemn "pacifism" as both a historical and a modern movement (some also leveling personal criticisms against Erasmus); and those who set the work within the context of the time and interpret it as a literary, religious and political tract that remains a true reflection of Erasmus' peacemaking. Into the first group fall J. A. Fernandez, "Erasmus on the Just War;" and John Mulryan, "Erasmus and War." This school of interpretation tends to label Erasmus and "pacifism" in general as "naive," "hedging," "inadequate," "con-

John Rinck.[80] The marks of his simmering dispute with the Paris theologians are clear, as are the dangers inherent in the university's opposition to his works.[81] Erasmus aims, therefore, both to refute the Lutherans' claim that the Turkish invasion is a divine punishment and a plot among Catholic leaders[82] and to stress his agreement with the general principle of the just war. At the same time, however, he also clearly states his preference for nonviolence. He makes no mistake that the Turks are rapacious, tyrannical, impious, and degenerate[83] and scoffs at those, including the Lutherans, who would prefer life under the Turks to that under Christian tyrants.[84] A Christian war against the Turks, led solely by the Emperor and joined by the great princes of a united Europe, if inevitable and if waged in a strictly Christian way, with as little bloodshed as possible, and with a true attempt to convert the Turks,[85] is acceptable to Erasmus. He asserts that he has never embraced the opinion of those who assert that the right of war is to be rejected by Christians and, in fact, that such a charge against him is "so absurd that one hardly needs to refute it."[86] Toward the end of the treatise he addresses the question in a passage that has puzzled interpreters and bears quotation in full:

---

fused," and Erasmus himself as a "coward." Into the second fall Maria Cytowska's analysis of Erasmus literary and ideological precedents in the Brethren of the Common Life ("Erasme et les Turcs"); Michael Heath's "Erasmus and War Against the Turks," an analysis of the work as a deeply spiritual meditation of the Psalms and thus an essentially "evangelical and irenic" piece; and Jean-Claude Margolin's "Erasme et la guerre contre les Turcs," an attempt to synthesize the work into the full religious and political context of Erasmus' career, drawing on the literary insights of both Heath and Cytowska.

Discussing Fernandez's analysis of Erasmus' *political* understanding of the potential of nonviolence, James Tracy (*Politics of Erasmus*, p. 151 n. 116) notes "what is 'flimsy' is not Erasmus' conception of the state, but Fernandez' understanding of Erasmus." Yet, despite their positions pro or con Erasmus and his "pacifism" in this work, all of the above scholars fail to examine or define the very point they seek to clarify: the assumed "pacifism" of their subject and the exact nature of this position, either in the past or the present. See above, nn. 3-6. Such assumptions also color the analysis in Gerlo, "Erasme conciliateur," pp. 383-84.

80. See Adams, *Valor*, pp. 298-99; Bense, p. 181.
81. See Erika Rummel, "A Reader's Guide to Erasmus Controversies," *Erasmus in English* 12 (1983): 13-19 at p. 16; idem, "Pride and Prejudice. Iacobus Stunica and the Homo Batavus," in *Catholic Critics* 1:145-77 and notes, 1:236-42; Bense, pp. 168-69, 176-81; Adams, *Valor*, p. 271. In 1531 the university formally condemned Erasmus' works as dangerous and blasphemous. Bense, p. 176 n. 50, acknowledges that he owes his use of the term "pacifism" in this context to Bainton, *Christian Attitudes.*
82. *Consultatio*, cols. 354B-355B, 366D-E.
83. Ibid., cols. 350D-353D.
84. Ibid., col. 364A-F.
85. Ibid., cols. 354E, 357E-358A, 368A-B.
86. Sunt enim qui in totum existimant Christianis interdictum bellandi ius, quam opinionem arbitror absurdiorem quam ut sit refellanda.... Ibid., 354A; see Brachin, p. 266.

Hereupon someone will accuse me, asking, "What are you getting at with this wordy sermon? Blurt it out, do you support fighting, or not?" If the Lord had spoken to me, I would announce it freely. Now it is easy to say what I would like, but it may not be the same in the future. Nevertheless, not being clairvoyant, nor knowing enough of the details of the affair, I hand this matter over to the judgment of monarchs to decide on more carefully. Nor do I advise against war, but I plead for my part that it be undertaken and waged auspiciously. For when we begin this most dangerous undertaking of all, it has to be that it either results in the greatest evil for all the Christian world, or that it brings the greatest happiness. What, therefore, shall we bear with impunity what the savagery of the Turks threatens against us and has done for so many ages, and does now, and will do? I admit this is difficult, but nevertheless, however difficult, it is better to bear if the Lord sees fit than to summon utter destruction upon ourselves.

As a first choice it would be desirable if we could subdue the power of the Turks just as the Apostles subdued all the nations of the world to the empire of Christ. This is the second choice: to effect this by force of arms in a way that they rejoice that they are conquered. This will come about especially if they see that Christianity is not a matter of words, but if they perceive in us souls and morals worthy of the Gospel; then, if outstanding preachers are sent into the field who do not seek their own gain but Jesus Christ's. At last, those who can not yet be allured, let them be left for a while to live under their own laws until little by little they grow one with us.[87]

---

87. Hic urgebit aliquis, quid, inquiens, agis hoc tam prolixo sermone? Dic exserte, censes bellandum an non? Si mihi loquutus esset Dominus, pronunciarem expedite. Nunc, quid optem proclive est dicere, quid futurum sit non item. Attamen nec praescius eventus, nec satis cognitas habens negocii circumstantias, monarcharum prudentiae materiam suppedito, vigilantius super hac re deliberandi. Nec bellum dissuadeo, sed ut feliciter et suscipiatur, et geratur, ago pro mea quidem virili. Quum enim negocium ordiamur omnium periculosissimum, aut in summum orbis Christiani malum exeat oportet, aut summam adferat felicitatem. Quid, feremus igitur impune quae Turcarum immanitas in nos et fecit tot seculis, et facit, et facturam minatur? Durum quidem fateor, sed hoc tamen quamvis durum ferre praestat, si ita visum est Domino, quam nobis panolethriam accersere. Illus in primis erat optabile: Si liceat Turcarum ditiones ita subigere, quemadmodum Apostoli cunctas mundi nationes subegerunt imperatori Christo. Proximum esto votum: sub armis hoc potissimum agere, ut se victos esse gaudeant. Ad id praecipue conducet, si viderint, Christianismum non esse verba, sed in nobis conspexerint animos ac mores Evangelio dignos. Tum si mittantur in messem integri praecones, qui non quaerant quae sua sunt, sed quae Iesu Christi. Postremo, hi qui nondum possunt allici, sinantur aliquandiu suis vivere legibus, donec paulatim nobiscum coalescant. Ibid., cols. 367B-368B.

For another version of this translation see Bainton, *Erasmus of Christendom*, p. 259. Bainton concludes, rather indecisively, on the issue: "The tract is mainly an excoriation of Christian princes for all the ills they have inflicted on each other. Just what does it add up to?" Bainton thus begs the question. His inability or unwillingness to resolve the issue is the natural outcome of his own analysis of Christian responses to war into three air-tight categories: the holy war, the just war, and pacifism. A position of nonviolent resistance, or active

Erasmus' conclusions therefore focus on several points: that waging war carries with it the danger of bringing on even greater evil than not, that nonviolent conversion is his first option; that even if fought, a crusade must be waged in such a manner that Christian conduct will persuade Turks to convert; and that, once conquered, Turks are to be left at peace so that the nonviolent process of conversion will take place spontaneously, a process that will, apparently, change hearts on *both* sides so that the Turks "grow one with us." Even while Erasmus concedes the possibility of armed struggle against the Turks, we have already seen, from the time of the *Handbook of the Militant Christian* through all the editions of his *Against War*, that waging truly Christian war "auspiciously" had meant only one thing: nonviolent struggle with the spiritual weapons provided by St. Paul. He thus nods to the just war tradition but only by reminding his readers of the true Christian position.

In this attitude toward external aggression Erasmus was combining two Christian viewpoints. First, he shared in the long tradition of nonviolent missionary work to the Islamic world that saw even the Turk as fully human, children of Abraham, worthy of grace and open to conversion.[88] In the last resort, however, the example of the martyrs takes first place. Just as the early Christians withstood the persecutions of the Roman emperors without resorting to violence, it is possible for Christians to retain their faith under oppression, to resist nonviolently.[89]

Yet if Christians are to renounce violence, how are they to remain true to their faith? Here Erasmus summons arguments from the second, humanist, tradition. Rejecting Luther's call for passive nonresistance, Erasmus had already reminded his readers that Christians must resist evil.[90] While admitting the possibility of the just war, he thus moves toward a theory of Christian nonviolent resistance to aggression, a very different idea and practice than the nonresistance associated with the early Luther and long misinterpreted by the modern term "pacifism."[91]

In sum, throughout the *Consultatio* Erasmus repeats the themes that he has stressed all his life: that war unleashes evil against both sides in a conflict, that Christians must first reform their own spiritual and political lives before embarking on any

---

peacemaking, as Erasmus proposes here, could well have resolved the interpretive difficulty but is thus outside the scope of Bainton's analysis.

88. See my *Catholic Peace Tradition*, pp. 88-96, 136-52 et passim; a n d *Annotated Bibliography*, pp. 165-88, 265-88, for a review of the literature and the issues.

89. *Consultatio*, col. 355D-E.

90. Ibid., col. 355B. See also the discussion of Erasmus' *Paraphrase on Romans* above, pp. 205-7.

91. See, for example, Johnson, *Quest*, passim; Guy Franklin Hershberger, *War, Peace and Nonresistance* (Scottdale, PA: and Kitchener, ONT: Herald Press, 1969), passim; Mulryan, p. 16; Margolin, "Erasme et la Guerre," p. 12.

crusade to spread Christianity,[92] that Christians should first follow the example of the Apostles so that their pure Christian lives will persuade the Turks to convert willingly, and that Christians' failure to behave as Christians will insure their failure against the enemy.[93] If they think they can lead a Christian life by slitting Turkish throats, Christians mock Christ and degenerate quickly into Turks themselves.[94]

Ultimately, when faced with unquestionable evil threatening Christendom, the modern problem of Hitler, or of the contemporary obsession with the "evil empire" and blood-thirsty tyrant, Erasmus focuses not on the issue of individual refusal to participate in war but on the over-riding scope of the "philosophy of Christ." He seeks peace and justice on a societal level born through individual conversion to these Christian norms and implemented through the adherence of peoples, rulers, and governments. He thus emphasizes not individual passivity or withdrawal but the realization that peacemaking must derive from the dynamic forces within each person who uses his or her informed will to adhere to the philosophy of Christ. Erasmus therefore stresses that the danger is not with the evil outside but with the Turk within, within each person, within each ruler and state of Christendom. Like More, he might have said "the Turk is but a shadow" of our own capacity for tyranny, oppression, greed, and violence.[95] Erasmus stressed the evils of the Turks, but he emphasized just as strongly that if Christians do not live as Christians there will be no difference between them and Turks.[96]

Thus, while his treatise tries to silence his critics and to bend to the fanatical pressures of the times, Erasmus remains true to his message of peacemaking: justice, unity, and true peace. The image of Christ, the Apostles, and the martyrs holds far more validity for him, even in his treatise against the Turks, than any crusade.

s

In conclusion we can say that Erasmus' thought changed very little over his career, and in fact remained essentially the same on matters of the immorality of war. On the question of the just war, Erasmus' thought shared most of the characteristics of the other Renaissance thinkers who rejected "nonresistance" as a position and accepted the theory of the just war but who saw little or no possibility of a just war in the real world, even when fought against so clear an enemy of Christendom as the Turks.

In his thinking on war and peace Erasmus, like More and Vives, was in reality discussing only one aspect of the Christian

92. *Consultatio*, cols. 353B, 365C-366D.
93. Ibid., cols. 357D-358F, 360E-361C. See also Brachin, p. 268; Cytowska, pp. 319-20.
94. *Consultatio*, col. 357E.
95. A point that he had made in his *Handbook*. See Dolan, pp. 73-74.
96. *Consultatio*, cols. 362D, 366D.

emphasis on peace and justice, but in such a way as to conform with the academic thought and political realities of the time and place. Thus the just war provided the framework for thought; but within this framework, theory and criticism explored the distinction between the ideal level of the just war and the reality of wars as they were fought. As is obvious in More's *Utopia,* through this critical dialectic the humanists were able to set up rhetorically and demonstrate in fact an irreconcilable tension between the ideals of a received tradition, which they rarely contradicted or criticized, and the realities of Christian practice. This rhetorical tension both showed up the limitations of theory and the hypocrisies and sinfulness of contemporary Christian society. Like Martin Luther King and the nonviolent civil rights movement of the 1960s, which made their appeal to the highest ideals of the American tradition, the humanists were able to use the ideal in order to criticize the contemporary practice. In both instances this irreconcilable tension showed up the inherent contradictions in the theory and pinpointed its practical failures.

In one direction this tension was resolved in the Lutheran teaching of passive nonresistance, emphasizing Romans 13 and taking nonresistance to evil rulers or aggressors as the punishment for sin. In the other direction the Catholic reaction was the condemnation of this Lutheran position, not of "pacifism" but of nonresistance, and the further codification of the just-war theory into the works of seventeenth-century thinkers like Vitoria and the Salamanca school.[97]

Thus while Erasmus remained fully consistent in his own thought and completely orthodox in his thinking on war and peace, his contrasts between this orthodoxy and the actual Christian praxis of peace and justice were so potent that his writings on the subject have remained of fundamental importance until the later twentieth century. In his drawing on the evangelical Christian tradition Erasmus was able to point toward a new paradigm of "nonviolence" that has arisen to replace the tension between the theory of just war and the actual conduct of war. Nonviolence has replaced both the just war and the "nonresistant" counter-position with a new model that resolves the tension and provides a new theory that recognizes the dynamics of growth, change and committed activism that were central to Erasmus' "philosophy of Christ."

97. See my *Catholic Peace Tradition,* pp. 162-64; and *Annotated Bibliography,* pp. 301-10.

XIV

Dressing Down the Dressed-Up: Reproving Feminine Attire in Renaissance Florence

RONALD RAINEY

The history of costume, not so long ago dismissed by serious historians as an antiquarian pastime and pursued primarily as a subcategory of art history, has in recent years won the attention and the interest of social historians. In particular, the regulation of dress during the Middle Ages and the Renaissance, at the national level in such places as France and England, and at the local level in the towns of Italy, Germany and Switzerland, has come to be seen as a useful avenue of investigation for social historians interested in the relations between various social groups in the social, cultural and economic contexts in which such regulation took place. Fernand Braudel, in commenting on the dress regulations of early modern France, points out that

> the history of costume is less anecdotal than would appear. It touches on every issue – raw materials, production processes, manufacturing costs, cultural stability, fashion and social hierarchy. Subject to incessant change, costume everywhere is a persistent reminder of social position.[1]

One aspect of the history of dress regulation that has received little attention from social historians, however, is what the regulation of feminine apparel tells us about the relations between the sexes in the Middle Ages and the Renaissance. My own research into the sumptuary legislation of Renaissance Florence,[2] and homiletical and literary sources of the period, indicates that in both legislative attacks on female attire and ostentation, and in contemporary denunciations of feminine dress from the pulpit, we can gain some insight into the attitudes of the Florentine patriarchy toward women.

---

1. Fernand Braudel, *The Structures of Everyday Life*, rev. ed., 3 vols. to date (New York: Harper & Row, 1981-), 1:311.
2. Ronald Eugene Rainey, "Sumptuary Legislation in Renaissance Florence," (Ph.D. diss., Columbia University, 1985).

Florentines of the Renaissance period were very much aware that dress played a role in announcing one's status, rank and dignity, and they attached a great deal of importance to appropriate attire. A chronicler of the Ciompi rebellion of 1378 declared that the artisans and members of the *popolo minuto* who demanded a role in communal government were not worthy of such an honor: beyond their lack of political experience and their vile demeanor, the chronicler complained that they were so poor they could scarcely dress themselves in a manner that was fitting for men of such rank.[3] Cosimo de' Medici complained of the slovenly way in which the sculptor, Donatello, dressed – inappropriate for a man of such *virtù* – and the wealthy patron made a gift to Donatello of a red cloak with a hood and a gown to be worn beneath the cloak, having the new outfit delivered in time for the sculptor to be appropriately attired for one of Florence's feast days. Donatello wore his new clothes once or twice but complained that the outfit seemed too dandified for him, and Cosimo was disappointed to learn that the sculptor put the new clothes aside and would not wear them again.[4] Machiavelli, in a famous letter of 1513, recounts that he spent his evenings in his country house, during his exile from Florence, reading the works of classical authors in his library. Before entering the library for "four long and happy hours" of study, Machiavelli reports that he removed his muddy everyday clothes and dressed himself as though he were about to appear before a royal court as a Florentine envoy: "Then decently attired, I enter the antique courts of the great men of antiquity who receive me with friendship."[5]

While the men who governed Florence made no bones about proclaiming their own status, rank and dignity through their attire, the women of Florence were not free to dress as they pleased. The city fathers were very much concerned about the expense involved in outfitting women with sumptuous garments and costly jewels, and from the end of the thirteenth century throughout the years of the Florentine Republic, and well beyond the republican regime, sumptuary laws were frequently enacted that imposed limits on expenditures for clothing, jewelry, wedding receptions and funeral display. Sumptuary enactments regulated the dress and celebration of both men and women, but the brunt of these paternalistic regulations fell upon women: while these laws included measures pertaining to both sexes, the rubric for dress regulations used in legislative documents was *Ornamenta mulierum* – "ornaments of women" – and while officials charged with enforcing the sumptuary laws were responsible

3.   Gene Brucker, *The Civic World of Early Renaissance Florence* (Princeton, NJ: Princeton University Press, 1977), p. 50 n. 166.
4.   E. H. Gombrich, "The Early Medici as Patrons of Art: A Survey of Primary Sources," in *Italian Renaissance Studies*, ed. E. F. Jacob (London: Faber & Faber, 1960), p. 288.
5.   Eugene F. Rice, Jr., *The Foundations of Early Modern Europe, 1460-1559* (New York: W.W. Norton, 1970), p. 66.

for prosecuting offenders of either gender, they were dubbed the *Ufficiali delle donne* – the "officials on women."

Let us begin our examination of dress regulations in Renaissance Florence by reviewing some measures in the sumptuary laws enacted by Florentine lawmakers in the fourteenth and fifteenth centuries to get an idea of the specific complaints about feminine apparel that the legislators had in mind. After looking at some of the laws, we can then examine how women were treated by the officials who enforced the sumptuary laws and what was being said about women by those who complained about the way in which they dressed.

Typically, the major portion of every Florentine sumptuary law enacted during the trecento and quattrocento concerned the regulation of *ornamenta mulierum*.[6] Some laws regulated the size of a woman's wardrobe, such as the statutes of 1322-1325, which allowed each Florentine woman to own no more than four *vestimenta* suitable for wearing outside the house, one of which could be made of *sciamito* (a costly silken fabric) or *scarlatta* (a woolen cloth tinted with expensive red dye), while the other three were to be of plain woolen cloth.[7] Most of the laws imposed limits on the number and value of rings and head ornaments, and restrictions were placed on the types of materials from which these could be made. There was a limit on the amount of silver that could be used in buttons, buckles, belts and other ornaments. Trains of dresses were not to exceed a certain length; and detailed specifications regulated plunging necklines, the width and length of detachable sleeves, and the quality and quantity of hemline decorations made of fur or scraps of silk. Costly silken fabrics, such as damask and brocade, and fancy ornamentation, such as embroidery or intaglio work, were subject to regulation. Foreign fashions, such as necklines "in the French style"[8] and pointed or saddle-shaped headgear "in the Flemish or French style"[9] were forbidden.

Florentine sumptuary laws were frequently revised, both to accommodate general fashion trends and to reflect particular fashion innovations. As one follows these revisions from the fourteenth into the early fifteenth century, one finds that there

6. There are roughly ninety documents preserved in the State Archives of Florence relating to the enactment of sumptuary laws from the period c.1280-1530, located in several different *fondi*. The following summary of the enactments of such laws is based on a reading of all of these documents.
7. *Statuti della Repubblica fiorentina*, ed. Romolo Caggese, 2 vols. (Florence: Galileiana, 1910-1921), 1:227-331; (*Statuto del Capitano del Popolo degli anni 1322-25*, Liber V, rubrica XIII, "De ornamentis perlarum, coronis vel vestibus non portandis").
8. Archivio di Stato di Firenze (hereafter cited as ASF), *Provv. Reg.* 140, fols. 68v-70v (28 April 1449): item 20 forbids necklines on dresses "che sono chiamati alla franciosa" and requires that they be adjusted "al modo honesto."
9. ASF, *Provv. Reg.* 146, fol. 365r (27 February 1455/56): "Item non possino portare cappucci cappelletti ne corna ne selle alla fiamingha o alla franzese in alcuno modo."

was a tendency on the part of the lawmakers to adjust the limitations on ornaments to allow for a somewhat greater degree of ornamentation in the later period than was the case earlier on. Trains of dresses were permitted to be a little longer, and a greater number of buttons and pearls was allowed in later regulations than in the earlier period. Throughout the fourteenth century, for instance, women were allowed to wear no more than two rings on the fingers of both hands at one time, but the statutes of 1415 permitted three rings at once, although only one of the rings could be decorated with a single pearl or precious stone. In 1439 a revised sumptuary law allowed three rings, with no limit on the number of pearls or precious stones, and brides were allowed to wear as many rings as they pleased at their wedding festivities. A regulation of 1449 increased the limit on rings to four per woman, and a further revision of 1464 permitted a married woman to wear no more than five rings at one time, while an unmarried girl was allowed to wear as many rings as she wished up until the time that she married. A reaction against these more liberalized sumptuary measures of the early quattrocento appeared in enactments of the 1470s and 1480s, when many of the earlier and more stringent limitations were restored.

Enforcement of the sumptuary laws, which will be discussed in greater detail below, tended to focus on different items of apparel at different times, apparently reflecting official concern about specific fashion innovations at any given moment: hence the enforcement officials' focus on headgear in one period, on particularly long sleeves in another, and on fur-trimmed cloaks and dresses in yet another. During the 1340s a cluster of prosecutions concerned men discovered wearing garments embellished with ruffles or pleats. This was unusual because men were rarely prosecuted for violating dress regulations, while the prosecution of women for such violations was fairly common. The prosecutions of the 1340s apparently reflected an attempt by communal officials to curb a growing fancy for ruffles on men's garments at the time; it is interesting, too, that this rare example of male prosecutions for dress code violations should have involved garments of a particularly "feminine" nature.

Turning our attention to the enforcement of the sumptuary laws of Florence, we find that communal officials attempted to discourage ostentation in feminine apparel by adopting a policy of harassment and bullying of Florentine women. In an enthusiastic account of the enactment of sumptuary measures in 1330, the Florentine chronicler Giovanni Villani indicates two methods of communal control in effect in his day over the garments and ornaments that Florentine women were allowed to wear.[10] He mentions, first of all, that women were required to render to a

---

10. Giovanni Villani, *Cronaca*, X.153, in *Croniche di Giovanni, Matteo e Filippo Villani*, 2 vols., Biblioteca Classica Italiana (Trieste: Lloyd-Austriaco, 1857), 2:350.

communal notary a description of garments that surpassed a certain value and that they already owned prior to the enactment of the 1330 ordinances. The notary was to enter the description in a register and then mark the garment with a leaden seal bearing a lily and a cross.[11] This seal indicated that the garments had been registered before the prohibitions took effect and was meant to prevent women from subsequently adding to their wardrobes. Anyone found wearing unmarked garments was subject to a fine.

Villani also reports that the law of 1330 provided for the appointment of an official, who came to be known as the *Ufficiale delle donne,* who was to search for women, men and children wearing forbidden ornaments and garments, and to impose heavy penalties on violators. In March 1330 a committee of six citizens elected a foreign notary – foreigners were preferred, presumably to guarantee impartiality – for a term of six months on communal salary.[12] He was to be provided with the authority to enforce these laws and a staff to assist him in discharging his duties. While there is little archival material surviving to document the activities of such officials in the earliest years of this office's existence, documentation for the enforcement of the sumptuary laws for the 1340s through the end of the fourteenth century is preserved in greater abundance in a series of judicial records in the Florentine State Archives.[13]

One set of documents records the appointment in January 1349 of Ser Donato di Piccolo di Giovanni of Monte Ramucino by the executor of the Ordinances of Justice as the executor's notary in charge of the office on women.[14] Donato was ordered to go out through the city and its environs for a period of six months investigating and searching for women and men wearing any ornaments or garments forbidden by law. If he found any violations, Donato was to report back to the executor and make a faithful report of such offenses.

After appointing such a notary to go out and search for violations, the executor would then order the town crier to go throughout the city and, after sounding a trumpet to get everyone's attention, to announce in a loud voice, in all the customary public places, a lengthy list of prohibitions. The list of these prohibitions, filled with the pettiest of details, ran for pages and

11.   ASF, *Esecutore* 83, fol. 27r (23 January 1346/47): Domina Tancia's lawyer explains that the dress that Tancia had been caught wearing had in fact been marked with the commune's seal, which he describes: "Quedam guarnachia...mercata fuit marco plumbeo habente ex utraque parte medium lilium et mediam crucem."
12.   ASF, *Liber fabarum* 14, fols. 57v-58r (26 March 1330).
13.   See *Guida generale degli Archivi di Stato italiani,* 3 vols. (Rome: Ministero per i beni culturali, 1983), 2:61, for a brief description of the office of the *Ufficiale delle donne degli ornamenti e delle vesti,* and of the documents preserved in the ASF pertaining to this office. Additional material pertaining to the enforcement of Florentine sumptuary laws is preserved in the *Esecutore* and *Giudice degli Appelli e Nullità fondi,* cited herein.
14.   ASF, *Esecutore* 116, fol. 2r (15 January 1348/49).

covered the offenses that these notaries were authorized to prosecute. A typical public announcement (thirteen pages long), made in July 1349,[15] included the following prohibitions: no one was to blaspheme the name of God, Jesus, the Virgin or the saints; no one was to make false money; no one was to carry defensive or offensive weapons; and no one was to go about the streets after curfew. These prohibitions were followed by ten items that specifically concerned women's ornaments. Garments or hats embellished with gold, silver, precious stones, pearls, mother-of-pearl, enamel or any silken embroidery were forbidden. Specific fabrics and styles were proscribed, as were furs, which were forbidden to be used as linings in cloaks or dresses. Only two rings were allowed to be worn by women at one and the same time, and only one of these rings should contain a gem or precious stone. Twelve items followed that regulated wedding celebrations, limiting the number of courses to be served, as well as the varieties of sweets to be distributed to guests, forbidding gifts of any kind from the guests and limiting the number of servants, trumpeters and jesters. Further regulations concerned banquets celebrating newly-struck knights, the amount of gifts and number of candles allowed at baptisms, and the weight of the candles to be used at funeral services. The town crier, as hoarse as he must have been after a full day of reciting thirteen pages' worth of such prohibitions, even had to announce publicly that the wicks of candles used at funerals could be made of no material other than cotton!

Once these officials had been appointed and the public had been notified about the regulations, so that no one could claim ignorance of the laws, the notaries began their daily patrol about town for violators. These notaries were scrupulous in accounting for their time and kept logbooks indicating when they went out investigating and searching. Even on days when no discoveries were made, entries in the notary's logbooks recorded that although the notary and his assistants had gone out looking for violations, nothing had been found. And when discoveries were made, the details of the violations were recorded in these logbooks. A representative example of the fairly detailed logs kept by a notary in charge of enforcing the sumptuary laws is found for the term of Ser Donato, whose commission by the executor in January 1349 was cited above.

On the same day that Donato received his commission, a notebook was opened up and maintained by Donato's assistant notary who had the responsibility of recording each day's findings. For the first three days of his term, Donato reported that, having gone out from the executor's palace, and having made the rounds of the city, and having gone to the churches of the city looking for anything done in violation of those matters contained in his commission, he came back having found no one guilty of such

15.   ASF, *Esecutore* 129, fols. 17r-23r (15 July 1349).

offenses.[16] On the fourth day, however, Donato and two of his men discovered three women in violation of the sumptuary laws. Two of these women were wearing silver head ornaments, one valued at more than six lire and the other valued at more than five gold florins, and neither of these ornaments was marked with the commune's seal. A third woman was wearing a party-colored woolen tunic (it was green and red), contrary to the commune's statutes. The names and addresses of the women were recorded, to be reported to the executor who would later impose fines for their violations.[17]

For the next two weeks the log is continued with daily entries indicating that Ser Donato had not made any discoveries, followed by a report that he had discovered Domina Lisa,[18] the wife of Giovanni di Francesco Magalotti (member of a leading patrician family who was later to play an active role in Florentine politics),[19] who was wearing a silver head ornament that had not been registered with the commune. Two more weeks passed before the notary cited a woman of the Florentine *contado* for having worn on her head a gilded silver *cerchiellum* valued at more than two florins and not marked with the commune's seal.[20] Several days later, Donato reported that he found Domina Geccha, wife of Rainerio di Grifo of the parish of S. Firenze, wearing three rings (one too many, according to the law).[21] While the notary was trying to write up his report about Geccha's offense, however, Pepino di Antonio Albizzi apparently intervened on the lady's behalf and caused Donato so much trouble that he was unable to complete his report. While we do not know if Donato was physically harmed in the altercation with the Albizzi ruffian, he did not report to work the next day, and it apparently took him some time to recover the nerve to make another report: the logbook continues with "nothing found" entries until the end of the month, when a woman of the parish of S. Trinità was cited for wearing a silver belt contrary to law.[22] Altogether during his six-month term of office, Ser Donato reported eighteen women in violation of the sumptuary laws and two cases of having been impeded by men in writing up his reports. In addition, a section in the back of this notebook indicates that Donato was also responsible during the same six months for having cited a

16. ASF, *Esecutore* 116, fol. 2r.
17. Ibid., fols. 2v-3r (18 January 1348/49).
18. Ibid., fol. 5r (3 February 1348/49).
19. Giovanni di Francesco Magalotti was a prominent member of the Ricci faction in the 1360s and served in the Signoria in May 1377. He was one of the eight men (Otto di Balìa) who directed the war effort against the papacy during the War of Eight Saints, 1375-1378. For mention of his career, see Gene Brucker, *Florentine Politics and Society, 1343-1378* (Princeton, NJ: Princeton University Press, 1962), pp. 63, 128, 199, 250, 256, 260 and 297-99.
20. ASF, *Esecutore* 116, fol. 6v (16 February 1348/49).
21. Ibid., fol. 8v (1 March 1348/49).
22. Ibid., fol. 11r (31 March 1349).

number of Florentine artisans for selling goods or services beyond
the prices established by the commune's statutes.[23]

Entries of sumptuary law violations in some volumes of such
logbooks include the location of the street patrol's encounter with
violators. In one such logbook from 1349, discoveries were made
outside the churches of S. Lorenzo, S. Maria Maggiore and S.
Reparata, near the Ponte Vecchio, next to the Tornaquinci loggia,
and in public streets throughout the city.[24] While Florentine
women may not have been altogether deterred from wearing
garments or ornaments in contravention of the sumptuary laws
simply because they risked harassment and prosecution by these
roving officials, the unpredictability of where these officials might
be encountered may well have made them more circumspect.

The feistier women of Florence did not readily submit to the
harassment of the officials who enforced the sumptuary laws; and
there is evidence to suggest that women who knew they were in
violation of the sumptuary laws were on the lookout for the
Ufficiale delle donne and did their best to avoid him when they saw
him coming. One case from 1359 involved Domina Lucia, wife of
Lorenzo Ziraldi of the parish of S. Liberata, who was cited for
having been discovered near the church of the Annunziata wearing a white dress of costly silken fabric. This dress was open at the
top and on the sides, and it had pleated ornaments contrary to the
sumptuary laws. Having been cited to appear before the judge
inquiring into such cases, Lucia's lawyer appeared in her behalf
and denied the charges against her. Women, incidentally, were
forbidden to appear personally in Florentine courts of law and had
to be represented either by professional procurators or by their
husbands or fathers. The lawyer, in outlining how he intended to
defend Lucia, explained that the whole matter was a case of
mistaken identity. On the day in question, Lucia was wearing a
gray dress that was not in any way outside the law. The problem
arose when Lucia was standing near the church, just as the notary
claimed she had been, but wearing the gray dress; she was standing next to another woman, whose name Lucia claimed not to
know, who was wearing the white dress with all the forbidden
trimmings. As the two women were standing near the church,
they saw the *Ufficiale delle donne* approaching. Apparently they
recognized the livery or "uniform" he was wearing – and, as
Lucia's lawyer explained, "out of fear of this official," the woman
in the white dress fled into the church to hide from the official
(law enforcement officials were forbidden to enter churches in the
course of their official responsibilities), and Lucia followed suit.
Later on, when Lucia emerged from the church, still wearing her
gray dress, the official accused Lucia of being that women who had

23. Ibid., fols. 22r ff.
24. ASF, *Esecutore* 121, fols. 2r-50v (August-November, 1349).

been wearing the forbidden white dress, of having escaped into the church, and of having changed into a different outfit![25]

Florentine women apparently gave the *Ufficiale delle donne* a hard time, as he went about town trying to discharge his duties, as a matter of routine. Franco Sacchetti tells of the frustrations of a notary charged with enforcing the sumptuary laws in the late fourteenth century. Messer Amerigo degli Amerighi of Pesaro was hired by the commune in 1384 as the *Ufficiale delle donne*, and he diligently went about his task by dispatching a staff of notaries to look for violators. Shortly after his appointment, however, the priors summoned him to ask why he was neglecting his responsibilities and why the streets were filled with women wearing fancier garments than ever before. Amerigo denied that he had been negligent in performing his duties and claimed that he had, in fact, been zealous in seeking violators, but he had found it very difficult to prosecute any of them because of the casuistry with which these women defended themselves.

If, for example, his notary encountered a woman wearing an embroidered head ornament, contrary to the ordinance governing the decoration of headgear, he would stop her and demand her name, since she was in violation of the law. But the woman, before the notary could jot down her name and address, would remove the band of embroidery, attached with a pin, and insist that the simple garland she was wearing on her head was not forbidden by law. When another was caught wearing an excessive number of buttons on her dress, she denied that she was wearing too many *bottoni*, but rather these decorations were *coppelle*, another word for "button" that was not used in the prevailing sumptuary regulations. She further argued that these ornaments could not be considered *bottoni* since there were no button holes corresponding to these *bottoni*. A sumptuary law of 1356 had included a requirement that all buttons had to correspond to button holes, but this measure was not included in the revised legislation of the 1370s and 1380s. The intention of the 1356 regulation had been, of course, to forbid decorative buttons that served no practical purpose. This woman turned that reasoning on its head by insisting that since the current law only set a limit on the number of functional buttons allowed, the regulation did not apply to decorative ornaments. A third woman was accused of wearing ermine, which was forbidden by law, but she insisted that the trim on her dress was of some other white fur, not forbidden in the prevailing legislation. These women seem to have been familiar with the details of the sumptuary laws and were able to talk their way out of prosecution. Indeed, Sacchetti marvels that the women of Florence could be such splendid "logicians" when they wanted to be.[26]

25. ASF, *Giudice degli Appelli e Nullità* 120, fols. 3r-4r (29 December 1359).
26. *Le Novelle di Franco Sacchetti*, ed. Enrico Bianchi (Florence: Adriano Salani, 1925), pp. 358-60 (novella 137).

Archival registers record judicial proceedings at which a number of Florentine women, through their male procurators, went to great lengths in contesting charges of sumptuary law violations brought against them. One woman argued that the garment she was prosecuted for wearing had been registered with communal officials, but when the entry was checked in the registry, it was found that the garment registered was described as being of a different color than the one she was wearing at the time of her offense. She went on the complain that the notary who entered the description must have made a mistake and instructed her lawyer to insist that the entry in the communal register be corrected.[27] Some women, cited for wearing headgear that exceeded the limitations on the quantity of silver allowed in such ornaments, brought appraisers to court to argue that the amount of silver did not, in fact, exceed the limits set by law.[28]

Some women did not deny the charges, but argued that they were exempt from such regulations. One such woman claimed that by virtue of being married to a foreigner, who was exempt from the Florentine regulations, she too was outside the jurisdiction of the Florentine sumptuary laws, and that she only had to prove that she was in fact married to this foreigner at the time of her violation.[29] Another denunciation for wearing a gilded silver head ornament was contested on the grounds that the young woman in question, a member of the Medici family, was only nine-and-a-half years old – most of the sumptuary laws only regulated the dress of women above the age of ten – and her defense rested on the testimony of numerous servants and neighbors who had to establish her actual age to the court's satisfaction.[30]

While a great number of Florentine women were harassed by the officials who enforced the sumptuary laws through encountering these officials in the streets, being subject to weighty fines[31] and having to go to great trouble and expense in defending themselves against allegations in court, the quality and form of the harassment was not the same for all women. At the top of the social scale, wives of knights, physicians, doctors of either civil or canon law, and foreigners were generally exempt from prohibitions in the sumptuary laws. At the bottom end of the social scale, there were separate regulations governing the dress of prostitutes and servant girls. Prostitutes were generally allowed to dress as they pleased, and most of the prohibitions against

27.   ASF, *Esecutore* 83, fols. 19v-24r (26 January 1347).
28.   See, e.g., ASF, *Esecutore* 92, fols. 16r-19r (6 September 1347).
29.   ASF, *Esecutore* 121, fols. 8r-9v (17 August 1349).
30.   ASF, *Giudice degli Appelli e Nullità* 117, filza 21, fols. 21r-30v (23 January 1343/44).
31.   While fines were generally paid for unmarried women by their fathers or guardians, and for married women by their husbands, the amount of the fine could be deducted from a woman's dowry at the time of restitution; and so, therefore, the brunt of the financial penalty for violating the sumptuary laws ultimately fell directly on the woman herself.

ornaments and fancy garments did not pertain to them; but prostitutes were required to identify themselves as such by wearing gloves on their hands and bells on their heads, attached either to their headgear or to their hair.[32]

Servant girls were required to cover their heads in public, but they were to wear only simple head coverings. Servant girls and nurses were forbidden to wear any hat or cap that was lined with any fur or costly fabric or that was adorned with any ornament or embroidery. Such women were also forbidden to wear slippers on their feet.[33] These slippers (pianelle) of which the sumptuary laws speak were probably the wooden platform shoes, also known as zoccoli, which came to cause something of a sensation in the fourteenth century because of their great height. Originally, these wooden shoes, with elevated soles and heels, were worn by stable boys and women carrying water in order to protect their feet from water, mud or anything else they would be likely to encounter in the streets. Such shoes enjoyed great popularity among Venetian ladies as protection from the muddy streets of Venice; and Venetian sumptuary laws regulated the height of such shoes. One Venetian law, which prohibited such zoccoli from exceeding one-half of a quarta (a quarter of an arm's length) in height, warned particularly of the danger to pregnant women who wore the high-heeled shoes: they risked losing their balance, falling, and having a miscarriage, and the preamble to this law recommended that pregnant women avoid wearing zoccoli.[34] While there may have been a practical purpose for wearing the high-heeled shoes in inclement weather in Florence, there was a growing fancy in fourteenth-century Florence for wearing these sandals simply for decoration. Boccaccio complained of those who "went about in zoccoli in dry weather," considering it an unnatural thing to do, and used the term derisively in referring to homosexual men.[35] A Florentine sumptuary law of 1377 forbade shoemakers and slipper-makers from keeping pianelle in their shops that were higher than one-sixth of a braccio (an arm's length); and shoemakers who were found keeping in their shops platform shoes that exceeded this height were subject to a fine of twenty-five lire.[36]

Not only did the dress regulations pertaining to prostitutes and servant girls differ from the regulations governing the dress of respectable women in Florence, but the form of punishment for prostitutes and servant girls who violated the sumptuary laws

32. See, e.g., ASF, Capitoli 12, fol. 69v (21 October 1377), "De meretricibus."
33. Ibid., fols. 60v-70r, "De famulabus."
34. M. Margaret Newett, "The Sumptuary Laws of Venice in the Fourteenth and Fifteenth Centuries" in Historical Essays by Members of the Owens College, ed. T. F. Tout and J. Tait (London: n.p, 1902), p. 274.
35. See Boccaccio's Decameron, giornata 5, novella 10, for the expression "andare in zoccoli per l'asciutto." Cf. Kenneth McKenzie, "Antonio Pucci's Le Noie," in Elliott Monograms in the Romance Languages and Literature 26 (1931): 31.
36. ASF, Capitoli 12, fol. 69v, "De calzolarijs."

differed as well. While the lawmakers had limited the degree of harassment that their wives, sisters and daughters might suffer at the hands of enforcement officials by forbidding the officials to touch the women,[37] there was no such ban on corporal punishment when it came to prostitutes or servant girls. A prostitute who was found in violation of the requirement that she wear gloves on her hands and a bell on her head was to pay a fine of ten lire; if she failed to pay such a fine within three days of her condemnation, she was to be flogged "throughout the public and customary places" and after having been flogged, she was to be released without having to pay the fine.[38] If a servant girl or nurse were found in violation of any of the regulations governing her attire, she was to be condemned to pay a fine of ten lire. If she failed to pay her fine within fifteen days of her condemnation, the servant girl was also to be flogged, but the punishment prescribed for a servant girl who failed to pay her fine was somewhat more severe than that prescribed for a prostitute who failed to pay hers. The servant girl was to be stripped naked before being flogged and having been stripped of all her clothes, she was to be flogged publicly, in the streets leading from the city jail to the Mercato Nuovo, and then around the marketplace and around the adjacent grain market of Orsanmichele, still naked, and flogged some more. After the enforcement officials decided that she had had enough, she was to be released, the flogging having been considered suitable punishment in lieu of the modest fine.[39] Flogging was never prescribed as a penalty for any other categories of women who violated the sumptuary laws or who neglected to pay fines as a result of such violations.

How can we account for all this harassment of Florentine women, sanctioned by their own fathers and husbands who, while not adverse to finery in their own wardrobes, took part in communal government after government that legislated against excess in *ornamenta mulierum* and provided for the enforcement of these laws? If we look outside the sumptuary laws themselves and consider what the moralists of Renaissance Florence were saying about women and how they framed their complaints about feminine ostentation in dress, we can better understand the motivation behind sumptuary legislation and the harassment of women that it inspired.

⚜

Many of the moralistic pronouncements about women's dress found in the episcopal edicts and sermons of Florence's bishops and preachers include the sorts of exhortations about modesty and submission that one might expect to find in homiletic literature

---

37. *Statuti 1322-25*, 1:228: "Et quod nulla mulier occasione longitudinis vestium tangatur per familiam domini Capitanei vel Potestatis vel Executoris."
38. ASF, *Capitoli* 12, fol. 69v.
39. Ibid., fols. 69v-70r.

throughout the medieval period. Such pronouncements were sometimes expressed as commentaries on passages from St. Paul – Paul's first letter to Timothy provided a useful text in this regard, especially the passage in which Paul directs women to dress themselves *"cum verecundia et sobrietate"* "modestly and soberly, not with twisted braids, or decked out with gold or pearls or expensive clothing."[40] In that passage he concludes that the appropriate ornamentation for a pious woman should be her good works, and he goes on to suggest that "a woman must be a learner, listening quietly and with due submission. I do not permit a woman to be a teacher, nor must woman domineer over man; she should be quiet."[41] Florentine moralists saw a similarity between Paul's audience – the rich women of Ephesus, which was a prosperous merchant community of the ancient world – and the women of their own merchant community in Florence, and they tailored their remarks to hit home with the wives and daughters of Florentine merchants, bankers and craftsmen.

In an episcopal constitution promulgated by Bishop Antonio d'Orso Biliotti of Florence in 1310, the bishop cited St. Paul's directive that women should dress modestly, declaring especially that women should cover their heads in church and in the bishop's presence; and he went on to point out the importance of submissiveness on the part of women, while at the same time warning against the dangers of consumerism: "Women should not talk in church, so that they might hear better and so that they might learn that those who consume will be paid in kind."[42] The same text from St. Paul served the Dominican friar of the late fifteenth century, Fra Girolamo Savonarola, as the starting point for a diatribe about superfluous ornamentation among Florentines of all descriptions:

> *Nec feratis aurum, nec margaritas, nec vestes pretiosas, nec crines tortos* – this is the life of a Christian woman; and St. Paul does not address these remarks to nuns, because he knew that they did not wear gems and gold, nor did he address rustic women of the countryside, who do not have the means to wear such things. *Dice, dunque, alle donne grande e a te, cittadina!* Do not wear gold or precious stones or garments or fancy hair-dos, but go about simply instead; and if these things are forbidden to ladies, how much more so is it forbidden to men to wear feminine ornaments, how much more so to religious, how much more so to

---

40. 1 Timothy 2:9-10. Cf. John Calvin, *Commentaries on the Epistles to Timothy, Titus and Philemon* in *Calvin's Commentaries*, translated from the Latin by Rev. William Pringle (Edinburgh: Calvin Translation Society, 1856), 21:65-67. It is interesting to note that in this commentary Calvin endorsed the enactment of sumptuary laws.

41. 1 Timothy 2:11-12.

42. Richard C. Trexler, "Synodal Law in Florence and Fiesole, 1306-1518," in *Studi e Testi*, 268 (Vatican City: Biblioteca Apostolica Vaticana, 1971), p. 229: "Igitur capiti propter prevaricationem primam, non libere, velamen imponant in episcopi presentia; in ecclesia non loquantur; audiant potius et discant, qui consumptionem insequitur, replebitur ex ea."

prelates of the Church, how much more so to monks, how much more so to the mendicant friars; otherwise, they are not living like Christians who have to account to God for all things.[43]

Elsewhere, commenting on the same passage in St. Paul, Savonarola aims his remarks in a different direction:

If the Apostle says that women should dress honestly, and he is speaking to those who are noble and wealthy women, telling *them* not to wear gems or gold (when he knows only too well that the poor do not have the means to wear such things), therefore how much more are these things prohibited to commoners and to the wives of artisans, and how much more so to *contadine* [the women of the countryside] and how much more so to religious women who are given to the service of Christ?[44]

Not only did preachers complain about ostentation in women's dress as a violation of the scriptural mandate that women be modest and submissive, but they also attributed specific failings among men to the taste for luxury among women. In introducing dress regulations in his episcopal constitution of 1310, for example, Bishop Biliotti chastised Florentines for seeking riches, often through immoral means, and for thinking that the pursuit of luxury was the most important part of their lives. Such pursuits not only endangered souls, he warned, but they were rendered meaningless by the squandering of fortunes on the unbridled ostentation of feminine attire. Biliotti complained that it was with the *spolia* of their greedy enterprises that Florentine merchants pampered their wives.[45] He seems to suggest a cause-and-effect relationship between the women's lust for ostentation and their husbands' pursuit of riches: curb the women's taste for luxury, he seems to imply, and their husbands might be saved from their sinful pursuit of money.

Another cause-and-effect relationship, linking the sins of Florentine men to women's ostentation in dress, was suggested by San Bernardino of Siena, preaching at the Franciscan church of S. Croce in Florence during the Lenten season of 1424. Bernardino took as his text the story of Lazarus and the rich man (from Luke 16), reminding his congregation that the rich man who had neglected poor Lazarus suffered eternal punishment for his greed and selfishness. Bernardino noted that while Lazarus begged for crumbs at the rich man's gate, the rich man feasted sumptuously everyday and he dressed in crimson and fine linen, "puffed up with pride" because of his fine apparel.[46] Bernardino then observed "that extravagant dress is not without mortal sin" and

43. *Edizione nazionale delle opere di Girolamo Savonarola* (Rome: A. Belardetto, 1955-1974), vol. 13 (*Prediche sopra i Salmi*, ed. Vincenzo Romano, 1969), p. 92.
44. Ibid., vol. 5 (Prediche sopra Giobbe), p. 383.
45. Trexler, "Synodal Law," p. 229.
46. *Le Prediche volgari di S. Bernardino da Siena*, ed. Ciro Cannarozzi, OFM (Pistoia: A. Pacinotti, 1934), 1:241.

warned his Florentine audience that "there is great danger in being puffed up with pride and in wearing crimson overgarments and fine linen undergarments, and garments made of fine Alexandrian linen, a cloth so soft and fine that the flesh (of those who wear such sumptuous fabrics) stays smooth and fat."[47] He chastised the women of Florence for asking their husbands to buy them more clothes than they needed,[48] and he noted that young men who might have taken wives were not doing so because of the expense required to dress them: "Who can afford such expenses?" San Bernardino asked.[49]

Bernardino was not the only one who noticed the trend among young Florentine men to postpone marriage during the first half of the fifteenth century; Florentine lawmakers enacted a number of measures in the early 1400s, including sumptuary laws, that were designed to remedy the new trend among men to marry later in life, and recent demographic studies confirm that Florentine men were indeed postponing marriage from their mid-twenties to their early thirties. On the basis of data collected from a number of *ricordanze* of Florentine families, it has been established that the average age for first marriage of men in Florence during the period 1351-1400 was 23.9, while the average age for first marriage of men during the period 1401-1450 was 30.9. The same study indicates that while Florentine men were postponing marriage until later in life, Florentine women were marrying younger. The average age for first marriage of women in Florence during the period 1351-1400 was 18.0, while the corresponding figure for the period 1401-1450 was 16.6.[50]

But late first marriage for men and early first marriage for women seems to have been the norm throughout Western Europe in the late Middle Ages; the trend was not restricted to Florence. It has been suggested that the explanation for this phenomenon was the desire for fewer heirs in order to prevent the disintegration of patrimony through excessive partitioning.[51] This explanation would suggest that a young man who postponed marriage until later in life did so deliberately and for a particular reason, namely, to preserve his family's patrimony, and not because he could not afford to get married. But San Bernardino and the lawmakers of Florence were convinced that ostentation in female apparel had something to do with the decision of Florentine men to postpone marriage, and they agreed that laws that regulated women's apparel would somehow remove an obstacle standing in the way of young men who wanted to marry.

---

47. Ibid., p. 244.
48. Ibid.
49. Ibid., p. 246.
50. David Herlihy and Christiane Klapisch-Zuber, *Les toscans et leurs familles* (Paris: Fondation nationale des sciences politiques, École des études en sciences sociales, 1978), p. 205, table 23.
51. David Herlihy, "The Medieval Marriage Market," *Medieval and Renaissance Studies* 6 (1976): 19.

What problems did the spiritual and civic leaders of Florence see in the decision of young men to marry later in life? There were three major concerns shared by churchmen and legislators alike, and all three of these concerns were rooted, or so they argued, in the unbridled taste for luxury among women. In the first place, fewer marriages meant fewer legitimate births; and Florence's city fathers saw a connection between restraining women's ornaments, thereby removing an obstacle standing in the way of men getting married, and the need to replenish the city's population. In one legislative document of the 1430s this connection is made clear when in the same breath the lawmakers chastised the women of Florence for squandering money on unnecessary ornaments and then reminded them of their duty to get married and bear children. In September 1433 the priors of Florence met to confirm the election of the newly chosen Officials on Women's Ornaments and to approve the sumptuary regulations drafted by these officials. At that meeting, the leading magistrates of Florence declared:[52]

> that these officials on women's ornaments have an honest desire, in great measure, to restrain the barbarous and irrepressible bestiality of women who, not mindful of the weakness of their nature, forgetting that they are subject to their husbands, and transforming their perverse sense into a reprobate and diabolical nature, force their husbands with their honeyed poison to submit to them. These women have forgotten that it is their duty to bear the children sired by their husbands and, like little sacks, to hold the natural seed which their husbands implant in them, so that children will be born. They have also forgotten that it is not in conformity with nature for them to decorate themselves with such expensive ornaments when their men, because of this, avoid the bond of matrimony on account of the unaffordable expenses, and the nature of these men is left unfulfilled. For women were made to replenish this free city and to observe chastity in marriage; they were not made to spend money on silver, gold, clothing, and gems. For did not God Himself, the master of nature, say this?: "Increase and multiply and replenish the earth and conquer it." [53]

A second way in which Florence's city fathers connected the reluctance of young men to get married with ostentation in feminine apparel involved the impact that expenses for providing a bridal trousseau for young girls had on the value of their dowry. Recent research into the medieval marriage market may shed some light on what the city fathers had in mind when complaining that Florentine men were avoiding matrimony because

52. ASF, *Deliberazioni dei Signori e Collegi, Ordinaria Autorità* 42, fols. 5v-6r. An English translation of a portion of this document appears in Gene Brucker, *The Society of Renaissance Florence: A Documentary Study* (New York: Harper & Row, 1971), pp. 180-81.
53. Genesis 1:28.

of the unaffordable expenses for women's ornaments. Professor David Herlihy has noted that

> late first marriage for men and early first marriage for women transformed the terms of matrimony in the late Middle Ages in forcing the fathers of nubile girls to engage in competitive bidding to attract reluctant grooms.[54]

In portraying the marriage market of the late Middle Ages in the terms of an auctioneer, depicting the fathers of young women bidding for the attention of young men by offering generous dowries, Herlihy's remarks prompt us to focus on the role of the dowry as an incentive to young men to take brides. Florentine dowries generally consisted of cash, minus the value of the woman's trousseau and any other wedding gifts that her family might have bestowed. It was not uncommon for husbands to invest the cash component of their wives' dowries in business enterprises; and it is certain that shrewd young men took into consideration the amount of cash offered, as part of a marriage agreement, before agreeing to the contract.

As Herlihy has suggested, late first marriage for men and early first marriage for women in the quattrocento had the effect of driving up the size of dowries as fathers of girls of marriageable age found it necessary to offer higher dowries in order to attract suitable husbands for their daughters. While dowries exceeding 500 florins were rare prior to the fifteenth century, it is not uncommon to encounter references to dowries ranging from 500 to 1000 florins in quattrocento documents.[55] But as the sumptuous standards of dress in the quattrocento increased the size of women's wardrobes and drove up the cost of the trousseau component of the dowry, the cash component of the dowry was reduced. Extravagance in women's apparel, then, had the effect of diminishing the real value of quattrocento dowries by increasing the cost of the trousseau, thereby making even the inflated dowries offered in the fifteenth century less attractive to prospective grooms.

The connection between extravagance in women's ornaments and the reluctance of young men to marry seems to have been based on the assumption that the attractiveness of dowries, meant to serve in the late medieval marriage market as an incentive to young men to take brides, was being diminished as the trousseau components of those dowries increased. As San Bernardino observed in that sermon of 1424, there were "thousands of young men who would take wives if it were not for the fact that they had to spend the entire dowry, and sometimes even more, in order to

54. Herlihy, "The Medieval Marriage Market," p. 19.
55. For the fourteenth century, see Isidoro Del Lungo, *La donna fiorentina del buon tempo antico*, 2d ed. (Florence: R. Bemporad, 1926), p. 61 n. 29. For the fifteenth century, see Lauro Martines, *The Social World of the Florentine Humanists, 1390-1460* (Princeton, NJ: Princeton University Press, 1963), pp. 201 ff.

dress the women."[56] Other documents of the period reflect the same concern. The priors of Florence enacted a provision in February 1463 in response to a petition received by the Florentine government from the citizens of the subject city of Pisa. It was brought to the lawmakers' attention by the citizens of Pisa that their city was very poor and

> that beyond their other difficulties, there are about 900 nubile girls, more than 300 of whom are twenty-four years of age and older, and many youths and men who might take these girls as wives instead remain without wives, as much as they wish to marry, on account of the great expenses that they would be required to make for the apparel and ornaments of married women, and especially because the dowries of these girls are so small, none of them having a dowry of more than 200 florins.[57]

The preamble to a sumptuary law enacted in April 1511 declared that the Signoria wanted "to impose once again some regulation and restraint on the inordinate and sumptuous apparel of women, both in their clothing and their ornaments, because the expenses for superfluous and unnecessary things had so increased that a good portion of the dowry is being consumed with little benefit to married men."[58] The sixteenth-century chronicler Giovanni Cambi noted that a sumptuary law of 1528, imposing limits on the cost of women's ornaments and forbidding the use of costly fabrics in women's apparel, had been enacted "so that husbands could use the dowries (they received from their wives) as capital."[59]

A third connection, linking feminine ostentation with the moral failings of men, was of great concern to moralists and legislators alike. In the same Lenten sermon of 1424 in which San Bernardino warned that, because Florentine women were demanding more clothes than they needed, young men who might have taken wives were not doing so, the preacher exclaimed, "And because of this, people are in need, and also sodomy increases."[60] Having noted the same cause-and-effect relationship between extravagance in women's apparel and the tendency of young men to avoid marriage that we found in other sources, San Bernardino further developed the connection to suggest that extravagance among women ultimately led to sexual immorality among men.

The lawmakers had already linked the issues of homosexuality and the decline in the number of marriages earlier in the fifteenth century. In 1403, when the commune established the office of the *Ufficiali dell'Onestà*, whose responsibility was the regulation of

56. *Le Prediche volgari di S. Bernardino da Siena*, 1:246.
57. ASF, *Provv. Reg.* 153, fols. 241v-242r (7 February 1462-63).
58. ASF, *Provv. Reg.* 201, fol. 15r (14 April 1511).
59. Giovanni Cambi, "Istorie di Giovanni Cambi, Cittadino Fiorentino," *Delizie degli eruditi italiani* 23 (1786): 19.
60. *Le Prediche volgari di S. Bernardino da Siena*, 1:246.

234

prostitution in the city, one of the reasons given for enacting measures in favor of prostitutes was to turn men away from homosexuality.[61] The sumptuary laws enacted in Florence during the fourteenth and fifteenth centuries, while imposing stringent limitations on the number of ornaments and types of fabrics permitted to ordinary women, generally allowed prostitutes a relative degree of freedom in ornamenting themselves. One historian of costume has suggested that by allowing prostitutes to dress as they pleased, the legislators reasoned that male clients of the prostitutes might be turned away from homosexuality.[62]

The notion that male homosexuals might be attracted to women who decorated themselves in fancy clothing and ornaments, *because* of the fancy clothing and ornaments, seems to have had some currency in quattrocento Florence. San Bernardino encountered this line of reasoning in reply to his complaints about the unseemly fashions of Florentine women. In a sermon delivered in Florence in 1425, Bernardino observed that when he had asked some married Florentine women why they dressed like prostitutes, they had replied that they did so in order to please their husbands. They wore lavish ornaments, they said, so that their husbands would find them more attractive and so that the men might not fall into sodomy. Bernardino objected to this line of reasoning, reminding the women that one was not permitted to commit any sin, even with the intention of achieving some good: "For what good would it be if one were to gain the world, but lose one's soul in the process?" he asked. He further argued that in reasoning in such a way, the women were being deceitful. It seemed to Bernardino that it was not for their husbands that the women dressed in their finest clothing: "At home, you dress like baker women, wearing rags," he said, "but save your finery for when you go outdoors." It was to please the men of the street, adulterers and philanderers, and not their husbands, that the women of Florence dressed up in their fancy ornaments, according to San Bernardino.[63]

By attaching specific social concerns affecting the community at large to the unbridled taste for ostentatious ornamentation among women – concerns about population decrease, the inflation of dowries and the reputedly increasing incidence of sodomy among men – the preachers and lawmakers were masking a deeply-rooted hostility toward women. For whether or not these connections that they made were valid or even logical, the language used by the moralists in denouncing feminine apparel goes far beyond a call for mere social reform. Recall the complaint in the 1433 legislation, cited earlier, about the need "to restrain the barbarous and irrepressible bestiality of women." Bestiality was what

61. Richard C. Trexler, "La prostitution florentine au XVe siècle: patronages et clientèles," *Annales E.S.C.* 36 (1981): 983-1015.
62. Rosita Levi-Pisetzky, *Storia del costume in Italia,* 4 vols. (Milan: Fondazione Giovanni Treccani degli Alfieri, 1964-1969), 2:173.
63. *Le Prediche volgari di S. Bernardino da Siena,* 2:141-42.

prompted women to violate nature through their unnatural adornment.

Bestiality was the part of a woman's "perverse nature" that needed to be curbed through dress regulations; and the preachers concocted a veritable bestiary of images when condemning particular fashions. Women wore dresses with daring décolletage, long trains trailing behind, and pointed headdresses adopted after the Flemish style; and Savonarola, in a sermon of the 1490s, likened such women to cows. He reminded his congregation that cows were foolish animals and then pleaded with the mothers of Florence not to allow their daughters to become like cows: rather, "let them go about with their breasts covered, and let them not wear tails like cows or have horns like cows."[64]

Savonarola was not alone in denouncing the length of trains on ladies' dresses. The trains of Florentine women's dresses had been getting longer during the quattrocento – changes in the sumptuary regulations point to this fashion trend when, for example, a law of 1439 limited the length of a woman's train to one-quarter of an arm's length,[65] while a revised law of 1449, only ten years later, set the limit at one-half of an arm's length; and women had apparently been wearing trains on their dresses that were even longer, since the law of 1449 required women to shorten the trains on garments already in their wardrobes to conform to the newly-set maximum length and prohibited them from acquiring any dresses in the future with trains that exceeded one-half of an arm's length.[66]   Already in the 1420s, San Bernardino was complaining about the long trains on Florentine women's dresses: "You, woman, who wear your dress with the tail of a serpent, just as Merlin prophesied that there would be a time when women wore the tails of serpents, and then we would all be in great danger, I say to you that it seems to me that this time has already begun!"[67]

The bishop of Florence, in his episcopal constitution of 1310, also contributed to this bestiary of images when reproving women for immodest dress and unnatural ornamentation. It was noted earlier that preachers sometimes offered their advice about how women should adorn themselves by quoting St. Paul. Bishop Biliotti also offered a warning to women about how they should *not* behave, and for this he turned to the Old Testament: Florentine women must not emulate Jezebel, who had led her husband into idolatry and was severely punished for her sin. The bishop recalled that Jezebel, with her hair decorated and dyed red, was thrown from the window of her palace and trampled upon by horses whose hooves were splattered with the wicked woman's

---

64.   *Edizione nazionale delle opere di Girolamo Savonarola*, vol. 15, *Prediche sopra Amos e Zaccaria*, ed. Paolo Ghiglieri (1971), pp. 323-24.
65.   Guido Morelli, *Deliberazione suntuaria del comune di Firenze, XIII aprile 1439* (Firenze, Stefanini-Morelli, 1881), p. 13.
66.   ASF, *Provv. Reg.* 140, fols. 68v-70v, Item 4.
67.   *Le Prediche volgari di S . Bernardino da Siena*, 1:244-45

blood.[68] In juxtaposing the images of Jezebel's dyed hair and the blood-splattered hooves of the horses that trampled upon her, Bishop Biliotti seems to have seen in Jezebel's horrible demise the judgment of God, not only on her wicked deeds, but on her unnatural ornamentation as well.

One last image, although not a bestial one, is taken from the sermon literature and is offered to suggest what our moralists held as the ideal of womanhood. Preaching during the Lenten season of 1427, this time back home in Siena, San Bernardino made reference to one of the most famous paintings of the Italian Renaissance, Simone Martini's *Annunciation*, now in the Uffizi in Florence, but at that time serving as the altarpiece for one of the side chapels of the cathedral of Siena, the chapel of Sant'Ansano. In the painting, the gilded Angel Gabriel kneels before an almost icon-like Virgin Mary, looking slightly distracted, perhaps a bit wistful, modestly clad and veiled and in the process of acceding to the ultimate demand of submission as the angel announces her role in the salvation of mankind. Bernardino asked his listeners:

> Have you seen that Annunciate (Virgin) that is in the Cathedral, at the altar of Sant'Ansano, next to the sacristy? Of a certainty, she seems to me to strike the most beautiful attitude, the most reverent and modest imaginable. Note that she does not look at the angel but is almost frightened. She knew that it was an angel; why was she troubled? What would she have done had it been a man! Take this as an example, you maidens.[69]

Women were being encouraged by the men of the day to be modest, submissive, to stay indoors, and, as the bishop of Florence had suggested a century earlier, to be quiet "so that they might hear better and so that they might learn...." What we learn from Bernardino's remark and the other moralistic pronouncements on women, it seems to me, is that although the religious and secular moralists of Renaissance Florence, in their complaints about the vanity of women, often linked ostentation in feminine apparel with very specific social problems of the day, the attitudes about women that fired both the preachers and the lawmakers had their roots in the same irrational distrust and visceral fears of women that continue to fuel misogyny even in our own day.

68. Trexler, "Synodal Law," p. 229.
69. Quoted by Keith Christiansen, in *Painting in Renaissance Siena, 1420-1500* (New York: H. N. Abrams for the Metropolitan Museum of Art, 1988), p. 4.

XV

Reconsidering Apprenticeship in Sixteenth-Century London*

STEVE RAPPAPORT

Apprenticeship was a crucial experience in the lives of most men who lived in London in the sixteenth century. At least two-thirds of the city's men had served apprenticeships when they were younger, living and working for seven or more years in households throughout the capital, learning from artisans and retailers the skills by which they would make their livings as adults. Serving an apprenticeship was also the route through which nearly nine of every ten men entered the world of citizens and members of livery companies, descendants of London's medieval gilds. The centrality of this experience in the lives of men was due in part to its length, to the amount of time men spent as apprentices.[1] When they finished their terms and set up their own shops, married and began to raise their own families, men had spent more than one-quarter of their lives as apprentices. And those were impressionable years, a time when a young man took stock of the world and of himself, tried to understand how the two fit together. Apprenticeship, then, played an important role in shaping men's personalities, their attitudes and perceptions, for as apprentices they learned more than the skills of a craft or trade. In sixteenth-century London, apprenticeship was a means by which men were socialized. Living in the households of their masters, apprentices were exposed to role models during those years that taught them what

* I would like to thank Maryanne Kowaleski who suggested that I write an essay on apprenticeship and then read an early draft, as well as Peter Laslett, Roger Schofield, and Tony Wrigley for their comments.
1. Three-quarters of London's adult males were citizens, and 87% of them had been apprentices when they were younger, and thus roughly two-thirds of all men had served apprenticeships. See Steve Rappaport, *Worlds Within Worlds: Structures of Life in Sixteenth-Century London* (Cambridge: Cambridge University Press, 1989), pp. 49-53, 291-95. The figure is probably even higher, since it is likely that many, if not most, men who were not citizens received vocational training through some form of apprenticeship as well, though not formally sanctioned by the city of London. For the length of apprenticeship and the age at which men completed terms, see pp. 244-45 and 251-54 below.

it meant to be a citizen and companyman, a father, the head of a household, a Londoner.[2]

London too derived many benefits from the institution of apprenticeship. Its importance as the principal means by which men received vocational training in early modern English cities is well known: as many as nine of every ten men in London learned how to bake bread, dress skins, lay bricks, make barrels by serving an apprenticeship.[3] As important to the city, however, was its function as a regulator of mobility, geographical and social. Each year in the middle of the sixteenth century London faced the formidable task of assimilating about 3000 people from all over England who streamed in through its gates. More than 1200 of these immigrants were young men who came to apprentice in the capital, and thus apprenticeship provided a means of regulating the immigration of male youths, perhaps a third of all immi-

2.   See Rappaport, *Worlds Within Worlds*, pp. 294-95; S. R. Smith, "The London Apprentices as Seventeenth-Century Adolescents," *Past and Present* 61 (1973): 149-61; and A. Yarbrough, "Apprentices as Adolescents in Sixteenth Century Bristol," *Journal of Social History* 13 (1979): 67-81. Nearly untouched by this experience, at least in the formal sense in which apprenticeship is usually understood, were women. No legal impediment barred females from serving as apprentices in London, but the names of fewer than 100 young women were found among tens of thousands of apprenticeship indentures from the Tudor period. Fewer still became citizens of London, but in this respect as well it was practice, not law, that denied women access to "the freedom." For women in early modern London, see N. Adamson, "Urban Families: The Social Context of the London Elite, 1500-1603" (Ph.D. diss., University of Toronto, 1983), pp. 245-50; V. B. Elliott, "Single Women in the London Marriage Market: Age, Status and Mobility, 1598-1619," in R. B. Outhwaite, ed., *Marriage and Society: Studies in the Social History of Marriage* (London: Europa Publications, 1981), p. 91; K. E. Lacey, "Women and Work in Fourteenth and Fifteenth Century London," in L. Charles and L. Duffin, eds., *Women and Work in Pre-Industrial England* (London: Croom Helm, 1985), pp. 46-48; and Rappaport, *Worlds Within Worlds*, pp. 36-42. At the same time, clearly women participated directly in London's economy, including a few who operated businesses of some size, though most female artisans and retailers were widows who ran shops left to them by their late husbands. Indeed, given the nature of preindustrial forms of production and the crucial role of the household as the center of economic activity, it is likely that in the early modern period most women were actively engaged in the production and distribution of goods and services, often working in shops alongside male members of the household. Thus the majority of London's women probably learned economic skills informally, outside the system of apprenticeship, and consequently were denied not only the benefits of occupational training but also the economic and political rights conveyed by citizenship and company membership, a status dependent in most cases upon completion of formal training in a craft or trade.
3.   For apprenticeship in early modern England, see M. G. Davies, *The Enforcement of English Apprenticeship: A Study in Applied Mercantilism 1563-1642* (Cambridge, MA: Harvard University Press, 1956); O. J. Dunlop and R. D. Denman, *English Apprenticeship and Child Labour: A History* (London: Fisher Unwin, 1912); A. Kussmaul, *Servants in Husbandry in Early Modern England* (Cambridge: Cambridge University Press, 1981); P. Laslett, "The Institution of Service," *Local Population Studies* 40 (1988): 55-60; Rappaport, *Worlds Within Worlds*, pp. 232-38, 291-322; S. R. Smith, "The Ideal and Reality: Apprentice-Master Relationships in Seventeenth Century London," *History of Education Quarterly* 21 (1981): 449-59.

grants, and of ensuring that upon their arrival they were situated in households of citizens, cared for by, and under the watchful eyes of, a master and mistress.[4] Through apprenticeship society also regulated the extent and speed of social mobility. Citizenship and company membership were prerequisites for exercising economic and political rights in London, and success of any sort was virtually impossible without these privileges.[5] Since apprenticeship was the principal route to the status of citizen and companyman, it was an important means of controlling who had access to economic, social, and political opportunities and the age at which those goals were attained. That control, however, could be exercised only if young men complied with the terms of apprenticeship, especially the obligation to serve the number of years to which they were bound in their indentures.

Every young man in London understood the logic of the institution of apprenticeship in its ideal form, for it was the moral of the legend of Dick Whittington, one of many rags-to-riches tales of apprentices who made good that became popular during the reign of Elizabeth: success was the reward for youths who finished their terms obediently, who for seven or more years fulfilled their responsibilities as apprentices and thus earned the rights and privileges of citizens and companymen. In practice, however, there was a considerable gap between the ideal and the real. Most apprentices did not finish their terms in the sixteenth century, and thus the ideal form of apprenticeship was the experience of less than one-half of the tens of thousands of young men who came from hamlets and villages throughout the realm to apprentice in the capital.[6] This does not mean that the system was not functioning properly. Rather, it suggests that apprenticeship was a complex phenomenon, one that took several forms and thus met different needs, both for society and for the young men who served as apprentices.

$\ast$

Having finished his apprenticeship, on Wednesday, 18 September 1549, Anthony Young was admitted into the Skinners' Company, sworn before the master and wardens in a simple ceremony at the company's hall on Dowgate Hill, a few hundred yards from the River Thames.[7] On that same day, or perhaps a few days later, he

4. Rappaport, *Worlds Within Worlds*, pp. 76-86, 294-95. See also V. B. Elliott, "Mobility and Marriage in Pre-Industrial England" (Ph.D. diss., University of Cambridge, 1978), pp. 220-33; Elliott, "Single Women," pp. 90-100; M. J. Kitch, "Capital and Kingdom: Migration to Later Stuart London," in A. L. Beier and R. Finlay, eds., *London 1200-1700: The Making of the Metropolis* (London: Longman, 1986), pp. 224-51.
5. Rappaport, *Worlds Within Worlds*, pp. 29-36.
6. Below, pp. 254-56.
7. London, Skinners' Hall, "Admission Books," vol. 1, fol. 78r. In this essay the careers of real men are used as vehicles for describing apprenticeship and other male experiences in London, though certain liberties were taken in telling their tales. Occasionally it is assumed that a man experienced an event

and his late master, William Hinton, walked to the Guildhall, the seat of London's municipal government and the focus of its ceremonial life, where Anthony Young was sworn a citizen or "freeman," his name enrolled in a leather-bound register. Though the Guildhall was located across town in the north of London, about two hundred yards from the wall, the walk there could not have taken long, fifteen or twenty minutes at most, for in the mid-sixteenth century London was still a small city, at least by continental standards. Nearly all of its roughly 70,000 inhabitants lived, worked, and raised their families within the walls that encircled an area of little more than a square mile.[8]

As a freeman, Anthony Young enjoyed economic and political rights that allowed him, among other things, to practice any craft or trade and to vote for municipal officials, and required him to pay taxes and to hold office in local government when called upon to serve. Assuming these rights and responsibilities, however, did not make Anthony a member of an elite. Approximately three-quarters of London's men, that is, males above the age of 25 years, were freemen. And, since citizenship could be obtained only by joining a company, three of every four men belonged to the roughly 100 companies that regulated most aspects of the city's economy, assumed responsibility for much of the work of government, and performed important social and judicial functions as well. At the same time, being a citizen did make him a member of a minority, amounting to about a fifth of the city's total population, for though legally women had the right to become citizens, there were very few freewomen in sixteenth-century London.[9]

Anthony's company, the Skinners, was one of the twelve "great companies," London's wealthiest and most prestigious companies, which dominated the capital's economy, especially its lucrative export trade, and provided most of its aldermen and common councilmen, i.e., members of the City's executive and legislative bodies respectively.[10] Skinners pursued a variety of activities involved in the manufacture and especially the sale of

---

that we know was typical of male careers, though it is not always possible to determine its date or even to verify that it happened to him at all. For example, we know the date when Anthony Young became a Skinner from the company's records, but not the date when he became a citizen, since nearly all of London's early modern citizenship rolls were destroyed by a fire at the Guildhall in 1786. We know from an extant fragment, however, when and how most men became citizens (see Rappaport, *Worlds Within Worlds*, pp. 23-25), and it is assumed that Anthony Young was typical in that regard.
8.   Rappaport, *Worlds Within Worlds*, pp. 61-67.
9.   Ibid., pp. 29-53.
10.   For great companies, see W. Herbert, *The History of the Twelve Great Livery Companies of London* (London: Guildhall Library, 1834-37; reprint ed., New York: Augustus M. Kelley, 1968). For the Skinners' Company, see A. Fox, *A Brief Description of the Worshipful Company of Skinners* (London: The Company, 1968); E. M. Veale, *The Fur Trade in the Later Middle Ages* (Oxford: Clarendon Press, 1966); J. F. Wadmore, *Some Account of the Worshipful company of Skinners of London* (London: Blades, East & Blades, 1902).

furs, retail and wholesale. Some were artisans who cut and stitched skins prepared by tawyers, others were retailers selling furs out of shops, often below their living quarters. Most Skinners, however, were importers and/or exporters of a wide range of skins, from ermine, marten, sable, and other furs that trimmed the cloaks of the wealthy, to commoner skins, such as rabbit, sheep, and squirrel, which for centuries had kept the English warm. Whether for domestic consumption or for export, the Skinners' Company nearly monopolized the manufacture and sale of furs in the capital.

Anthony Young entered the world of citizens and company-men at what was to some degree a time of uncertainty and ferment, especially in religion and politics. Edward VI, England's first Protestant king, who succeeded his father, Henry VIII, in January 1547, was not quite twelve years old in September 1549, and royal minorities were often times of trouble. Indeed, during the previous summer the duke of Somerset, who ruled in Edward's stead as Protector of the realm, had faced not one but two rebellions.[11] To make matters worse, the late 1540s were also a time of war with Scotland and France and of severe inflation, when prices nearly doubled in less than a decade. [12]

Still, in most respects 1549 was a reasonably good year for a young man in London to set out on his own. Driven by the demands of an expanding population and a threefold increase in exports of cloth, the city's economy thrived during the first half of the sixteenth century. The enormous increase in cloth exports was especially important because approximately one-third of London's men were employed in finishing and marketing cloth, most of which was bound for Antwerp whence it was reexported to consumers in western Europe. Cloth exports reached their zenith in 1550 when a record 133,000 cloths were shipped overseas, but then fell by a third in the next two years and, despite a brief recovery in 1554, the great Tudor boom in cloth exports had spent itself by the time Elizabeth took the throne in 1558. The subsequent decline in cloth exports hurt London's economy, especially in the cloth-finishing industry where complaints about unemployment mounted.

Overall, however, the economic picture during the Elizabethan decades was far from bleak. The structure of London's economy gradually changed during the second half of the sixteenth century, becoming more diversified and thus less dependent upon commerce, and consequently many jobs lost in the wake of the collapse of the cloth export boom were made good by increases in employment in other sectors of the economy. For example, as the national government became more centralized, its administration larger, and the social life of the court more extravagant, the capital benefited increasingly from its proximity to Westminster. Similarly, London was becoming the legal and

11. A. Fletcher, *Tudor Rebellions*, 3d ed. (London: Longman, 1983), pp. 40-68.
12. Rappaport, *Worlds Within Worlds*, pp. 131-35.

financial center of the realm as well as the focus of a social season that by the early seventeenth century would last from October through June of the following year. In addition to providing employment directly for lawyers, bankers, and other professionals, these developing functions attracted thousands of people to the capital each year, and the money they spent there stimulated employment indirectly as well. It is likely, then, that during the reign of Elizabeth employment expanded considerably in the distributive, professional, and service sectors of London's economy and probably in the luxury crafts and trades as well. If so, then these were relatively good years for a Skinner, a purveyor of a popular luxury good, and indeed they seem to have been for Anthony Young, whose career began in 1549.[13]

Forty-two years later, in August of 1591, Anthony Young was laid to rest in his burial pit in the south aisle of the church of Saint Peter Cornhill, in which parish he had lived for approximately 30 years. He was 68 years old when he died, or so the parish clerk noted in the register of burials.[14] If that age is correct, and it probably is, then Anthony Young was 26 years old when he swore the oaths of freemen and Skinners. That is, in fact, the average age at which men in London finished their apprenticeship terms and thus crossed what was an important threshold in their lives.[15] This rather late age at completion of apprenticeship was the result in part of the City's efforts to delay the age at which men became citizens and companymen. In 1556 the common council passed an act barring young men under the age of 24 years from becoming freemen and requiring that apprentices be bound to terms of sufficient length to ensure that no man was admitted into the freedom below the minimum legal age. The crown followed suit seven years later when the Statute of Artificers mandated that men "shall be of the age of 24 years at the least" when they finish their apprenticeships.[16]

Municipal and national legislation reflects the contemporary view that a man under the age of 24 years was still an adolescent, possessing neither the skills nor the maturity to set up shop, run a business, teach apprentices.

> Until a man grows unto the age of 24 years, he (for the most part though not always) is wild, without judgement, and not of sufficient experience to govern himself, nor (many times) grown unto the full or perfect knowledge of the art or occupation he professes, and therefore has more need still to remain under

13. Ibid., pp. 87-122.
14. G. W. G. Leveson Gower, ed., *A Register of...Saint Peeters upon Cornhill* (London: The Harleian Society, 1877), p. 138.
15. Rappaport, *Worlds Within Worlds*, pp. 322-29.
16. London, London Corporation Records Office (LCRO), Letter Book S, fols. 97v-99r. The Statute of Artificers is printed in R. H. Tawney and E. Power, eds., *Tudor Economic Documents*, 3 vols. (London: University of London, 1924), 1:338-50.

244

government, as a servant and learner, than to become a ruler, as a master or instructor.

Youths were not old enough to assume parental responsibilities either, yet "some take wives and before they are 24 years of age have three or four children, which often they leave to the parish where they dwell to be kept," compounding the burden of poor relief, a problem that concerned the crown increasingly during Elizabeth's reign.[17] London's aldermen too were troubled by the "overhasty marriages and oversoon setting up of households of and by the youth and young folks...[who] marry themselves as soon as ever they come out of their apprenticehood, be they never so young and unskillful."[18]

More than anything else, what concerned the crown and the City were the social, economic, and political consequences of unemployment caused in part by the numbers of artisans and retailers growing faster than the rate at which the economy was expanding. To avoid substantial increases in unemployment, a balance was needed between the supply of and demand for economic opportunities, and it was by strengthening the institution of apprenticeship that national and municipal authorities sought to correct what they believed was a growing imbalance between the two. About the supply of economic opportunities early modern society could do very little, for the economic resources of a community – a parish, a town, the nation – were finite, capable of expansion but not without limit, and it was difficult to legislate economic growth, although that did not prevent governments from trying. Authorities could do nothing to stop or even slow the substantial increase in population during the sixteenth century, but the demand for economic opportunities *was* subject to some governmental control, at least in towns where corporate bodies could regulate numbers of artisans and retailers by means of licensing and other powers. Because apprentices were barred from accepting wages during their terms and thus constituted a dependent labor force, it was through the institution of apprenticeship that municipal authorities exerted some control over the numbers of men who were economically independent and the age at which they attained that status. Lax enforcement of a seven-year apprenticeship as a requirement for economic independence meant fewer apprentices and/or shorter terms, and that in turn led to an increase in the numbers of men competing for a limited range of economic opportunities. Thus governments in early modern England strove to preserve the traditional seven-year term because the institution of apprenticeship played a crucial role in limiting the size of the pool of artisans and retailers and thus in maintaining a balance between their numbers and economic opportunities.

17. From a "Memorandum on the Statute of Artificers," printed in Tawney and Power, *Tudor Economic Documents*, 1:354-56.
18. London, LCRO, Letter Book S, fol. 97v.

By means of legislation, therefore, national and municipal authorities sought to protect the livelihoods of established artisans and retailers by ensuring that a glut of younger men did not compete with them for employment. The crown asserted that it acted for precisely that reason, arguing that failure to complete a minimum seven-year apprenticeship term was "a means whereby the number of artificers do so multiply that one of them do as it were eat out and consume another." If apprentices were required to remain in service until they were at least 24 years old, the crown argued, "many ancient householders should not fall into decay and distress as they do, nor be driven to live upon the alms of parishes as they are." London's aldermen expressed similar sentiments when they claimed that a minimum age requirement for freedom admission would remedy the "great poverty, penury, and lack of living" among the city's freemen.[19] The solution, then, was to strengthen the institution of apprenticeship through which authorities regulated numbers of artisans and retailers, and that indeed is what the crown and the aldermen attempted to do. It is impossible, of course, to evaluate the success of measures adopted by municipal and national authorities. We know, however, that London's companies cooperated in enforcing the minimum age requirement for company membership and thus for citizenship, for often an apprentice was denied permission to become a companyman "for that he is not of the age of 24 years." And success is suggested by the fact that in the years after passage of the acts of common council in 1556 and of parliament in 1563 few complaints were voiced in London about "overhasty marriages and oversoon setting up of households of and by the youth and young folks."[20]

After finishing his apprenticeship and joining the Skinners' Company in September 1549, Anthony Young probably worked as a wage laborer or "journeyman" for two or three years, once again living in his employer's household and thus able to save the bulk of his wages, and then he set up his own shop. That, at least, is the picture that emerges from a reconstitution of the careers of more than 100 men who finished their apprenticeships in the early 1550s, just a few years after Anthony did.[21] The overwhelming majority of these men eventually became householders, independent craftsmen and retailers who ran businesses of various sizes throughout the capital: two-thirds of the men were still living in London a decade after they became citizens and companymen, and four of every five men had shops of their own. Though one quarter of the men needed six or more years to become householders and a few as many as 14 years, most men achieved that goal in much less time, especially men who, like Anthony Young, be-

19.   "Memorandum on the Statute of Artificers," pp. 355-56; London, LCRO, Letter Book S, fol. 97v.
20.   Rappaport, *Worlds Within Worlds*, pp. 324-26.
21.   For the rate and speed of mobility to the status of householder, see Rappaport, *Worlds Within Worlds*, pp. 329-45.

longed to great companies. It took most men in minor companies nearly four years to accumulate the capital needed to rent a shop, to purchase tools and raw materials, but most great companymen needed less than two years, probably because they came from wealthier families and thus could tap parental and other resources.

Unfortunately we do not know when Anthony Young became a householder, though he was in business for himself by February 1556 when he engaged his first apprentice, seven years after becoming a Skinner. Like some men in London, it may have taken him six or seven years of journeywork in order to save enough money to open a shop of his own, or he may have spent a few years building up his business before taking on his first apprentice. It is also possible that he spent the early 1550s working overseas, perhaps as a factor for another Skinner in London. From 1556 Anthony Young's career progressed in a manner typical of men who lived in Elizabethan London. He had only one apprentice working in his shop during his early years, for not until 1565 did he engage another apprentice, an interval of nine years. Thereafter intervals between apprentices shortened: he engaged an apprentice in 1568 and then again in 1572. Like most shops in sixteenth-century London, therefore, his appears to have been small, consisting of himself, one or two apprentices, and perhaps a journeyman.[22]

We have no record of Anthony Young's marriage, but we know that he was married by 1 May 1564 when the register of Saint Peter Cornhill records the christening of a son, Thomas, the first of his six children born in the parish.[23] It is likely, however, that he married several years earlier, at about the time that he set up his own shop, for in early modern England these two final steps in the transition to adulthood – marriage and establishment of a household – were linked closely and for men in London occurred at about the age of 28 or 29 years.[24] If so, then he and his wife lived elsewhere for a few years before moving to Saint Peter Cornhill, a moderately wealthy parish in the center of London. It was an ideal place for a Skinner to live and have a shop, for in the parish was Leadenhall Market, one of the capital's most important public markets where goods of every description were sold in shops and stalls. Perhaps the move to such a prosperous and centrally located section of London reflects an improvement in his status. It certainly appears that way, for in the mid-1560s, when he seems to have moved, Anthony Young began engaging apprentices more frequently, suggesting that he was more successful.

$

---

22. London, Skinners' Hall, "Admission Books," vol. 1, fols. 97r, 128r, 137r, 153r. For the size of shops, see Rappaport, *Worlds Within Worlds*, pp. 242-44.
23. Leveson Gower, *Saint Peeters upon Cornhill*, pp. 11-13, 15, 17.
24. Rappaport, *Worlds Within Worlds*, pp. 326-29.

It is to the first of those apprentices that we must now turn. His name was Hamlet Cook, and he hailed originally from Colton, Staffordshire, a small village in the northern midlands about eight miles east of Stafford in the Vale of Trent.[25] His father was a husbandman, a term used by contemporaries to describe a small to middling farmer who worked anywhere from five to fifty acres of land. It is impossible to determine his father's social status precisely, for by that definition nearly half the farmers in Tudor England were husbandmen, from men who were really cottagers, without enough land to support a family, to substantial farmers who prospered over the years by selling a modest surplus in an era of rising agricultural prices and thus would soon be considered yeomen by their neighbors. Nonetheless, gentlemen, yeomen, and husbandmen belonged to rural status groups that were ordered hierarchically in terms of wealth, power, and prestige and were perceived by contemporaries as components of a formal hierarchy, providing historians with a useful means of exploring the effects of wealth and status in early modern England.[26]

Hamlet began his apprenticeship with Anthony Young on Christmas Day, 1565, and thus he probably set out for London sometime during the autumn of that year. The trip must have taken some time, for the village of Colton was more than 125 miles from London, though Hamlet was fortunate in that his home lay less than 20 miles from the main road between Manchester and London. That Hamlet came from so far away was not unusual. Indeed most of London's apprentices journeyed from distant places, at least in early modern terms, travelling an average of 115 miles in the early 1550s to learn their crafts and trades in the capital. In an age when travel and communications over even tens of miles was slow and difficult, the fact that two-thirds of 876 immigrants who became citizens in 1551-53 hailed from homes at least 80 miles from London is remarkable. Though some of these young men may have set out for the city one day without knowing what they would find there when they arrived, most of them (or more likely their parents) must have made arrangements for an apprenticeship before committing themselves to so lengthy a journey. Networks of relatives and friends across England may have provided one means of arranging apprenticeships in the capital. London was a city of immigrants – only one-sixth of its citizens were born there – and thus most English people probably had a friend or relative living there or at least knew someone who did, a person who might be willing to assist a provincial youth in his search for a master in the capital. The importance of networks of friends and kin is suggested by the fact that 15 percent of more than 700 Londoners

25. London, Skinners' Hall, "Admission Books," vol. 1, fol. 128r.
26. See D. Cressy, "Describing the Social Order of Elizabethan and Stuart England," *Literature and History* 3 (1976): 29-44; L. Stone, "Social Mobility in England, 1500-1700," *Past and Present* 33 (1966): 17-22; K. Wrightson, *English Society 1580-1680* (New Brunswick, NJ: Rutgers University Press, 1982), pp. 17-38.

who engaged apprentices during the sixteenth century had at least one apprentice during their lives with the same surnames as themselves.[27]

One can only wonder about how Hamlet Cook felt when he walked through one of the city's gates for the first time. Surely he had never seen anything like it, for London was unlike any other city in the realm. Norwich, England's second-largest city, was not even one-fifth the size of London; and Stafford, the market town nearest to Hamlet's home in Colton, probably had about a thousand inhabitants. As he wandered the streets of the capital looking for the house where he would live for the next seven or eight years, it must have been exciting to see and hear things so far beyond the realm of his experiences. Had he ever seen a building as tall as Saint Paul's Cathedral, or a street like Cheapside, lined with stalls selling things he had never seen, from places he did not even know existed, or wharves where ships with names like the *Unicorn*, the *Flying Ghost*, and the *Grace of God* waited to be unloaded? At the same time, he must have felt apprehensive as well, but fortunately for Hamlet at Anthony Young's house he would find many things that would alleviate his anxieties and facilitate his assimilation into London society. In addition to a roof over his head and food on the table, Hamlet would have a family, a household, a routine, the material and immaterial structures of life that eased the transition from country to town and assuaged the fears and anxieties that must have been among the emotions that he felt on that autumn day. The city of London benefited as well, for the institution of apprenticeship was a funnel through which passed so many of its male immigrants, regulating that male migration and thus mitigating some of the problems often caused by very high rates of immigration.[28]

Once he found Anthony Young's house and settled in, Hamlet Cook discovered that in some respects little had changed. As an apprentice, his status in the household was childlike. Since he earned no wages, he was totally dependent upon his master and mistress for food, clothing, shelter, and other material needs; and they were responsible for his behavior *in loco parentum*. This could not have been easy for Hamlet, for when he began his term he was no longer a boy but a young man about 19 years old, the average age at which males in London began apprenticeships. From 1572 through 1594 the Carpenters' Company recorded the ages at which 1317 apprentices began their terms, and their average age was 19.5 years. The overwhelming majority were in their late teens and early twenties: more than half were aged 18 to

27. Rappaport, *Worlds Within Worlds*, pp. 76-81.
28. For the socializing functions of apprenticeship, see n. 2 above. For the problems caused by immigration, see n. 4 above; A. L. Beier, "Social Problems in Elizabethan London," *Journal of Interdisciplinary History* 9 (1978): 203-21; A. L. Beier and R. Finlay, "Introduction: The Significance of the Metropolis," in *London 1500-1700*, pp. 9-22; Rappaport, *Worlds Within Worlds*, pp. 64-67, 76-77, 84-86, 294-95.

20 years, three-quarters between the ages of 17 and 21 years. Similarly, around the turn of the seventeenth century 232 apprentices in 40 of London's companies averaged 18.9 years when they began their terms.[29]

Presumably one of the first things that Hamlet Cook did upon his arrival at Anthony Young's house was to sign his apprenticeship indenture. In it he promised that he

> his said master faithfully shall serve, his secrets keep, his lawful commands everywhere gladly do. He shall not commit fornication nor contract matrimony within the said term. He shall not play at cards, dice, tables or any other unlawful games. He shall not haunt taverns nor playhouses, nor absent himself from the master's service day or night unlawfully.[30]

If he did not fulfil his responsibilities or otherwise failed to observe the terms of his indenture, Hamlet could be punished severely by his master and/or the Skinners' Company. On 29 August 1567 William Smith, apprentice with Richard Corbin, Pewterer,

> in example of other apprentices was whipped in the hall for that contrary to honesty when his master put him in trust to watch [the shop] for him, he opened his master's door and did let a harlot into his master's house, where he had to do with her by his own confession.

Six years later an apprentice named Robert Coles confessed to stealing cloths from his master's shop and he "was openly punished in the hall before divers and sundry householders and apprentices." Ultimately, however, it was the master who was responsible for an apprentice's behavior, a point made clear by the Clothworkers' Company in 1538. Having received complaints about the behavior of Clothworkers' apprentices, the company's governors warned householders to keep their apprentices indoors. Permission to leave the house could be granted only if a master knew "whither [his apprentice] goes and in what company he goes in," and masters were instructed to ensure that apprentices "neither haunt taverns nor alehouses nor bowling alleys nor no other suspicious places." If an apprentice violated these rules, "the charge to be laid to the said master to be punished for the said apprentice."[31]

At the same time, the indenture was a contract to which his master was bound as well, and thus it guaranteed Hamlet Cook certain rights:

29. Rappaport, *Worlds Within Worlds*, pp. 295-97.
30. Young's indenture has not survived, but it probably used the standard language printed in [P. E. Jones], *The Corporation of London: Its Origin, Constitution, Powers and Duties* (London: Corporation of London, 1950), p. 90. For the rights and responsibilities of apprentices, see Rappaport, *Worlds Within Worlds*, pp. 232-38.
31. London, Guildhall Library (GL) MS. 7090, vol. 2, fol. 56v; London, Clothworkers' Hall, "Court Orders," vol. 1, fol. 72r; vol. 2, fol. 177r.

> The said master his said apprentice shall teach and instruct or cause to be taught and instructed, finding unto his said apprentice meat, drink, apparel, lodging and all other necessaries, according to the custom of the City of London.[32]

If his master failed to abide by the terms of the indenture an apprentice had the right to complain to the company's governing body, the court of assistants, or even to the chamberlain's court of the City of London. In practice these authorities appear to have responded to apprentices' grievances, such as the Merchant Taylors' governors who ordered Peter Towers to provide his apprentice, Peter Potts, with "meat, drink, lodging, apparel, washing, and other necessaries fit for an apprentice to have." Of great importance to apprentices was their masters' responsibility to train them properly in their craft or trade. In 1568 John Bashe complained that he was "not sufficiently instructed in his science" and the Drapers' court fined his master, Cuthbert Marshall, two pounds, the equivalent of about two months' income. William Hamlet was dismissed from the Cooper's livery, the company's elite, because his apprentice, Edward Pettiver, had learned "little or nothing at all of his trade" in four years' time.[33] Companies looked after apprentices in other ways. In 1566, for example, the Pewterers ordered George Ross "to see his apprentice's leg healed and the surgeon fully contented." Every master craftsman and retailer in London was bound by his freeman's oath to pay all fees to make an apprentice a citizen and companyman at the end of his term, and it was customary to provide him with money and/or goods, often clothing and tools worth three or more pounds, a substantial sum in the sixteenth century. If the master was too poor or otherwise unable to fulfil this obligation, his company often paid the costs. Clothworkers paid 15s. 8d. in 1560 "for the making free of William Redwick, for that his master that he served with died poor and not able to pay the charges." Twenty years later Merchant Taylors gave William Curtis £4 10s. "to apparel him therewith" because his master "is lunatic and has no reason."[34]

In his indenture Hamlet Cook promised to serve Anthony Young as an apprentice for eight years, and in that respect he was typical of apprentices in sixteenth-century London. Hamlet was one of 276 young men whose indentures were enrolled by the Skinners' Company from 1563 through 1569.[35] Two-thirds of the apprentices were bound to terms of eight (37 percent) or nine (29

32. [Jones], *Corporation of London*, p. 90.
33. London, Drapers' Hall, "Court of Assistants' Minute Books," vol. 8, fol. 32r; London, GL, MS. 5602, vol. 1, fols. 136v-37v; London, Merchant Taylors' Hall, "Court Minute Books," vol. 4, fol. 218v. Householders in Elizabethan London probably earned about £10-15 a year, though this is a very rough estimate (see Rappaport, *Worlds Within Worlds*, p. 221 n. 16).
34. London, Clothworkers' Hall, "Renter and Quarter Wardens' Accounts," vol. 1, 1560/1, fol. 4r; London, GL, MS. 7090, vol. 2, fol. 44r; London, Merchant Taylors' Hall, "Court Minute Books," vol. 2, fol. 112r.
35. London, Skinners' Hall, "Admission Books," vol. 1, fols. 121v-42r.

percent) years, one-fifth (19 percent) to seven-year terms, and 15 percent committed themselves to terms of ten or more years, including one young man who promised to serve for 13 years. A similar distribution of terms was found among 207 Skinners' apprentices who began their terms in the late 1540s and early 1550s, but 138 young men bound to Butchers in the 1580s committed themselves to shorter terms: nearly nine-tenths promised to serve for seven (66 percent) or eight (22 percent) years, compared with about one-half of the Skinners' apprentices who began terms twenty years earlier.[36] Most young men admitted into these two companies after completing their apprenticeships had served full terms, training for about the number of years stipulated in their indentures. Skinners' apprentices enrolled in the 1560s served from six to eleven years, averaging 8.5 years, and three-quarters served at least as many years as they had promised to serve in their indentures. The terms of 56 Butchers' apprentices engaged in the 1580s averaged 7.7 years, nearly a year shorter than the terms served by Skinners' apprentices, and all but six served full terms at least.[37]

Shorter terms for Butchers in the 1580s may indicate a general tendency in London for apprenticeships to decrease in length during Elizabeth's reign, or perhaps it reflects variations in the amount of time required to train Skinners and Butchers. A study of 180 young men apprenticed in the 1540s, however, found no significant variations in lengths of training periods required by seven crafts and trades. A more likely explanation is that it is due to differences between great (Skinners) and minor (Butchers) companies, though the study of apprentices in the 1540s does not support this conclusion either.[38] As we will see later, it was the master rather than the apprentice who benefited most from a lengthy term. Presumably the prestige of serving with masters in the twelve great companies and the greater income potential

36. London, GL, MS. 6440, vol. 2, unfol.; London, Skinners' Hall, "Admission Books," vol. 1, fols. 70r-84v. Skinners' apprentices promised to serve for 7 (22%), 8 (35%), 9 (25%), and 10+ (19%) years.
37. Footnotes will report results of tests of the statistical significance of differences between groups of men, chiefly to determine whether it is reasonable to generalize from observations in samples (such as apprenticeship terms served by 118 Skinners and 56 Butchers) to the populations from which the samples were drawn (such as the thousands of Skinners and Butchers who lived in Tudor London). Here, for example, a t-test established that the difference between the average terms served by Skinners (mean = 8.5, s.d. = 0.95) and Butchers (mean = 7.7, s.d. = 0.85) *is* statistically significant, that is, there is *no* measurable chance or probability (p = 0.00) that the difference between the samples does *not* reflect a difference between the populations from which they were drawn. Readers who do not consult footnotes may assume that a difference between samples is discussed in the text only when the probability is at least 95% that it *does* reflect a difference between the populations from which the samples were drawn. Footnotes will also report a measure of the strength of a relationship if it is statistically significant (here $eta^2 = 0.14$), and quantitative information not reported in the text.
38. Rappaport, *Worlds Within Worlds*, pp. 319-20.

offered by careers in related crafts and trades intensified the competition for apprenticeships in those companies, perhaps allowing great companymen to demand lengthier terms from prospective apprentices. Somewhat surprising is the conclusion from this and other studies that a man's family background – whence he came, the social status of his father, whether his father was alive, whether he followed his father's occupation – had no effect at all on the number of years he served.[39] Thus it appears that the length of apprenticeship terms in London was determined chiefly by the attitudes or needs of individual masters and apprentices, factors that have no consistent pattern.

꜡

There is another respect in which Hamlet Cook was typical of the young men who came from all parts of England to apprentice with artisans and retailers in London: he did not finish his apprenticeship term. Fewer than one-half (46 percent) of 276 Skinners' apprentices whose indentures were enrolled from 1563 to 1569 eventually became citizens of London and members of the Skinners' Company, nearly identical to the completion rate of 44 percent among 138 young men who began apprenticeships with Butchers in the 1580s. Though the difference is slight, these apprentices were actually *more* inclined to finish their terms than most apprentices in Tudor London: only 41 percent of 44,169 apprentices engaged by men in 15 companies from 1490 through 1599 completed their terms. There was little variation in completion rates among these companies, with rates in all but four companies averaging 37 to 47 percent across those eleven decades, nor were there significant differences between great and minor or economic types of companies. Mortality could not have been responsible for this very high rate of attrition among apprentices, for in a group of young men beginning apprenticeships at the same time no more than 10 percent would die during the course of a seven- or eight-year term. Consequently with one-tenth dying and two-fifths completing their terms, approximately one-half of the young men who began apprenticeships in sixteenth-century London simply abandoned their training at some point during their service.[40]

What happened to Hamlet Cook? It is impossible to say. Indeed as it turns out, we know less about apprenticeship than we had thought, for though we can reconstruct many of the experi-

39. Among Skinners' apprentices enrolled in 1563-9, no differences in terms served by 19 native Londoners (8.6 years) and 104 immigrants (8.7); or by sons of 13 gentlemen (8.8), 25 yeomen (8.9), and 29 husbandmen (8.7). Among Butchers' apprentices enrolled in 1585-8, no differences in terms served by 5 native Londoners (7.6) and 47 immigrants (7.6); or by 36 men whose fathers were alive (7.7) and 15 men whose fathers were dead (7.6); or by 6 men whose fathers were butchers (7.8) and 41 whose fathers were not butchers (7.7). Rappaport, *Worlds Within Worlds*, pp. 321-22.
40. Rappaport, *Worlds Within Worlds*, pp. 311-13.

ences of apprentices who completed their training, the two-fifths who neither died nor left London before their terms ended, we know very little about what happened to the *majority* of men who began apprenticeships in sixteenth-century London: those who did *not* complete their terms. We know, for example, that Hamlet Cook came from a village in the northern midlands, that his father was a husbandman, and that he began his apprenticeship in the household of a Skinner on Christmas Day, 1565. We may assume that one day around then Anthony Young took Hamlet Cook to the Skinners' hall where he was presented to the company's master and wardens to show them that he was "free born and of true kindred and right and clean of limbs." There his name and what we know about his family background was recorded in the Skinners' *Admission Books*, his master paid a fee of 2s. 6d. for his enrollment, and in a simple ceremony Hamlet swore the oath of an apprentice, promising "by my faith and troth to be obedient unto the master and wardens of the fellowship."[41] That, however, is all that we know about not only Hamlet Cook but also most of the tens of thousands of other young men who began apprenticeships in sixteenth-century London but never completed their terms. Why did so many of them leave? Had they intended all along to leave London after a few years' training? If not, then what made them change their minds?

The family backgrounds and experiences of apprentices bound to serve 276 Skinners and 138 Butchers were analyzed to shed some light on this subject, but the results provide unequivocal answers to none of those questions. Knowing whence a man came is no help in predicting whether he would serve his full term. Completion rates varied somewhat among men from different regions of England, but no clear or intelligible pattern emerges. Not surprisingly, native Londoners were more inclined than immigrants to finish their terms, though here too the results are ambiguous. Among Butchers' apprentices, only two-fifths of 126 immigrants but all of six native Londoners completed apprenticeships.[42] Native Londoners bound to serve Skinners also tended more than immigrants to complete their apprenticeships, but the difference is not substantial (58 and 45 percent respectively).[43] Indeed what is surprising is the fact that 42 percent of 33 native Londoners did *not* finish their terms. Presumably many immigrants terminated their training because they chose to return home, or heard of opportunities elsewhere, or decided that life in the capital was unappealing. Londoners, however, had roots in the capital – family, friends, and the like – including contacts that might prove valuable in promoting their carers, and

---

41.   Information about what Hamlet Cook did and probably did when he became an apprentice is from London, Skinners' Hall, "Admission Books," vol. 1, fol. 128r; London, GL, MSS. 5807 and 16,981.
42.   Chi-square test(X^2) p = 0.01, phi (ϕ) = 0.25.
43.   58% of 33 native Londoners and 45% of 234 immigrants did not finish their terms, but the difference is not statistically significant (X^2p = 0.26).

they must have been more reluctant than immigrants to leave. Maybe not. Perhaps young men then, like many youths today, craved new experiences and thus seized the first opportunity, such as a chance to work or to study far from home, to leave London and strike out on their own. Or perhaps they abandoned their apprenticeships but not their city, choosing instead to claim citizenship and membership in their father's company by patrimony, the right of any young man or woman born to a citizen.

Differences in the family backgrounds of these 414 apprentices also shed little light on why some chose to finish their terms. Whether a man's father were alive when his indenture was signed made no difference among 132 Butchers' apprentices.[44] The 153 sons of gentlemen, yeomen, and husbandmen who apprenticed with Skinners had virtually identical completion rates (43 to 47 percent),[45] though father's social status did make a difference among Butchers' apprentices: 54 percent of 28 sons of husbandmen served their full terms, but only two of thirteen sons of yeomen finished their apprenticeships.[46] Coming from wealthier families than sons of husbandmen and thus presumably able to draw upon greater financial resources and a wider network of contacts throughout England, the career options of yeomen's sons were probably more numerous. Sons of husbandmen, on the other hand, were less independent economically and thus perhaps more inclined to make their way in London, and that may explain why their completion rate (54 percent) was well above the average for young men who began apprenticeships in the sixteenth century. Finally, the length of the terms to which apprentices were bound in their indentures was not associated with variations in completion rates: young men who promised to serve nine or more years were as likely to finish their apprenticeships as men bound to shorter terms.[47]

Though we cannot explain why some men finished their apprenticeships and others did not, the consequences of their decisions are clear. Because so many more young men began apprenticeships than finished, about two and a half times as many, the number of apprentices living in London was considerable. In the middle of the sixteenth century more than 7000 young men were serving apprenticeships at any one time, from the 1400 men just beginning their terms to the nearly 600 men in their last year of service, amounting to more than one-tenth of London's entire population and about a third of the roughly 22,000 males who either were citizens and companymen or were apprenticed with

44. 41% of 96 men whose fathers were alive and 47% of 36 men whose fathers were dead finished their terms ($X^2p = 0.63$).
45. 43% of 30 sons of gentlemen, 47% of 55 sons of yeomen, and 43% of 68 sons of husbandmen finished their terms ($X^2p = 0.87$).
46. $X^2p = 0.05$, $\phi = 0.36$.
47. Completion rates were similar for 134 Butchers' apprentices who served 7 (41% of 88 apprentices), 8 (43% of 30), and 9 or more years (50% of 16): $X^2p = 0.79$; and also for 272 Skinners' apprentices who served 7 (35% of 51), 8 (50% of 101), 9 (53% of 78), and 10 or more years (38% of 42): $X^2p = 0.15$.

them. This was, however, a highly transient population. With more than 800 apprentices dying or abandoning their terms each year and nearly 600 finishing their training, the annual turnover amounted to one-fifth of the 7250 apprentices learning crafts and trades in London in the middle of the sixteenth century.[48]

The most significant consequence of a low completion rate, however, concerns the impact of the institution of apprenticeship beyond London's walls. In the sixteenth century youths like Hamlet Cook came from all over England to learn crafts and trades in households of the city's freemen, but fewer than half of them settled there permanently, and thus it is clear that Londoners were training a share of the nation's non-agricultural labor force living elsewhere. In the middle of the century nearly 1300 young men arrived in the city annually to begin apprenticeships, but each year nearly 800 youths left London and headed for villages and towns throughout the realm, bringing to local economies their skills learned in the capital.[49] Where did they go? It is unlikely that many youths went from London to other cities in England, for in regional and even county urban centers citizenship was a prerequisite for setting up shop as an artisan or retailer.[50] Thus most of these young men probably went to the roughly 750 market towns in early modern England, each serving the surrounding countryside not only as a market where husbandmen and yeomen sold agricultural produce, but also as a place where farmers purchased goods made by local artisans. Though most market towns were home to from 600 to 1000 people and served relatively small hinterlands, their inhabitants pursued a wide range of occupations: wills and inventories from 19 of Norfolk's 28 market towns record 57 different occupations, including representatives from all occupational groups. It is true that most inhabitants of market towns worked as farmers, but people engaged chiefly in crafts and trades often amounted to a sizable proportion of their populations. About a quarter of the

48. Rappaport, *Worlds Within Worlds*, pp. 232-34.
49. This includes more than 700 apprentices who abandoned their terms and probably left London (total annual attrition of 823 apprentices minus the mortality of 106 apprentices) and about 75 young men who left London within 2 years of finishing their terms (12.6% of 574 apprentices who finished terms each year), computed from figures in Rappaport, *Worlds Within Worlds*, pp. 76-77, 232-34, 311-15, 329-33.
50. A. Dyer, *The City of Worcester in the Sixteenth Century* (Leicester: Leicester University Press, 1973), p. 124; W. T. MacCaffrey, *Exeter 1540-1640. The Growth of an English Country Town*, 2d ed. (Cambridge, MA: Harvard University Press, 1975), p. 73; D. M. Palliser, "The Trade Gilds of Tudor York," in *Crisis and Order in English Towns 1500-1700*, P. Clark and P. Slack, eds. (Toronto: University of Toronto Press, 1972), p. 87; C. Phythian-Adams, "Ceremony and the Citizen: The Communal Year at Coventry 1450-1550," in *The Early Modern Town*, P. Clark, ed. (London: Longman, 1976), p. 107; J. Pound, *Tudor and Stuart Norwich* (Chichester, Sussex: Phillimore & Co., 1988), p. 46; M. Reed, "Economic Structure and Change in Seventeenth-Century Ipswich," in *Country Towns in Pre-Industrial England*, P. Clark, ed. (Leicester: Leicester University Press, 1981), pp. 120-21.

men who lived in Oakham, for example, a small market town in Rutland about 50 miles east of Colton where Hamlet Cook grew up, were engaged in non-agricultural occupations, including men who worked in victualling, cloth, leather, construction, and metal crafts, and even a minstrel.[51]

The ramifications of a low completion rate among apprentices are wider still, for London was not the only city that functioned as a vocational training center in early modern England. If, as it appears, a high rate of attrition among apprentices was common in English cities, then each year thousands of young men left tens of cities after receiving several years' training in a craft or trade.[52] Clearly vocational training was another important function of urban centers in early modern England. How important was this educational function? What proportion of the nation's rural, non-agricultural labor force was trained in its cities? One way to provide a very rough answer that question, an order of magnitude, is to estimate the number of men added to that labor force annually to account for its attrition due to mortality and its natural increase, and then to compare that figure with an estimate of the number of apprentices who left cities each year. It is estimated that in the 1520s England's rural, non-agricultural population amounted to 18.3 percent of its total population of 2.4 million, that is, there were approximately 440,000 people *not* living in cities who depended upon employment other than farming.[53] Since people trained in cities were young men, the labor force they entered was the adult male labor force, defined here as males aged 22 to 64 years, amounting to about 22 percent of that rural, non-agricultural population.[54] Assuming a mortality

51. P. Clark and P. Slack, *English Towns in Transition 1500-1700* (Oxford: Oxford University Press, 1976), pp. 17-25; A. Everitt, "The Marketing of Agricultural Produce," in *The Agrarian History of England and Wales. Volume IV 1500-1640,* J. Thirsk, ed. (Cambridge: Cambridge University Press, 1967), p. 478; J. Patten, *English Towns 1500-1700* (Folkestone, Kent: Wm. Dawson & Sons, 1978), pp. 168-69; J. F. Pound, *Tudor and Stuart Norwich*, pp. 1-5.
52. We do not know how many apprentices failed to complete terms in cities other than London, but we do know how many apprentices never became citizens, and it is likely that many of them left the cities where they served before completing their terms: about two-thirds of all apprentices in Bristol (A. Yarbrough, "Apprentices as Adolescents in Sixteenth Century Bristol," p. 80 n. 48); one-half of 183 apprentices in Chester during 1558-1625 (D. M. Woodward, "Sources for Urban History. I. Freemen's Rolls," *Local Historian* 9 [1971]: 92-93); 44% of 1192 apprentices in Norwich during 1576-1600 (J. F. Pound, *Tudor and Stuart Norwich*, pp. 48-50); and only 45 of 375 apprentices in York in 1450-1500 (H. Swanson, "The Illusion of Economic Structure: Craft Guilds in Late Medieval English Towns," *Past and Present* 121 [1988]: 46).
53. E. A. Wrigley, *People, Cities and Wealth: The Transformation of Traditional Society* (Oxford: Basil Blackwell, 1987), p. 170, Table 7.4. I assume a total urban population (including London, which I estimate at 60,000) in the 1520s of about 190,000 (see n. 56 below), larger than Wrigley's estimate of 130,000, and that reduces his estimate of the size of the rural, non-agricultural population from 450,000 to 440,000.
54. Age limits of the rural, non-agricultural labor force in early modern England are, of course, extremely difficult to define. Twenty-two years is used

rate of 24 per 1000 and a growth rate of 0.9 percent per year, 3200 men were needed annually to make up for the attrition due to mortality (2328 men) and the increase (873 men) in a labor force of 97,000 adult males.[55] How many men left England's cities each year after receiving some vocational training? In the 1520s approximately 130,000 people lived in 27 towns with at least 3000 inhabitants.[56] Assuming that both the proportion of apprentices in their populations and the completion rate among apprentices were roughly the same as in London, every year about 1500 young men failed to complete terms. Adding the roughly 700 youths who left London annually, approximately 2200 young men in England abandoned apprenticeships each year.[57] England's largest

---

here for the lower limit because men in London (and perhaps other cities) probably abandoned terms at their midpoint (see pp. 259-60 below), when they were about 22 years old (Rappaport, *Worlds Within Worlds*, pp. 295-98, 322), and thus it was at about that age that they entered a labor force elsewhere. Regarding the upper limit, 65 years is often considered the average age at which people became economically dependent; see R. Pressat, *The Dictionary of Demography*, C. Wilson, ed. (Oxford: Basil Blackwell, 1985), p. 56; E. A. Wrigley and R. S. Schofield, *The Population History of England 1541-1871: A Reconstruction* (London: Edward Arnold, 1981), pp. 443-50; P. Slack, *Poverty and Policy in Tudor and Stuart England* (London: Longman, 1988), pp. 78-85. Using data from a model North, level 4 life table from A. J. Coale and P. Demeny, *Regional Model Life Tables and Stable Populations*, 2d ed. (New York: Academic Press, 1983), p. 222, r = 10.00, and assuming equal numbers of males and females, males aged 22 to 64 years accounted for 21.9% of the total rural, non-agricultural population.

55. The mortality rate for males aged 22 to 64 years was computed from model North, level 4 age-specific mortality rates (Coale and Demeny, *Model Life Tables*, p. 222, r = 10.00); the growth rate (compounded annually) was computed from figures in Wrigley, *People, Cities and Wealth*, p. 170, Table 7.4. From 1520 to 1600 the annual rate of growth in England's rural, non-agricultural population (0.87%) was faster than the rate in its total population (0.67%).

56. C. Phythian-Adams, *Desolation of a City: Coventry and the Urban Crisis of the Late Middle Ages* (Cambridge: Cambridge University Press, 1979), p. 12, Table 3, estimated that 123-141,000 people lived in 27 towns with populations of 3000 or more in the 1520s. P. Corfield, "Urban Development in England and Wales in the Sixteenth and Seventeenth Centuries," in *Trade, Government, and Economy in Pre-Industrial England. Essays Presented to F. J. Fisher*, D. C. Coleman and A. H. Johns, eds. (London: Weidenfeld, 1976), p. 222, estimated that 95-113,000 people lived in 21 towns with populations of 3000 or more in the 1520s, while Wrigley, *People, Cities and Wealth*, p. 160, Table 7.1, restricted his calculation of England's urban population to 9 towns with populations of at least 5000. Phythian-Adams' estimate is used here because he includes towns, such as Lincoln and Canterbury, that had gilds and probably served as vocational training centers for their regions. Indeed, by that criterion other towns that even he excluded, such as Abingdon, Beverley, and Rye, ought to be included as well. See Clark and Slack, *English Towns in Transition*, pp. 28-29, 108-9; Swanson, "Craft Guilds in Late Medieval English Towns."

57. For the number of apprentices in mid-Tudor London and their completion rate, see pp. 254 and 256 above. If we assume stable demographic and other characteristics, and if 800 young men left London annually in the 1550s when the population was about 70,000 (see n. 49 above), then about 700 left each year in the 1520s when the population was about 60,000. Comparable figures are not available for other English cities, and thus we must assume that if 700

cities, therefore, provided at least some vocational training for more than two-thirds of the 3200 men who each year entered the adult male labor force living outside of cities and employed in non-agricultural occupations.[58]

Why did some men abandon their apprenticeships and leave London? In the experiences of 414 Butchers' and Skinners' apprentices there was no consistent pattern that explains why some completed their terms and others did not, or allows us to construct a profile of the type of youth who was likely to serve out the term to which he was bound. There is one thing, however, about which we can speculate: the effects of apprenticeship itself upon the rate at which men completed their terms. Men who did not complete their training probably left London at about the midpoint of their terms, after four or five years, for the system of apprenticeship encouraged men *not* to complete their training. The first half of a term was worth more to an apprentice than his master. An apprentice had a great deal to learn then, but he was not yet skilled enough to do much more than menial tasks. Thus during those early years his master paid the bulk of the costs of his education by providing him with room, board, and time spent training him. As an apprentice's skills developed, however, his labor became increasingly valuable to his master. As a writer in the 1570s put it, "one year's service at the latter end is worth more than four at the beginning,"[59] and indeed men in London were willing to pay quite a bit of money for apprentices who had served several years but whose masters had died or for other reasons could no longer train them. In 1585 Thomas Powell, a Carpenter, agreed to pay John Lyff two shillings a week for his apprentice, John Saunders, who was halfway through the fourth year of his term, though Lyff reserved the right to Saunders' last year of service. Hiring a semiskilled carpenter would have cost Powell twice as much, about four or five shillings a week, so this was a considerable savings, though it must be remembered that he had to pay for the apprentice's room and board as well. Three years later another Carpenter, John Billing, was willing to pay three

---

young men left London each year in the 1520s, then about 1500 emigrated annually from 27 towns with a combined population of 130,000.

58.   Based on several assumptions which cannot be tested empirically, the figure computed here (69%) is a very rough estimate of the proportion of the rural, non-agricultural labor force that received some vocational training in English towns. Other assumptions would produce different estimates. For example, estimates of the size of England's urban population in the 1520s by Corfield (104,000) and Wrigley (70,000) yield figures of 60% and 46% respectively. On the other hand, using model North, level 5 and 6 life tables, based on less severe mortality schedules (life expectancies from birth of 27 and 30 years respectively, compared with 25 years for level 4), yield figures of 72% and 74% respectively. Finally, reducing the upper limit of the labor force to 60 years, preferred by Wrigley and Schofield, *Population History of England*, p. 443, yields a figure of 76%.

59.   "Memorandum on the Statute of Artificers," p. 356.

pounds for the two and a half years remaining of the term of Thomas Medcalf, also in the fourth year of his apprenticeship.[60] Consequently it was during the latter half of a term that a master received the greatest compensation for teaching a young man a craft or trade, and for that reason it was in the master's interest to prolong the length of an apprenticeship.

It was in the apprentice's interest as well to serve his full term, thereby gaining a "greater knowledge and perfection in the art or occupation that he was brought up in."[61] But that was not really the issue. In society's view what mattered most was that by serving out his years an apprentice fulfilled his contractual obligation to his master, for it was chiefly during the second half of his term, when he was most skilled, that he repaid his master for his education. Thus a young man owed it both to himself and to his master to finish his apprenticeship. Indeed in its ideal form the logic of the institution of apprenticeship was compelling, for it not only facilitated the transmission of vocational skills and other types of knowledge from one generation to the next, but also provided a means by which two generations cared for each other. When it worked properly, "the aged should be guides unto the youth," teaching them not only how to finish cloth or bake bread but also what it meant to be an adult, a parent, the member of a community. To pay for their education "young men should work to sustain the aged who were their bringers up," remembering that one day they in turn would be masters and "should themselves enjoy the like commodity by those that should rise under them." Many apprentices, however, probably saw things differently. Barred from accepting wages for labor that became more and more skilled as his term wore on, an apprentice may have reached a point when he preferred to exchange his labor for money instead of further refinement of his skills. Indeed at about the midpoint of his term he may have felt skilled enough to earn his living as a journeyman or even to set up his own shop, but either step meant leaving London, for there he could do neither unless he completed his term and became a freeman and member of a company.[62] Completing his apprenticeship provided a man with additional skills and citizenship, but apparently half the young men who began apprenticeships in London in the sixteenth century chose instead to leave the city and practice their crafts and trades elsewhere in England, careers for which they had been trained substantially in the capital.

♣

60.   B. Marsh and J. Ainsworth, eds., *Records of the Worshipful Company of Carpenters*, 5:142, 157, 173, 212, 217, 226; 6:145, 176, 199, 243, 253. A semiskilled carpenter earned 10d. a day in the 1580s.
61.   Quotations in this paragraph are from "Memorandum on the Statute of Artificers," pp. 356-57.
62.   Rappaport, *Worlds Within Worlds*, pp. 29-36.

Like Hamlet Cook, John Bowyer began his apprenticeship on Christmas Day, 1565. Bowyer was the son of a gentleman from Ranton, a village in Staffordshire about 14 miles west of Colton where Hamlet Cook was raised. Unlike Cook, however, Bowyer served all nine years of his term and was sworn a Skinner on Friday, 4 February 1575, one of five men admitted into the company on that day.[63] We will never know why Hamlet Cook and John Bowyer chose different courses. It is frustrating (and, I suppose, humbling) for this historian, armed with powerful computing and statistical tools, to realize that in some cases the past must remain murky, that quantifiable factors such as whence a man came or his fathers' social status affected but did not determine completely what was in the end a very personal decision. For men in their early twenties apprenticeship cannot have been an easy experience: seven or more years of labor that for much of the time was menial and perhaps grueling, of total dependence at an age consumed by the search for an independent identity, of sexual repression, of childlike status when one is yearning for adulthood. And London had its problems. The wonderment felt by Hamlet Cook when first he gazed upon Saint Paul's Cathedral or the stalls in Cheapside may have given way within a few years to loathing for the noise and the filth, and thus to longings for the clean air and the quiet of the countryside in which he remembered wandering when he was younger. Or perhaps he left London reluctantly, lured to a Yorkshire hamlet or a Cornish village by an offer too good to pass up or a woman too attractive to refuse. Was he driven from London or enticed by opportunities elsewhere? We will never know why Hamlet Cook left, but perhaps that is best. Too pat, too tidy, leaving little room for human agency and even less for the miraculous, history without mystery is reductionism, though I shall never stop wondering where Hamlet Cook went.

---

63.   London, Skinners' Hall, "Admission Books," vol. 1, fols. 127v, 162.

XVI

Venereal Hermeneutics:
Reading Titian's *Venus of Urbino*

DAVID ROSAND

Titian's *Venus of Urbino*, one of the most familiar images in Western art, has come to stand for both the sensuality and the classicism we ascribe to the culture of the High Renaissance, its low as well as its high life.[1] More recently, it has become the field for critical battle over ways of perceiving and understanding the imagery of the past, our modes of response and interpretation. That conflict has inevitably colored our perception of the picture, forcing certain issues to the fore. Any attempt at an *explication de tableau* must, therefore, assume some degree of methodological self-consciousness.[2] There is a further complication. Our view of the *Venus of Urbino* has been screened by an event of the mid-nineteenth century: Manet's *Olympia*, which was so conspicuously inspired by Titian's picture, and the scandal that attended its public exhibition in 1865. Whatever the desired focus of our historical vision, it is impossible for us to ignore this intrusion. We must acknowledge that Manet's pictorial commentary has affected our sense of the interpretive possibilities inherent in its Renaissance model.

Indeed, our consideration of Titian's painting may legitimately begin in the nineteenth century, when the picture's reception becomes increasingly problematical. The *Venus of Urbino* has long been a high point on the tourist's obligatory rounds of the galleries of the Uffizi. By way of introducing some of the basic hermeneutic problems surrounding the picture, I offer as an opening text the response of one such observer, an American traveller abroad. Upon entering the Uffizi, he reports,

> you proceed to that most-visited little gallery in the world – the Tribune – and there, against the wall, without obstructing rag or

---

1. Harold E. Wethey, *The Paintings of Titian*, vol. 3. *The Mythological and Historical Paintings* (London: Phaidon, 1975), p. 203f., cat. no. 54; Mina Gregori et al., *Tiziano nelle gallerie fiorentine* (Florence: Centro Di, 1978), pp. 125-35, cat. no. 30, with exhaustive bibliography.
2. Cf., most recently, David Freedberg, *The Power of Images: Studies in the History and Theory of Response* (Chicago and London: University of Chicago Press, 1989), pp. 13-21 et passim.

leaf, you may look upon the foulest, the vilest, the obscenest picture the world possesses – Titian's Venus. It isn't that she is naked and stretched out on a bed – no, it is the attitude of one of her arms and hand. If I ventured to describe that attitude, there would be a fine howl – but there the Venus lies, for anybody to gloat over that wants to – and there she hag a right to lie, for she is a work of art, and Art has its privileges.

Our American tourist then makes his contribution to the dossier on the picture's *Rezeptionsgeschichte:* "I saw young girls stealing furtive glances at her; I saw young men gaze long and absorbedly at her; I saw aged, infirm men hang upon her charms with pathetic interest." And he concludes his outburst by reconciling himself to the power of the aesthetic and taking one final stab at historical explanation:

There are pictures of nude women which suggest no impure thought – I am well aware of that. I am not railing at such. What I am trying to emphasize is the fact that Titian's Venus is very far from being one of that sort. Without any question it was painted for a bagnio and it was probably refused because it was a trifle too strong. In truth it is too strong for any place but a public Art Gallery.

This splenetic account of a visit to the Uffizi is by Mark Twain, from *A Tramp Abroad* (published in 1880).[3] It was professionally inspired by what in a Renaissance context we might call a *paragone*, a comparison between the visual arts and literature – more specifically, between the moral courtesy extended to each by society, by Victorian society. "Art," the author observes in his opening attack, "is allowed as much indecent licence to-day as in earlier times – but the privileges of Literature in this respect have been sharply curtailed within the past eighty or ninety years."[4]

Mark Twain's satiric outrage at the blatant nakedness of Titian's lady on the couch, then, is a kind of oblique First Amendment defence. But the issues it raises – or, better, exemplifies – go to the heart of more traditional debates in visual hermeneutics. How, indeed, are we to read this picture? How respond to this image of the female body? Can our response be validated in any way? Can we speak of intention? If so, whose? The culture's? The artist's? The picture's? If the questions seem obvious, the answers are less so.

The problems begin with the painting itself, for critics do not readily agree on just who or what is being depicted. Nor is recourse to the scant historical documentation of much help. One immediate question concerns the identity of the young woman herself. Is this "Venus" in fact a Venus? Or is she one of the

3.   Mark Twain, *A Tramp Abroad* (Toronto: Rose, 1883), p. 357.
4.   In this respect, I wonder if Leo Steinberg, who properly notes the displacement of response in this passage, is not a bit too harsh in his indictment of the author of *Huckleberry Finn*: see "Art and Science: Do They Need to be Yoked?" *Daedalus* 115, 3 (Summer 1986): 10f.

celebrated courtesans of Venice, a *cortigiana onesta*, or merely a common whore, a *cortigiana meretrice*, called up from the *calli* to pose for the painter friend of the infamous Pietro Aretino?[5] Some art historians have taken this as the central question, that which contains *in nuce* all the others; in the identity of the painter's model, they assume, lies the resolution of the entire interpretive challenge.[6] For all its obvious interest and relevance, the question itself, however, merely displaces the issue – or, worse, confounds it by the simplistic confidence of its own positivism, the prosaic literalism of its historicizing pretension.

As a more direct introduction to the painting, we might adduce another nineteenth-century text, published only three years before Mark Twain's. This is the description of the *Venus of Urbino* by Crowe and Cavalcaselle in their classic *Life and Times of Titian* (1877):

> Lying as nature shaped her, with her legs entwined, at the foot of a deep green hanging, on a muslin sheet, that covers a ruby tinged damask couch, her left arm reposes on her frame, her right supporting her on cushions, whilst the hand is playing with a chaplet of flowers. We may fancy her to have bathed and to be waiting for the handmaids, who are busy in the room, one of them having raised the lid of a chest and taken a dress out, whilst a second stoops to select another. Meanwhile a little dog lies curled up on the couch....
>
> Not after the model of a Phryne [the Athenian courtesan said to have posed for Apelles], nor yet with the thought of realizing anything more sublime than woman in her fairest aspect, did Titian conceive of this picture. Nature as he presents it here is young and lovely, not transfigured into ineffable noblesse, but conscious and triumphant without loss of modesty.[7]

We recognize the inevitable passage of description into interpretation. Unlike the American tourist, the Victorian art historians have no difficulty with the license claimed by Art. It is exactly such license that permits their indulgent participation in Titian's painting, that allows them to enjoy publicly the charms of his Venus – "if," as they themselves wonder, "Venus be an appropriate name." Their account of the picture brings it to a

---

5. On the topic in general, see Paul Larivaille, *La vie quotidienne des courtisanes en Italie au temps de la Renaissance* (Paris: Hachette, 1975); and Lynne Lawner, *The Lives of the Courtesans: Portraits of the Renaissance* (New York: Rizzoli, 1987); and *Il gioco dell'amore: le cortigiane di Venezia dal Trecento al Settecento*, exh. cat. (Venice: Berenice, 1990). See also Gaetano Cozzi, "La donna, l'amore e Tiziano," in *Tiziano e Venezia: Convegno internazionale di studi* (Vicenza: N. Pozza, 1980), pp. 47-63.

6. Cf. especially Charles Hope, "Problems of Interpretation in Titian's Erotic Paintings," in *Tiziano e Venezia*, pp. 117-20; and Hans Ost, "Tizians sogenannte 'Venus von Urbino' und andere Buhlerinnen," in *Festschrift für Eduard Trier*, ed. J. Müller-Hofstede and Werner Spies (Berlin: Mann, 1981), pp. 129-49.

7. J. A. Crowe and G. B. Cavalcaselle, *The Life and Times of Titian*, 2d ed. (London: Murray, 1881), 2:389f.

more licit life than did Mark Twain's. "What the painter achieves," they continue,

> is the representation of a beauteous living being whose fair and polished skin is depicted with enamelled gloss, and yet with every shade of modulation which a delicate flesh comports; − flesh not marbled or cold, but sweetly toned; and mantling with life's blood, flesh that seems to heave and rise and fall with every breath. Perfect distribution of space, a full and ringing harmony of tints, atmosphere both warm and mellow, are all combined in such wise as to bring us in contact with something that is real, and we feel as we look into the canvas that we might walk into that apartment and find room to wander in the grey twilight into which it is thrown by the summer sky that shows through the coupled windows.[8]

With delicate avoidance of the all too obvious focal point of the composition, the Victorian critics manage to sublimate the sensual in the aesthetic with a decorousness that we can only admire, I think, for its self-control. And their aesthetic prophylaxis returns us to a fundamental question: Just what kind of painting is this deliberate display of female flesh?

It is not without interest that the first serious effort to locate the picture's significance historically, to articulate its iconography and set it within a specific social context, was in effect the by-product of scholarship on Manet. To understand the meaning of *Olympia*, Theodore Reff quite naturally felt obliged to come to terms with its inspiring image.[9] Against the provocation of a tableau of a French prostitute, a brazen pictorial gesture calculated to *épater le bourgeois*, Titian's nude was recognized as a model of domestic virtue. The *Venus of Urbino* was seen as a marriage picture, the goddess of love characterized by her surrounding attributes as the protectress in particular of marital love. She holds a bunch of roses; and on the window ledge in the background a myrtle plant, in perpetual bloom, is pointedly silhouetted against the glowing sky. These floral symbols, traditionally associated with Venus, combine to define the very special kind of love she here represents: the fruitful passion of licit love, not the quickly sated and sinful lust of the body but the permanent bond of conjugal affection. The little dog curled up at her feet in contented slumber overtly signifies the ideal of marital fidelity − its trusting nature having become so much more poignant for us in light of its feline transformation in Manet's painting. The enframed background scene of maids at an open *cassone*, a marriage chest, offers a naturalistic anecdotal comment on the

8. Ibid., 2:390f.
9. Theodore Reff, The Meaning of Titian's Venus of Urbino," *Pantheon* 21 (1963): 359-66. On Manet's picture, cf. idem, *Manet: Olympia*, Art in Context (London: Allen Lane, 1976); and T. J. Clark, *The Painting of Modern Life: Paris in the Art of Manet and His Followers* (Princeton, NJ: Princeton University Press, 1984), pp. 77-146.

symbolism of the main motif that would seem to confirm the social significance of the image.[10]

Other aspects of the *Venus of Urbino*, as well, seem to confirm its generic status as a marriage picture. Before considering them, however, we must acknowledge one potentially embarrassing issue. If Titian's canvas was indeed painted to celebrate a marriage, then whose wedding was it? And this returns us to its history. We assume that the painting was acquired in 1538 by Guidobaldo II della Rovere, then duke of Camerino and subsequently of Urbino. On March 9, 1538, Guidobaldo wrote to his agent in Venice that he was most anxious to take possession of two paintings still in Titian's studio, a portrait of himself and a picture of a nude woman ("il ritratto mio e la donna nuda").[11] Unfortunately, the duke was short of funds and proposed to borrow from his mother, Eleonora Gonzaga. The duchess was agreeable and wrote to her son on April 14 that she was having the portrait sent to him (three days earlier it was reported as not yet finished).[12]

The following month, on May first, Guidobaldo was still anxious to obtain the other picture, "the nude woman," which remained in the painter's shop and which the duke feared Titian might sell to someone else. By the ninth of May the picture was still undelivered, and the reason seems to have been that Titian, for his part, was rather anxious about payment; at least, the ducal agent reported his guarantee to the painter that his master was good for it.[13] Exactly when Guidobaldo finally possessed his "donna nuda" the extant documents do not actually reveal.[14]

On the basis of this archival situation, two major objections to an epithalamic interpretation of the *Venus of Urbino* have been registered. First, that the Venus of Urbino is no Venus – since the letter of March 9 refers to her only as a naked woman. Second, that this painting of 1538 cannot possibly be a marriage picture – since Guidobaldo's marriage (to the ten-year-old Giulia Varana of Camerino) occurred four years earlier, in 1534. Moreover (the argument runs), if the picture had been so specifically com-

---

10.   Hope's attempt to discredit any symbolic association of the attributes in the *Venus of Urbino* seems arbitrary and forced, and historically naive ("Problems of Interpretation," p. 118). The same floral attributes, myrtle and roses, plus a fertilizing Cupid, characterize Venus in another epithalamic painting, a remarkable picture by Lorenzo Lotto recently acquired by the Metropolitan Museum. Instead of the dog, clinging ivy around the tree behind Venus symbolizes commitment and fidelity. See Keith Christiansen, "Lorenzo Lotto and the Tradition of Epithalamic Paintings," *Apollo* 124 (September 1980): 166-73.

11.   Georg Gronau, *Documenti artistici urbinati* (Florence: Sansoni, 1936), p. 93, doc. XXXI.

12.   Ibid., docs. XXXII, XXXIII.

13.   Ibid., p. 94, docs. XXXV, XXXVI.

14.   The immediately subsequent correspondence indicates that Guidobaldo continued to have difficulties in paying Titian for pictures: see, in particular, his letter of July 30, 1539 (ibid., p. 95, doc. XLII).

missioned by Guidobaldo, then it is unlikely that he would have so feared losing it to another buyer.[15] The highly circumstantial nature of these objections pretends to a certain historical verifiability, the appeal to the supposedly unproblematic truth of documents. In any event, I propose to shift the ground of the debate by offering the picture itself as the essential document.

What kind of picture is the *Venus of Urbino*? Format and iconography – that is, shape and subject: the horizontal rectangle of its field and the reclining female nude – both relate the canvas to a larger group of pictures, including others by Titian himself. Most famously, Titian's "donna nuda" represents a variation on an invention by Giorgione, the *Sleeping Venus* in Dresden. Evidently painted for Girolamo Marcello, in whose house it was seen in 1525 by Marcantonio Michiel, the Dresden picture was actually completed by Titian. Michiel records "the canvas with a nude Venus sleeping in a landscape with Cupid" as by the hand of Giorgione, but he notes explicitly that "the landscape and Cupid were finished by Titian."[16]

Although the Cupid is no longer visible, X-radiography has confirmed its original existence at the feet of the goddess, holding a symbolically loaded little bird. Jaynie Anderson has elegantly demonstrated the epithalamic nature of this imagery, tracing the motif of the sleeping Venus back to classical literature, Claudian in particular.[17] Within the ancient tradition of epithalamia, Venus is found at rest in her sacred landscape; roused by Cupid, she prepares herself for the mortals' wedding where she will serve as *pronuba*, the patroness of marriage. The wedding of Girolamo Marcello and Morosina Pisani took place on October 9, 1507, and it is plausibly suggested that Giorgione's canvas was commissioned for that occasion.

Commissioned, but evidently not delivered. It would seem likely that the painting was still incomplete when Giorgione died in the plague of 1510. Like other pictures presumably left behind in his studio, the *Sleeping Venus* was brought to completion by a surviving artist.[18] Marriage pictures, we might infer, did not always arrive on time.[19]

15. These objections have been voiced most forcefully by Hope, "Problems of Interpretation," pp. 117-20.
16. "La tela della Venere nuda, che dorme in uno paese cun Cupidine, fu de mano de Zorzo da Castelfranco; ma lo paese e Cupidine furono finiti da Tiziano." From *Notizia d'opere di disegno*, ed. Gustavo Frizzoni (Bologna: N. Zanichelli, 1884), p. 169. Further on the picture: Terisio Pignatti, *Giorgione*, 2d ed. (Milan: Alfieri, 1978), pp. 111f., cat. no. 23.
17. Jaynie Anderson, "Giorgione, Titian and the Sleeping Venus," in *Tiziano e Venezia*, pp. 337-42.
18. The other notable example is *The Three Philosophers* in Vienna (Pignatti, *Giorgione*, pp. 108f., cat. no. 19). Describing the canvas in the house of Taddeo Contarini in 1525, Michiel observes that it was begun by Giorgione and finished by Sebastiano del Piombo (*Notizia*, ed. Frizzoni, pp. 164f.).
19. For the moment I pass over alternative reconstructions of the situation – such as that suggested by Anderson: namely, that Titian (then presumably

A quarter of a century later Titian recalled his Giorgionesque intervention in the *Venus of Urbino*. He awakened and domesticated Giorgione's dreaming deity. Brought indoors, this nude stresses less her classical poetic pedigree than her contemporary social function. And her blatant address to the viewer, invitation by sight as well as touch, reinforces even as it complicates that dimension of the image in the world. Although Giorgione had reinvoked an antique type of Venus – as well as of Ariadne – reclining in a landscape, the distended female nude had already found her natural pictorial field in the quattrocento: in the painted panels inside the lids of *cassoni*, those trousseau chests whose decorations often celebrated uxorial virtue or dynastic generation.[20] It is precisely the furniture format of those panels that is recalled in another painting by Titian, one that can be documented to a very particular marriage.

This is the painting generally known as *Sacred and Profane Love* (Rome, Galleria Borghese). Although it too has had to withstand more than its share of scholarly attention, at least here we are certain of the picture's patronage and purpose, for two coats of arms affirm the joining of two families.[21] The more prominently displayed, above the foundation spigot in the relief of the transformed sarcophagus, is that of Niccolò Aurelio. More discretely hidden, inlaid at the bottom of the silver bowl, are the arms of the Bagarotto family of Padua. Niccolò Aurelio, then secretary to the Venetian Council of Ten, was married to Laura Bagarotto in May of 1514.[22]

---

nineteen years old) was called in to assist Giorgione because the older master had his hands full with official commissions in 1507.
20. These recumbent female nudes were usually paired with male counterparts. See Paul Schubring, *Cassoni: Truhen und Truhenbilder der italienischen Frührenaissance* (Leipzig: Hiersemann, 1915), nos. 156, 157, 184, 185, 289, 290. We observe the conflation of these couples into single horizontal fields in late quattrocento images, such as Botticelli's *Mars and Venus* (London, National Gallery) and the similar composition by Piero di Cosimo (Berlin-Dahlem, Staatliche Museen), which may indeed be marriage pictures: see E. H. Gombrich, "Botticelli's Mythologies: A Study in the Neo-Platonic Symbolism of his Circle," in *Symbolic Images: Studies in the Art of the Renaissance* (London: Phaidon, 1972), pp. 66-69; also Edgar Wind, *Pagan Mysteries in the Renaissance*, rev. ed. (Harmondsworth and Baltimore: Penguin Books, 1967), pp. 89-91. Further on *cassoni* paintings, see E. H. Gombrich, "Apollonio di Giovanni: A Florentine Cassone Workshop seen through the Eyes of a Humanist Poet," in *Norm and Form: Studies in the Art of the Renaissance* (London: Phaidon, 1966), pp. 11-28; Ellen Callmann, *Apollonio di Giovanni* (Oxford: Clarendon Press, 1974); Brucia Witthoff, "Marriage Rituals and Marriage Chests in Quattrocento Florence," *Artibus et Historiae* 5 (1982): 43-59.
21. See Wethey, *The Paintings of Titian*, 3:175-79, cat. no. 33.
22. The bride, a widow embarking upon a second marriage, was the daughter of a prominent Paduan rebel who had been executed for treason by the Venetians in 1509; the proposed marriage occasioned some comment, therefore, and necessitated official state approval. In recording the event in his diaries, "una cosa notanda," Marin Sanudo adds, "et par habi auto licentia dal Principe, consieri e Ca[p]i di X; *tamen* di questo molto se parloe." See *I Diarii*, ed. Rinaldo Fulin et al. (Venice: F. Visentini, 1879-1903), 18:199 (17 May 1514).

Erwin Panofsky has given the *Sacred and Profane Love* its canonical interpretation, confirming the Neoplatonism of the received title.[23] His reading, however, has hardly gone unchallenged. Recently, the debate over the exact nature of the iconography of the picture has reached a particularly feverous pitch, as serious scholars – in what can only be described as anti-Panofsky hysteria – have vehemently argued against any philosophical, especially Neoplatonic, dimension to the painting. Insisting on what they call "straightforward" interpretation, these critics reject the reading of the image as a representation of twin Venuses, terrestrial and celestial, or, as described in the early seventeenth century, "Beltà disornata e Beltà ornata." Instead, they prefer a more prosaic path. Forced by the presence of Cupid into acknowledging the identity of the nude figure, at least, as Venus, they see the clothed beauty as the bride herself; the painting is thus to be retitled "Laura Bagarotto at the fountain of Venus."[24] The extraordinary acuity – not to say fantasy – of physiognomic perception necessary to distinguish between these two faces is, I confess, beyond my powers, especially since their features grace any number of *belle donne* in Titian's work of this period. To call this *beltà ornata* a portrait of Laura Bagarotto is as wishful as the nineteenth-century recognition of the *Venus of Urbino* as a portrait of Eleonora Gonzaga, duchess of Urbino and mother of the patron – as wishful and blind.

At this point in my argument, it is enough to insist upon the essential dialogic structure of the composition of *Sacred and Profane Love* and to recognize in that structure a fundamental guide to its meaning: the two beauties stand to each other as terms of an equation.[25]

Titian's *Sacred and Profane Love* affirms the existence of one pictorial category directly relevant to an understanding of the *Venus of Urbino*: the marriage picture. The category itself, however, can be liberated from the restrictions of historical circumstances to assert its own generic independence, its existence as a recognizable formal type per se. The *cassone* panel of the quattrocento preserved the social context of the image by setting it in furniture that would continue to fulfill a social function. As an

---

The relevant passages from Sanudo are cited in Wethey, *The Paintings of Titian*, 3:177.

23. Panofsky addressed the picture several times in the course of his career: *Hercules am Scheidewege und andere antike Bildstoffe in der neueren Kunst*, Studien der Bibliothek Warburg, 18 (Leipzig: Teubner, 1930), pp. 173-80; *Studies in Iconology: Humanistic Themes in the Art of the Renaissance* (1939), (New York: Harper & Row, 1962), pp. 150-60; *Problems in Titian, Mostly Iconographic* (New York: New York University Press, 1969), pp. 110-19.

24. Cf. Hope, "Problems of Interpretation," pp. 115-17; and idem, *Titian* (London: Jupiter Books, 1980), pp. 34-36; also Edward Fry, "In Detail: Titian's *Sacred and Profane Love*," *Portfolio* 1 (October-November 1979): 34-39.

25. I have commented on the implications of such pictorial structure in "Panofsky, Tiziano e le strutture pittoriche," in *Iconologia e oltre: Seminario internazionale* (in press).

easel picture, such as Giorgione's, the image of Venus gained a certain independence and, we might say, flexibility of function. Whatever its originating cause, its continued existence and significance necessarily became, over time, less dependent on that cause. So, too, the image-type itself came to enjoy a meaning and an appeal beyond the socially legitimizing marital context. "Marriage pictures" could be painted without marriages – although we can hardly rule out the possibility that the *Venus of Urbino* may indeed have been commissioned on the occasion of the wedding of 1534.

There is another genre of picture that is equally relevant, one that is, however, more difficult to fix with such documentary clarity. This comprises pictures of beautiful women, usually coming down to us without name or title, in various states of deshabille. The highest example of the type is Titian's own *Flora* (Florence, Uffizi), who so identifies herself by the flowers she offers.[26] Flora was both goddess and courtesan, and Flora was one of the names adopted by Venetian courtesans when they entered the profession. Another name that appears frequently among the sixteenth-century lists of courtesans in Venice is Laura – ironic homage to the idolized Petrarchan *madonna*.

In this light, we can hardly accept the reading of Giorgione's *Laura* (Vienna, Kunsthistorisches Museum), displaying herself before the floral declaration of her name, as the portrait of a good Venetian matron.[27] Palma Vecchio, to judge by the number of extant works, seems to have made a specialty of this type of imagery, "fantasy pieces," as Crowe and Cavalcaselle called them *(quadri di fantasia)*.[28] Even the aged Giovanni Bellini was called upon to contribute. Whether or not his lady at her toilet (Vienna, Kunsthistorisches Museum) is a Venus or the portrait of someone's *favorita*, whether or not she is susceptible of allegorization as Vanitas, her primary appeal is clear.[29] On a basic level – that is, on the first level of Erwin Panofsky's synoptical table of interpretation – the "object of interpretation" is "primary or natural subject matter." And the "equipment [necessary] for interpreta-

26. Wethey, *The Paintings of Titian*, 3:154-56, cat. no. 17; also, David Rosand, *Titian* (New York: H. N. Abrams, 1978), p. 82, pl. 11.

27. See Jaynie Anderson, "The Giorgionesque Portrait: From Likeness to Allegory," in *Giorgione: Atti del convegno internazionale di studio* (Castelfranco Veneto: Banco Popolare di Asolo e Montebelluna, 1979), pp. 153-58. On the character herself, see Julius S. Held, "Flora, Goddess and Courtesan," in *De Artibus Opuscula XL: Essays in Honor of Erwin Panofsky*, ed. Millard Meiss (New York: New York University Press, 1961), pp. 201-18.

28. Crowe and Cavalcaselle, *Life and Times of Titian*, 1:391. On Palma's "molti ritratti di Dame con ornamenti e vesti all'antica" (Ridolfi), see Philip Rylands, *Palma il Vecchio: L'opera completa* (Milan: Mondadori, 1988), pp. 103-26.

29. Bellini's painting is discussed, with specific reference to its sensuous appeal and in the context of Titian's art, by Rona Goffen, *Giovanni Bellini* (New Haven and London: Yale University Press, 1989), pp. 252-57.

tion," to stay with Panofsky's outline, is "practical experience (familiarity with objects and events)."[30]

Crowe and Cavalcaselle faced the hermeneutic problem with their usual Victorian tact. They wondered about Titian's Flora whether she was

> one of those ladies of light fame who survived to be copied by Rubens under the name of courtezan. The lover of art [they concluded] may now say it is a matter of little consequence. The "Flora," if nothing more, is a lovely ideal which ranges far above the realms to which her earthly lot would seem to bind her.[31]

And the moral generosity of these art historians – however patronizing its tone – inflected critical response, once again, into aesthetic sublimation: the delicate sensuality of their description, its loving attention to detail, pays full tribute to the effect of Flora on her admirers.

Not quite so delicate is the more recent verdict of a contemporary English art historian. Charles Hope concludes, "The implication is that these pictures [and he is referring to both the Flora and the Venus of Urbino] were for the most part mere pinups, and that the girls were seen as little more than sex objects....[32]

It is true that in one of the very few early references we have to a picture like the Venus of Urbino, a reclining nude by Savoldo in the house of Andrea Odoni, the invaluable Marcantonio Michiel locates it in the bedroom over the bed: "La Nuda grande destesa da drietto el letto...."[33] But that hardly diminishes its cultural position. Rather, it would seem to confirm its higher talismanic function: to conceive a child under the sign of Venus increases the chance, presumably, of generating beauty. A century earlier Leon Battista Alberti had recommended that in the bedroom of the master of the family and his wife there be hung only images of "dignity and handsome appearance; for they say that this may have a great influence on the fertility of the mother and the appearance of future offspring."[34]

---

30.   Panofsky, *Studies in Iconology*, pp. 14-15 – slightly modified in "Iconography and Iconology: An Introduction to the Study of Renaissance Art," in *Meaning in the Visual Arts: Papers in and on Art History* (Garden City, NY: Doubleday, 1957), pp. 40-41. For further comment on the hierarchy of this interpretive scale, see Rosand, "Panofsky, Tiziano e le strutture pittoriche."
31.   Crowe and Cavalcaselle, *The Life and Times of Titian*, 1:271.
32.   Hope, "Problems of Interpretation," p. 119.
33.   *Notizia d'opere di disegno*, ed. Frizzoni, p. 160.
34.   "Ubi uxoribus conveniant, nonnisi dignissimos hominum et formosissimos vultus pingas monent; plurimum enim habere id momenti ad conceptus matronarum et futuram spetiem prolis ferunt." From *De re aedificatoria* IX.iv, ed. Giovanni Orlandi (Milan: Polifilo, 1966), 2:805. The English translation is from Leon Battista Alberti, *On the Art of Building in Ten Books*, trans. Joseph Rykwert, Neil Leach, Robert Tavernor (Cambridge, MA: MIT Press, 1988), p. 299. The two sixteenth-century Italian translations are worth quoting for their directness: "Ammoniscono che si dipingano belle faccie de huomini ove concorrono le moglie con li mariti à generare. Il che molto importa che le matrone faccino belli figliuoli," in *I dieci libri de l'architettura di Leon Battista de gli*

Whatever its ostensible source in the antique *Venus pudica*, the gesture of the Venus of Urbino, even more than that of her Giorgionesque prototype, hardly serves the cause of modesty. It was just this gesture that Mark Twain could not bring himself to describe for fear "there would be a fine howl."[35] The Venetian Venus rather calls attention to her genitals, and that focus is still more precisely fixed by the central vector of the hanging curtain in the *Venus of Urbino* – part of the tectonic grid against which her curves are so deliberately measured.[36] Not covering but rather stimulating, this gesture, as Rona Goffen has recently suggested, confirms the licit nature of sexuality in these images; its invitation is to love within marriage, its allusion to the generative function of such love – the procreation of beauty.[37]

To call these images "mere pin-ups" must strike us as more than just a flippant response from the twentieth century, more than just an easy way of accommodating a complex past to what can only seem a simplistic present. It represents a willful act of critical irresponsibility, a failure to confront the very hermeneutic issues it pretends to resolve with such casual aplomb. Such reduction of meaning is predicated on a vacuation of the possibilities of meaning from the image, a denial of its cultural resonance. To deny a Renaissance picture of a nude woman her mythological garb is indeed to turn her out into the streets. It is also to deny the complexity and vitality of Renaissance culture, most especially its appropriation of the classical as a way of dealing with the present. This argument – and I must apologize for dwelling so long on what Leonardo in his notebooks would refer to as "the adversary" – claims to found itself on a close reading of the documents.

Alberti Fiorentino, trans. Pietro Lauro (Venice: V. Vangris, 1546), p. 200. "Ma nelle camere dove i padri delle famiglie hanno a dormire con le lor' moglie, avertiscasi che non vi si dipinga se non volti di huomini, o di donne bellissime, & honorati & dicono che questo importa grandemente quanto allo ingravidare, delle matrone, & quanto alla bellezza della futura progenie," in *L'Architettura di Leon Battista Alberti*, trans. Cosimo Bartoli (Florence: L. Torrentino, 1550), p. 334. Further on this topos, see Freedberg, *The Power of Images*, pp. 2-4, citing passages from St. Augustine to Giulio Mancini (*Considerazioni sulla pittura*, c.1617), who expands upon Alberti.

35.   In a letter of 1864, Swinburne anticipated Twain's response, but with less ambivalent enthusiasm: "As for Titian's Venus – Sappho and Anactoria in one – four lazy fingers buried dans les fleurs de son jardin – how any creature can be decently virtuous within thirty miles of it passes my comprehension." The passage is cited by David Freedberg in the chapter "The Senses and Censorship," in *The Power of Images*, p. 345.

36.   For a sensitive structural analysis of the picture, see Daniel Arasse, *Tiziano: Venere d'Urbino* (Venice: Arsenale, 1986).

37.   Rona Goffen, "Renaissance Dreams," *Renaissance Quarterly* 40 (1987): 683-706, esp. 697-701. Observing that Giorgione's Venus "denotes not the act of love but the recollection of it," S. J. Freedberg then suggested, in a note, "that this is the interpretation of Giorgione's placing of the left hand, quite different in meaning from its presumable antique source in the *Venus Pudica* type." See *Painting in Italy 1500-1600*, Pelican History of Art (Harmondsworth and Baltimore: Penguin, 1971), pp. 85, 476 n. 25.

With regard to the *Venus of Urbino,* this means the correspondence of Guidobaldo della Rovere and his attempt to acquire the painting he apparently ordered some time before 1538 but was having some difficulty affording. His reference to "la donna nuda" is really quite adequate descriptively, and yet this has been read as an indication of the picture's non-subject: "It is surprising," we are told, "that Guidobaldo should have referred to the picture merely as 'la donna nuda' if he really meant 'la Venere'."[38] So runs the argument. But such efficient references, like those in inventories or in Marcantonio Michiel's notes, were hardly meant to be interpretive epitomes; they were, rather, functional identifying labels, indications of pictures seen. And "the nude woman" affords a most satisfactory description of the "object of interpretation." The reference is to its "primary or natural subject matter" – the base level of Panofsky's synoptical table – and represents the beginning, not the end, of interpretation.

Guidobaldo's "donna nuda" leads us back to the question of pictorial genre and the conception of such pictures. Another letter and another painting expand the discussion. The letter, written from Venice in 1544 (September 20) by Giovanni della Casa to Cardinal Alessandro Farnese, is filled with sarcastic allusions to members of the Farnese circle as well as to a number of paintings by Titian. Among the latter is one, nearly finished, being done for the cardinal himself, "una nuda," to which della Casa devotes special attention. Declaring that the picture will particularly excite a certain member of the curia (Umberto Gambara), he then compares it explicitly with the *Venus of Urbino.* The nude now on Titian's easel, he writes, makes that of the duke of Urbino seem like a Theatine nun. Onto this nude body Titian joked about attaching the head of a well-known Roman courtesan and Farnese favorite (Camilla Pisana) – presumably when he himself arrived in Rome, which would be the following year (October 1545-May 1546). The painter was in fact most anxious to please the Farnese, for he was hoping to guarantee a benefice for his son Pomponio; his jesting offer to add the features of a *favorita* might well have been an especially appreciated gesture. Della Casa concludes his comments with praise of the painter's personality and recommends him most highly to the cardinal.[39]

38. Hope, "Problems of Interpretation," p. 118.
39. "...ha presso che fornita, per commession di Vostra Signoria Reverendissima, una nuda, che faria venir il diavol adosso al Cardinale San Sylvestro; et quella che Vostra Signoria Reverendissima vide in Pesaro nelle Camere del Signor Duca d'Urbino è una teatina appresso a questa; et vole appicciarle la testa della sopradetta cognata, pur che'l benefitio venga. Verrà a Roma et per tutto, et non è giuocco si strano, che non sia per farlo, e petitione di questo benefitio. Et senza burla, è valente persona et affettionatissima servitore di Nostro Signore et di Vostra Signoria Reverendissima, et io glielo raccomando quanto posso più efficacemente." The letter was republished and discussed by Charles Hope, "A Neglected Document about Titian's 'Danae' in Naples," *Arte veneta* 31 (1977): 188f.

The painting in question is the *Danae*, part of the Farnese collection now in the Gallerie di Capodimonte in Naples.[40] Here there is no doubt about its subject matter: the shower of gold and the presence of an encouraging Cupid confirm the identity of the heroine in the tower, ravished by Jupiter in his gilded potency. This nude is more actively engaged than her Urbinate cousin; turned into her own narrative situation, she manifests a richer sensuality. Titian's brush has moved closer to its role as tactile surrogate, giving us a lusher feast of flesh. Whether or not she makes the *Venus of Urbino* seem like a Theatine nun, Giovanni della Casa's comparison was hardly fortuitous. As X-radiography of the Naples canvas has revealed, Titian constructed this composition on the basis of the earlier design. Beneath the final version we find the essential structure of the *Venus of Urbino*, recognized most notably in the background opening and the kneeling maid at the *cassone*.[41]

It was evidently Titian's habit to preserve compositional inventions in this way, maintaining a record of a completed painting in the form of a newly begun canvas, blocked in *(abbozzata)*, a sketch awaiting further realization.[42] In the course of realizing a second redaction, as we see in the case of the Farnese picture, he might actually modify it, and the old composition would evolve into a new variation of the theme. How far this particular canvas had evolved when della Casa saw it in 1544 is difficult to say, but we may imagine that it still acknowledged its origins in – if not as – the *Venus of Urbino*, and thus inspiring the writer's salacious comparison. Titian brought the canvas *in medias res* to Rome, where he finished it in the studio provided for him in the Belvedere – the site of one of the great encounters of art history, according to Vasari: there Michelangelo visited the Venetian painter, saw the *Danae*, and upon leaving, offered his grudging praise of Titian along with his critique of painters in Venice.[43]

Whether or not Giovanni della Casa saw a composition already representing the rape of Danae in Titian's studio in

40.   Wethey, *The Paintings of Titian*, 3:132f., cat. no. 5.

41.   The X-rays were taken and published by Ludovico Mucchi, "Radiografie di opere di Tiziano," *Arte veneta* 31 (1977): 297-304. Mucchi did not recognize the relationship of the Naples *Danae* to the *Venus of Urbino*, and the significance of his X-radiography has, unfortunately, gone unnoticed. Cf. the entry on the painting in the recent exhibition catalog, *Tiziano* (Venice, 1990), pp. 267-69, cat. no. 40, which fails even to mention Mucchi's publication.

42.   See the still fundamental study of Titian's workshop practices by E. Tietze-Conrat, "Titian's Workshop in His Late Years," *Art Bulletin* 26 (1946): 76-88.

43.   Giorgio Vasari, *Le vite de' più eccellenti pittori, scultori ed architettori* (1568), ed. Gaetano Milanesi (Florence: Sansoni, 1878-85), 7:447. Hans Tietze, "An Early Version of Titian's Danae: An Analysis of Titian's Replicas," *Arte veneta* 8 (1954): 199-208, had suggested that Titian carried an unfinished canvas with him to Rome to be brought to completion there; although his attribution in this particular case is unconvincing, Tietze's intuition regarding Titian's practice has proved quite accurate.

Venice, it is clear from the final painting that the nude he did see was fully capable of being inflected into such a mythological narrative. Indeed, thanks both to della Casa's letter and to the confirming X-rays, we can follow just such a transformation: the receptive object of our (masculine) attention, "la donna nuda" of the *Venus of Urbino*, becomes the more responsive objective of Jupiter's passion. That declension – from passive to active, from iconic to narrative – attests at once to the potentiality of meaning in such images, as the two related paintings in effect comment upon and define one another.

"La donna nuda," we may say, exists as a foundational structure, a generic sign latent with a range of significance – from *una Venere mondana*, goddess of base passion, to the celestial deity of divine love. And the Neoplatonic hierarchy of Venuses articulated just such a range of venereal possibilities. Indeed, the usefulness and appeal of the scheme lie precisely in its ability to accommodate that range of experience, from low bestial lust to the highest spiritual aspiration to union with the divine.

We need not ascribe to Titian any profound commitment to Neoplatonism to recognize how much he profited from the hermeneutic potential of the system. His long series of variations on the basic Giorgionesque invention of the reclining Venus may be read as a commentary on that potential. Some time ago (at the Titian *convegno* of 1976), I reviewed the motivations and implications of Titian's thematic variations, and I refrain from rehearsing an old publication here.[44] Suffice it to say that while these later compositions, eventually including serenading courtiers, complicate the basic theme in fascinating ways, that complexity builds upon the kinds of hierarchies and alternatives we have been discovering – between high and low values, communal and personal, the sacred and the profane, the licit and the libidinous. Within the spread of these extremes lies what we may call the arena of interpretation: a hermeneutic space whose boundaries are defined by a complex of coordinates – historical, cultural, critical, phenomenological – a space filled with potential, latent with possibilities of meaning.

We can see, then, just how the *Venus of Urbino* functions within such an arena, how it depends upon and exploits that potential. The picture operates on an equivocal scale of values, and from that very ambivalence derives its richness of experience. The image's direct appeal is blatant: a naked woman offering herself. This is what Panofsky would have called "*primary or natural* subject matter." And yet she is clothed in cultural convention – as the frustrated Mark Twain had to acknowledge. A nude woman, in painting, was seen as a Venus as easily and naturally as the lover or sonneteer saw his beloved as a Laura –

---

44.   David Rosand, "*Ermeneutica Amorosa*: Observations on the Interpretation of Titian's Venuses," in *Tiziano e Venezia*, pp. 375-81; for a different reading of the situation, cf. Hope, "Problems of Interpretation," pp. 111-24.

and it is worth recalling that Vasari had no trouble in recognizing the divinity of Titian's naked lady.[45] Generic expectation conditions vision and interpretation. This would be the second level of Panofsky's synoptical table: "*secondary* or *conventional* subject matter, constituting the world of *images, stories* and *allegories*."

But we are not dealing with a simple hermeneutic algebra of nude = Venus. In paintings like this one such elementary symbolic equations hardly do justice to the situation. This is no emblem; it is not in an allegorical mode – as is, for example, Bronzino's more obviously programmatic complex of Venus and Cupid with modifying attendants (National Gallery, London).[46] Rather than a mystery to be unriddled, decoded, it represents an invitation to participation, an invitation that engages the imagination on several levels.[47] Indeed, it is out of the interplay of intellectual response and sexual fantasy, of social function and private satisfaction, that the possibilities of meaning in the *Venus of Urbino* emerge.

At the third and highest level of Panofsky's table the object of interpretation is "*intrinsic meaning* or *content*, constituting the world of '*symbolical*' *values*." On this level we move beyond analysis to seek in "specific *themes* and *concepts*" the expression of "essential tendencies of the human mind." We tend to assume that such iconological reach is upward, toward the higher spiritual level of a hierarchy, from the literal through the moral and allegorical to, finally, the anagogical sense. All of these senses are, of course, historically circumscribed.

Taking advantage of Panofsky's notion of "essential tendencies," however, I would like to suggest an additional, somewhat different, dimension or direction for our search for meaning: toward the artist and the act of painting itself. What did it mean to Titian to paint such an image? Addressing that question, Paul Valéry could conclude:

> When Titian arranges a purely carnal Venus, softly stretched out...in all the fullness of her perfection as goddess and subject

45.   Vasari, *Le vite*, ed. Milanesi, 7:443: "...una Venere giovanetta a giacere, con fiori e certi panni sottili attorno molto belli e ben finiti." Representing a late revival of Renaissance interpretive instincts, Stefano Ticozzi quite naturally read the *Venus of Urbino* in Platonizing terms: of the two maids in the background he observed, "vanno da un cassone traendo le vesti che devono nascondere ai profani sguardi tanta beltà." See *Vite dei pittori Vecellj di Cadore* (Milan: Stella, 1817), p. 168f.
46.   On Bronzino's picture, see Panofsky, *Studies in Iconology*, pp. 86-91; also Michael Levey, "Sacred and Profane Significance in Two Paintings by Bronzino," in *Studies in Renaissance and Baroque Art Presented to Anthony Blunt* (London: Phaidon, 1967), pp. 30-33.
47.   Our task is not a "game of unriddling the mysteries of the past," as E. H. Gombrich formulates it in his essay on "Aims and Limits of Iconology," in *Symbolic Images*, p. 21. Rejecting the very idea of levels of meaning, Gombrich would restrict us to a search for a presumed "dominant meaning, the intended meaning or principal purpose of the picture" (p. 15) – an unacceptable limitation, in my view.

for paint, it is obvious that, for him, to paint meant to caress, a conjunction of two voluptuous sensations in one supreme act in which self-mastery and mastery of his medium were identified with a masterful possession of the beauty herself in every sense.[48]

Nor is this merely a twentieth-century perception imposed upon the past. We can recast it into more historical terms. One late sixteenth-century witness describes the painter's total absorption in the human subjects of his art:

> when he wanted to draw or paint some figure, and had before him a real woman or man, that object would so affect his sense of sight and his spirit would enter into what he was representing so that he seemed conscious of nothing else.[49]

The concept itself is a Neoplatonic commonplace, involving especially the lover and the object of desire: "The lover is moved by the beloved object as the senses are by sensible objects; and they unite and become one and the same thing." That is the way it was formulated toward the beginning of the sixteenth century by Leonardo da Vinci, hardly a committed Platonist.[50]

Vision and desire, representation and possession: these are terms of a psychosexual dynamics of painting that we know best and acknowledge most readily in the art of Picasso. But they are no less valid for picture-making in the past. The phenomenology of painting, the act of projecting another being onto canvas, implicates a level of meaning that must demand our attention. It is on this level that viewer and artist meet most directly, for we do assume, in some basic sense, that what we project into the image, or read out of it, is what the artist put into it. To ignore that encounter is to deny a fundamental dimension of meaning, that which is both historically based – in that it represents past moments of creation – and most essentially available to us.[51]

≵

48. Paul Valéry, "The Nude," in *Degas, Manet, Morisot*, trans. David Paul in *The Collected Works of Paul Valéry* (New York: Pantheon, 1960), 12:48.
49. Antonio Persio, *Trattato dell'ingegno dell'huomo* (Venice: Aldine Press, 1576), p. 98: "...[il] gran Titiano padre del colorire; il qual, secondo ho udito di sua bocca, & di quegli che sono ritrovati presenti à suoi lavori, quando volea disegnare o colorir alcuna figura, tenendo avanti una donna o un huomo naturale, cotal oggetto cosi movea la vista corporale di lui, & il suo spirito cosi penetrava nell'oggetto di chi ritirava, che facendo vista di non sentire altra cosa, che quella, veniva a parere à circostanti d'esser andato in ispirito." We owe our awareness of this important passage to Charles Hope, *Titian*, p. 170.
50. Jean Paul Richter, ed., *The Literary Works of Leonardo da Vinci*, 2d ed. (London: Oxford University Press, 1939), no. 1202.
51. I have discussed some of these issues in *The Meaning of the Mark: Leonardo and Titian*, The Franklin D. Murphy Lectures, 8 (Lawrence, Kansas: Spencer Museum of Art, 1988).

In summary, I would like to invoke another text from our own century, by perhaps our most pictorial poet. It is a text that, more completely and satisfyingly than Panofsky's platonizing synoptical table, addresses the several aspects of the hermeneutic problem – the reality and ideality of the image, the absence and presence of its maker, being itself in the world – and from their tensions and contradictions defines the arena of response and interpretation. It presents us with three propositions in the form of projections: A) the image, as its primary or natural subject matter; B) our idealizing of it, investing it with symbolical values; C) our recognition of the artist in it; and then, finally, our return to "things as they are." The poem is Wallace Stevens' "So-And-So Reclining on Her Couch."[52] I offer it as a lecture with slides.

> On her side, reclining on her elbow.
> This mechanism, this apparition,
> Suppose we call it Projection A.
>
> She floats in air at the level of
> The eye, completely anonymous,
> Born, as she was, at twenty-one,
>
> Without lineage or language, only
> The curving of her hip, as motionless gesture,
> Eyes dripping blue, so much to learn.
>
> If just above her head there hung,
> Suspended in air, the slightest crown
> Of Gothic prong and practick bright,
>
> The suspension, as in solid space,
> The suspending hand withdrawn, would be
> An invisible gesture. Let this be called
>
> Projection B. To get at the thing
> Without gestures is to get at it as
> Idea. She floats in the contention, the flux
>
> Between the thing as idea and
> The idea as thing. She is half who made her.
> This is the final Projection, C.
>
> The arrangement contains the desire of
> The artist. But one confides in what has no
> Concealed creator. One walks easily
>
> The unpainted shore, accepts the world
> As anything but sculpture. Good-bye,
> Mrs. Pappadopoulos, and thanks.

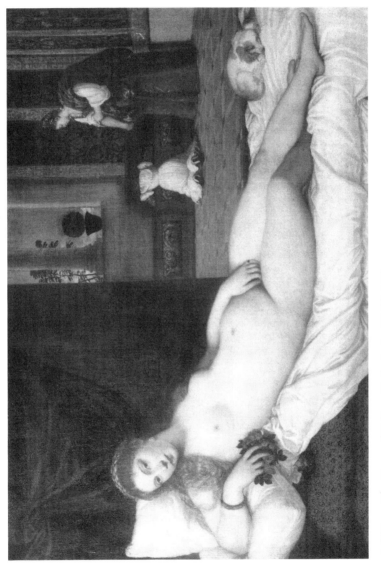

1. Titian. *The Venus of Urbino*. Galleria degli Uffizi, Florence.

XVII

The Pamphlet
As a Source for French History,
1559-1572

LEONA ROSTENBERG

An eye-witness account of a specific event remains the most valid source for the historian. By reason of its brevity and pertinence, the pamphlet reflects the essence of an event. Close to political parley and military maneuver, the pamphleteer has, in the manner of the latter-day reporter, assembled the facts of a specific happening or the qualities of an individual. Thus an accumulation of pamphlets reflects the multi-faceted history of a particular age.[1]

It is difficult to assess the influence of the pamphlet press upon the immediate events in France in the years 1559 to August 1572. The fighting Frenchman far eclipsed the reading Frenchman. The reading public was extremely limited, but it was occasionally incited by a broadside nailed to a town hall or the circulation of a violent, incendiary tract. Yet the spate of pamphlets written by both sides of the French wars of religion, a vital outpouring of the printing press, remains of great social, political, and religious significance. These

---

1.   For a detailed history of the period, see James Westfall Thompson, *The Wars of Religion in France 1559-1576* (New York: Frederick Ungar, 1909). For an analysis of some of the pamphlets, see Henry Hauser, *Les Sources de l'histoire de France: XVIe siècle*, 4 vols. (Paris: Picard, 1906-1915), notably vol. 3; J. R. Moreton MacDonald, *A History of France*, 3 vols. (London: Methuen & Co., 1915), notably vol 2.; Emile Picot, ed., *Catalogue des Livres Composant La Bibliothèque De Feu M. Le Baron James Rothschild*, 5 vols. (Paris: D. Morgand, 1884-1920; New York: Franklin Reprint, n.d.). For bibliography and location of pamphlets, see Robert O. Lindsay and John Neu, *French Political Pamphlets 1547-1648* (Madison, WI: University of Wisconsin Press, 1969), hereafter cited as *L-N*. For recent scholarship on the subject see Jean Bérenger, "Les Armées françaises et les Guerres de Religion," *Revue Internationale d'Histoire Militaire* 55 (1983): 11-28; Barbara Diefendorf, "Prologue to a Massacre: Popular Unrest in Paris, 1557-1572," *American Historical Review* 90, 5 (1985): 1067-91; R. J. Knecht, *The French Wars of Religion, 1559-1598* (London and New York: Longman, 1989); Jean Hippolyte Mariejol, *Catherine de Medicis: 1519-1589* (Paris: J. Tallandier, 1979); Pierre Miquel, *Les Guerres de Religion* (Paris: Fayard, 1980); Ian R. Morrison, "François de la Noue, les Guerres de Religion et la Tolérance Religieuse," *Bibliothèque d'Humanisme et de Renaissance* 48, 1 (1986): 71-84; and N. M. Sutherland, *The Huguenot Struggle for Recognition* (New Haven: Yale University Press, 1980).

pamphlets reflect daily life, social needs, religious bias, battles, births, deaths, royal succession, the authority of the queen-mother, the struggles of her sons. As we will be using the term "pamphlet" here – as a published broadside, printed and disseminated in multiple copies – they also appeared in a variety of genres: edicts of the crown, orations of royal sycophants, harangues of politicians, and fulminations of Catholic and Huguenot prelates. In short, they relate the soul of Valois France during the civil wars.

This brief paper will therefore attempt to demonstrate how the student of the period can use pamphlets as one important source to trace these events, personalities, and positions. It will use the chronological unfolding of events as a matrix upon which to place these sources within a comprehensible context. However, it makes no pretense of reconstructing these events from the pamphlet sources but hopes only to highlight significant examples of the genre to introduce the reader to their nature and variety and to lead students to more detailed research.

$$\text{\textbf{\textit{ϟ}}}$$

Despite its attempts at paternalism and continuity, the Valois monarchy confronted a nation divided by political faction, religious turmoil and civil war. To these issues the press readily responded, spewing forth a succession of pamphlets. We will begin our survey in 1559, at the beginning of the civil struggle known as the Wars of Religion.

In anticipation of a pending marital alliance, the wedding of Marguerite, sister of King Henry II of France, to Philibert Emmanuel, duke of Savoy, the great poet Ronsard wrote his *Discovrs à tréshavlt et tréspvissant prince, monseignevr le dvc de Savoye. Chant pastoral à madame Marguerite, duchesse de Savoye.* On the very day of this union between France and Savoy festivities for a more significant alliance were planned in Paris: the troth of Elizabeth, daughter of the French monarch, to Philip II, king of Spain. These royal celebrations were cancelled by the fatal accident suffered by King Henry II. At a royal joust held in honor of the double event Henry was mortally wounded by the lance of Gabriel de Lorges, sieur de Montgomery, captain of the king's Scottish guard. Henry's demise a few days later became rich largesse for the waiting press, which issued elegy and tribute to the fallen monarch. Examples of the type published include the *Tvmvlvs Henrici secvndi gallorvm regis christianiss.* of Joachim du Bellay; *Henrici II. Gallorvm regis christianiss. epitaphia* by the poet Auger Ferrier; and a detailed narrative of the services and interment, *Les trespas, & ordre des obseqves, funerailles & enterrement de feu de...memoire le Roy Henrici devxiesme... secours des affligez* by Francis of Signac, seigneur de la Borde.[2]

Following his coronation at Rheims on 18 September 1559, the sickly Francis II became king of France. His reign of a little over a year was marked by a spate of edicts concerned with domestic and

2.   *L-N*, nos. 164, 126, 128, 167.

military matters and the ever-increasing threat of the Huguenot minority. A good example of an edict that appeared in printed form and can therefore be grouped among the pamphlets cited here is the *Lettres Patentes...par lesqvelles en forme d'edict, sur la diligente inquisition & iustice de ceux qui font conuenticules & assemblées illicites, & pvnition des iuges negligens de ce faire* and the *Lettres patentes...à l'encontre des conuenticules & assemblées des heretiques*.[3]

The administration of the young monarch was threatened not only by the demands of an ever stronger Huguenot party under the leadership of Louis I de Bourbon, prince of Condé, and the popular admiral of France, Gaspard de Coligny, but also by a powerful mutual opponent, Francis, duke of Guise, supported by his brother, Charles, cardinal of Lorraine. The Guise family made no secret of its pretensions to rule France, a solidly Catholic realm. The party issued a series of propaganda tracts, of which our anonymous example, *Brieve remonstrance des estats de France, au roy leur souuerain seigneur. Sur l'ambition, tyrannie, & oppression du tout intollerable des de Guyse,* excoriates what it portrays as Guise ambition and brutality.[4]

In March 1560 Guise henchmen detected a so-called Protestant plot against the royal family entrenched at Amboise. Subsequently several of the Huguenots involved were hanged from the crenellated walls of the chateau. Despite Guise triumph, Francis II, guided by his mother, issued a general amnesty, the *Edict dv roy svr le grace et pardon à ceulx qui ont esté aux assemblées et en armes es enuirons de la ville d'Amboise,*[5] which in printed form demonstrates the use of the pamphlet as a source for formal policy statements. Another example of this type would have to include the *Mandement dv roy pour faire assembler certains personnages des chascune prouince pour consulter les moyens du Concile General, reformation de l'église, et conuocation des estats.*

In the hope of national reconciliation and some recognition of the Huguenot party, the Estates General were summoned to a meeting at Orléans at the close of 1560. A large folding plate depicting the seating of the three estates enhances *La Description dv plant dv théâtre faict à Orléans, pour l'assemblée des trois estats,* also from 1560. This pamphlet, however, is more of a news story than an official report and shows the multiple forms of the pamphlet that can document a single event.

At Orléans Guise followers gathered in the hope of crushing the Huguenots and Condé. Violence was averted, however, by the untimely death of Francis II.[6] With the demise of her eldest son, Catherine de' Medici became queen regent of France for her twenty-year-old son, Charles IX. The queen quickly determined to strengthen the Huguenot position as a balance against overweening Guise pretension. In keeping with this policy, a conference was summoned at Poissy in October 1561 to settle religious differences. Despite the

3.   *L-N*, 204, 132.
4.   *L-N*, 169.
5.   *L-N*, 190.
6.   *L-N*, 181, 171.

harangues and speeches of Catholic and Huguenot prelates, the Council of Poissy failed. The two parties remained far apart.[7] Nevertheless, the participants issued a series of pamphlets that illustrate the usefulness of the genre as a source for political and intellectual history. A twenty-page pamphlet treats orations and issues discussed. It is entitled *Ample discours des Actes de Poissy, Contenant le commencement de l'assemblée, l'entrée & issue du colloque des prélats de France, et ministres de l'éuangile, l'ordre y garde; ensemble la harangue du roy Charles IX. Auec les sommaires, poincts des oraisons de monsieur le chancelier Theodore de Besze et du cardinal de Lorraine.* At the same time, two separate printings of the *First* and *Second Oration* of Theodore de Bèze, arch-lieutenant of Calvin, appeared anonymously.

Pamphlets were also valuable for one of the most venerable forms of war-time propaganda: the atrocity narrative. *Discours au vray et en abbregé de ce qui est dernierement aduenu à Vassi, y passant monseigneur le duc de Guise* related the violence perpetrated by the duke of Guise against the Huguenot community of Vassy, a small town in the diocese of Chalons-sur-Marne. The narrative is to the point: returning from Germany, Francis, duke of Guise, observed a group of Huguenots at prayer in a barn outside the town. Infuriated, Guise ordered his men to sack the town and to murder each and every one of the offenders and to continue to kill all Huguenots within the town. This slaughter at Vassy, on 1 March 1562, was followed by similar incidents at Cahors, Sens, Auxerre and Tours. Civil war had begun, and the pamphleteers rose to the occasion.[8]

Three examples must suffice to illustrate the use of the pamphlet as a call to arms for the defense of God and cause. Applauded in Paris as a hero, Francis of Guise rallied his forces with the *Arrest et ordonnance de la Court de Parlement sur la permission aux communes, tant des villes que villages, de prendre les armes contre les pilleurs d'églises & maisons & faiseurs de conuenticules & assemblées illicites,* a pamphlet that reflects crown reaction to Huguenot political and military action. Members of the minority faith rallied around Condé, who in 1562 published his *Traicte d'association faicte par monseigneur le prince de Condé auec les princes, cheualiers de l'ordre, seigneurs...autres de tous estats qui sont entrez...en la dicte association, pour maintenir l'honneur de Dieu, le repos de ce royaume, & l'estat & liberté du roy, sous le gouuernement de la royne sa mere.* Huguenot respect for the role of the queen-mother is here declared, but little respect for the military action of Huguenots is displayed in the pamphlet of Gabriel Dupreau, *Harangve sur les causes de la gverre entrepris contre les rebelles, & seditievx, qui en forme d'hostilité ont pris les armes contre le roy en son royaume; & mesme des causes d'ou prouuiennent toutes autres calamitez... qui iournellement nous suruiennent.*

Despite hope for success, the armies of Condé and the king of Navarre suffered repeated defeat at Toulouse, Mans and the lengthy siege of Rouen. Ronsard's *Discovrs des misères du temps* reviews the

7.   *L-N,* 219, 220, 221.
8.   *L-N,* 274.

suffering and misery of the time[9] and demonstrates how the pamphlet could reflect the realities of conflict.

The Huguenots snatched a glimmer of hope when on 18 February 1563 Francis of Guise was assassinated. Suspicion veered toward Coligny, who disavowed any involvement in a lengthy protest entitled *Response à l'interrogatoire qu'on dit auoir este fait a vn nommé Iean de Poltrot, soy disant seigneur de Merey, sur la mort de feu duc de Guyse.* Coligny used the pamphlet to assuage public opinion and to place the blame for the deed upon his own hired henchman, Jean Poltrot, sieur de Merey. The great Huguenot admiral of France did not disguise his glee at the death of his enemy, Francis of Guise: "Cette mort est le plus grand bien que pouvoit arriver a ce royaume, à l'église de Dieu, et particulierement à moy et à toute ma famille,"[10] records a frank piece of pamphlet reportage.

Doubtless, equally relieved by the removal of Guise, Catherine de' Medici sought to placate the Huguenots, and on 19 March 1562 Charles IX issued his *Edict sur la pacification des troubles de ce royaume,* the Edict of Amboise, an act most favorable to the minority faith. The terms of peace permitted members of the reformed party to pursue their faith in all towns – with the exception of Paris – where it had formerly prevailed. A town was selected in every bailiwick where the gospel might be read, and all nobles enjoying high justice could permit preaching on their estates.[11] We have included it among the pamphlet literature discussed here because its printed form serves as clearcut evidence of the penetration of government decrees among the population as a whole.

In the hope of uniting a nation torn by religious and political strife, the king, his mother and younger brother, Henry, duke of Anjou, toured the French provinces from 1564 to 1566. The royal suite held court at Lorraine, Poitou, Picardy, and Champagne. Wherever they sojourned the visitors confronted the desolation of war, famine, plunder, a people bereft, malnourished, hopeless.

The pamphlet literature reflects the impact of this devastation upon royal policy and public communication. For those seeking shelter the government issued an *Ordonnance dv roy, sur la police et reglement des bois, tant des forests qu'autres: soit pour edifices, cercles, eschallatz, chauffages, & autres quelzconques.* With looting and marauding widespread, owners and keepers of small hostelries were advised to take precautions by the government in the *Declaration...sur le reiglement des hosteliers, tauerniers & cabaratiers & pris des viuvres en chasque faison de l'année.*

Travelling from one province to another, the royal family was made aware of increasing antagonism toward the Huguenots. In a pamphlet that resembles modern investigative reporting an aristocrat of Maine describes the harassed Huguenot situation in his *Remonstrance envoyée au roy par la noblesse de la Religion Reformée du*

9. *L-N*, 278, 271, 276, 356.
10. *L-N*, 314. Coligny's statement is quoted in MacDonald, *History*, 2:59.
11. *L-N*, 334. For a full discussion of the Edict of Amboise, see Knecht, *French Wars of Religion*, pp. 26-27; Thompson, *Wars of Religion*, p. 191.

païs & comté de Maine, sur les assassinats, pilleries, saccagements de maisons, seditions, violements de femmes & autres exces horribles commis depuis la publication de l'edit de pacification...le x. iour d'Aoust. 1564.[12]

Upon his return to Paris the young king and his entourage found the city besieged by Huguenots who engaged in fierce combat at St. Denis. Here the stout constable of France, Anne de Montmorency, was slain. The printed pamphlet of the constable's last words, *Epitaphes svr le tombeav de havt et pvissant seigneur Anne duc de Montmorency*, gives an excellent example of the use of print as a creator of popular heroes and legends.

In the hope of reducing bloodshed, Charles IX issued another *Edict...svr la pacification des trovbles de ce royavme.* In March 1568 the Peace of Longmujeau granted the Huguenots limited toleration and practice of their faith.[13] Official indulgence of the Huguenots was short-lived, however. Alarmed by their growing strength and increasing demands, in December 1568 Catherine de' Medici decided to kidnap Condé and Coligny, an enterprise that failed.

The press, aware of the chaotic condition of the country, issued a variety of pamphlets in a variety of genres that reflect the sense of crisis. *Remonstrance av pevple de Paris, de demevrer en la foy de levrs ancestres* by the poet Francis of Belleforest; and an eight-page anonymous pamphlet, *Complaincte et querimonia des pauures labovrevrs suyuant la calamité du temps present sur da [sic] pacem*, treats the problems of daily life. A Catholic author analyzes current problems in the *Discours Catholique, sur les causes & remedes des malheurs intentés au roy, & eschens à son peuple, par les rebelles caluinistes.* Condé published his *Protestations*, while Coligny, protesting any taint of treason, was attacked by Antoine Fleury in the *Responce a vn certain escrit, pvblié par l'admiral & ses adherens, pretentans couurir & excuser la rupture qu'ils ont fait de l'edit de la pacification, & leurs nouueau remuemens & entreprinses contre l'estat du roi, & le bien & le repos de ses subiects.*[14]

The pamphlet literature also mirrors the growing importance of the press as creators and molders of political and religious positions. The Catholic press of Jean Dallier, Jean Bonfons, Victoire Sertenas and others was challenged to some small degree by the La Rochelle establishments of the Huguenots Barthélemy Berton and the Haultin family. Berton circulated Protestant polemics from 1562 to 1573; the Haultins were active from 1571 to 1623. Berton imprints include *Letters & Requests of the Prince of Condé, Lettres de tréshavte, trésvertueuse & tréschrestienne princesse, Iane royne de Nauarre* (Jeanne d'Albret) addressed to the king, queen-mother and Elizabeth of England; and the *Sommaire discovrs svr la rvptvre et infraction de la paix roy [sic] pvbliqve, & sur les moyens que tient le Cardinal de Lorraine, pour subuertir l'estat de la France & en inuestir l'Espagnol*, an exposé of the

12. *L-N*, 392, 371, 401.
13. *L-N*, 513, 583; for the Peace of Longmujeau in March 1568, granting Huguenots limited tolerance see Knecht, *French Wars of Religion*, p. 40; Thompson, *Wars of Religion*, pp. 345-50.
14. *L-N*, 460, 563, 564-565, 568.

ambitious schemes of the cardinal of Lorraine to encourage Spanish influence and machination. The satirical attack of Pierre du Quignet upon the intrigue of the cardinal of Lorraine is to be attributed to the press of Berton.[15]

The propaganda efforts of a La Rochellois printer-publisher may have slightly disconcerted the queen-mother, who confronted an even greater threat in the person of the eighteen-year-old Henry of Guise, a counterpart of his late father and the leader of a band of enthusiastic followers, extreme Catholics prepared to challenge existing law and order. Catherine de' Medici may have enjoyed some respite when the Huguenots suffered defeat at the Battle of Jarnac (March 1569) and the prince of Condé was brutally murdered. The event is described in the *Epitaphes de Louis de Bourbon Prince de Condé*.[16]

Oscillating between Catholic superiority and Huguenot threat, Catherine de' Medici decided to placate the latter constituency once again. In November 1570 she arranged the marriage between her son Charles IX and Margaret, daughter of the Emperor Maximilian II, a lady known for her reform proclivity. Further, she urged her son Henry, duke of Anjou, to woo a lady of greater stature, Elizabeth I, queen of England, a courtship of little success. Yet the Treaty of Saint Germain won great concessions to the Huguenot party, ending the Third Civil War. This was followed by the suggestion that the Valois princess Marguerite marry the Huguenot leader Henry of Navarre.

For the wedding of her son Henry to the daughter of Catherine de' Medici, Jeanne d'Albret arrived at the Valois court in March 1572. On 9 June she died suddenly. Rumor pointed to the tactics of the queen-mother, who at the Florentine court of her father had familiarized herself with the art of poison and other methods of quick dispatch. By this time Catherine had decided to rid France of all Huguenots, including Coligny, an evil influence upon her son, the king. The ensuing Huguenot massacre can be attributed to the design and determination of Catherine de' Medici.

With the ringing of the tocsin on 24 August 1572 Coligny and one thousand of his followers in Paris, and an additional ten thousand Huguenots in France, were destroyed. A few propaganda pamphlets justify the horror and perfidy of this deed, such as the *Discovrs sur les causes de l'execution faicte de personnes de ceux qui auoient coniuré contre le roy & son estat. Declaration du roy, de la cavse et occasion de la mort de l'admiral, autres ses adherens & complices, dernièrement aduenue en ceste ville de Paris, le xxiiii. iour du resent moys d'Aoust. M.D.LXXII*, published by Jean Dallier at the Sign of the White Rose on the bridge of St. Michel, is the royal justification of the defenestration of Coligny

15. *L-N*, 564, 627, 637, 648. For a detailed study on Berton, see Eugénie Droz, *Barthélemy Berton, 1563-1572. L'Imprimerie à La Rochelle* (Geneva: Droz, 1960). For the work of the Haultin family, see Louis Desgraves, *Les Haultin, 1571-1623. L'Imprimerie à La Rochelle* (Geneva: Droz, 1960).
16. For the debacle of the Third Civil War, see *L-N*, 649; Michel Pernot, *Les Guerres de Religion en France, 1559-1598* (Paris: Sedes, 1987); Thompson, *Wars of Religion*, pp. 349-77.

and his fellow Huguenots from the Louvre. In contrast, an anonymous press issued a lament for Coligny with tender poems in Greek, Latin and French, the *Epicedia illvstri heroi Caspari Colignio...beato Christi martyri, variis lingvis doctis piisqv. poetis decantata.*[17]

The Huguenot extermination failed. Catherine's favorite son, the future Henry III, was assassinated in 1589, to be succeeded by a former Huguenot, the converted Henry IV, who in 1598, by the publication of the Edict of Nantes, granted toleration to the Huguenots.

17.   *L-N*, 723, 725, 729.

XVIII

The Origins of Columbia University's Collection of Medieval and Renaissance Manuscripts

ROBERT SOMERVILLE

Columbia University owns more than five hundred western medieval and Renaissance manuscripts.[1] This collection has not received the attention that it merits, and is less well known than comparable holdings at other institutions. The following remarks can draw some much deserved attention to this assembly of treasures, although a proper picture of its growth would require more research than so far has been possible.[2] The glimpse that follows concerns the late nineteenth and early twentieth centuries and barely touches the single most important moment in this history, that is, the extraordinary donation of over three hundred manuscripts by George A. Plimpton in 1936.

    "Book rarities we esteem as luxuries, but as gifts – we appreciate more what we cannot afford to buy." So wrote, in his annual report for the year 1884, the Columbia College Librarian Melvil Dewey.[3] Dewey, a visionary and strong-willed man who

---

1.   The author is grateful to Kenneth Lohf and his staff in the Rare Book and Manuscript Library at Columbia for help at many points in the preparation of these remarks (special thanks are due to Rudolph Ellenbogen and to Jane Rodgers). Paul Oskar Kristeller, as always, generously shared his unsurpassed erudition about manuscripts; and Olha Della Cava of the School of Library Service, and Hollee Haswell of the Columbiana Collection, kindly answered various questions about the University's history, libraries, and alumni.

2.   A shortened form of this article was presented at the annual Columbia University Medieval-Renaissance Studies Colloquium on March 31, 1990 (with the dedicatee of the present volume in the audience).

3.   *Librarian's Report* (1884): 17; cited in Linderman, "History" = Winifred B. Linderman, "History of the Columbia University Library, 1876-1926" (Ph.D. diss., Teachers College, Columbia University, 1959), p. 114. The following other abbreviations will be used throughout: BC = *Bibliotheca Columbiana*; *Catalogue* = *Catalogue of Officers and Graduates of Columbia University*, 15th ed. (New York: Columbia University, 1912); CLC = *Columbia Library Columns*; CUQ = *Columbia University Quarterly*; De Ricci = Seymour J. De Ricci (with the assistance of W. J. Wilson), *Census of Medieval and Renaissance Manuscripts in the United States and Canada*, 3 vols. (New York: H.W. Wilson, 1935-40); Facilities = special number of CLC (n.d. [1974]), titled *Rare Books and*

left a permanent legacy on library service in the form of his Dewey Decimal Classification system, was College Librarian for six years, from 1883-89.[4] This was a period of unusual significance in the history of book collections at Columbia College, which then was located at Madison Avenue and 49th Street, for a new library building was being constructed. Previously the College Library was, as Winifred B. Linderman characterized it in her history of the Columbia Library, "a collection of little used books in a second story room over the chapel...a fairly typical college library situation for that period."[5] The new facility was occupied by October 1883 and provided an opportunity, as Dr. Linderman wrote, of pulling together and classifying collections "that had been accumulated without policy or plan over a long period of time."[6]

There also had been losses. In 1861 Librarian William A. Jones, describing the origins of the King's College Library, spoke of several significant benefactions.[7] But he then remarked that:

> Many, if not most, of the rare old tomes forming these collections were dispersed during the war – from 1776 to '84 – when the College was closed as an Academic retreat, and used as a hospital for the soldiery.

Writing in 1862, Jones related that when in the year 1857 Columbia moved uptown to 49th Street from its original location at Park Place, a box of books, "it has always been supposed, must have fallen from the cart *in transitu*."[8] But, notwithstanding such setbacks, by 1883 Columbia owned one of the ten largest college libraries in the country,[9] and some significant collections had been bequeathed by alumni or donated by friends of the College. It is with one of these gifts – the Phoenix bequest – that a history of

---

Manuscripts at Columbia: Their Facilities and Use; Jones, *Library* = William A. Jones, *Columbia College Library* (New York: Columbia University, 1861); *Manuscript Collections* = *Manuscript Collections in the Columbia University Libraries* (New York: Columbia University, 1959); Simkhovitch, "Rariora" = V. G. Simkhovitch, "University Library Collections: Monumenta and Rariora," CUQ 13 (1911): 172-82, published separately as *The Libraries of Columbia University* (New York: Columbia University, 1911); *Rare Book Library* = Kenneth Lohf & Rudolph Ellenbogen, *The Rare Book and Manuscript Library of Columbia University* (New York: Columbia University, 1985).

4.   See Linderman, "History," pp. 87-177, for Dewey's tenure at Columbia, esp. pp. 107 ff. ("Classification and Cataloging"), and 177 ff. ("Dewey the Man").

5.   Ibid., p. 84.

6.   Ibid., p. 175.

7.   Jones, *Library*, p. 9.

8.   William A. Jones, *Librarian's Report* (1862): 8-9.

9.   Linderman, "History," p. 46: in 1876 Columbia possessed the seventh-largest college collection in the U.S., behind Harvard, Yale, Brown, University of Virginia, Cornell, and Northwestern, but ahead of Amherst and the College of New Jersey.

Columbia's rare books and medieval and Renaissance manuscripts properly could commence.[10]

Some parameters should be inserted. "Medieval and
Renaissance manuscripts" will be taken here to include manuscript books or substantial parts of such books and documents that
were written by hand, on parchment or on paper, in Latin or in
Western vernacular languages, before the year 1600. This makes
clear that Columbia's significant holdings of, for example, papyri,
Hebrew manuscripts, or incunables are not at issue.[11] It must be
noted, however, that medieval and Renaissance manuscripts
often arrived at the University within collections containing
other things, including manuscripts written after the year 1600. In
a significant way, therefore, the history of Columbia's accumulation of pre-seventeenth-century Western manuscripts is the
history of several extraordinary and multifarious book collections.

In 1880 the library of the late Professor Henry J. Anderson, who
had been a professor and trustee, was purchased by the
Association of Alumni and presented to the College.[12] Then
quickly thereafter came the Phoenix bequest, from Stephen
Whitney Phoenix, Columbia College class of 1859, Law School
class of 1863.[13] The fortunes of the Whitney and the Phoenix
families enabled Stephen to live a gentlemanly existence free
from pecuniary concerns, and his library reflected his interests in
literature, history and particularly the history of New York,[14] in
travel, and antiquities. The Phoenix Bequest – as the Anderson
library demonstrates – was not the first private library to find its
way to Columbia, but it overshadowed all predecessors in size and
significance (and the fact that Phoenix also left $500,000 to the
College would help to earn him a special benefactorial memory).[15]
Kenneth Lohf has written that the Phoenix bequest brought to

10.   At many points herein further research in hitherto unstudied library
records, preserved in the Columbiana Collection or elsewhere, could yield new
information.
11.   For a good overview of Columbia's "rare book" holdings see *Facilities*, and
also *Rare Book Library*, passim. For medieval manuscripts defined to exclude
documents, see Hellmut Lehmann-Haupt, "Rare Books in the University," CUQ
28 (1936): 195 n. 1.
12.   See Linderman, "History," p. 66. For Anderson see *Catalogue* 28, and n. 26
below.
13.   For Phoenix see Linderman, "History," p. 69, and also *Facilities* 8
(although the information provided there about Phoenix being a founder and
president of the Grolier Club is mistaken); *Rare Book Library*, p. 12; and
Rudolph Ellenbogen, "The Many Lives of Phoenix," CLC 31 (November 1981):
19-28.
14.   Phoenix willed his art collection to the Metropolitan Museum, and his
library of genealogical books to the New York Historical Society: Ellenbogen,
"Phoenix" p. 28. Cf. George H. Baker, "Special Collections in the Columbia
College Library I. – the Phoenix Collection," *Columbia Literary Monthly* 2 (Oct.
1892): 6-14, for Phoenix' library, where it is noted that he left the "purely
historical" portion of his library to the New York Historical Society; cf.
Simkhovitch, "Rariora," pp. 173-75.
15.   Frederick Paul Keppel, *Columbia* (New York: Oxford University Press,
1914), p. 73.

Columbia its first "collector's library,"[16] and among the more than 7000 items in this rich collection were a Caxton, a First Folio Shakespeare, manuscripts written by Nathaniel Hawthorne and Robert Fulton, and, germane to the present purpose, at least one late medieval manuscript, the beautiful fifteenth-century Phoenix Book of Hours.[17]

The Phoenix Book of Hours is not the first manuscript owned by Columbia, although it is difficult to be certain what was. William Jones, writing in 1861, conjectured that a "Latin translation of Herodotus, folio, 1475, is we believe, the oldest book in the collection."[18] He also described a "*Missal, 1484,* in capital preservation," as the second-oldest book in the collection.[19] Was Jones speaking only of printed books, or did he not know of any book, printed or manuscript, in the Columbia collection older than the incunable of Herodotus?

The question of identifying the first medieval-Renaissance manuscript owned by any library is complicated in one way by a formal consideration: manuscript pages can be used as backing for, or can be found bound into, early printed books. It becomes a matter of definition to decide whether or not a printed book with pre-seventeenth-century manuscript pages included thus counts as "a manuscript." Such a hybrid could qualify as the first manuscript owned only if it contained a substantial part of a manuscript, and not merely a few pages – that is to say, only if a reader could be aware of handling a portion of a manuscript, and not merely a printed book with manuscript pages used to buttress the binding or as end leaves.

What manuscript(s) can be placed in the Columbia Library earlier than the date of the bequest of the Phoenix Book of Hours, i.e., earlier than 1881? One volume certainly can, and although there might also be other candidates, the honor of being the first manuscript owned by Columbia may well belong to a book that already was in the library in 1874. In that year the college published a printed catalog 412 pages long, arranged alphabetically (but providing no call numbers).[20] Under the heading "Psalterium" (p. 219), a bound volume is described, containing an early sixteenth-century printed Psalter, plus various liturgical pieces, including one designated "Horae Beatae Marie Virginis MS."[21]

16.   *Rare Book Library,* p. 12; see also Simkhovitch, "Rariora," pp. 173-75.
17.   MS BP096 F (De Ricci, no. 47) – see Jane Rosenthal, *A Selection of Medieval and Renaissance Manuscripts at Columbia University* (New York: Columbia University, 1981), no. 8.
18.   *Library,* p. 22. This work can be identified today in the Rare Book Library as Incunabulum H-89 (Rome: Arnoldus Pannartz). In fact, Columbia owns two copies of this volume, but one derives from the Phoenix Collection.
19.   Ibid., p. 14.   This today is Columbia, Rare Book Library M-697 (Nuremberg: Georg Stuchs).
20.   *Catalogue of the Books and Pamphlets in the Library of Columbia College* (New York: Columbia University, 1874).
21.   The Psalter was published in Paris, in 1512, by Bertholdt Reinboldt.

Using the chronological files in the Rare Book and Manuscript Library, this work has been traced. Housed in Rare Books, it bears the shelfmark X.096.C286 (21318) and contains a printed Psalter, extending for 130 folios, flanked on either side by liturgical material in manuscript, including 15 folios at the beginning from a fifteenth-century (?) book of hours.[22] Some of the texts in manuscript following the Psalter suggest a Franciscan provenance,[23] and throughout the handwritten portions of the book decorative initials occur, although the best art work therein is the damaged illumination on fol. 1r, an isolated manuscript page bound into the book in front of the Hours of the Virgin. This volume was rebound within the last century, but a note inside the front cover, in a nineteenth-century (?) hand, relates, from what evidence it is impossible to say, that the present mélange of material originally had been bound together in the early sixteenth century at Basel. This composite volume once belonged to George Templeton Strong (†1875), Columbia College class of 1838 and a trustee from 1853; and Strong's name – perhaps his signature – appears in the upper right-hand corner of the first folio.[24] The printed catalog proves that it was in the Columbia collection by 1874, seven years before the Phoenix bequest. A cautious claim can be advanced, therefore, that the first medieval-Renaissance manuscript owned by Columbia has been identified.

Any attempt to delve into the history of Columbia's earliest holdings of medieval-Renaissance manuscripts is hampered by the fact that until well into the twentieth century no specific department of rare books existed to oversee the acquisition and preservation of such treasures. Bequests and donations made to the library contained both manuscripts and printed books. Not all collections, however, were as noteworthy and obviously valuable as was that from Stephen Whitney Phoenix, and the policy at

---

22. De Ricci, 1267 (no. 46), gave the shelfmark as B.096.C (21318), which should be corrected as above. He noted the presence of printed material in the book, and also the volume's connection to George T. Strong, for whom see below. The numbers in parentheses, which occasionally accompany shelf marks for manuscripts cited here, probably are accession numbers of some sort. It has not, however, been possible to use those designations to arrive at dates for when various items entered Columbia's collections.

23. Following the Psalter is a portion of a *Diurnale fratrum minorum secundum Consuetudinem Romane curie*, followed by material introduced as *Sancte Clare capitula et responsoria brevia dicuntur de communi virginum*.

24. *Catalogue*, p. 114 for Strong. Following the catalog of 1874, it can be demonstrated that the book was by that date at Columbia, but De Ricci assumed that the volume arrived after the posthumous sale of Strong's library in 1878 (although he did note that the item cannot be identified in the sale catalog, *Catalogue of the Books, Manuscripts, etc. of the late George Templeton Strong* [New York: C.C. Shelley, 1878]). Inside the front cover the date "5/29/1901" appears. This could not be when the volume was cataloged and more likely indicates when the book was rebound (cf. De Ricci, 1267), which also could explain the note that follows the date – "reb. 3.00" – probably indicating the price paid for the rebinding work.

Columbia was not to keep gift collections together but to catalog the items therein separately.[25]

Manuscript material could lie hidden in donated collections and be unearthed and catalogued only long after it arrived at the University. Because of the erratic nature of the surviving records, particulars about the time and circumstances of many donations and bequests have become opaque.[26] MS X615.R.24 (De Ricci no. 24), for example, listed in the De Ricci *Census* as sixteenth-century, written in German, containing "Medical Recipies," was cataloged May 15, 1905 and contains an indication that it was at that point "Found," presumably among printed books somewhere in the library system.[27]

No specific information has come to light about how whatever manuscripts owned were preserved in the library built on 49th Street in the 1880s. A part of the Phoenix Collection was kept together, however; and in 1884 Dewey spoke of it being housed on the fourth floor of the library.[28] Other rarities could have been preserved in adjacent space, but this is speculation. On December 7, 1895, however, only slightly more than a decade after completion of the 49th Street library, the cornerstone was laid on Morningside Heights for a splendid new library, designed by the renowned architectural firm of McKim, Mead, and White – a library that was to be the central building of a new campus for Columbia.[29] On June 12, 1897 the 49th Street facility was closed; and less than four months later, on October 4, Low Memorial Library, named in memory of the father of the facility's chief benefactor, Columbia President Seth B. Low, opened its doors to users.

No particular space was designated in Low Library for rare books and manuscripts, but by 1899 Columbia had a new librarian.

25. Linderman, "History," p. 191. Columbia's policies at the time probably were no different than those at most other colleges and universities.
26. Consider MS X.133.K.75 (De Ricci, no. 1), a two-volume German work, dated in 1589, and listed in the *Census* as Philippus Knodius, *Reconditae philosophiae monumenta*, which contains a Columbia bookplate indicating that it is from "Dr. Anderson's Collection." This probably refers to Henry James Anderson (†1875), Columbia College 1818, and M.D. in 1824 (*Catalogue*, p. 28), who was professor of mathematics and astronomy, and whose library came to Columbia, as previously indicated, in 1880. But caution is necessary, for *Catalogue*, p. 983 lists nearly fifty Andersons who were associated with Columbia from the time of its foundation into the early twentieth century. (N.b., that H. J. Anderson was referred to as "Dr. Anderson" in a report of the Columbia College librarian, "Statement of the Librarian" [1857], p. 6.) It can be pointed out that Knodius also occurs, noted as "a Schlammersdorph," as the author of a treatise on geomancy found in Lindau, Stadtbibl., MS P 132: Paul Oskar Kristeller, *Iter Italicum*, vol. 3 (Leiden: Brill, 1983), p. 598.
27. As late as the mid-1930s, in a job description for an assistant in the Rare Book Department, it is noted that the person was to "recommend transfers of special or rare volumes still on the open shelves of the general library in South Hall (i.e., Butler Library)": Rare Book and Manuscript Library, Library Office Files, 1927-1942, R-Sea: Rare Book Department to 1937.
28. *Librarian's Report* (1884): 28.
29. See Linderman, "History," pp. 214-22, for Low Memorial Library.

James Hulme Canfield was a lawyer and former professor of law at the University of Kansas, who resigned the presidency of Ohio State University to become University Librarian at Columbia.[30] He was a man of enormous ability and prestige, who, indeed, almost simultaneously with his appointment at Columbia was under consideration by President McKinley for the post of Librarian of Congress.[31] McKinley chose someone else, and Canfield's tenure at Columbia must be counted as a pivotal moment for the history of the development of the University's rare book and manuscript tradition. Although he went on record in 1900 as saying that the Columbia Library was not a museum and could spend little money on "bibliophilic eccentricities," in 1901 he seems to have reversed his ground somewhat, pointing out the value of having what he called a "bibliographical museum."[32] The idea was prompted by the success of a long showing that year of the Phoenix collection in one of the Low Library galleries. Canfield said that he doubted that many knew that Columbia possessed rare and beautiful volumes, such as the Phoenix Book of Hours, and he proposed the creation of a bibliography department to manage and display such rarities, and to attract gifts.

Clearly this was an idea whose time had come, for Canfield received support at the highest possible level in the University. Acting President Nicholas Murray Butler, in February 1902, actually vacated his office in Room 307 Low Library to make space for this newly created department. The Phoenix Collection was removed from what was termed the Phoenix Gallery – it has not been possible to determine exactly where this was[33] – and cases from the gallery were hauled into Room 307. Other shelving was also constructed, and V. G. – for Vladimir Grigorievitch – Simkhovitch (1874-1959), later famous as professor of economic history at Columbia, was appointed bibliographer in charge of the operations of the department, including mounting exhibits and scanning catalogs of second-hand book dealers with an eye to new acquisitions.[34]

30. Ibid., p. 254.
31. Ibid., p. 256.
32. Ibid., p. 303, citing the *Librarian's Report* for 1900, p. 355, (and 1906, p. 238), and 345-47, citing the *Librarian's Report* for 1901, pp. 221-23, for the "bibliographical museum."
33. Writing in 1931, William Linn Westermann, "The Columbia University Collection of Greek Papyri," CUQ 23 (1931): 276, noted that the papyri were housed in a special gallery of the library, but gave no details. Further information about these developments could be at hand in the published Reports of the University Librarian from the first decades of this century. Linderman, "History," had access to those documents, but the author has been unable to find copies.
34. Linderman, "History," p. 287, comments on Simkhovitch's "hobby" of reading catalogs of dealers in second-hand books. Simkhovitch (1874-1959), was appointed lecturer in Russian history in 1904, and was professor of economic history at Columbia from 1915-42 ("Memorial Moment," Faculty of Political Science, April 22, 1960 – preserved in the Columbiana Collection).

By 1902, therefore, Columbia had made an official entry of sorts into the world of rare book and manuscript libraries, although it would be nearly thirty more years until a specific department in the library system was created to manage this material.[35] But the "bibliographical museum" made it possible for some of the University's treasures to be put on display; and exhibitions were mounted, including presentation of material from the manuscript collection of J. P. Morgan.[36] Acquisitions were made;[37] and Simkhovitch worked at generating publicity for the books and manuscripts in his domain.[38] At times his enthusiasm exceeded his expertise for, writing in 1911 of manuscripts in the collection, he noted that "the oldest...is a ninth century manuscript of St. Jerome's Vita Pauli primi heremitae."[39] The manuscript he was describing, X.208.J.48 (320658) (De Ricci, no. 3), obtained in 1902, actually is a fifteenth-century book, written in 1436, to be precise, as a colophon on fol. 177v, which Simkhovitch missed, indicates.[40] In the same article Simkhovitch did note what probably was the earliest manuscript in Columbia's collection at that time. This is a late twelfth- or early thirteenth-century English book, purchased in 1901, containing a variety of texts, including Lawrence of Durham's *Hypognosticon,* and Ailred of Rievaulx' *De spirituali amicitia.*[41]

The collection continued to grow. In February 1912, for example, Professor Wendell T. Bush donated a mid-twelfth-century manuscript of Gregory the Great's *Homilies on Ezekiel.* This manuscript, X.878.G86 Q (De Ricci, no.36), once had been part of the library of the great English bibliophile Sir Thomas Phillipps (*olim Phillippicus* 2774) and survives today with twelfth-century board covers and original stitching. A note inside the front cover of the book reveals that it had been purchased, presumably by the peripatetic Bush, for £16.[42]

---

35. *Rare Book Library,* p. 17.
36. E.g., Vladimir G. Simkhovitch, "Exhibition of Illuminated Manuscripts," CUQ 4 (1901-2): 191-92, with reference to the "bibliographical collection;" cf. CUQ 9 (1906-7): 44, for the term "bibliographical room." For exhibitions of non-Columbian material, see Linderman, "History," pp. 347-48.
37. The listings for Columbia in De Ricci, 1258-69, indicate numerous items that were purchased very early in the twentieth century: e.g., nos. 2, 4, 12, 14, 16-17, 19-20, 22, etc.
38. Cf. "Rariora."
39. Ibid., p. 176.
40. De Ricci, 1258-59, gives the correct date but does not mention the colophon, written by a scribe who identifies himself as *Zammateus Veronensis.*
41. MS X.878.L.43 (318539) (De Ricci, no. 38). For Lawrence of Durham see *The Dictionary of National Biography,* vol. 11 (Oxford: Oxford University Press, 1973), pp. 689-91. This manuscript was unknown to the editor of the critical edition of Ailred's treatise: J. Dubois, *Aelred de Rievaulx, L'amitié spirituelle* (Bruges-Paris: Éditions C. Beyaert, 1948), pp. xcv-xcvi.
42. For Wendell T. Bush, see Horace L. Friess, "Professor Bush and His Collection of Religion and Culture," CUQ (April 1941): 159-64, whose collection now is in large part housed in the Department of Religion, 628 Kent Hall. The evaluation of the manuscript's boards and binding was made by Michael

The history of the "bibliographical museum" in Low Library was, in one sense, a history of motion. Crowded conditions in Low were a fact of life from the very beginning; and surviving records reveal a series of opinions and temporary remedies for locating both the Phoenix Collection and other rare books and manuscripts.[43] The collection's expansion continued, both through the purchase of individual items, and by donations, and by the process of discovering and pulling manuscripts out of larger collections that came to the University. The details of its growth in the early decades of the twentieth century form a complex history that remains to be assembled.[44] Worthy of note, even in passing, however, are the following: the Joan of Arc collection, donated in 1920 by Acton Griscom;[45] the acquisition in 1924 of the autograph manuscript of the unpublished sixth book, c.1550, of Sebastiano Serlio's *Tutte l'opere di architettura;*[46] two fifteenth-century Latin manuscripts from the Seligman Collection on economic history, which was purchased by the University in 1929;[47] late medieval and Renaissance documents and account books, in various languages, from the Montgomery Library of Accountancy, presented to the Business School Library from 1924-28;[48] the acquisition in 1933 by the Law Library of a thirteenth-

---

Gullick and is preserved on a sheet inside the manuscript, and in the files of the Rare Book and Manuscript Library.

43.   For various pieces of information about the movement of the Phoenix Collection and other rare books and manuscripts see, e.g., Linderman, "History," p. 467; and a suggestion made by Isadore G. Mudge (Reference Dept.), to the University Librarian, and the recommendation made in 1916 by the Committee on the Rearrangement of Library Collections (both found in the Rare Book and Manuscript Library, Library Office Files, Corresp. 1890-1926, box 146). Cf. the *Report of the Acting Librarian for the Academic Year Ending June 30, 1916*, p. 353 – this is clearly part of a larger report of some sort; the copy cited here is found bound together with other Library Reports (*Librarian's Reports, 1910-1935*), in the Columbiana Collection, under the call number CPC.

44.   A survey of information about the various collections of manuscripts at Columbia can be found in *Manuscript Collections; Facilities;* and *Rare Book Library.* The most useful orientation for the holdings in medieval and Renaissance manuscripts is in vol. 5 of Paul Oskar Kristeller, *Iter Italicum,* soon to be published.

45.   De Ricci, nos. 48-52; see BC 1 (April 1933): 4-5; and *Rare Book Library,* p. 15. Griscom is an intriguing figure, and the files of Columbiana yield the following information. He received a B.A. degree from Columbia in 1913, an M.A. in 1916, and was active as a historian and an Anglican clergyman. In 1937 he resigned from the active ministry and entered the world of finance, becoming a bond broker. He lived in High Point, NJ; but Kenneth Lohf recalls that he moved to Arizona and was still alive in 1954. It has been impossible to learn a date of his death, and it is just possible that he remains alive.

46.   Now housed in Avery Library. Linderman, "History," p. 503, calls this one of the most important manuscript owned by Columbia. See *Manuscript Collections,* p. 80.

47.   Ibid., pp 15-16; De Ricci, 1821.

48.   *Rare Book Library,* p. 15; De Ricci, 1270-72. The Montgomery collection was put on deposit in Special Collections (the forerunner of the Rare Book and Manuscript Library), in 1956, and formally transferred in 1974. See also

century manuscript of Bracton's *De legibus et consuetudinibus Angliae*;[49] and the donations of rare books, scientific instruments, documents, and manuscripts by Professor David E. Smith to both Teachers College and the newly established Rare Book Department at the University. Upon its establishment in 1930, this department was given quarters in Rooms 505 and 506 of Schermerhorn Hall, although not all books were transferred out of Low, and by 1934 Rare Books was moved back into Low Library.[50]

Kenneth Lohf has written that the action of the trustees in 1930 in creating a Rare Book Department perhaps was stimulated by expectations of gifts.[51] At the moment when the Department was established, in fact, negotiations were under way with Samuel S. Dale for the donation of his library on weights and measures; and David Smith's intention to present to Columbia his distinguished collection was known. But even with these additions, and even taking account of manuscripts that arrived in the 1940s and later, i.e., manuscripts from the library of the American Type Founders Company of Jersey City, from the library of the Classicist, Professor Gonzalez Lodge, or from the descendants of Park Benjamin,[52] the Columbia collection of medieval and Renaissance manuscripts would be interesting but second rate. What moved it into the first rank was the acquisition in the early 1930s of 317 medieval and Renaissance manuscripts from the library of George Arthur Plimpton.

Plimpton was a close friend of David Smith and had served as president of the Friends of the Library of Columbia University after its establishment in 1928.[53] Although an Amherst alumnus, he had long taken an interest in Columbia, and in education on Morningside Heights in general. He was instrumental in the founding of Barnard College and had served as a trustee both at

---

Exhibition of Selected Books and Manuscripts from the Montgomery Library of Accountancy (n.p. 1937).
49.   MS B.72; BC 1 (April 1933): 7-8.
50.   See the letter from Roger Howson, University Librarian, dated November 17, 1930: Rare Book and Manuscript Library, Library Office Files, 1927-42, R-Se, Rare Book Dept. to 1937. (The author is grateful to Bernard Crystal of Rare Books for calling this material to his attention.) See also BC 2 (December 1934): 5. For Smith and his library see BC 1 (April 1933): 3-4; 3 (June 1936): 5-6; De Ricci, 1273-79. Sorting out the details of the donations of the Smith collections of manuscripts and documents is a complicated process that cannot be attempted here: see *Manuscript Collections*, p. 83, for some of this material; and Paul Oskar Kristeller, *Iter Italicum*, vol. 5 (in press) for further details.
51.   For what follows see *Rare Book Library*, p. 17.
52.   Details about these acquisitions will not be given here; but further information can be obtained in *Rare Book Library*, pp. 19-21, and in the files of the Rare Book and Manuscript Library. A special study of Lodge has been published: Bernard R. Crystal, "Gonzalez Lodge: Apostle of the Classical Tradition," CLC 29 (Feb. 1980): 3-13.
53.   For much of what follows see *Rare Book Library* 16; BC 1-3 (April 1933-June 1936): passim.

Barnard and at Union Theological Seminary. He was a serious collector – of Highland black-faced sheep, Civil War artifacts, cigar-store wooden Indians, and especially of books and manuscripts.[54]

Plimpton had been chairman of the board of Ginn and Co., the famous textbook publishers, and his entire library comprised more than 16,000 volumes. He was especially interested in the history of education – what he referred to as "our tools of learning" – and his collection has been described as "a collection of notable treatises on the liberal arts."[55] His library had been on deposit in Low Library from 1932 and was formally presented to the University shortly before his death in 1936.[56] It is impossible to encompass in a précis the wonders contained therein but, straying a bit afield from medieval and Renaissance manuscripts, mention can be made of Melanchthon's copy of Homer, inscribed to him by Martin Luther; Erasmus' copy of Herodotus; and one of the earliest items – and one of the most remarkable – a cuneiform tablet, written in Old Babylonian script, sometime between 1900 and 1600 B.C., presenting a mathematical text resembling the Pythagorean Theorem.[57]

In conclusion, a word can be said about one of Plimpton's medieval manuscripts. MS 58 was written in southern France in the second third of the ninth century, according to Bernhard Bischoff, and comprises a collection of theological texts, including the *Liber ecclesiasticorum dogmatum* of Gennadius of Marseille and texts of Gregory the Great. The book may have served as a bishop's or priest's handbook, and similar collections exist in manuscripts elsewhere.

Among the files in the Rare Book Library concerning the Plimpton Collection is a list of prices that Plimpton paid for some of his books. He bought MS 58 in 1931 or '32 from a dealer in Holland for $3,354. This seems to be a very high price and is, in fact, the highest of any of the two dozen or so prices given on the list. The cheapest was $15, for what is now Plimpton MS 122 – four folios of a thirteenth-century manuscript of Statius. The high figure for MS 58 probably is explained by the fact that the book was sold, following the dealer's advertisement, as a collection of treatises "which may have some connection with Alcuin."[58] Alcuin probably had nothing to do with this volume, but his name and his significance for the Carolingian Renaissance might have seduced Plimpton, the collector of "tools of learning," and the price tag would have been incidental.

Exactly why he bought that particular manuscript probably never can be known for certain, but Plimpton's acumen and

54. Francis T. P. Plimpton, "The Wide-Ranging Collector: George Arthur Plimpton," CLC (Nov. 1960): 1-8.
55. See *Rare Book Library*, p. 17; BC 4 (August 1937): 1.
56. Ibid.
57. Mary C. Hyde, "History of the Library Friends and the Phoenix Story of Columbia," CLC 20 (May 1971): 12; *Rare Book Library*, p. 7.
58. *Rotulus* 1 (1931): 24-29.

activity as a book collector on many fronts often has been documented.[59] The princely donation to Columbia of a very great part of this library, with its incunables and more than 300 Western medieval and Renaissance manuscripts, is a high point in the University's rich tradition of interest in the Middle Ages and the Renaissance. From the obscurity surrounding George Templeton Strong's "Psalterium" in the late nineteenth century, Columbia had come to possess by the 1930s a dazzling accumulation of *monumenta* from the centuries between the fall of Rome and modern times.

59. See, very recently, Sören Edgren, "George Arthur Plimpton and His Chinese Collection," CLC 40 (November 1990): 14-23.

INDEX

Frontinus, *Strategemata* 64
Fulton, Robert 292
Gambara, Umberto 274
Gennadius of Marseille, *Liber ecclesiasticorum dogmatum* 299
Genua, Marcantonio 152
Geoffrey of Vinsauf 119; *Poetria nova* 119
Gesner, Conrad, *Bibliotheca universalis* 142
Ghiberti, Lorenzo 13-14; Baptistry Doors (Florence) 13
Gil, Jacob 180, 192-93, 195
Gilbert, William 56
Giorgione 268, 271; *Laura* 271; *Sleeping Venus* 268-69
Gonzaga, Eleonora 267, 270
Gouffier, Artus 42-43; Aymar 42
Grammont, Gabriel de 40
Granada 161, 166-68
Gratian 119-20
Gregory of Nazianzus 83-84
Gregory the Great, St. 299; "Homilies on *Ezekiel*" 296
Gregory XII, pope 63
Gregory XIII, pope 190
Grifo, Domina Geccha 223; Rainerio di 223
Grijalva, Juan de 134
Griscom, Acton 297
Grosseteste, Robert 115; see also *Stans puer ad mensam*
Guilds 239-61; see also individual companies
Guise family 283; see also Francis, duke of Guise
Hallam, Henry 2
Harangve sur les causes de la gverre... 284
Hastings castle 1-2, 4-7
Haultin family 286
Hawthorne, Nathaniel 292
Hebrews 84
Hegendorff, Christoph 124
Hemmerlin, Felix 131
Henry II, king of France 282
Henry III, king of France 288
Henry IV, king of England 2, 3, 6; see also Henry of Bolingbroke
Henry IV, king of France 288
Henry VIII, king of England 209-10, 243
Henry of Bolingbroke 1, 4-7; see also Henry IV of England

Henry of Burgundy 107
Henry of Guise 287
Henry of Navarre 287
Henry, duke of Anjou 285, 287
Herodotus 292, 299
Homer 79, 81, 83, 299; *Iliad* 78-79, 81-82
Homeric lexicon 82
Homeromanteion 81-82
Honorius III, pope 163
Hugh of St. Victor 113-14; *De institutione novitiorum* 113-15, 120
Humbert of Romans 114
Ignatius, St., *Regulae modestiae* 127
Innocent IV, pope 89, 163
Innocent VIII, pope 24, 26-27, 31-32, 173
Irenaeus, *Adversus Haereses* 80
Isabella, queen, *Testament* 133
Ive, William 193
Jarnac, battle of 287
Jerome, St., *Vita Pauli primi heremitae* 296
Joachim du Bellay, *Tvmvlvs Henrici secvndi gallorvm regis christianiss.* 282
Joan of Arc collection 297
John of Fruttuaria 113
John of Garland, *Parisiana poetria* 119
John of Gaunt 1, 4
John of Wales 114-15, 120, 122
John XXII, pope 179-80, 182, 191; *Cum inter nonnullos* 191
John XXIII, pope 60
Jouffroy, Jean, cardinal 177-78, 180, 185, 187, 195
Lancaster, house of 1-7
Las Casas, Bartolomé de, 134; *Apologética historia sumaria* 133-34
Lauretano, Michele 128
Lawrence of Durham, *Hypognosticon* 296
Leo X, pope 205
Leonardo da Vinci 273, 278
León 161, 163, 165-68, 171, 174
Lerma, Don Juan de 170
Lettres de tréshavte, trésvertueuse & tréschrestienne princesse, Iane royne de Nauarre 286
Lettres patentes...à l'encontre des conuenticules & assemblées des heretiques 283
Lettres Patentes...par lesqvelles en forme d'edict 283
Liber Vagatorum 190

This Book Was Completed on February 17, 1991
at Italica Press, New York, New York and
Was Set in Palatino. It Was Printed on
55 lb Glatfelter Natural Paper with a
Smyth-Sewn, Case Binding by
McNaughton & Gunn
Ann Arbor, MI
U. S. A.
* *
*